COLLECTION DEVELOPMENT
AND
COLLECTION EVALUATION

A Sourcebook

by
MICHAEL R. GABRIEL

The Scarecrow Press, Inc.
Lanham, Md., & London

British Library Cataloguing-in-Publication data available

Library of Congress Cataloging-in-Publication Data

Gabriel, Michael R.
  Collection development and collection evaluation : a
sourcebook / by Michael R. Gabriel.
     p.   cm.
  Includes index.
  ISBN 0-8108-2877-4 (acid-free paper)
    1. Collection development (Libraries)—United
States. 2. Collection development (Libraries)—United
States—Evaluation. I. Title.
Z687.2.U6G33 1995
025.2′1′0973—dc20   94-7697

For
Holly and Kara

TABLE OF CONTENTS

v

ACKNOWLEDGMENTS

I am indebted to the American Library Association for granting permission to reprint certain standards and guidelines relating to collection development and evaluation. Appreciation also is due to the libraries that granted permission to cite collection development policies as general examples of the genre.

Michael R. Gabriel
Northern Illinois University

INTRODUCTION

Collection development and collection evaluation activities are steadily growing in importance in all types and sizes of libraries, and many writers whose works are cited in this sourcebook believe there will be continued significant growth during the 1990's.

Collection development gained increased stature in the preceding two decades as many libraries reorganized administrative functions to include the position of "Collection Development Librarian," at senior levels in the institution. Where libraries once assigned collection duties to acquisition heads, or reference managers, or library directors, now collection management officers increasingly direct the work of circulation, serials, acquisitions, and even cataloging departments, often administering the activities of many different selectors or subject specialists among the library staff.

The speed with which collection management (as it is now frequently called) has gained stature is all the more remarkable given the fact that collection development did not enjoy its own distinctive subject heading in the publication *Library Literature* until 1988. Up until that time citations relating to selection of materials or to management of collections appeared under the headings Acquisitions, Book Selection, Book Collections, etc., and the field did not earn its own specialized journals until 1976–78, with *Collection Building* and *Collection Management*.

Despite its relatively late start as a unique activity in libraries, collection development was an early subject of research for leading library personalities, building over the course of many years a very rich store of literature. Interesting for its theoretical insights, and of utilitarian value for its practical advice, such literature established the core concerns of the specialty. As an archive the writings show a progression of ideas about managing collections from Lyle and Tauber's day right on up to analyses of present-day library functions and cogent predictions for the year 2000 and beyond. The writings are invaluable to librarians just entering the field, to researchers interested in the evolution of collection practices, and to librarians in positions of responsibility for acquisitions, circulation, and collection management who wish to employ proven techniques in their daily work. Such works cover the spectrum of core activities: Needs assessment, Development of written policies, Selection of materials, Acquisitions, Weeding, and Evaluation. All these basic components of collection management are extensively covered in the writings of librarians during the previous forty years. And the last component—Evaluation— appearing at the end in works by Edward Evans and others, is now thought by many observers to rank first among equals during the present day.

Assessing the strengths and weaknesses of library collections, the crux of evaluation, is such an important part of the collection manager's work that it rates a special chapter of its own. The use of checklists and bibliographies to compare holdings, application of the Conspectus approach to delineate collection building subject-by-subject, and recent advances in computer techniques that broaden the scope of analyses while compressing the time needed to accomplish evaluations—all have an importance that justifies special treatment in this book.

This sourcebook is divided into sections on Collection Development and on Collection Evaluation. Each section summarizes the most significant publications on these topics, followed by exhaustive bibliographies of the extant literature. Because acquisitions is such an integral part of collection management, Part 3 of the sourcebook is a comprehensive bibliography on acquisitions work in libraries. Some writings date to the 1950's, but the preponderance of published literature is in the 1970's and 1980's.

In addition to the comprehensive bibliographies, this Sourcebook contains representative samples of collection development policies from various types and sizes of libraries, plus guidelines and standards established by professional organizations for the subjects of collection development and collection evaluation. Following Part 5 is a broad glossary of terms relating to collection management and to library resource sharing in general.

Each bibliographic citation is arranged alphabetically by author in the sections of comprehensive bibliographies, so that readers searching for a specific writer may turn to those sections following Parts 1, 2, and 3.

Subject access to entries in the Sourcebook is provided in the Subject Index at the end of the book. All bibliographic citations are preceded by entry numbers (starting with 1 and proceeding to 1899), and readers using the Index are directed to these unique entry numbers for rapid and convenient access to information about all areas of collection development, collection evaluation, and acquisitions work in libraries.

PART ONE

COLLECTION DEVELOPMENT

Collection development is a term representing the process of systematically building library collections to serve study, teaching, research, recreational, and other needs of library users. The process includes selection and deselection of current and retrospective materials, planning of coherent strategies for continuing acquisition, and evaluation of collections to ascertain how well they serve user needs. Collection development activities historically have received prominent mention in the writings of published librarians, but in recent years greater attention has centered on this speciality, with a concomitant rise in the number of published writings, and of workshops and conferences devoted to collection development.

Collection development embraces a myriad of library operations ranging from selecting individual titles for purchase to withdrawal of expendable materials. In Guy Lyle's day, the term collection development had not yet come into general usage, but descriptions of this activity were an important segment of Lyle's treatise on college libraries. Lyle asserted that "to provide a plentiful supply of good and useful books is the college library's *raison d' être*,"[1] and he believed that book selection and acquisitions work demanded attention because library collections are the core around which sound teaching and related educational activities take place.

In similar fashion, Wilson and Tauber delineated "Acquisition Policies and Procedures,"[2] and described how university librarians are "increasingly concerned with growth in the size and complexity of collections, as well as the concomitant problems of *supplying materials to support individual university courses* (emphasis added), and the number and character of journals and special types of materials required for research by the various departments and schools. Important, too, is the construction given to specialization in collecting as a part of cooperative enterprises."[3]

Wilson and Tauber set forth the principles on which collection development should rest, i.e., acquisition programs must ensure developing a collection of materials "adequate to meet the demands which the university

3

makes upon it,"[4] and these demands will be dictated by specific university functions: conservation of knowledge, instruction, research, publication, extension, and service. Of all functions, the three most important in the authors' minds were conservation, instruction, and research. And these three in large measure will persist in determining the policies a given university should follow in collection development.

More recent monographic treatments of collection development amplify the programmatic aspects of acquisitions work and related activities. A good example of this approach is the work of G. Edward Evans,[5] who asserts that collection development is a universal process in which librarians acquire diverse materials to meet patron demands. This continuous process consists of six definable elements:

1. Community analysis (users)
2. Policies
3. Selection
4. Acquisition
5. Weeding
6. Evaluation

Evans sees a sequential relationship among these elements, with community analyses (surveys, needs assessment, etc.) leading to clearly defined policies for both collection development and for selection, which in turn lead to guidelines for choosing items for inclusion in the collection. Collection policies encompass a wider range of topics than do selection policies, including guidelines to assist in decision-making on which items to purchase as well as related issues such as gifts, weeding, and library cooperation. In time, nearly every item acquired by acquisition librarians "outlives its original value to the library"[6] and must be weeded from the main collection. To a limited extent, weeding is an evaluation process, but evaluation ranges over a plethora of techniques and systems whose variety and importance is increasingly emphasized by collection developers.

Galvin and Lynch[7] provide a valuable perspective on the first of Evans's six definable elements of collection development. Community analysis is considered as a planning function essential to collection development. As the academic community changes, so must library collections change to meet new priorities. Hiring patterns for new faculty, altered university goals and objectives, creation and elimination of academic programs, the development of new methods of scholarship—all influence collection development policies. And if inadequate attention is paid to such shifts in the academy, the authors point out that "fiscal resources will be wasted, and academic units and individual scholars without adequate access to an appropriate level of library support will be frustrated."[8]

Community analysis gives birth to the second of Evans's elements: Collection development policies. The American Library Association has made available an excellent reference document, *Guidelines for Collection Development,*[9] the first chapter of which presents "Guidelines for the Formulation of Collection Development Policies."[10] The Guidelines identify essential elements of written statements for collection development policy, and establish a standard terminology and structure for use in the preparation of such policies. Although not equally applicable to all libraries, the Guidelines were formulated to serve libraries of all kinds and sizes. By drafting individual policies, libraries produce tools that enable selectors to work toward defined goals and thus to use funds wisely in shaping strong collections, to inform library staff and users concerning the scope and nature of existing resources and plans for continual development of collections, and to provide information that will help to provide objective evidence for use in the budgetary allocation process so as to inform and satisfy competing university clienteles.

Collection development policies must also contain instructions for de-selection, for comparing resources of different institutions, for starting cooperative plans, and for establishing collecting levels by individual form, discipline, subject area, or language.

The third element of collection development—selection—usually is a decentralized decision-making process in academic libraries, with responsibility assigned to a variety of selectors such as bibliographers, reference librarians, branch librarians, departments, individual faculty members, or committees of faculty.[11] Selection is governed by broad influences arising from university and library conditions, including allocation budgets, relative emphasis on current versus retrospective purchases, the adoption of specialized purchasing and approval plans, and the interaction of the many individuals involved in the collection development process.

For an excellent, detailed analysis of selection, Bonk and Magrill[12] supply extensive guidelines covering what they term "traditional principles of selection." These are

(a.) **"Select the Right Materials for the Library's Readers."** This demands that individual libraries decide whether to select for present clientele only, or also for some hypothetical potential clientele.

(b.) **"See to it that No race, Nationality, Profession, Trade, Religion, School of Thought, or Local Custom is Overlooked."** Employing this principle dictates that a library buys in such areas even if members of these particular groups are not active, present users of library resources. They are, however, potential users, and possible future interests should be anticipated.

(c.) **"Every Library Collection Should Be Built up According to a Definite Plan on a Broad General Foundation."** This approach rests on the idea that every library collection has inherent needs separate from the direct needs of its primary clientele, and that collection developers have "a responsibility to the collection itself and should" work "to balance it and round it out." Collections should contain resources on varied topics irrespective of whether or not groups in the community are actively interested in those subjects. In an era of limited funding for libraries, this principle may be said to be observed more in the breach than in practice.

(d.) **"Demand is the Governing Factor in Selection."** This principle is the converse of the preceding idea of "inherent needs," because librarians here are acquiring materials present readers need and request, rather than attempting to develop a well-rounded collection or to buy for potential instead of actual users.

(e.) **"Materials Acquired Should Meet High Standards of Quality in Content, Expression, and Format."** Developers applying this viewpoint would concentrate on accuracy, authoritative quality, effective expression, significance, sincerity of author's purpose, and responsibility of author's opinion. Anything that failed to meet these standards, even if in heavy demand, would be rejected.

Bonk and Magrill have developed additional library guidelines for selection primarily, but not exclusively, intended for public libraries. The authors also supply valuable advice for organizing selection activities in university libraries.[13]

The fourth element of Evans's collection development program is *acquisitions.* As a library operation, acquisitions work is inextricably bound up with and flows from selection. Acquisitions covers the broad processing functions of ordering, billing, payment, receiving, checking, and related business operations. Magrill and Hickey's work on *Acquisitions Management and Collection Development in Libraries*[14] is an excellent introduction to the general functions of an acquisitions unit. The authors list and define the fundamental tasks of such units as they vary from library to library, depending on the type and size of the institution. The virtues of statistical analysis also are stressed, both for the continual satisfactory performance of the acquisitions unit and for monitoring up-to-date knowledge on the status of materials budgets.

Weeding, the fifth of Evans's elements, is covered extensively in sources previously mentioned. However, a number of additional works should be mentioned, including

Mosher,[15] Reed,[16] Slote,[17] Ash,[18] Farber,[19] Fussler,[20] Gosnell,[21] Rouse,[22] Thompson,[23] and Totten.[24]

The sixth and concluding item comprising Evans's collection development process is evaluation. The author places evaluation in the center of the collection developer's universe:

> For purposes of collection development the following definition will be used: The process of identifying the strengths and weaknesses of a library's materials collection in terms of patron needs and community resources, and attempting to correct existing weaknesses, if any. This requires the constant examination and evaluation of the library's resources and the constant study of both patron needs and changes in the community to be served.[25]

Additional works on evaluation appear in Chapter Two.

In recent years much greater attention and importance has been attached to "collection management," which often encompasses acquisitions work, circulation, interlibrary loans, and the traditional functions of collection development. Increasingly, libraries appoint a "Collection Management Librarian" at a senior level to coordinate the above activities.

Ferguson[26] outlined what he considered to be the central functions of collection management, then suggested various models of organization to allow flexibility. Bobick[27] produced a SPEC Kit on organizational patterns of collection management work among ARL libraries that provides extensive position descriptions, organization charts, and training aids. Cogswell[28] cited what he believed to be the eight vital activities of collection management, identified half a dozen organization models for libraries, and then evaluated the efficiency of the models when paired with collection management activities. Cubberly[29] addressed the difficulties of librarians who have divided responsibilities in smaller libraries, and who can not do full justice therefore to their collection duties. The author recommends a separate unit for collection development activities even in medium-sized libraries. Sohn[30] also surveyed various organizational models among ARL libraries, and found that most libraries had separate collection development departments but very few assigned full-time duties to selectors. Most librarians responsible for selecting books and periodicals had primary job responsibilities that took them out of line supervision in collection management departments. Bryant[31] offered a detailed background examination of the progression of collection management in libraries, and addressed the management problems that arise with part-time selectors. The author listed seven configurations for collection development across a broad spectrum of library types:

1. Collection development that is performed by a single librarian
2. Separate subject-oriented segments of the library, each of which has its own collection developer who may or may not report to a collection development officer (other than the director)
3. Collection development that is the function of a committee that reviews suggestions from patrons and staff, making final purchase decisions
4. A group of librarians who come together to perform collection development activities and then disperse to their primary assignments throughout the library
5. A unit of full-time or part-time collection developers that is subsumed by a larger division of the library
6. A unit of collection developers that is separate from other divisions of the library, or
7. The collection development unit that subsumes one or more other library functions, such as acquisitions, special collections, or interlibrary loan.

Much potential for controversy exists concerning the best configuration; 1 for the library and its collections; 2 for the collection development operation; 3 for the collection development officer; and 4 for the individual collection developer. In the final analysis, however, whatever works best in a specific library should prevail without regard for whether the organization was created by evolution or by careful analysis of collection development as an organizational function.

Divided responsibilities for selection attracted much additional attention throughout the decade. Null[32] argued that compromises must be agreed upon if part-time selectors are to achieve the time and support needed to develop and manage coherent collections. His evaluation centered on the work of reference librarians who have dual assignments for development. And Vidor[33] evaluated a business school collection to find whether librarians were more effective selectors than faculty. Results were inconclusive.

Bucknall[34] provided an overview of the problems of maintaining collection management in a centralized office, rather than a decentralized structure. Schad[35] noted that dual responsibility selectors often failed to balance their work between collection development and other duties. The author advocated a use of matrix organization where traditional line hierarchy is improved by lateral lines of authority. And Hay[36] reviewed the history of the use of subject specialists, which started with area and language specialists during the Second World War and continued with specialists for academic disciplines afterward. Hay evaluates the successes and difficulties of subject specialists in German, British, Third World, and American libraries.

Osburn[37] supplied an excellent overview of the history of collection development work in libraries. His work shows the close relationship between organizational structures and the importance of constructing clear and concise policy statements for collection management. Atkinson[38] stated that the primary objective of a policy is to set the current and future directions of collecting, with emphasis on guidelines that will enable individual selectors to understand and to intelligently treat the specific areas for which they are responsible. Other works of interest for those who strive to construct meaningful policies are Krueger,[39] who provided useful guidelines; Rawlinson,[40] who explicated selection policies at a public library system; Kemp,[41] who compiled written policies with appropriate forms and procedures used by school libraries nationwide; Bostic,[42] who reaffirmed that written collection policies are fundamental to intelligent support of academic programs in the university; Bullard,[43] who offered an insightful look at the political ramifications inherent in collection development policies and the importance of involving teaching faculty and administration in the drafting of such policies; Hoolihan,[44] who demonstrated the drafting of policies for highly specialized collections in the university; Dienes,[45] who provided helpful procedures for libraries that are just beginning the process of drafting policy statements; and Scarborough,[46] who was adept at outlining what is necessary to cover theoretic and practical issues that separate collection building for ethnically diverse populations (African American, American Indian, Asian, and Chicano) from other traditional models of policy statements.

During the latter half of the decade of the 80's, prices of library materials became an alarming issue for collection development officers. The most critical component of this controversy was serials, the literature on which is summarized annually in "Year's Work in Serials," *Library Resources and Technical Services*. Another excellent source for prices of library materials is the *Bowker Annual of Library and Book Trade Information*. A number of excellent articles address price concerns of librarians in the 1980's, among them Cargill,[47] who provided an overview of the main components of pricing library materials; Facente,[48] who explicated the methods publishers use to set the prices of books and other items; and Loe,[49] who argued that the fundamental shifts caused by the Thor Power Tool tax case drastically affected the size of print runs for academic books and consequently pushed general book prices higher. In a fascinating survey of American and German library expenditures over a period of 100 years, Danton[50] discovered that budget increases for libraries did not equal the demands placed upon collections by increasing numbers of students, courses, faculty, and published books. Edelman and Muller[51] circulated data on library material budgets, in addition to much other information on selection methods in different types of libraries, uses of reviews, and methods of acquisition;

Martin[52] supplied a summary of library attempts to acquire and build special collections, while Alessi[53] compared various sources of data for pricing materials in the U.S. and U.K. Boissonnas[54] reviewed other studies of discriminatory pricing practices of publishers, Hendrickson[55] examined background factors that directly or indirectly influence costs of books, Schrift[56] revealed the methods by which some publishers set prices of individual titles, and Clark[57] enumerated the many methods librarians have employed to cope with rapidly escalating prices of books and serials.

White[58] increasingly took a proactive stance for libraries coping with staggering price increases. He warned scholarly publishers that financial pressures caused by such increases were likely to change the friendly relationship that had existed for so long between librarians and publishers[58]. Other writers offered advice on methods of coping with punitive budget demands, among them Lynden,[59] who recommended that individual libraries complete local price studies for materials; Laughrey,[60] who reported on similar studies finished at the University of Michigan; Welsch,[61] who analyzed external factors including statistics on the size of published literature when preparing budgets; and Werking,[62] who analyzed various methods of allocating materials budgets. And in a follow-up by Lynden[63] the sometimes positive effects of tight budgets are pointed out, forcing librarians to evaluate collection priorities and to become better consumer advocates. Shaughnessy[64] believed, instead, that escalating costs produced a crisis for library administrators, while Cargill[65] showed how insufficient funds could deleteriously affect a library's entire processing activity. Niles[66] provided a provocative analysis of the political ramifications of making allocations to academic departments for acquisition of materials, and Dowd[67] analyzed the differences that exist between public service functions and the archival responsibilities of libraries, with concommitant conflicts in budget allocation. Hunter[68] explored the pricing trends of serial literature and the possible emergence of electronic journals, and Byrd[69] used the "Commons' metaphor to illustrate how escalating prices are an insoluble crisis for libraries in an era of dwindling resources, while individual rewards (especially tenure) for increasing the number of serials and other publications is so great there is little likelihood that countervailing pressures will have any significant impact. And Lynden[70] contributed again with two additional very useful works, on the methods needed to gather and supply information for successful budget requests, and an analysis of one research library's total budget with emphasis on the growth of published literature and attendant cost increases.[71]

Collection-development focus on audiovisual resources suffered for many years in comparison with monographs and serials. Nowhere is this better illustrated than in the number and variety of published works on these respective topics. Gradually, however, a change was noticeable from the days when 16mm film, slides, filmstrips, etc., received perfunctory evaluation by librarians. As video gained popularity, it began to displace other audiovisual formats, as was often true of the new technologies of CD-ROM, laser disc, computer software, and electronic journals, books, and newsletters. In this work we are interested primarily in the latter innovations. The transformation of printed books and journals into electronic formats is one of the paramount issues for collection management librarians in the 1990's. Already a significant literature exists on this subject. Johnson[72] provided a summary of the ACRL standards for audiovisual services and collections, Galloway[73] described the rapid increase in technological innovations affecting academic libraries, and Lagana[74] made a strong case for the importance of all nontraditional collections. Roose[75] explored the advent of CD-ROM technology and its potential to displace traditional methods of communication and archival preservation, Calmes[76] reaffirmed the value of microfilm for archival work in comparison with newer technologies like CD-ROM, which are too new to enjoy adequate testing, and Lynch[77] supplied an excellent overview of electronic media and their vast potential for less expensive and faster transmission of research results in addition to alleviation of space and preservation problems.

A report from the Association of Research Libraries[78] placed new electronic technologies in an environment of diminished resources for traditional library materials at the same time that a fascinating array of new technologies appeared on the horizon. The principal challenge confronting research librarians was perceived to be a problem of supplying scholars with research materials in paper while coming to grips with demands for electronic formats. In addition, the new formats required new dollars since they infrequently displaced paper media, while requiring more specialized and technologically proficient reference librarians to interpret new resources for users. Poole[79] argued for acquisition of electronic data bases and other new technologies drawn on regular material budgets, while Dowd[80] and others strongly disagreed. Sack[81] implored librarians to utilize the advantages available in new technologies to create libraries without walls, or where access is stressed rather than the heretofore imperative of collecting widely and often comprehensively in several disciplines of study and research.

Bratton[82] conducted a valuable survey of health educators to determine their needs with audiovisual resources, while Webb[83] concentrated on the best methods of building adult video collections. Gatten[84] described the wealth of CD-ROM offerings available to librarians and reviewed specific products, while Stewart[85] outlined selection criteria utilized by one academic library when purchasing CD-ROMs. Cargill[86] continued with a sobering look at the impact of CD-ROMs on budgets, and Ferguson[87] provided criteria for collection developers to use in selecting CD-ROMs and other new technologies that are truly beneficial to librarians rather than selecting new technologies merely as fads to be discarded promptly when something newer arrives on the doorstep. Buckland's[88] view encompassed all media as integral to a library's collecting mission and to scholarship and research, in general, thus the materials budget must contain room for all formats. And Nissley,[89] in an interesting approach to consumerism, encouraged librarians to judiciously buy and use new communication technologies as a spur to manufacturers to produce appropriate equipment for libraries.

Alley[90] believed that the introduction of CD-ROM would have profound consequences for libraries, especially its dangerous impact on already strained budgets. Welsch[91] offered the idea of a special collection development workstation to aid selection of materials in an era of expanding technologies, while Johnson[92] discussed several problem areas arising from the impact of CD-ROM and newer formats. Robinson[93] followed up with additional insight on this topic. Demas[94] outlined procedures for integrating electronic media in modern libraries so as to create a reasonable mix of new and traditional formats. Intner's[95] focus in this regard was on computer software, and the criteria to be used in selection. And Reed-Scott[96] explored the effect that so many of these new technologies had on keeping collection development policies up-to-date and workable.

Downes[97] predicted only gradual growth for electronic technologies vis-à-vis printed books and journals, and Rice[98] showed how libraries will shift to an emphasis on access rather than on ownership, with universities building local collections of research on a wide range of topics and with commercial publishers providing entry to external data bases. An interesting model of this scenario already exists at Carnegie-Mellon University, described by Arms.[99] And, for a broad perspective, the outlook of Atkinson[100] is instructive for a glimpse of what the future holds for electronic libraries and collection development. Atkinson sees a radical shift as the Gutenberg Era fades into the Electronic Age, as librarians structure operations around three basic functions:

> The first function is the obvious one of mediation. The library will clearly need to maintain and enhance its ability to identify needed information in appropriate databases, and to assist users in the downloading of such information . . . The advent of the online era should at least provide us with the opportunity to reconnect these two essential and adjacent components of library service.

The second function will be primary record definition. This is the equivalent of traditional collection development, as I have briefly been trying to describe it. The purpose of this function will be to create a stable database by downloading discrete, carefully selected online publications. Fulfilling that function will require, as it does now, considerable subject knowledge, i.e., an understanding of the content and significance of the constantly evolving network of public data from which the selected publications are to be downloaded.

The final function I envision in the electronic library has no real equivalent today. I will call it, for want of a better designation, secondary record definition. This will be the library's uploading function. When a scholar at an institution has written something which is deemed by a select group of peers to be worth communicating broadly to other scholars, that communication should take place by the library's uploading that publication into the library database, thus disseminating it to other libraries, and thereby to other scholars, throughout the nation and the world. The ultimate purpose of the library is to provide bibliographic support for education and to serve as a basis for communication among scholars—in short, to disseminate significant information. In the predominately paper era, we rely heavily upon commercial publishing for that purpose, but such commercial publishing is merely a means to achieving that ultimate end, and already that particular means is becoming economically prohibitive and technically unnecessary. The library, in conjunction with the computer center and the academic press, must assume direct responsibility for disseminating information among scholars. Providing scholars with the channels through which to communicate, working with scholars to establish the technical and bibliographical standards and procedures for online publication in this fashion, these are responsibilities which should therefore also be assumed by the library in the online era.

Librarians working in crowded and underfunded institutions of the 1980's and 1990's, where cooperative collection development is viewed as a necessity, may not realize how early cooperative arrangements were formed among American libraries.

Of course, the early work of the American Library Association centered on cooperative efforts. And at the turn of the century, in 1899, the Library of Congress under the leadership of E.C. Richardson emphasized the importance of cooperation when buying new books so that libraries would supplement, not duplicate, each other.[101] Ten years later the librarians of McGill and Harvard universities raised two issues of cooperation that would be central issues for the future. The first[102] was to establish regional libraries whose sphere of influence would embrace large geographical areas and who would aid local libraries while maintaining cooperative arrangements with all other large regional libraries. The second was to construct cooperative arrangements for central storage and bibliographic coverage of books, especially the gathering of union catalogs and bibliographies to show the locations of individual works.

Weber[103] provided an excellent history of cooperative programs among academic libraries. One of the earliest collection development projects was a 1913 acquisitions trip by the Northwestern University librarian, who acquired thousands of South American books and newspapers for a half-dozen academic institutions. After the Second World War the Library of Congress shipped a million books from Europe to American libraries under the Cooperative Acquisitions Project for Wartime Publications. In 1948, the Universal Serial and Book Exchange (USBE) was formed, and in the same year, the Farmington Plan saw the beginning of an acquisitions program to ship foreign materials of research value to libraries in the United States. In 1951, the Center for Research Libraries inaugurated a program for joint buying and for deposit of research collections; in 1956 the Foreign Newspaper Microfilm Project started operations; and in 1959 the Latin American Cooperative Acquisitions Program started to benefit forty academic libraries in the U.S. Two years later passage of Public Law 480 enabled 300 academic libraries to acquire many thousands of publications throughout the world. And in 1973, the Research Libraries Group (RLG) composed of four of the most prestigious American libraries, formed a partnership to counter problems of economic restraint and financial uncertainty. Coordinated collection development was one of the principal programs of RLG, and the creation of the RLG Conspectus had far-reaching effects as more and more libraries used the Conspectus approach to define areas of collection development, evaluation, and preservation.

Sohn[104] continued with a follow-up overview of cooperative collection development, in which many local and regional Conspectus projects are described, as is the North American Collections Inventory Project (NACIP). The goals of the NACIP were to ensure the:

> Availability of a standard for collection description and assessment for the identification of North American collection strengths and weaknesses;
> Development of a mechanism to locate needed research materials more expeditiously;
> Development of the capacity to relate local collection development policies to collection levels at other institutions and to serve as the basis for cooperative collection development, both nationally and regionally;
> Development of the capacity to relate collection development strengths to cataloging and preservation needs and to serve as the basis for cooperative cataloging and preservation efforts, again both nationally and regionally;
> Support for emerging coordinated retrospective conversion projects; and
> Enhancements of individual libraries' collection management programs. Analysis of conspectus data will lead to identification of collection strengths and weaknesses, contribute to the preparation of collection development policies, and improve budget allocation decisions.

In the same year, Luquire[105] published an excellent monograph on cooperative collection development, which is especially useful for its detailed examinations of several successful regional projects. Hewitt[106] described the long-term cooperative arrangement between Duke University and the University of North Carolina, and several other writers commented on effective cooperative

projects among libraries of different type and size. Ballard,[107] however, voiced reservations about the future of
cooperation among public libraries because of the library's clientele insisting upon rapid, convenient access
to materials in local collections. Hewitt[108] supplied background on several cooperative programs among large
research libraries, while Branin[109] reviewed recent cooperative arrangements and some of the roadblocks libraries
experienced. Dougherty[110] developed a model for timely
resource sharing between two or more libraries, Boisse[111]
cited the Center for Research Libraries (CRL) for its outstanding contributions to resource sharing, Rutledge[112]
offered a procedure for evaluating the cost effectiveness of
memberships in CRL, Michalak[113] cited the efficacy of
closer cooperation between collection management people and interlibrary loan officers, and Jaramillo[114] surveyed the introduction of new technologies that have
done much to enhance cooperative collection development.

Sartori[115] covered the necessary conditions to be met if
cooperative serials projects are to be realized, Cruse[116]
performed the same service for map collections, Hamilton[117] described cooperative collection efforts among Oregon libraries, as did Pettos[118] for Northern California, and
Mosher[119] contributed a well-reasoned explication of the
prevailing trends in cooperation, with libraries gradually
leaning toward a client/access centered mission as opposed to collection-driven management. Mosher[120] followed with a plea for more individual cooperation among
bibliographers as opposed to collaboration among libraries. And Dowd[121] described four types of cooperative
programs, the first of which addressed the need to extend
access to research materials.

A milestone for cooperative collection development
was the inauguration in 1990 of an annual ADVANCES IN
LIBRARY RESOURCE SHARING[122], which concentrated
on the work being done each year in bibliographic networks, cooperative acquisitions, and coordinated collection building. Despite one assertion that electronic pub-

lishing will render resource sharing obsolete, most observers believe that significant achievements have occurred from cooperation agreements, and that much additional benefit will accrue to collaboration efforts of librarians in the years to come.

NOTES PART ONE

1. Lyle, Guy. *The administration of the college library.* New York: H.W. Wilson, 1961. p. 232.
2. Wilson, Louis and Maurice Tauber. *The university library.* New York: Columbia University Press, 1956.
3. *Ibid.,* 346.
4. *Ibid.,* 348.
5. Evans, G. Edward. *Developing library collections.* Littleton: Libraries Unlimited, 1979. p. 21.
6. *Ibid.*
7. Galvin, Thomas and Beverly Lynch. *Priorities for academic libraries.* Washington: Jossey-Bass, 1982.
8. *Ibid.,* 53.
9. Perkins, David. *Guidelines for collection development.* Chicago: American Library Association, 1979.
10. *Ibid.,* 1–8.
11. Cline, Hugh and Loraine Sinnott. *Building library collections.* Lexington: Lexington Books, 1981.
12. Bonk, Wallace and Rose Magrill. *Building library collections.* 5th edition. Metuchen: Scarecrow Press, 1979. pp. 4–12.
13. *Ibid.,* 27.
14. Magrill, Rose and Doralyn Hickey. *Acquisitions management and collection development in libraries.* Chicago: American Library Association, 1984.
15. Mosher, Paul. "Managing library collections: the process of review and pruning," *Collection Development in Libraries,* edited by R.D. Stueart and G.B. Miller. Greenwich: JAI Press, 1980.
16. Reed, Mary. "Identification of storage candidates among monographs," *Collection Management* 3:203–214. Summer/Fall 1979.
17. Slote, Sidney. *Weeding library collections.* Littleton: Libraries Unlimited, 1982.

18. Ash, Lee. *Yale's selective book retirement program.* Hamden: Anchor Books, 1963.
19. Farber, Evan. "Limiting college library growth: bane or boon?" *Journal of Academic Librarianship* 1:12–15. November 1975.
20. Fussler, H.H. and J.L. Simon. *Patterns in the use of books in large research libraries.* Chicago: University of Chicago Library, 1969.
21. Gosnell, Charles. "Obsolescence of books in college libraries." *College and Research Libraries 5:* 115–125. March 1944.
22. Rouse, Roscoe. "Within library solutions to book space problems." *Library Trends* 19:299–310. January 1971.
23. Thompson, James. "Revision of stock in academic libraries." *Library Association Record* 75:41–44. March 1973.
24. Totten, Herman. "Selection of library material for storage: a state of the art." Library Trends 19:341–351. January 1971.
25. Evans, 1979, p. 28.
26. Ferguson, Anthony. "University library collection management using a structural-functional systems model." *Collection Management* 8:1–14. Spring 1986.
27. Bobick, James. *Collection development organization and staffing in ARL libraries.* Washington: Association of Research Libraries, 1987.
28. Cogswell, James. "The organization of collection management functions in academic research libraries." *Journal of Academic Librarianship* 13:268–76. No. 5, 1987.
29. Cubberly, Carol. "Organization for collection development in medium-sized academic libraries." *Library Acquisitions: Practice and Theory* 11:293–323. No. 4, 1987.
30. Sohn, Jeanne. "Collection development organizational patterns in ARL libraries." *Library Resources and Technical Services 31:*123–134. April–June 1987.
31. Bryant, Bonita. "The organizational structure of collection development." *Library Resources and Technical Services* 31:111–122. April–June 1987.
32. Null, David. "Robbing Peter . . . Balancing collection development and reference responsibilities." *College and Research Libraries 49:*448–52. 1988.
33. Vidor, David and Elizabeth Futas. "Effective collection development: Librarians or faculty." *Library Resources and Technical Services* 32:127–36. 1988.
34. Bucknall, Carolyn. "Organization of collection develop-

ment and management in academic libraries." *Collection Building* 9:11–17. No. 3–4, 1989.

35. Schad, Jasper. "Managing collection development in university libraries that utilize librarians with dual responsibility assignments." *Library Acquisitions, Practice and Theory* 14:165–71. 1990.

36. Hay, Fred. "The subject specialist in the academic library: A review." *Journal of Academic Librarianship* 16:11–17. 1990.

37. Osburn, Charles. *"Collection development and management." Academic Libraries: Research Perspectives.* Chicago: American Library Association, 1990.

38. Atkinson, Ross. "The language of the levels: Reflections on the communication of collection development policy." *College and Research Libraries* 47:140–149. March 1986.

39. Krueger, Karen. "Guidelines for collection management." *Collection Management in Public Libraries,* edited by Judith Serebnick. Chicago: American Library Association, 1986.

40. Rawlinson, Nora. "The approach to collection management at Baltimore County Public Library." *Collection Management in Public Libraries* edited by Judith Serebnick. Chicago: American Library Association, 1986.

41. Kemp, Betty. *School library and media center acquisitions policies and procedures.* Phoenix: Oryx Press, 1986.

42. Bostic, Mary. "A written collection development policy: To have and have not." *Collection Management* 10:89–103. Nos. 3–4, 1988.

43. Bullard, Scott. "Read my lips: The politics of collection development." *Library Acquisitions, Practice and Theory* 13:251–53. 1989.

44. Hoolihan, Christopher. "Collection development policies in medical rare book collections." *Collection Management* 11:167–79. Nos. 3–4, 1989.

45. Dienes, Frances. "Collection development policies: Are they a good thing or a necessary evil?" *New Zealand Libraries* 46:5–7. June 1989.

46. Scarborough, Katherine. "Collection development policies for ethnic groups." *Library Journal* 116:44–47. June 15, 1991.

47. Cargill, Jennifer. "Today's primary issue: Pricing and costs of library materials." *Library Acquisitions, Practice and Theory* 10:227–28. No. 3, 1986.

48. Facente, Gary. "An overview of American publishing for librarians." *Library Resources and Technical Services 30:*57–67. January–March, 1986.

49. Loe, Mary. "Thor tax ruling after five years." *Library Acquisitions, Practice and Theory 10:*203–218. No. 3, 1986.

50. Danton, J. Periam. "University library book budgets 1860, 1910, and 1960." *Library Quarterly 57:*284–302. July 1987.

51. Edelman, Hendrik and Karen Muller. "A new look at the library market." *Publishers Weekly 231:*30–35. May 29, 1987.

52. Martin, Rebecca. "Special collections: Strategies for support in an era of limited resources." *College and Research Libraries 48:*241–46. May 1987.

53. Alessi, Dana. "Books across the waters." *Pricing and Costs of Monographs and Serials.* New York: Haworth, 1987.

54. Boissonnas, Christian. "Differential pricing of monographs and serials." *Pricing and Costs of Monographs and Serials.* New York: Haworth, 1987.

55. Hendrickson, Kent. "Pricing from three perspectives." *Pricing and Costs of Monographs and Serials.* New York: Haworth, 1987.

56. Schrift, Leonard. "Truth in vending." *Pricing and Costs of Monographs and Serials.* New York: Haworth, 1987.

57. Clark, Lenore. "Materials costs and collection development in academic libraries." *Pricing and Costs of Monographs and Serials.* New York: Haworth, 1987.

58. White, Herbert. "Scholarly publishers and librarians: A strained marriage." *Scholarly Publishing 19:*125–29. 1988.

59. Lynden, Fred. "Prices and discounts." *Library Acquisitions, Practice and Theory 12:*255–58. 1988.

60. Laughrey, Edna. "Projecting materials costs: Basis for effective decision making." *Pricing and costs of Monographs and Serials.* New York: Haworth, 1987.

61. Welsch, Erwin. "Price versus coverage: Calculating the impact on collection development." *Library Resources and Technical Services 32:*159–63. 1988.

62. Werking, Richard. "Allocating the academic library's book budget." *Journal of Academic Librarianship 14:*140–44. 1988.

63. Lynden, Fred. "The impact of the rising costs of books and journals on the overall library budget." *Journal of Library Administration 10:*81–98. No. 1, 1989.

64. Shaughnessy, Thomas. "Management strategies for financial crises." *Journal of Library Administration 10:*3–15. 1989.

65. Cargill, Jennifer. "Budgeting constraints: The impact on technical services." *Journal of Library Administration 10:* 39+ No. 1, 1989.
66. Niles, Judith. "The politics of budget allocation." *Library Acquisitions, Practice and Theory 13:*51–55. 1989.
67. Dowd, Sheila. "Fee, fie, foe, fum: Will the serials giant eat us?" *Journal of Library Administration 10:*17–38. 1989.
68. Hunter, Karen. "Economic and technological trends in journal publishing." *Library Acquisitions, Practice and Theory* 14:121–26. 1990.
69. Byrd, Gary. "An economic Commons tragedy for research libraries: Scholarly journal publishing and pricing trends." *College and Research Libraries 51:*184–95. 1990.
70. Lynden, Fred. "Cost analysis of monographs and serials." *Journal of Library Administration 12:*19–40. No. 3, 1990.
71. Lynden, Fred. "Library materials budget justifications." *Book Research Quarterly 5:*68–74. Winter 1989–90.
72. Johnson, Margaret. "Guidelines for audiovisual services in academic libraries." *College and Research Libraries News* 47:333–35. May 1986.
73. Galloway, Margaret, et al. "The expanding universe of special formats." *College and Research Libraries News* 47:650–54. November 1986.
74. Lagana, Gretchen. "Beyond the book: Collection development and the special collections librarian." *Energies for Transition* by D.A. Nitecki. Chicago: American Library Association, 1986.
75. Roose, Tina. "The new papyrus: CD-ROM in your library." *Library Journal* 111: 166–67. September 1986.
76. Calmes, Alan. "New confidence in microfilm." *Library Journal* 111:38–42. September 15, 1986.
77. Lynch, C.A. and E.B. Brownrigg. "Library applications of electronic imaging technology." *Information Technology and Libraries* 5:100–105. June 1986.
78. *The Changing Systems of Scholarly Communication.* Washington: Association of Research Libraries, 1986.
79. Poole, Jay and Glorianna St. Clair. "Funding online services from the materials budget." *College and Research Libraries* 47:225–29. May 1986.
80. Dowd, Sheila et al. "Reactions to funding online services from the materials budget." *College and Research Libraries* 47:230–37. May 1986.

81. Sack, John. "Open systems for open minds. Building the library without walls." *College and Research Libraries* 47:535–44. November 1986.

82. Bratton, Barry et al. "Selection and acquisition of audiovisual materials by health professionals." *MLA Bulletin* 75:355–61. October 1987.

83. Webb, Ruth. "The $5000 video collection." *Library Journal* 112:34–40. May 15, 1987.

84. Gatten, Jeff et al. "Purchasing CD-ROM products considerations for a new technology." *Library Acquisitions, Practice and Theory* 11:273–81. No. 4, 1987.

85. Stewart, Linda. "Picking CD-ROM's for public use." *American Libraries* 18:738–40. October 1987.

86. Cargill, Jennifer. "CD-ROM databases and other new information formats: Their acquisitions." *Acquisitions, Budgets and Materials Costs.* edited by Sul Lee. New York: Haworth, 1988.

87. Ferguson, Anthony. "Assessing the collection need for CD-ROM products." *Library Acquisitions, Practice and Theory* 12:325–32. 1988.

88. Buckland, Michael. "Library materials; paper, microform, database." *College and Research Libraries News* 49:117–122. 1988.

89. Nissley, Meta. "Optical technology: Considerations for collection development." *Library Acquisitions, Practice and Theory* 12:11–15. 1988.

90. Alley, Brian. "Robbing Peter." *Technicalities* 9:1+ September 1989.

91. Welsch, Erwin. "Back to the future—A personal statement on collection development in an information culture." *Library Resources and Technical Services* 33:29–36. January 1989.

92. Johnson, Peggy. "CD-ROM: Issues in acquisitions." *Technicalities* 9:6–8. March 1989.

93. Robinson, Barbara. "Managing change and sending signals in the marketplace." *Library Acquisitions, Practice and Theory* 13:217–25. 1989.

94. Demas, Sam. "Mainstreaming electronic formats." *Library Acquisitions, Practice and Theory* 13:227–32. 1989.

95. Intner, Sheila. "Selecting software." *Library Acquisitions, Practice and Theory* 13:233+ 1989.

96. Reed-Scott, Jutta. "Information technologies and collection development." *Collection Building* 9:47–51. Nos. 3–4, 1989.

97. Downes, Robin. "Electronic technology and access to infor-

mation." *Journal of Library Administration* 12:51–61. No. 3, 1990.

98. Rice, Patricia. "From acquisitions to access." *Library Acquisitions, Practice and Theory* 14:15–21. 1990.

99. Arms, William. "Electronic publishing and the academic library," *Publishing and the Next Generation.* Washington: Society for Scholarly Publishing, 1990.

100. Atkinson, Ross. "Text mutability and collection administration." *Library Acquisitions, Practice and Theory* 14:355–58. 1990.

101. Richardson, Ernest. "Cooperation in lending among college and reference libraries." *Library Journal* 24:32–36. May 1899.

102. Gould, Charles. "Regional libraries." *Library Journal* 33:218–19. June 1908.

103. Weber, David. "A century of cooperative programs among academic libraries." *College and Research Libraries* 37:205–21. May 1976.

104. Sohn, Jeanne. "Cooperative collection development: A brief overview." *Collection Management* 8:1–9. Summer 1986.

105. Luquire, Wilson. *Coordinating Collection Development: A National Cooperative Perspective.* New York: Haworth, 1985.

106. Hewitt, Joe. "Cooperative collection development programs of the Triangle Research Libraries Network." *Coordinating Cooperative Collection Development,* edited by Wilson Luquire. New York: Haworth, 1985.

107. Ballard, Thomas. *The Failure of Resource Sharing in Public Libraries and Alternative Strategies for Service.* Chicago: ALA, 1986.

108. Hewitt, Joe and John Shipman. "Cooperative collection development among research libraries in the age of networking." *Advances in Library Automation and Networking.* 1:189–232. 1987.

109. Branin, Joseph. "Issues in cooperative collection development: The promise and frustration of resource sharing," *Issues in Cooperative Collection Development,* edited by June Engle. Atlanta: SLN, 1986.

110. Dougherty, Richard. "A conceptual framework for organizing resource sharing and shared collection development programs." *Journal of Academic Librarianship* 14:287–91. 1988.

111. Boisse, Joseph. "CRL membership: The library director's perspective." *Library Administration, Practice and Theory* 12:399–402. 1988.

112. Rutledge, John and Luke Swindler. "Evaluating membership in a resource sharing program. The CRL." *College and Research Libraries* 49:409–24. 1988.

113. Michalak, Sarah. "Visions for the future on resource sharing." *PNLA Quarterly* 53:4. 1988.

114. Jaramillo, George. "Computer technology and its impact on collection development." *Collection Management* 10:1–13. Nos. 1–2, 1988.

115. Sartori, Eva. "Regional collection development of serials." *Collection Management* 11:69–76. Nos. 1–2, 1989.

116. Cruse, Larry. "New tools for collaborative map collection development." *Information Bulletin of the Western Association of Map Libraries* 20:215–20. June 1989.

117. Hamilton, Paula and Hugh Feis. "A model of cooperative collection development practices for academic libraries." Technicalities 9:9–11. August 1989.

118. Pettos, William. "Cooperative collection development: The Northern California experience." *Collection Building* 9:3–6. No. 2, 1989.

119. Mosher, Paul. "Cooperative collection development: Collaborative independence." *Collection Building* 9:29–32. Nos. 3–4, 1989.

120. Mosher, Paul. "Collaborative interdependence: The human dimensions of the Conspectus." *IFLA Journal* 16:327–31. 1990.

121. Dowd, Sheila. "Library cooperation: Methods, models to aid information access." *Journal of Library Administration* 12:63–81. No. 3, 1990.

122. *Advances in Library Resource Sharing.* Westport: Meckler, 1990.

COMPREHENSIVE BIBLIOGRAPHY ON COLLECTION DEVELOPMENT

123. Aaron, S.L. "The collection developer's link to global education." *School Library Media Quarterly.* pp. 35–43. Fall, 1990.
124. Agnew, Grace et al. "Faculty AV materials use and collection planning at Georgia State." *Collection Management.* pp. 1–2. 1989.
125. Allen, G.G. and Lee Tat. "The development of an objective budget allocation procedure for academic library acquisitions." *Libri.* pp. 211–221. September, 1987.
126. Alley, Brian. "Cooperative collection development: A national perspective." *Technicalities.* pp. 10+. October, 1985.
127. Alley, Brian and J.S. Cargill. "Inventory and selection techniques for large unorganized collections." *Library Acquisitions, Practice and Theory.* pp. 23–28. Nov. 1, 1978.
128. Allison, A.M. "Managing collections in an automated network environment." *Collection Building.* pp. 24–32. Nov. 2, 1988.
129. Altran, S. "Collection development in practice in an independent school." *Catholic Library World,* pp. 110–112. October, 1982.
130. Amir, M.J. and W. B. Newman. "Information: Unlimited demands, limited funds." *Collection Management,* pp. 111–119. Spring, 1979.
131. Anderson, C. "Spreadsheet programs and collection development." *Wilson Library Bulletin,* pp. 90+. September, 1990.
132. Anderson, L.W. "Feasibility study for establishing cooperative programs for state academic libraries." *Library Research in Progress,* p. 5. March, 1963.
133. Angel, Michael and Carol Budnick. "Collection development and acquisitions for service to off-campus students."

Library Acquisitions, Practice and Theory, pp. 13–24. Nov. 1, 1986.

134. Archer, J.D. "Preorder searching in academic libraries: A bibliographic essay." *Library Acquisitions, Practice and Theory.* pp. 139–144. Nov. 2, 1983.

135. Ash, Lee. "Farmington Plan junk." *Library Journal.* p. 3050. September 15, 1960.

136. Asheim, Lester. "Facets of book selection." *Mountain Plains Library Quarterly.* pp. 3–4. Spring, 1960.

137. Asheim, Lester. "The librarian's responsibility—not censorship but selection," in *Freedom of Book Selection* by F.J. Moshier. Chicago: American Library Association, 1964.

138. Asheim, Lester. "Problems of censorship in book selection." *Bay State Librarian.* pp. 5–9. Winter, 1962.

139. Atkinson, R.W. "The language of the levels: Reflections on the communication of collection development policy." *College and Research Libraries.* pp. 140–149. March, 1986.

140. Atkinson, R. W. "Old forms, new forms—the challenge of collection development." *College and Research Libraries.* pp. 507–520. September, 1989.

141. Atkinson, R. W. "Preparation for privation—the year's work in collection management." *Library Resources and Technical Services.* pp. 249–262. July, 1988.

142. Atkinson, R.W. "Preservation and collection development—toward a political synthesis." *Journal of Academic Librarianship.* pp. 98–103. May, 1990.

143. Atkinson, R.W. "The role of abstraction in bibliography and collection development." *Libri.* pp.201–216. September, 1989.

144. Atkinson, R.W. "Selection for preservation—a materialistic approach." *Library Resources and Technical Services.* pp. 341–353. October-December, 1986.

145. Avant, John. " Slouching toward criticism." *Library Journal.* pp. 4055–4059. December 15, 1971.

146. Axford, H. William. "Economics of a domestic approval plan." *College and Research Libraries.* pp. 368–375. September, 1971.

147. Baatz, Wilmer. "Collection development in 19 libraries of the Association of Research Libraries." *Library Acquisitions, Practice and Theory.* pp. 85–121. No. 2, 1978.

148. Bain, Chris and Bernice Casey. "State-private contract for library resource sharing." *Special Libraries.* pp. 332–336. September, 1978.

149. Baker. S.L. "Does the use of a demand oriented selection policy reduce overall collection quality?" *Public Library Quarterly.* pp. 29–49. Fall, 1984.

150. Baker, S.L. "Research related to client-centered collection development." *Unabashed Librarian.* p. 3. No. 66, 1988.

151. Ballard, T.H. *The Failure of Resource Sharing in Public Libraries and Alternative Strategies For Service.* Chicago: American Library Association, 1986.

152. Barcus, T.R. and V.W. Clapp. "Collecting in the national interest." *Library Trends.* pp. 337–355. April, 1955.

153. Barker, J.W. "Acquisitions and collection development 2001." *Library Acquisitions, Practice and Theory.* pp. 243–248, 1988.

154. Barker, J.W. "Acquisitions in the West." *Library Acquisitions, Practice and Theory.* pp. 5–43. No. 1, 1991.

155. Baughman, James. "Toward a structural approach to collection development." *College and Research Libraries.* pp. 241–248. May, 1977.

156. Baughman, R. "Our growing collections." *Columbia Library Columns.* pp. 39–45. November, 1959.

157. Baughman, R. "The selection and acquisition of rare books and related materials at Columbia University." *Library Resources and Technical Services.* pp. 271–278. Fall, 1958.

158. Beckerman, E.P. "Administrator's viewpoint—collection development in an urban setting: Case study and responses." *Collection Building.* pp. 35–44. Winter, 1984.

159. Beckerman, E.P. "A few thoughts on collection development." *Collection Building.* pp. 2–4. Summer, 1984.

160. Beilby, M.H. and G.T. Evans. "Information system for collection development in SUNY—a progress report." *Collection Management.* pp. 217–228. Fall, 1978.

161. Beilke, Pat and F.J. Sciara. *Selecting Materials for and about Hispanic and East Asian Children and Young People.* Hamden: Library Professional Publications, 1986.

162. Belland, John. "Factors influencing selection of materials." *School Media Quarterly.* pp. 112–119. Winter, 1978.

163. Bender, Ann. "Allocation of funds in support of collection development in public libraries." *Library Resources and Technical Services,* pp. 45–50. Winter, 1979.

164. Bendix, D. *Some Problems in Book Selection Policies and Practices in Medium Sized Public Libraries.* Urbana: University of Illinois Library School, 1959.

165. Bennett, Scott. "Current initiatives and issues in collection management." *Journal of Academic Librarianship.* pp. 257–261. No. 10, 1984.

166. Bennion, Bruce. "The use of standard selection sources in undergraduate library collection development." *Collection Management.* pp. 141–152. Summer, 1978.

167. Bentley, S. and D. Farrell. "Beyond retrenchment: The reallocation of a library materials budget." *Journal of Academic Librarianship.* pp. 321–25. January, 1985.

168. Berninghausen, David. "Antithesis in librarianship— social responsibility vs. the Library Bill of Rights." *Library Journal.* pp. 3675–3681. November 15, 1972.

169. Berry, John. "Some collecting issues never go away—the medium is not the message." *Library Journal.* p. 4. April 15, 1989.

170. Berry, John. "Two kinds of popular demand in reference to book selection." *Library Journal.* p. 1691. September 15, 1982.

171. Bertalan, F.J. "Selection and reference use in the special library." *Library Trends.* pp. 143–156. July, 1966.

172. Biggs, Mary and Victor Biggs. "Reference collection development in academic libraries: A survey." *Reference Quarterly.* pp. 67–79. Fall, 1987.

173. Billman, B.V. and P. Owens. "School and public library cooperation: A prerequisite for cooperative collection development." *Collection Management.* pp. 183–195. Fall, 1985.

174. Blaske, V.L. "The role of reviews and reviewing media in the selection process." *Collection Management.* pp. 1–40. No. 1, 1989.

175. Blow, B.L. and L. Waddle. "Book selection primer." *English Journal.* pp. 76–79. January 1, 1974.

176. Bob, M.L. "Principles of library non-selection." *New York Library Association Bulletin.* pp. 1+. May, 1976.

177. Boblick, James. *Collection Development Organization and Staffing in ARL Libraries.* Washington: ARL, 1987.

178. Bone, Larry. "The future of book selection and collection building." *Catholic Library World.* pp. 66–68. September, 1975.

179. Bonk, Wallace and Rose Magrill. *Building Library Collections.* 5th edition. Metuchen: Scarecrow Press, 1979.

180. Bostic, M.J. "Written collection development policy—to have and have not." *Collection Management.* pp. 89–103. No. 3–4, 1988.

181. Boyer, Calvin and Nancy Eaton. *Book Selection Policies in American Libraries.* Austin: Armadillo Press, 1971.

182. Boylan, Ray. "Scholarly citadel in Chicago: The Center for Research Libraries." *Wilson Library Bulletin.* pp. 503–506. March, 1979.

183. Branin, J.J. "Information policies for collection development librarians." *Collection Building.* pp. 19–23. No. 3–4, 1988.

184. Bratton, Barry et al. "Selection and acquisition of audio-visual materials by health professionals." *MLA Bulletin.* pp. 355–361. October, 1987.

185. Brenni, V.J. "Book selection and the university library." *Catholic Library World.* pp. 425–429. March, 1967.

186. Brewer, Karen et al. "A method for cooperative serials selection and cancellation through consortium activities." *Journal of Academic Librarianship.* pp. 204–208. September, 1978.

187. Bridges. A.E. "Scholarly book reviews and collection development—a case study in American history." *Journal of Academic Librarianship.* pp. 290–293. November, 1989.

188. Briggs, D.R. "Gift appraisal policy in large research libraries." *College and Research Libraries.* pp. 505–507. November, 1968.

189. Broadus, R.N. *Selecting Materials For Libraries.* New York: H.W. Wilson, 1973.

190. Broderick, Dorothy. "Censorship reevaluated." *Library Journal.* pp. 3816–3818. November 15, 1971.

191. Broderick, Dorothy. "Focus on youth: The non-person gap in public library collections." *Collection Building.* pp. 33–35. Spring, 1983.

192. Broderick, Dorothy. "I may, I might, I must—some philosophical observations on book selection policies." *Library Journal.* pp. 507–510. February 1, 1963.

193. Broude, Jeffrey. "Journal deselection in an academic environment—comparison of faculty and librarian choices." *Serials Librarian.* pp. 147–166. Winter, 1978.

194. Brownson, C.W. "Mechanical selection." *Library Resources and Technical Services.* pp. 17–29. January, 1988.

195. Brownson, C.W. "Modeling library materials expenditure—Initial experiments at Arizona State University." *Library Resources and Technical Services.* pp. 87–103. January, 1991.

196. Bryant, Bonita. "Allocation of human resources for collection development." *Library Resources and Technical Services.* pp. 149–162. April, 1986.

197. Bryant, Bonita. "Automating acquisitions—the planning process." *Library Resources and Technical Services.* pp. 285–298. October, 1984.

198. Bryant, Bonita. "Collection development policies in medium sized academic libraries." *Collection Building.* pp. 6–26. No. 2, 1980.

199. Bryant, Bonita. "The organizational structure of collection development." *Library Resources and Technical Services.* pp. 111–122. April, 1987.

200. Buckeye, Nancy. "A plan for undergraduate participation in book selection." *Library Resources and Technical Services.* pp. 121–125. Spring, 1975.

201. Buckland, Michael. "The roles of collections and the scope of collection development." *Journal of Documentation.* pp. 213–226. September, 1989.

202. Budd, John and Kay Adams. "Allocation formulas in practice." *Library Acquisitions, Practice and Theory.* pp. 381–390, 1989.

203. Buis, E. "Collection development policies." *Collection Management.* pp. 11–26. No. 3, 1990.

204. Bullard, Scott. "Collection development in the Electronic Age." *Library Acquisitions, Practice and Theory.* pp. 209–240. No. 3, 1989.

205. Bullard, Scott. "Education Rita: Part 2-training for collection development." *Library Acquisitions, Practice and Theory.* pp. 243–245. No. 4, 1985.

206. Bullard, Scott. "Read my lips—the politics of collection development." *Library Acquisitions, Practice and Theory.* pp. 251–253. No. 3, 1989.

207. Burr, Robert. "Evaluating library collections—a case study." *Journal of Academic Librarianship.* pp. 256–260. November, 1979.

208. Busha, Charles. "Intellectual freedom and censorship—the climate of opinion in Midwestern public libraries." *Library Quarterly.* pp. 283–301. July, 1972.

209. Butler, Meredith. "Electronic publishing and its impact on libraries: A literature review." *Library Resources and Technical Services.* pp. 41–58. 1984.

210. Buzzard, Marion. "Writing a collection development pol-

icy for an academic library." *Collection Management*. pp. 317–328. Winter, 1978.

211. Buzzard, Marion and John Whaley. "Serials and collection development." *Drexel Library Quarterly*. pp. 37–49. Winter, 1985.

212. Bryant, Bonita. "The organizational structure of collection development." *Library Resources and Technical Services*. pp. 111–122. April, 1987.

213. Byrd, C.K. "Collecting collections." *Library Trends*. pp. 434–436. April, 1961.

214. Byrne, N. "Selection and acquisition in an art school library." *Library Acquisitions, Practice and Theory*. pp. 7–11. No. 1, 1983.

215. Byrnes, M.M. "Preservation and collection management—some common concerns." *Collection Building*. pp. 39–45. No. 3–4, 1988.

216. Cabatu, C. "Selection and acquisition of materials on the social sciences." *ASLP Bulletin*. pp. 46–51. June–September, 1960.

217. Cabeceiras, James. *The Multimedia Library: Materials Selection and Use.* New York: Academic Press, 1978.

218. Cahalan, T.H. "Regional cooperation in the acquisition of foreign dental periodicals." *MLA Bulletin*. pp. 30–33. January, 1957.

219. Caldiero, Wendy. "The selection and use of children's audiovisual materials in public libraries." *Catholic Library World*. pp. 212–215. March–April, 1986.

220. Calhoun, J.C. and J.K. Bracken. "Automated acquisitions and collection development in the Knox College Library." *Information Technology and Libraries*. pp. 246–256. September, 1982.

221. "California schools state their book selection policies—How one state achieved this objective." *School Libraries*. pp. 18–21. March, 1957.

222. Callison, D. "A review of the research related to school library media collections." *School Library Media Quarterly*. pp. 57–62. Fall, 1990.

223. Callison, D. "School library collection development policies in Indiana." *Indiana Libraries*. pp. 5–10. No. 2, 1990.

224. Cargill, J.S. "Collection development policies—an alternative viewpoint." *Library Acquisitions, Practice and Theory*. pp. 47–49. No. 1, 1984.

225. Cargill, J.S. "Today's primary issue—pricing and costs of library materials." *Library Acquisitions, Practice and Theory.* pp. 227–228. No. 3, 1986.

226. Carlson, J.F. "Book selection and the small college library." *Learning Today.* pp. 37–43. Fall, 1971.

227. Carlson, W.H. "Cooperation: An historical review and a forecast." *College and Research Libraries,* pp. 5–13. January, 1952.

228. Carpenter, E.J. "Collection development policies based on approval plans." *Library Acquisitions, Practice and Theory.* pp. 39–43, no. 1, 1989.

229. Carpenter, E.J. "Collection development policies: The case for." *Library Acquisitions, Practice and Theory.* pp. 43–45. No. 1, 1984.

230. Carpenter, E.J. "Toward interdisciplinarity in literacy research—some implications for collection development." *Collection Management.* pp. 75–85. No. 1, 1990.

231. Carrigan, D.P. "Librarians and the dismal science." *Library Journal.* pp. 22–25. June 15, 1988.

232. Carter, M. and W.J. Bonk. *Building Library Collections.* 2nd edition. New York: Scarecrow Press, 1964.

233. Caskey, J.D. "Alan Ginsberg in a high school library?" *Arkansas Libraries.* pp. 3–4. March, 1982.

234. Cass, R. "For public librarians—notes toward a science of selecting books that don't die on the shelf." *Unabashed Librarian.* p. 5. Winter, 1975.

235. Cassell, Mary. "Bare bones adult nonfiction collection." *Unabashed Librarian.* pp. 21–26. no 45, 1982.

236. Castagna, Edwin. "Censorship, intellectual freedom and libraries." *Advances in Librarianship.* New York: Seminar Press, 1971.

237. Caswell, L.S. "Grief and collection development." *Library Acquisitions, Practice and Theory.* pp. 195–199. No. 3, 1987.

238. Cave, R. "Translations and book selection problems." *Library World.* pp. 32–35. August, 1960.

239. Caywood, C. "Nonprint media selection guidelines." *Journal of Youth Services in Libraries.* pp. 90–94. Fall, 1988.

240. Cerny, R. "When less is more—issues in collection development." *School Library Journal.* pp. 130–131. March, 1991.

241. Chamberlin, C.E. "Issues in book and serial acquisition:

Old problems, new solutions." *Serials Review.* pp. 94–95. Winter, 1984.

242. Chiang, K.S. "Software and collection development—part 2." *Technical Services Quarterly.* pp. 17–20. No. 3, 1990.

243. Churukian, A.P. "Current national bibliographies from the Near East as collection development tools." *Library Resources and Technical Services.* pp. 156–162. Spring, 1979.

244. Clapp, V.W. "Cooperative acquisitions." *College and Research Libraries.* pp. 99–100. April, 1947.

245. Cline, Hugh and Loraine Sinnott. *Building Library Collections.* Lexington: Lexington Books, 1981.

246. Cline, L. "Collection management, academic libraries, and service." *Show Me Libraries.* pp. 50–53. October–November, 1984.

247. Cochran, P.A. et al. "Research library collections in a changing universe." *College and Research Libraries.* pp. 214–224. May, 1984.

248. Coffin, L.C. "P.L. 480 in Africa." *Law Library Journal.* pp. 34–40. February, 1967.

249. Cogswell, J.A. "The organization of collection management functions in academic research libraries." *Journal of Academic Librarianship.* pp. 268–276. November, 1987.

250. Cohen, Jacob and Kenneth Leeson. "Sources and uses of funds of academic libraries." *Library Trends.* pp. 25–46. Summer, 1979.

251. Cohen, L.M. "Collection development in Alabama's academic libraries." *Collection Management.* pp. 43–60. Nos. 3–4, 1988.

252. Cohen, L.M. "Resource sharing and coordinated collection development in the network of Alabama academic libraries." *Collection Management.* pp. 149–162. Nos. 3–4, 1988.

253. Coleman, Kathleen and Pauline Dickinson. "Drafting a reference collection policy." *College and Research Libraries.* pp. 227–233. May, 1977.

254. "Collection development against the grain." *Technicalities.* pp. 12–13. December, 1985.

255. Conway, S. et al. "Selection and acquisitions manual development." *Medical Library Association Bulletin.* pp. 54–58. January, 1979.

256. "Cooperative acquisitions project: Some second thoughts." *Connecticut Libraries.* pp. 1–2. November, 1982.

257. "Cooperative collection development in the Illinois Library and Information Network." *Illinois Libraries.* pp. 566–570. September, 1979.

258. Copeland, A.T. "Philosophy journals as current book selection guides." *College and Research Libraries.* pp. 455–460. November, 1966.

259. Corbett, E.M. "Collection development in a liberal arts college library." *Bookmark.* pp. 27–31. Fall, 1982.

260. Coscarelli, W.F. "Acquisition of French language monographic materials." *Collection Management.* pp. 45–53. Spring, 1986.

261. Cox, S. "Preconference 1984: Collection management in public libraries." *Library Acquisitions, Practice and Theory.* pp. 233–241. No. 4, 1984.

262. Creth, S.D. "The organization of collection development—a shift in the organization paradigm." *Journal of Library Administration.* pp. 67–85. No. 1, 1991.

263. Cronin. J.W. "Library of Congress National Program for acquisitions and cataloging." *Libri.* pp. 113–117. 1966.

264. Crush, Marion. "Deselection policy—how to exclude everything." *Wilson Library Bulletin.* pp. 180–181. October, 1970.

265. Cubberly, Carol. "Organization for collection development in mid-sized academic libraries." *Library Acquisitions, Practice and Theory.* pp. 297–323. No. 4, 1987.

266. Curley, A. and D. Broderick. *Building Library Collections.* 6th edition. Metuchen: Scarecrow Press, 1985.

267. Curol, H. and A. Harms. "Using choice on cards for collection development at McNeese." *LLA Bulletin.* pp. 117–120. Winter, 1987.

268. Curran, N.E. "Yours for the ordering." *Wilson Library Bulletin.* pp. 342–344. December, 1962.

269. Current, C.E. "Acquisition of maps for school and other small libraries." *Wilson Library Bulletin.* pp. 578–583. February, 1971.

270. Daily, Jay. *The Anatomy of Censorship.* New York: Marcel Dekker, 1973.

271. Daly, Sally. "Happiness is good selection techniques." *Catholic Library World.* pp. 226+. March–April, 1987.

272. Dane, Chase. "Selection and reference use in the school library." *Library Trends.* pp. 87–92. July, 1966.

273. Danton, J.P. *Book Selection and Collections—A Compar-*

ison of German and American University Libraries. New York: Columbia University Press, 1963.

274. Danton, J.P. "Subject specialist in national and university libraries with special reference to book selection." *Libri.* pp. 42–58, No. 1, 1967.

275. Danton, J.P. "University library budgets 1860, 1910, and 1960: Introduction to an inquiry." *Library Quarterly.* pp. 384–393. July, 1983.

276. Darling, R.L. "Selection and reference use in the school library." *Library Trends.* pp. 87–92. July, 1966.

277. David, C.W. and Rudolf Hirsch. "Importations of foreign monographs under the early influence of the Farmington Plan." *College and Research Libraries.* pp. 101–105. April, 1950.

278. Davis, C.R. "The compleat collection developer." *New Horizons for Academic Libraries.* New York: Saur, 1979.

279. Davis, Mary. "Model for a vendor study in a manual or semi-automated acquisitions system." *Library Acquisitions, Practice and Theory.* pp. 553–60. No. 1, 1979.

280. Day, R. and J. Angus. "Off campus acquisitions at Deakin University." *Library Acquisitions, Practice and Theory.* pp. 43–53. No. 1, 1986.

281. DeGennaro, Richard. "Austerity, technology, and resource sharing: Research libraries face the future." *Library Journal.* pp. 917–923. May 15, 1975.

282. DeGennaro, Richard. "Copyright, resource sharing, and hard times—A view from the field." *American Libraries.* pp. 430–435. September, 1977.

283. DeGennaro, Richard. "Escalating journal prices—time to fight back." *American Libraries.* pp. 69–74. February, 1977.

284. Deller, A.M. "Your book/media selection policy—a public relations opportunity." *Michigan Librarian.* p. 5. Summer, 1973.

285. Demas, S.G. "Mainstreaming electronic formats." *Library Acquisitions, Practice and Theory.* pp. 227–232. No. 3, 1989.

286. Demas, S.G. "Software and collection development, part 1." *Technical Services Quarterly.* pp. 13–16. No. 3, 1990.

287. DeVilbiss, M.L. "Approval built collection in the medium sized academic library." *College and Research Libraries.* pp. 487–492. November, 1975.

288. DeWald, Ernest. "Map procurement in government agencies." *Special Libraries.* pp. 175–178. May–June, 1953.
289. Dick, M.H. "Standing book orders." *Library World.* pp. 95–99. January, 1958.
290. Dickinson, Dennis. "Subject specialists in academic libraries: Once and future dinosaurs." *New Horizons for Academic Libraries.* New York: Saur, 1979.
291. Dimalanta, C. "Selection and acquisition of library materials in pure and applied sciences." *ASLP Bulletin.* pp. 74–78. June–September, 1960.
292. Dixon, J. "Book selection, racism and the law of the land." *Assistant Librarian.* pp. 94+. July–August, 1979.
293. Dobbyn, Margaret. "Approval plan purchasing in perspective." *College and Research Libraries.* pp. 480–484. November, 1972.
294. Donahue, M.K. et al. "Collection development policy making." *Collection Building.* pp. 18–21. Fall, 1984.
295. Dorst, T. "Statewide cooperative collection development." *Illinois Libraries.* pp. 17–18. January, 1987.
296. Dougherty, Richard. "A conceptual framework for organizing resource sharing and shared collection development programs." *Journal of Academic Librarianship.* pp. 287–291. 1988.
297. Doughty, F.W. "Selection criteria: Science books for children." *Horn Book.* pp. 195–200. April, 1965.
298. Douglas, J.W. "Selection principles: A beginner's guide." *New Library World.* pp. 274–275. December, 1973.
299. Dowd, Sheila. "Fee, fie, foe, fum—will the serials giant eat us?" *Journal of Library Administration.* pp. 17–38. 1989.
300. Dowd, Sheila. "Major collection components and policies of the CRL." *Library Acquisitions, Practice and Theory.* pp. 403–405. 1988.
301. Dowlin, Ken. *The Electronic Library.* New York: Neal-Schuman, 1984.
302. Downs, Robert. "Collection development for academic libraries—an overview." *North Carolina Libraries.* pp. 31–38. Fall, 1976.
303. Downs, Robert. "Report on Farmington Plan program." *College and Research Libraries.* p. 143–145. March, 1962.
304. Drazniowsky, R. "Bibliographies as tools for map acquisition and map compilation." *The Cartographer.* pp. 138–144. December, 1966.

305. Dudley, C.C. "Microcomputer software collection development." *Choice.* pp. 704–705. January, 1986.
306. Dudley, N. "Some of the effects of computerization on collection management in American university libraries." *IATUL Proceedings.* pp. 51–55. No. 18, 1986.
307. Dunlap, Connie. "Automated acquisition procedures at the University of Michigan Library." *Library Resources and Technical Services.* pp. 192–202. Spring, 1967.
308. Eaglen, Audrey. "The warning bookmark—selection aid or censorship." *Library Acquisitions, Practice and Theory.* pp. 65–71, no. 3, 1979.
309. Eaton, E.M. and M.H. Mahar. "Selection and organization of library materials for modern language programs." *School Life.* pp. 14–17. May, 1960.
310. Edelman, Hendrik and G. Tatum. "Development of collections in American university libraries." *College and Research Libraries.* pp. 222–245. May, 1976.
311. Ehikhamenor, F.A. "Formula for allocating book funds: The search for simplicity and flexibility." *Libri.* pp. 148–161. June, 1983.
312. Emmens, C.A. "Cooperative purchasing of video." *School Library Journal.* p. 42. February, 1983.
313. Erlandson, J.A. and Y. Boyer. "Acquisition of state documents." *Library Acquisitions, Practice and Theory.* pp. 117–127. No. 2, 1980.
314. Erlich, Martin. "Pruning the groves of Libraro." *Wilson Library Bulletin.* pp. 55–58. September, 1975.
315. Eshelman, L. "French adult book selection." *Ontario Library Review.* pp. 91–96. June, 1975.
316. Espenshade, Ed. "Maps for the college library." *College and Research Libraries.* pp. 132–137. April, 1947.
317. Espenshade, Ed. "No one source for acquiring maps." *Library Journal.* pp. 431–436. March 15, 1950.
318. Esterquest, R.T. "Aspects of library cooperation." *College and Research Libraries.* pp. 203–208, May, 1958.
319. Esterquest, R.T. "Building library resources through cooperation." *Library Trends.* pp. 257–283. January, 1958.
320. Evans, G. Edward. "Book selection and book collection usage in academic libraries." *Library Quarterly.* pp. 297–308. July, 1970.
321. Evans, G. Edward. *Developing Library and Information Center Collections.* Littleton: Libraries Unlimited, 1987.

322. Evans, G. Edward. *Developing Library Collections.* Littleton: Libraries Unlimited, 1979.

323. Evans, G. Edward. "Limits to growth, or the need to weed." *California Librarian.* pp. 8–15. April, 1977.

324. Evans, G. Edward. "Review essay—shaping library collections for the 1980's." *Collection Management.* pp. 61–69. Fall, 1982.

325. Evans, R.W. "Collection development policy statement." *Collection Management.* pp. 63–73. Spring, 1985.

326. Fahy, T.W. and S.A. Bosch. "A model of the publishing universe within which collection development operates." *Serials Review,* pp. 7–10. No. 2, 1989.

327. Fain, E. "Selection and soapboxes: An ideological primer." *Wilson Library Bulletin.* pp. 136–139. October, 1977.

328. Farber, Evan. "Limiting college library growth: bane or boon?" *Journal of Academic Librarianship.* pp. 12–15. November, 1975.

329. Farber, Evan and William Miller. "Collection development from a college perspective. Comment and response." *College and Research Libraries.* pp. 325–328. July, 1979.

330. Farrell, D. "The NCIP option for coordinated collection management." *Library Resources and Technical Services.* pp. 47–56. January, 1986.

331. Feng, T.Y. "The necessity for a written collection development statement." *Library Resources and Technical Services.* pp. 39–44. Winter, 1979.

332. Ferguson, A.W. "University library collection development and management using a structural-functional systems model." *Collection Management.* pp. 1–14. Spring, 1986.

333. Fiels, Keith. "Coordinated collection development in a multitype environment." *Collection Building.* pp. 26–31. No. 2, 1986.

334. Fineman, C.S. "Madame Signoret's lament and West European library collections." *Collection Management.* pp. 15–25. Spring–Summer, 1983.

335. Fiske, Marjorie. *Book Selection and Censorship: A Study of School and Public Libraries in California.* Berkeley: University of California Press, 1959.

336. Fiste, D. "Practical aspects of collection development."

Library Acquisitions, Practice and Theory. pp. 33–64. No. 1, 1989.

337. Flanagan, Leo. "Defending the indefensible—the limits of intellectual freedom." *Library Journal.* pp. 1887–1891. October 15, 1975.

338. Fletcher, J. "Selecting scholarly books." *Library Journal.* p. 1677. September 15, 1978.

339. Folke, C. "Selective bibliography on school materials selection and censorship." *Wisconsin Library Bulletin.* pp. 37–41. Spring, 1981.

340. Follett, Charles. "FLB's side of the story." *Library Acquisitions, Practice and Theory.* pp. 73–75. No. 3, 1979.

341. Forcier, P.C. "Building collections together—The Pacific Northwest Conspectus." *Library Journal.* pp. 43–45. April 15, 1988.

342. Forcier, P.C. "LIRN Grant initiates collection development planning." *PNLA Quarterly.* p. 21. Winter, 1986.

343. Ford, K.E. "Interaction of public and technical services: Collection development as common ground." *Journal of Library Administration.* pp. 41–53. No. 1, 1988.

344. Ford, Stephen. *Acquisition of Library Materials.* Chicago: American Library Association, 1973.

345. Forinash, M.R. "Materials selection for adult basic education collections." *Drexel Library Quarterly.* pp. 14–32. October, 1978.

346. Fraley, Ruth. "Publishers vs. wholesalers: The ordering dilemma." *Library Acquisitions, Practice and Theory.* pp. 9–13. No. 1, 1979.

347. Francis, J.P. "Some observations on book selection." *New Library World.* pp. 131–133. August, 1984.

348. Frankie, S.O. "Collection development in academic libraries." *Catholic Library World.* pp. 103–109. October, 1982.

349. *Freedom of Book Selection.* Chicago: American Library Association, 1954.

350. Frizzell, M. "Book selection in a cooperative group." *North County Librarian.* pp. 8–10. March, 1963.

351. Furnham, Adair. "Book reviews as a selection tool for librarians: Comments from a psychologist." *Collection Management.* pp. 33–43. Spring, 1986.

352. Fussler, Herman et al. "Acquisition policy—A symposium." *College and Research Libraries.* pp. 363–372. October, 1953.

353. Futas, Elizabeth. "Conference goers' guides to collection building." *Collection Building.* pp. 62–71. No. 2, 1981.

354. Futas, Elizabeth. "Issues in collection development: Ready reference collections." *Collection Building.* pp. 46–48. No. 3, 1981.

355. Galloway, R.D. "Cooperative acquisitions for California's libraries." *California Librarian.* pp. 183–187. July, 1963.

356. Galloway, R.D. "Library cooperation at the grass roots: A regional intertype library network in the San Joaquin Valley." *Journal of Academic Librarianship.* pp. 430–433. January, 1979.

357. Galvin, Thomas and A. Kent. "Use of a university library collection: A progress report on a Pittsburgh study." *Library Journal.* pp. 2317–2320. November 15, 1977.

358. Galvin, Thomas and Beverly Lynch. *Priorities for Academic Libraries.* San Francisco: Josey-Bass, 1982.

359. Ganly, J. "The European Community—sources of information for 1992." *Collection Building.* pp. 26–31. No. 1, 1990.

360. Gardner, C.A. "Book selection policies in the college library: A reappraisal." *College and Research Libraries.* pp. 140–146. March, 1985.

361. Gardner, Richard. *Library Collections: Their Origins, Selection, and Development.* New York: McGraw Hill, 1981.

362. Garg, K.C. and S.P. Gupta. "Collection development and management in special libraries in India." *Collection Management.* pp. 103–112. Summer, 1986.

363. Gaunt, M. "Machine readable literary texts: Collection development issues." *Collection Management.* pp. 87–96. Nos. 1–2, 1990.

364. Gaver, M.V. *Background Readings in Building Library Collections.* Metuchen: Scarecrow Press, 1969.

365. Gensel, S. and A. Powers. "Collection development and the special library." *Bookmark.* pp. 11–15. Fall, 1982.

366. Gerhardt, L.N. "Getting ahead takes more than a 4% increase in book budget." *School Library Journal.* p. 82. March, 1988.

367. Gerhardt, L.N. "Selection overtime." *School Library Journal.* p. 2. April, 1985.

368. Getz, M. "Economics—managing the collecting effort." *Bottom Line.* pp. 41–43. No. 1, 1989.

369. Getz, M. "The economics of research libraries—present

state and future prospects." *IFLA Journal.* pp. 299–305. No. 4, 1989.

370. Gibb, I.P. "Foreign book procurement, the decennial Farmington Plan survey and afterwards." *Journal of Documentation.* pp. 1–9. March, 1960.

371. Giblon, D.L. "Materials selection policies and changing adult needs." *Catholic Library World.* pp. 378–379. April, 1982.

372. Gillespie, J.T. "Selection tools for school libraries." *Catholic Library World.* pp. 269–270. May–June, 1988.

373. Gingerich, M. "Effective acquisition program for the religious archives." *American Archivist.* pp. 515–518. October, 1966.

374. Gleason, M.L. "Training collection development librarians." *Collection Management.* pp. 1–8. Winter, 1982.

375. Gleaves, E.S. "Carter and Bonk revisited—review of recent collection development literature." *Collection Management.* pp. 79–85. Spring, 1987.

376. Glicksman, Maurice. "Changing patterns of scholarly communications—implications for libraries." *Library Acquisitions, Practice and Theory.* pp. 341–346. 1990.

377. Gluck, Harold. "Maps practically for the asking." *Journal of Geography.* pp. 36–39. January, 1940.

378. Godden, Irene. *Collection Development and Acquisitions, 1970–1980: An Annotated, Critical Bibliography.* Metuchen: Scarecrow Press, 1982.

379. Goehner, D.M. "Allocating by formula: The rationale from an institutional perspective." *Collection Management.* pp. 161–173. Fall–Winter, 1983.

380. Gold, Steven. "Allocating the book budget." *College and Research Libraries.* pp. 397–402. September, 1975.

381. Goldblatt, M.A. and B.D. Reams. "Cooperative acquisitions among law libraries." *Law Library Journal.* pp. 657–667. no. 4, 1984–85.

382. Gore, Dan. *Farewell to Alexandria: Solutions to Space, Growth and Performance Problems of Libraries.* Westport: Greenwood Press, 1976.

383. Gore, Dan. "The view from the Tower of Babel." *Library Journal.* pp. 1599–1605. September 15, 1975.

384. Gorman, G.E. "Collection development and acquisitions in a distance learning environment." *Library Acquisitions, Practice and Theory.* pp. 9–66. No. 1, 1986.

385. Goyal, S.K. "Allocation of library funds to different departments of a university." *College and Research Libraries.* pp. 219–222. May, 1973.
386. Graham, J.W. "Where to find college sports information." *RQ.* pp. 381–391. Spring, 1989.
387. Grannis, F. "Book selection for the blind." *Catholic Library World.* pp. 491–496. April, 1969.
388. Grannis, F. "Philosophical implications of book selection for the blind." *Wilson Library Bulletin.* pp. 330–339. December, 1968.
389. Grant, J. "Purpose and value of the RTSD guidelines in collection development." *Bookmark.* pp. 20–23. Fall, 1982.
390. Gration, Selby and Arthur Young. "Reference-bibliographers in the college library." *College and Research Libraries.* pp. 28–34. January, 1974.
391. Gregory, V.L. "Development of academic library budgets in selected states with emphasis on the utilization of formulas." *Journal of Library Administration.* pp. 23–45. No. 1, 1990.
392. Grieder, Ted. *Acquisitions: Where, What and How.* Westport: Greenwood Press, 1978.
393. Groesbeck, J. "U.N. documents and their accessibility." *Library Resources and Technical Services.* pp. 313–318. Summer, 1966.
394. Grover, M.L. "Collection assessment in the 1980's." *Collection Building.* pp. 23–26. No. 4, 1987.
395. Guappone, R.A. et al. "Integrating electronic publishing into the concepts and practices of collection development." *Library Acquisitions, Practice and Theory.* pp. 327–329. 1990.
396. Gwinn, Nancy. "A National Periodicals Center: Articulating the dream." *Library Journal.* pp. 2166–2169. November 1, 1978.
397. Haar, J.M. "The reference collection development decision—will new information technologies influence libraries' collecting patterns?" *Reference Librarian.* pp. 113–124. No. 22, 1988.
398. Hacken, R.D. "Current trends in the planning and development of Northern European collections." *Collection Management.* pp. 69–87. Fall–Winter, 1983.
399. Haertle, Robert. "Coordinating collections in the Milwaukee area," in *Making Cooperation Work,* Library Journal Special Report #9. New York: R.R. Bowker, 1979.

400. Hagler, Ronald. "Selection and acquisition of books in six Ontario public libraries in relation to the Canadian publishing system." PhD thesis. University of Michigan, 1961.
401. Haight, A.L. *Banned Books.* New York: R.R. Bowker, 1958.
402. Haines, H.E. *Living With Books—The Art of Book Selection.* New York: Columbia University Press, 1950.
403. Hale, C.E. "Library consumerism—a need for concerted action saying no to exorbitantly high book and periodical prices." *Technicalities.* pp. 8–9. May, 1984.
404. Hall, Blaine. "Writing the collection assessment manual." *Collection Management.* pp. 49–61. Fall–Winter, 1984.
405. Hamaker, Charles. "Costs and the serials information chain: Containing the impact on library budgets." *Journal of Library Administration.* pp. 99–113. 1989.
406. Hamer, E.E. "Conferences in Europe on shared cataloging and acquisition programs." *Library of Congress Information Bulletin.* pp. 721–722. November 17, 1966.
407. Hamilton, P.A. and H. Feiss. "A model of cooperative collection development policies for academic libraries." *Technicalities.* pp. 9–11. August, 1989.
408. Hamilton, P.A. and T.L. Weech. "Give them what they want or give them what they should have: Survey of attitudes about quality vs demand debate in collection development." *Illinois Libraries.* pp. 284–289. April, 1987.
409. Hamlin, A.T. "Impact of college enrollments on library acquisition policy." *Liberal Education.* pp. 204–210. May, 1966.
410. Hannaford, William. "Tilting at windmills—selection in college libraries." *Collection Management.* pp. 31–35. Nos. 1–2, 1990.
411. Hardesty, Larry. "Book selection for undergraduate libraries: A study of faculty attitudes." *Journal of Academic Librarianship.* pp. 19–25. March, 1986.
412. Harloe, B. "Achieving client-centered collection development in small and medium-sized academic libraries." *College and Research Libraries.* pp. 344–353. May, 1989.
413. Haro, R.P. "Book selection in academic libraries." *College and Research Libraries.* pp. 104–106. March, 1967.
414. Hart, Harold. *Censorship: For and Against.* New York: Hart, 1971.
415. Hartz, F.R. "Selection of school-media materials." *Catholic Library World.* pp. 425–429. May, 1976.

416. Hattendorf, L.C. "The art of reference collection development." *RQ.* pp. 219–229. Winter, 1989.
417. Haviland, Virginia. "Building the foundation—the book collection." *Library Trends.* pp. 14–23. July, 1963.
418. Hayes, R.M. "Summary of the Institute on Collection Development for the Electronic Library." *Library Acquisitions, Practice and Theory.* pp. 359–370. 1990.
419. Haywood, C.R. "Old, bold librarians: An acquisitions program to fit the library college." *Library College Journal.* pp. 11–14. Summer, 1968.
420. Hazen, Don. "Collection development, collection management, and preservation." *Library Resources and Technical Services.* pp. 3–11. March, 1982.
421. Headings, B.E. "The formulation of a book budget policy for a small college library." *Wilson Library Bulletin.* pp. 389–391. January, 1952.
422. Heard, J.N. "Suggested procedures for sharing acquisitions in academic libraries." *Louisiana Library Association Bulletin.* pp. 17–21. Spring, 1972.
423. Heinzkill, R. "The literary canon and collection building." *Collection Management.* pp. 51–64. Nos. 1–2, 1990.
424. Heinzkill, R. "Retrospective collection development in English literature: An overview." *Collection Management.* pp. 55–65. Spring, 1987.
425. Heitshu, Sara and J.T. Leach. "Developing serials collections in the 1990's." *Collection Building.* pp. 53–59, Nos. 3–4, 1989.
426. Helen, S.N. "Book purchasing for a small college library." *Catholic Library World.* pp. 147–152. December, 1957.
427. Hellenga, R.R. "Departmental acquisitions policies for small college libraries." *Library Acquisitions, Practice and Theory.* pp. 81–84. Nos. 2, 1979.
428. Hendricks, D.D. "Interuniversity council cooperative acquisitions of journals." *Texas Library Journal.* pp. 269+. November, 1971.
429. Hernon, Peter and Jory Purcell. *Developing Collections of U.S. Government Publications.* Greenwich: JAI Press, 1980.
430. Herzog, K.S. "Collection development for the electronic library." *Computers in Libraries.* pp. 9–13. November, 1990.
431. Hewitt, J.A. "Education for acquisitions and serials librarianship." *Library Acquisitions, Practice and Theory.* pp. 185–194. Nos. 3, 1987.

432. Hewitt, Joe. "Impact of networks on collection development." *Library Acquisitions, Practice and Theory.* pp. 209–216. 1977.
433. Hill, B.N. "New England academic librarians writing seminar: Collection development: The right and responsibility of librarians." *Journal of Academic Librarianship.* pp. 285–286. November, 1977.
434. Hitchcock, K.A. "Collection management in the 80's: Where are we now?" *Library Acquisitions, Practice and Theory.* pp. 3–12. No. 1, 1985.
435. Hodge, Elizabeth. "Book selection practices in the nation's schools." *School Libraries.* pp. 111–115. March, 1957.
436. Hodge, S.P. et al. "Formulating an integrated library government documents collection policy." *Government Information Quarterly.* pp. 199–213. nos. 2, 1989.
437. Hodowanec, G. "Literature obsolescence, dispersion, and collection development." *College and Research Libraries.* pp. 421–423. November, 1983.
438. Hodson, J. "Development of a local database for collection development and SDI." *Small Computers in Libraries.* pp. 28–29. January, 1988.
439. Hoffman, Andrea. "Collection development programs in academic libraries: An administrative approach." *Bookmark.* pp. 121–125. Spring, 1979.
440. Hoffman, H.H. "Cooperative acquisitions in German research libraries." *Library Quarterly.* pp. 249–257. July, 1964.
441. Holicky, B.H. "Collection development vs. resource sharing: View from the small academic library." *Journal of Academic Librarianship.* pp. 146–147. July, 1984.
442. Holley, R.P. "Modest proposal on modern literature collection development." *Journal of Academic Librarianship.* pp. 91+. May 1979.
443. Holter, C.S. "Selecting books for young adults." *Catholic Library World.* pp. 170–171. January–February, 1986.
444. Hoolihan, C. "Collection development policies in medical rare book collections." *Collection Management.* pp. 167–169. Nos. 3–4, 1989.
445. Horney, Karen. "Building Northwestern's core." *Library Journal.* pp. 1580–1583. May 1, 1971.
446. *How Baltimore Chooses: Selection Policies of the Enoch Pratt Free Library.* Baltimore: The Library, 1973.

447. Howard, G.S. "High-low collection building." *School Library Journal.* pp. 120–121. October, 1982.
448. Hulbert, Linda and David Curry. "Evaluation of an approval plan." *College and Research Libraries.* pp. 485–491. November, 1978.
449. Hulfish, J.W. "Audiovisual media for librarians." *Illinois Libraries.* pp. 99–103. February, 1965.
450. Immroth, B.F. "Limiting what students read: Books and other learning materials in our public schools - how they are selected and removed." *Texas Library Journal.* pp. 113. Winter, 1981.
451. Intner, Sheila. "Selecting software." *Library Acquisitions, Practice and Theory.* pp. 233+ 1989.
452. Ionesco, M. "Regional cooperation for research collections." *Collection Building.* pp. 7–11. No. 2, 1988.
453. Jacobs, P.I. "Nonprint materials - a low-cost treasure for libraries." *Library Journal.* pp. 58–59. November 15, 1989.
454. Jacobson, Susan. "The Q Formula - comments." *Library Acquisitions, Practice and Theory.* pp. 307–09. No. 4, 1986.
455. Jaramillo, G.R. "Computer technology and its impact on collection development." *Collection Management.* pp. 1–13. Nos. 1, 1988.
456. Jenkins, F. "The acquisition of scientific and technological materials." *Library Trends.* pp. 414–421. April, 1955.
457. Johnson, Edward. "Financial planning needs of publicly supported academic libraries in the 1980's." *Journal of Library Administration.* pp. 23–26. Fall–Winter, 1982.
458. Johnson, J.M. "Government publications and collections development policies." *Illinois Libraries.* pp. 477–79. November, 1989.
459. Johnson, Jean. "Collection management for off-campus library services." *Library Acquisitions, Practice and Theory.* pp. 75–84. No. 1, 1987.
460. Johnson, M.A. "Collection development officer - a reality check." *Library Resources and Technical Services.* pp. 153–160. April, 1989.
461. Johnson, M.A. "The future has arrived prematurely - MRDF and collection development." *Technicalities.* pp. 10–13. September, 1989.
462. Johnston, M. and J. Wekert. "Selection advisor - an expert system for collection development." *Information Technology and Libraries.* pp. 218–225. September, 1990.

463. Jones, A. "Resource sharing in an electronic age - past, present, and future." *Catholic Library World.* pp. 104–106. November–December, 1989.

464. Jones, C.L. "Cooperative serial acquisition program: Thoughts on a response to mounting fiscal pressures." *Medical Library Association Bulletin.* pp. 120–123. April, 1974.

465. Jones, H. and R. Lawson. "Intellectual freedom and materials selection." *School Media Quarterly.* pp. 113–116. Winter, 1973.

466. Jordan, R.T. "Eliminate the middleman in book ordering." *Library Journal.* pp. 327–329. January 15, 1961.

467. Kaegbein, P. "National collection building in the Federal Republic of Germany." *Journal of Academic Librarianship.* pp. 81–85. May, 1987.

468. Kanazawa, M. "Organization theory and collection management in libraries." *Collection Management.* pp. 43–57. No. 1, 1991.

469. Kaplan, L. "Public Law 480." *ACLS Newsletter.* pp. 8–9. March, 1966.

470. Katz, William. "Class and selection." *Collection Building.* pp. 34–36. No. 3, 1985.

471. Katz, William. *Collection Development: The Selection of Materials for Libraries.* New York: Holt, Rinehart, 1980.

472. Katz, William. *Magazine Selection: How to Build a Community-Oriented Collection.* New York: R.R. Bowker, 1971.

473. Kebabian, J.S. "Book appraisals." *Library Trends.* pp. 466–470. April, 1961.

474. Keder, J. "Using the campus network for ILL and book orders." *Library Software Review.* pp. 250–251. September–October, 1989.

475. Keller, George. *Academic Strategy: The Management Revolution in American Higher Education.* Baltimore: Johns Hopkins Press, 1983.

476. Kelly, G.J. "The development of acquisitions and collection services for off-campus students in Northeastern Ontario." *Library Acquisitions Practice and Theory.* pp. 47–66. No. 1, 1987.

477. Kennedy, Gail. "Relationship between acquisitions and collection development." *Library Acquisition Practice and Theory.* pp. 225–232. No. 3, 1983.

478. Kent, Allen. "Library resource sharing networks - how to make a choice." *Library Acquisitions Practice and Theory.* pp. 69–76. 1978.

479. Kent, Allen. *Resource Sharing in Libraries: How, Why, When, Next Action Steps.* New York: Dekker, 1974.
480. Kephart, J.E. "Spending library book funds." *Catholic Library World.* pp. 558–560. May, 1969.
481. Kilton, Thomas. "Out-of-print pronouncement in academic libraries." *Collection Management.* pp. 113–134. Fall–Winter, 1983.
482. Kim, David V. and Wilson, C.A. *Policies of Publishers - A Handbook for Order Libraries.* Scarecrow Press, 1989.
483. King, Jack. "Collecting business records." *American Archivist.* pp. 387–390. July, 1964.
484. Kingery, R.E. "Latin American cooperative acquisition project." *Stechert-Hafner Book News.* pp. 65–66. February, 1960.
485. Kleberg, Tonnes. "Cooperation in acquisitions." *Library Journal.* pp. 4319–4322. November 15, 1963.
486. Kemp, Betty. *School Library and Media Center Acquisition Policies and Procedures.* Phoenix: Oryx Press, 1986.
487. Koenig, Dorothy. "Rushmore at Berkeley: The dynamics of developing a written collection development policy statement." *Journal of Academic Librarianship.* pp. 344–350. No. 7, 1982.
488. Kohl, David. *Acquisitions, Collection Development and Collection Use: A Handbook for Library Management.* Santa Barbara: ABC-CLIO, 1985.
489. Kohl, David. *Circulation, Interlibrary Loan, Patron Use, and Collection Maintenance.* Santa Barbara: ABC-CLIO, 1986.
490. Kohut, Joe. "Allocating the book budget: A Model." *College and Research Libraries.* pp. 192–199. May, 1974.
491. Kohut, Joe and John Walker. "Allocating the book budget - Equity and economic efficiency." *College and Research Libraries.* pp. 403–410. September, 1975.
492. Kosa, Geza. "Book selection tools for subject specialists in a large research library." *LRTS.* pp. 13–18. Winter, 1975.
493. Kosa, Geza. "Book selection trends in American academic libraries." *Australian Library Journal.* pp. 416–424. November, 1972.
494. Kovacs, B. *The Decision-Making Process for Library Collections.* Westport, CT: Greenwood, 1990.
495. Kraft, Donald and Richard Polacsek. "A journal worth measure for a journal selection decision model." *Collection Management.* pp. 121–139. Summer, 1978.

496. Krarup, Agnes. "Book selection policies in the Pittsburgh public schools." *School Libraries.* pp. 24–28. March, 1957.

497. Kreimeyer, V.R. "Washington's cooperative collection development project." *PNLA Quarterly,* pp. 26–28. Spring, 1989.

498. Kroll, R.H. "The place of reference collection development in the organization structure of the library." *Resource Quarterly.* pp. 96–100. Fall, 1985.

499. Kornick, David. "A regional cooperative acquisition program for monographs." *Medical Library Association Bulletin.* pp. 297–301. July, 1979.

500. Kornick, David. "Preventing wastelands: A personal statement." *Library Journal.* pp. 483–87. February 15, 1980.

501. Kujoth, J.S. *Libraries, Readers, and Book Selection.* Scarecrow Press, 1969.

502. Kull, B. "Evaluating materials: Preventing and selection of media materials." *Media Spectrum.* pp. 6+. No. 2, 1982.

503. Kumar, S. "Sources for the selection of British Government Publications." *Annals of Library Science.* pp. 115–118. September, 1962.

504. Ladenson, A. "Budget control of book purchases and binding expenditures in large public libraries." *Library Resources and Technical Services.* pp. 47–58. Winter, 1960.

505. Lake, A.C. and J.S. Dunn. "Book selection standards - education or communication?" *Wilson Library Bulletin.* pp. 672–676. April, 1963.

506. Lancaster, Fredrick et al. "The changing face of the library: A look at libraries and librarians in the year 2001." *Collection Management.* pp. 55–77. Spring, 1979.

507. Lane, David. "New York case study 3 - METRO Cooperative Acquisition Program." *Multitype Library Cooperation.* New York: Bowker, 1977.

508. Laughlin, M. "Principles for the principal in selection of materials for a school library." *Learning Today.* pp. 57–59. Winter, 1980.

509. Leaver, R.A. "Hymnals, hymnal companions, and collection development." *Notes.* pp. 331–354. December, 1990.

510. Lee, Sul. *Serials Development: Choices and Strategies.* Ann Arbor: Pierian Press, 1981.

511. Leggett, M. "Developing an Indiana business directory collection." *Indiana Libraries.* pp. 32–37. No. 2, 1990.

512. Lein, E. "Suggestions for formulating collection development policy statements for music score collections in academic libraries." *Collection Management.* pp. 69–101. Winter, 1987.

513. Lenzini. R.T. and T.P. Koppel. "CARL and collection development: Building on a strong foundation." *Colorado Libraries.* pp. 14–17. March, 1990.

514. Leon, S.J. "Book selection in Philadelphia." *Library Journal.* pp. 1081–89. April 1, 1973.

515. Leon, S.J. "Survey of the handling of certain controversial adult materials by Philadelphia area libraries." *Pennsylvania Library Association Bulletin.* pp. 195+. July, 1972.

516. Leonard, Virginia. "Book selection in Grosse Points - where school librarians advise the public library." *ALA bulletin.* pp. 627–29. June, 1966.

517. Leonhardt, T. "Collection development and acquisitions: The division of responsibility." *RTSD News.* pp. 73–75. No. 6, 1984.

518. Logan, George. "New Orleans Public Library reviews its gifts." *Library Journal.* pp. 2093–2096. September 15, 1957.

519. Losee, Robert. "A decision - theoretic model of materials selection and acquisition." *Library Quarterly.* pp. 269–283. July, 1987.

520. Lucas, T.A. "Verifying the Conspectus - Problems and progress." *College and Research Libraries News.* pp. 199–201. March, 1990.

521. Lucker, Jay K. "Library Resources and bibliographic control." *College and Research Libraries.* pp. 142–53. March, 1979.

522. Lugnire, Wilson. *Coordinating Cooperative Collection Development: A National Perspective.* Haworth Press, 1986.

523. Lunati, R. *Book Selection: Principles and Procedures.* Scarecrow Press, 1975.

524. Lyle, Guy. *The Administration of the College Library.* New York: H.W. Wilson, 1961.

525. Lynden, Frederick. "Collection management by automation." *Library Acquisitions, Practice and Theory.* pp. 177–183. No. 2, 1989.

526. Lynden, Frederick. "Library materials budgeting in the private university library: Austerity in action." *Advances in Librarianship.* New York: Academic Press, 1980.

527. Machlup, F. "Our libraries: Can we measure their hold-

ings and acquisition?" *AAUP Bulletin.* pp. 303–307. October, 1976.

528. Machovec, G. "The retention of print sources in view of electronic databases." *Colorado Libraries.* pp. 26–28. September, 1990.

529. Magarrell, Jack. "Research libraries' collections hit hard by inflation." *Chronicle of Higher Education.* pp. 18. January 22, 1979.

530. Magrill, Rosemary and Mona East. *Collection development in large university libraries.* Advances in Librarianship. New York: Academic Press, 1978.

531. Magrill, Rosemary. "Collection development and preservation in 1979." *LRTS.* pp. 247–273. 1980.

532. Magrill, Rosemary. "Collection development and preservation in 1980." *LRTS.* pp. 244–266. 1981.

533. Magrill, Rosemary. "Collection development in 1981." *Library Resources and Technical Services.* pp. 240–253. July, 1982.

534. Mahler, J.H. "Selection and reference use in the public library." *Library Trends.* pp. 93–106. July, 1966.

535. Maichel, Karol. "The Russian Exchange Program at Columbia University." *Library Resources and Technical Services.* pp. 254–258. Fall, 1958.

536. Maihl, V.R. "Cooperation in book buying and lending." *PLD Reporter.* pp. 39. November, 1956.

537. Mancall, J.C. "Unchanging factors in the searching environment: Collections, collectors, and users." *School Library Media Quarterly.* pp. 84–89. Winter, 1991.

538. Mancini, D. "Implementing a collection development policy." *Georgia Librarian.* pp. 92–94. November, 1985.

539. Martin, Lowell. "The future of the urban main library." *Library Trends.* pp. 774–87. April, 1972.

540. Martin, M.S. "A future for collection management." *Collection Management.* pp. 1–9. Fall–Winter, 1984.

541. Mason, Harold. "Beating the brush for books - the dealers sources of supply." *College and Research Libraries.* pp. 21–29. January, 1961.

542. Massman, Virgil and David Olson. "Book selection: A national plan for small academic libraries." *College and Research Libraries.* pp. 271–279. July, 1971.

543. Maxin, Jacqueline and Frances Chilson. "Cooperative purchasing by a New York 3 R's Council." *Serials Librarian.* pp. 299–305. Spring, 1978.

56   Collection Development and Collection Evaluation

544. Mazer, Norma. "Çomics, codes, and censorship." *Top of the News.* pp. 167–170. January, 1976.
545. Mazzola, A.L. "Developing collection in school library media centers." *Bookmark.* pp. 6–10. Fall, 1976.
546. McAnally, A.M. "Recent development in cooperation." *College and Research Libraries.* pp. 123–132. April, 1951.
547. MacCann, Donnarae. "Children's books in a pluralistic society." *Wilson Library Bulletin.* pp. 154–162. October, 1976.
548. McCarthy, S.A. "Centralization and decentralization at Cornell." *College and Research Libraries.* pp. 334–338. September, 1961.
549. McClellan, A.W. "Accessibility and other problems of book provision." *Library World.* pp. 275–281. May, 1962.
550. McCrum, B.P. "Book selection in relation to the optimum size of a college library." *College and Research Libraries.* pp. 138–142. April, 1950.
551. McCullogh, Kathleen. "Approval plans: Vendor responsibility and library research: A literature survey and discussion." *College and Research Libraries.* pp. 368–81. September, 1972.
552. McDaniel, J.A. "Leading the way. In-house collection development training for new selectors." *Library Acquisitions, Practice and Theory.* pp. 293–95. No. 3, 1989.
553. McDonald, David et al. "Sequential analysis: A methodology for monitoring approval plans." *College and Research Libraries.* pp. 329–334. July, 1979.
554. McGrath, William. "Relationship between hard-soft, pure-applied, and life-nonlife disciplines and subject books use in a university library." *Information Processing and Management.* pp. 17–28. 1978.
555. McGrath, William. "Two models for predicting subject circulation." *American Society for Information Science Journal.* pp. 264–68. September, 1979.
556. MacIver, I. "The exchange of publications as a medium for the development of the book collection." *Library Quarterly.* pp. 491–502. October, 1938.
557. McLaren, M. "Full acquisition systems at University of Kentucky." *Library Acquisitions, Practice and Theory.* pp. 247–250. No. 3, 1990.
558. McNeill, E. "Book selection policy." *Assistant Librarian.* pp. 30–32. March, 1978.
559. McPheron, Judith. "Overdue: On to the tumbrels, or let's

put quality in its rightful place." *Wilson Library Bulletin.* pp. 446–47. February, 1975.

560. Meachen, E. and G.R. Scharnfennorth. "Cooperative collection management in higher education." *Illinois Libraries.* pp. 46–52. January, 1989.

561. Measel, W. and L. Crawford. "School children and book selection." *American Libraries.* pp. 955–957. October, 1971.

562. Melin, Nancy. *The Serials Collection: Organization and Administration.* Ann Arbor: Pierian Press, 1982.

563. Mercer, A.E. "Cooperative book buying in the Waikato." *New Zealand Libraries.* pp. 133–135. July, 1961.

564. Merritt, LeRoy. *Book Selection and Intellectual Freedom.* New York: H.W. Wilson, 1970.

565. Merritt, LeRoy. *Reviews in Library Book Selection.* Detroit: Wayne State University Press, 1958.

566. Metcalf, Keyes. "Survey of possible cooperation among the larger academic and public libraries in Maine." *Library Research in Progress.* p. 8. March, 1961.

567. Metz, Paul. "Collection development in academic libraries - new media, new choices." *Journal of Academic Librarianship.* pp. 298+. November, 1987.

568. Metz, Paul. *The Landscape of Literature: Use of Subject Collections in a University Library.* Chicago: ALA, 1983.

569. Metz, Paul and Bela Foltin. "A social history of madness, or who is buying this round? Anticipating and avoiding gaps in collection development." *College and Research Libraries.* pp. 33–39. 1990.

570. Meyer, B.J. and J.T. Demos. "Acquisition policy for university libraries - selection or collection?" *Library Resources and Technical Services.* pp. 395–99. Summer, 1970.

571. Miele, A.W. and S.O. Medina. "Collection development in Alabama's public libraries - a statewide perspective." *Collection Management.* pp. 103–112. Fall–Winter, 1983.

572. Miller, E.P. and J.P. Cohen. "Collection development in a multi-system cooperative." *Library Acquisitions, Practice and Theory.* pp. 329–333. No. 4, 1986.

573. Miller, K.G. "Do libraries get religion?" *Library Journal.* pp. 1941–43. October 15, 1982.

574. Miller, William and Stephen Rockwood. "Collection development from a college perspective." *College and Research Libraries.* pp. 318–324. July, 1979.

575. Monroe, M.E. "Library's collection in a time of crisis." *Wilson Library Bulletin.* pp. 372–374. January, 1962.

576. Moon, B.E. "Development of special collections - problems of constructing networks." *INSPEL.* pp. 168–178. No. 3, 1983.

577. Moon, Eric. *Book Selection and Censorship in the Sixties.* New York: R.R. Bowker, 1969.

578. Moore, C. "Core collection development in a medium-sized public library." *Library Resources and Technical Services.* pp. 37–46. January, 1982.

579. Moran, Michael. "Concept of adequacy in university libraries." *College and Research Libraries.* pp. 85–93. March, 1978.

580. Moran, Robert. "Library cooperation and change." *College and Research Libraries.* pp. 268–274. July, 1978.

581. Mosher, Paul. "Collection development in research libraries: The search for quality, consistency, and system in collection development." *LRTS.* pp. 16–32. Winter, 1979.

582. Mosher, Paul. "Collection development to collection management: Toward stewardship of library resources." *Collection Management.* pp. 41–48. Winter, 1982.

583. Mosher, Paul and Marcia Pankake. "Guide to coordinated and cooperative collection development." *Library Resources and Technical Services.* pp. 417–431. October, 1983.

584. Moskowitz, M. "Collection development and the college library: A state of the art review." *Collection Building.* pp. 5–10. Summer, 1984.

585. Muller, Hans. "Administration of book funds in college libraries." *MA Thesis.* University of Chicago, 1941.

586. Muller, Hans. "Management of college library book budgets." *College and Research Libraries.* pp. 320–326. September, 1941.

587. Mullikan, A.G. "Library staff participation in book selection in an academic library." *Tennessee Librarian.* pp. 11–14. Winter, 1983.

588. Mulliner, K. "The acquisition allocation formula at Ohio University." *Library Acquisitions, Practice and Theory.* pp. 315–27. No. 4, 1986.

589. Munby, A.N. "Acquisition of manuscripts by institutional libraries." *Bibliographical Society of America Papers.* pp. 1–15. 1960.

590. Munn, Robert. "Collection development vs. resource sharing: Dilemma of the middle level institutions." *Journal of Academic Librarianship.* pp. 352–53. January, 1983.
591. Munn, Robert. "Cooperation will not save us." *Journal of Academic Librarianship.* pp. 166–67. July, 1986.
592. Murphy, C. "The online catalog: A tool for collection management." *School Library Media Quarterly.* pp. 154–57. Spring, 1987.
593. Myrick, W.J. "Library materials selection and ordering practices in New York State." *New York Library Association Bulletin.* pp. 1+. October, 1977.
594. Naylor, B. "Survival of the fittest - collection management after the Enright Report." *Library Association Record.* pp. 140. March, 1991.
595. Neikirk, Harold. "Automated acquisitions and the shared database - A meeting of the RTSD discussion group on automated acquisitions/in-process control systems." *Library Acquisitions Practice and Theory.* pp. 89–107. No. 2, 1983.
596. Nelma, W. "Toward effective book selection." *Tennessee Librarian.* pp. 129–130. Fall, 1976.
597. Nelson, Anne. "How my hometown library failed me?" *Library Journal.* pp. 317–319. February 1, 1978.
598. Nelson, B.K. "Automated acquisitions in small academic libraries." *Library Acquisitions, Practice and Theory.* pp. 351–59. No. 4, 1989.
599. New, Doris and R.Z. Ott. "Interlibrary loan analysis as a collection development tool." *Library Resources and Technical Services.* pp. 275–283. Summer, 1974.
600. Newman, Wilda and Amir Michlean. "Report literature: Selecting versus collecting." *Special Libraries.* pp. 415–424. November, 1978.
601. Nisonger, T.E. "Collection development." *Indiana Libraries.* pp. 1–68. No. 2, 1990.
602. Nissley, M. "Optical technology - consideration for collection development." *Library Acquisition, Practice and Theory.* pp. 11–15. No. 1, 1988.
603. Nitecky, A. "Polish books in America and the Farmington Plan." *College and Research Libraries.* pp. 439–449. November, 1966.
604. Norman, R.V. "Method of book selection for a small public library." *RQ.* pp. 143–145. Winter, 1977.

605. Null, D.G. "Robbing Peter . . . Balancing collection development and reference responsibilities." *College and Research Libraries.* pp. 448–452. September, 1988.

606. Nzotta, B.C. "Acquisition policy in a developing economy: A case study of Nigerian state libraries." *Collection Building.* pp. 3–8. No. 4, 1985.

607. Oberg, L.R. "Evaluating the conspectus approach for smaller library collections." *College and Research Libraries.* pp. 187–196. May, 1988.

608. O'Brien, Pat. "Cooperative collection and sharing." *Illinois Libraries.* pp. 110–112. February, 1978.

609. O'Connell, J.B. "Collection evaluation in a developing country: A Mexican case study." *Libri.* pp. 44–64. March, 1984.

610. O'Connell, T.F. "Creation of a Canadian research library." *Canadian Library Journal.* pp. 132–135. March, 1969.

611. Oertel, Dieter. "Coordinating the acquisitions of research libraries in the Federal Republic of Germany." *UNESCO Bulletin for Libraries.* pp. 285–289. September–October, 1963.

612. O'Halloran, C. "Library book selection." *Show Me Libraries.* pp. 3–4. February, 1982.

613. Okpokwasili, N.P. and M.L. Bundy. "A study of selection-acquisition policies of agricultural libraries in the U.S." *Libri.* pp. 319–330. December, 1989.

614. Olson, L.E. "Blind spots in collection development." *Top of the News.* pp. 371–76. Summer, 1985.

615. O'Neil, Robert. "Libraries, librarians, and First Amendment freedoms." *Human Rights.* pp. 295–312. Summer, 1975.

616. Orne, J. "Current trends in collection development in university libraries." *Library Trends.* pp. 197–334. October, 1966.

617. Orne, J. "Newspaper resources of the Southeastern region: An experiment in coordinated resource development." *Southeastern Libraries.* pp. 226–35. Winter, 1971.

618. Osborn, Andrew. "Development of library resources at Harvard." *Harvard Library Bulletin.* pp. 197–212. Spring, 1955.

619. Osborn, Andrew. *Serial Publications: Their Place and Treatment in Libraries.* Chicago: American Library Association, 1980.

620. Osburn, Charles. *Academic Research and Library Resources.* Westport: Greenwood Press, 1979.

621. Osburn, Charles. "Collection development - the links between scholarship and library resources." *New Directions for Higher Education.* pp. 45–54. September, 1982.

622. Osburn, Charles. "Impact of collection management practices on intellectual freedom." *Library Trends.* pp. 168–182. Summer-Fall, 1990.

623. Osburn, Charles. "New directions in collection development." *Technicalities.* pp. 1–4. February, 1982.

624. Osburn, Charles. "Planning for a university library policy on collection development." *International Library Review.* pp. 209–224. No. 9, 1977.

625. Osburn, Charles. "Some practical observations on the writing, implementation, and revision of collection development policies." *Library Resources and Technical Services.* pp. 7–15. Winter, 1979.

626. Osgood, T.S. "Let the kids choose their own books." *English Journal.* pp. 57–58. February, 1979.

627. Paddock, C. "Gifts and exchanges." *Louisiana Library Association Bulletin.* pp. 127–130. Summer, 1957.

628. Pafford, J.H. "Book selection in the university library." *UNESCO Bulletin for Libraries.* pp. 12–16. January, 1963.

629. Pankake, Marcia. "Coordinated collection development: The librarian's progress from this world to that which is to come." *Library Acquisitions, Practice and Theory.* pp. 93–98. No. 2, 1985.

630. Pankake, Marcia. "From book selection to collection management: Continuity and advance in an unending work." *Advances in Librarianship.* New York: Academic Press, 1984.

631. Pankake, Marcia. "Progress in the Pacific Northwest: A report on the regional collection management and development institute." *Library Acquisition, Practice and Theory.* pp. 135–39. No. 2, 1986.

632. Parish, David. "Consideration in state document collection building." *Documents to the People.* pp. 34–36. January, 1982.

633. Parker, Jean. "Scholarly book reviews in literature journals as collection development sources for librarians." *Collection Management.* pp. 41–57. No. 1–2, 1989.

634. Parr, V.H. "Case study: A collection development policy for an academic library endowed enrichment area and collection." *Collection Management.* pp. 83–92. Fall-Winter, 1984.

635. Pasterczyk, C.E. "Checklist for the new selector." *College and Research Libraries News.* pp. 434–35. 1988.

636. Perdue, A. "Conflicts in collection materials." *Library Acquisition Practice and Theory.* pp. 123–26. No. 2, 1978.

637. Perez, Ernest. "Acquisition of out-of-print materials." *Library Resources and Technical Services.* pp 42–59. Winter, 1973.

638. Perkins, David. "Writing the collection development manual." *Collection Management.* pp. 37–47. Fall, 1982.

639. Perkins, H.A. "Exchange and gifts." *MLA Bulletin.* pp. 407–417. July, 1962.

640. Pettos, William and Henry Bates. "Cooperative collection development: An inexpensive project in Northern California." *Collection Management.* pp. 59–67. No. 1–2, 1989.

641. Phelps, R.H. "Selecting materials for science-technology libraries." *Special Libraries.* pp. 89–92. March, 1953.

642. Phillips, F. "Developing collection policies for manuscript collections." *American Archivist.* pp. 30–42. Winter, 1984.

643. "Philosophy of collection development - Tucson Public Library." *Unabashed Librarian.* pp. 3. No. 43, 1982.

644. Piccolo, C. "Collection development media multiplication." *Library Resources and Technical Services.* pp. 175–177. April, 1989.

645. Pickett, A.S. "Faculty participation in book selection." *Indiana Librarian.* pp. 32–35. June, 1960.

646. Piele, Linda. "Selecting software for microcomputer centers." *Wilson Library Bulletin.* pp. 23–26. June, 1986.

647. Pierce, Thomas. "An empirical approach to the allocation of the university library book budget." *Collection Management.* pp. 39–58. Spring, 1978.

648. Pike, M.H. "Distribution of the book budget within the library system and between the main library and branches." *ALA Bulletin.* pp. 108–110. September 15, 1942.

649. Pinnell-Stephens, J. "Local conspectuses applications." *PNLA Quarterly.* pp. 22–23. Spring, 1989.

650. Piternick, Anne. "Problems of resource sharing with the community." *Journal of Academic Librarianship.* pp. 153–158. July, 1979.

651. Pojman, P.E. "Collection development in elementary school libraries - current practice." *Catholic Library World.* pp. 262–65. May–June, 1987.

652. Polacheck, D. "Method of adult book selection for a public library systems." *RQ.* pp. 231–33. Spring, 1977.

653. Pollett, M. "Criteria for science book selection in academic libraries." *Collection Building.* pp. 42–47. No. 3, 1982.

654. Pope, Michael. *Sex and the Undecided Librarian.* Metuchen: Scarecrow Press, 1974.

655. Porter, R.E. "How to select an atlas." *Library Journal.* pp. 3747–3750. November 1, 1961.

656. Potter, W.G. "Modeling collection overlap on a microcomputer." *Information Technology and Libraries.* pp. 400–407. December, 1983.

657. Powell, W.S. "Local materials for reference - their acquisition and administration." *Southeastern Librarian.* pp. 293–296. Winter, 1961.

658. Propas, S.W. "Cincinnati collection management and development institute." *Library Acquisitions, Practice and Theory.* pp. 51–64. No. 1, 1984.

659. Quimby, D.W. "Unity College starts a library." *Maine Library Association Bulletin.* pp. 3–4. November, 1967.

660. Quinn, K. "Using DIALOG as a book selection tool." *Library Acquisition, Practice and Theory.* pp. 79–82. No. 1, 1985.

661. Ramakrishna, Rao. "Library cooperation in the U.S." *Bibliographical Indian Librarian.* pp. 19–26. June 26, 1962.

662. Rawlinson, N.K. "Bring ALA back to basics - new collection development units reveal ALA structural problems." *Library Journal.* pp. 6. August, 1990.

663. Rawlinson, N.K. "Collection building - more than reviews the business of publishing and human nature." *Library Journal.* pp. 64. May 15, 1989.

664. Reed-Scott, I. "Information technologies and collection development." *Collection Building.* pp. 47–51. Nos. 3–4, 1988.

665. Reeves, F.W. "The administration of the library book budget." *Library Quarterly.* pp. 268–278. July, 1932.

666. Reid, D. "Drafting a written book selection policy." *Wilson Library Bulletin.* pp. 48–49. September, 1960.

667. Reid, Marion. "Coping with budget adversity - the impact of the financial squeeze on acquisitions." *College and Research Libraries.* pp. 266–272. May, 1976.

668. Reid, R.C. "Fee based services and collection development in an academic library." *Drexel Library Quarterly.* pp. 54–67. Fall, 1983.

669. Reidelbach, J.H. and G. Shirk. "Selecting an approval plan vendor." *Library Acquisitions, Practice and Theory.* pp. 177–260. No. 3, 1985.

670. Reiser, T.J. and A.H. Scott. "Coordinated collection development in Chicago." *Illinois Libraries.* pp. 21–25. January, 1989.

671. Rice, Barbara. "The development of working collections in university libraries." *College and Research Libraries.* pp. 309–312. July, 1977.

672. Rice, Pat. "From acquisitions to access." *Library Acquisitions, Practice and Theory.* pp. 15–21. 1990.

673. Richards, J.H. "Academic budgets and their administration, 1962." *Library Trends.* pp. 415–426. April, 1963.

674. Richards, J.H. "Allocation of book funds in college libraries." *College and Research Libraries.* pp. 379–380. October, 1953.

675. Rider, Fremont. "The future of the research library (reprint). *College and Research Libraries.* pp. 49–55. January, 1989.

676. Ring, R. "Budgeting for collection development." *Collection Building.* pp. 25–28. Nos. 3–4, 1988.

677. Roberts, M. and K.J. Cameron. "Barometer of unmet demand—ILL analysis and monographic acquisitions." *Library Acquisitions, Practice and Theory.* pp. 31–42. No. 1, 1984.

678. Robinson, B.M. "Managing change and sending signals in the marketplace." *Library Acquisitions, Practice and Theory.* pp. 217–225. No. 3,1989.

679. Rochester, M.K. "The ABN database: Sampling strategies for collection overlap studies." *Information Technology and Libraries.* pp. 190–196. September, 1987.

680. Root, N.J. "Decision making for collection management." *Collection Management.* pp. 93–101. Spring, 1985.

681. Rossi, J. Gary. "Library approval plans: A selected annotated bibliography." *Library Acquisitions, Practice and Theory.* pp. 3–34. No. 1, 1987.

682. Rotbowicz, R. and K. Nabors. "Collection development in academics libraries." *Show Me Libraries.* pp. 30–35. October–November, 1984.

683. Rowell, John. "A total book selection process." *Wilson Library Bulletin.* pp. 190–196. October, 1966.

684. Rozsa, G. "International exchange of publications with Afro-Asian Countries." *UNESCO Bulletin for Libraries.* pp. 141–143. May, 1962.

685. Russell, R.C. "Collection development in a municipal public library." *North Carolina Libraries.* pp. 35–38. Spring, 1985.

686. "Rutgers acquires crime collection." *Wilson Library Bulletin.* pp. 88. October, 1984.
687. Rutledge, J. "Collecting contemporary European literature for a reserach library." *Collection Management.* pp. 1–13. Spring–Summer, 1983.
688. Rutledge, J. and L. Swindler. "The selection decision: Defining criteria and establishing priorities." *College and Research Libraries.* pp. 123–131. March, 1987.
689. Rutstein, J.S. "Collection development confronts the 90's." *Colorado Libraries.* pp. 5–22. March, 1990.
690. Rutstein, J.S. "National and local resource sharing: Issues in cooperative collection development." *Collection Management.* pp. 1–16. Summer, 1985.
691. Rutstein, J.S. "The present and future withering away of collection development." *Colorado Libraries.* pp. 43–44. September, 1986.
692. Rutstein, J.S. and E. Fuselez-McDowell. "Cultural literacy and college students - new challenges for academic libraries and collection development." *Colorado Libraries.* pp. 6–9. March, 1990.
693. Ryland, John. "Collection development and selection: Who should do it?" *Library Acquisition: Practice and Theory.* pp. 13–17. No. 1, 1982.
694. Sabzwari, I.H. "National Exchange Centre." *Pakistan Library Review.* pp. 44–47. March, 1961.
695. Safran, Franciska. "Defensive ordering." *Library Acquisition Practice and Theory.* pp. 5–8. No. 1, 1979.
696. Sager, Donald. "A National Periodicals Center: Too Limited a goal." *American Libraries.* pp. 465–66. September, 1979.
697. Sampson, Gary. "Allocating the book budget: Measuring for Inflation." *College and Research Libraries.* pp. 381–83. September, 1978.
698. Sanborn, F.M. "Example of regional cooperation in West Angeles." *California Librarian.* pp. 41–44. January, 1960.
699. Sanders, N.P. "Review of selected sources in budgeting for collection managers." *Collection Management.* pp. 151–59. Fall–Winter, 1983.
700. Santavicca, E.F. "Best collection development articles." *Library Acquisition, Practice and Theory.* pp. 319–321. No. 4, 1989.
701. Sasse, M. and P.A. Smith. "Automation and collection development - threat or promise." *Colorado Libraries.* pp. 10–13. March, 1990.

702. Sattley, H.R. "Problem areas in book selection: What they imply for all librarians." *Library Journal.* pp. 3120–3123. September, 1962.
703. Saunders, C. "Choosing for children." *Assistant Librarian.* pp. 37–40. March, 1978.
704. Savage, Noel. "A National Periodicals Center - the debate in Arlington." *Library Journal.* pp. 1108–1115. May 15, 1979.
705. Scarborough, K.T. "Collection for the emerging majority." *Library Journal.* pp. 44–47.June 15, 1991.
706. Schad, Jasper. "Allocating materials budgets in institutions of higher education." *Journal of Academic Librarianship.* pp. 328–32. January, 1978.
707. Schad, Jasper. "Managing collection development in university libraries that utilize librarians with dual responsibility assignments." *Library Acquisitions, Practice and Theory.* pp. 165–171. No. 2, 1991.
708. Schad, Jasper and N.E. Tanis. *Problems in Developing Academic Library Collections.* New York: R.R. Bowker, 1974.
709. Schad, Jasper and R.L. Adams. "Book selection in academic libraries: A new approach." *College and Research Libraries.* pp. 437–42. September, 1969.
710. Schenck, W.Z. "The year's work in acquisition and collection development, 1988." *Library Resources and Technical Services.* pp. 326–337. July, 1990.
711. Scheppke, J.B. "Management of book selection procedures in public libraries." *Texas Library Journal.* pp. 18–19. Spring, 1984.
712. Scheppke, J.B. "Public library book selections - A heretical view." *Unabashed Librarian.* pp. 5–6. No. 52, 1984.
713. Schmid, T.M. "Cooperative acquisitions." *Idaho Librarian.* pp. 5–9. January, 1974.
714. Schmidt, G. "Building blocks for statewide collection development." *Colorado Libraries.* pp. 10+. December, 1982.
715. Schmidt, G. "Collection management in public libraries: Preconference report." *RTSD News.* pp. 67–69. No. 6, 1984.
716. Schmidt, K. "Capturing the mainstream: Publisher-based and subject-based approval plans in academic libraries." *College and Research Libraries.* pp. 365–69. July, 1986.
717. Schmidt, K.A. "Lives of noisy desperation - year's work in

collection development." *Library Resources and Technical Services.* pp. 433–43. October, 1990.

718. Schmitt, J.P. and S. Saunders. "Assessment of choice as a tool for selection." *College and Research Libraries.* pp. 375–80. September, 1983.

719. Schuman, Patricia. "Concerned criticism or casual cop-outs? Face children's books sections and supplements." *Library Journal.* pp. 245–248. January 15, 1972.

720. Schwartz, Charles. "Book selection, collection development and bounded rationality." *College and Research Libraries.* pp. 328–43. May, 1989.

721. Scott, R.L. "Books for college libraries on microfiche." *Microform Review.* pp. 33–35. Winter, 1979.

722. Scudder, M.C. "Using choice in an allocation formula in a small academic library." *Choice.* pp. 506–511. June, 1987.

723. Secor, J.R. "Issues and Trends in 1988." *Library Acquisition, Practice and Theory.* pp. 329–334. No. 4, 1989.

724. Shaffer, K.R. *The Book Collection - Policy Case Studies in Public and Academic Libraries.* Hamden: Shoestring, 1961.

725. Shaughnessy, Thomas. "From ownership to access - a dilemma for library managers." *Journal of Library Administration.* pp. 1–7. No. 1, 1991.

726. Shaw, W.M. "A journal resource sharing strategy." *Library Research.* pp. 19–29. Spring, 1979.

727. Shearer, K.D. "Applying new theories to library selection." *Drexel Library Quarterly.* pp. 73–90. Spring, 1983.

728. Shearer, K.D. "Selector as gatekeeper." *Public Libraries.* pp. 91–93. Fall, 1981.

729. Sheel, P. "Exchange of publications in south and South East Asia." *Annals of Library Science.* pp. 52–54. June, 1958.

730. Shepard, M.D. "Cooperative acquisitions of Latin American materials." *Library Resources and Technical Services.* pp. 347–360. Summer, 1969.

731. Sherrer, J. "Collection development in Colorado academic libraries." *Colorado Libraries.* pp. 25–29. March, 1982.

732. Shirk, Gary. "Allocation formulas for budgeting library materials: Science or procedure?" *Collection Management.* pp. 37–47. Fall–Winter, 1984.

733. Shoemaker, S. "Collection management - current issues." *Collection Building.* pp. 1–74. No. 3–4, 1988.

734. Shubert, J.F. "Coordinated academic libraries collection development program." *Bookmark.* pp. 3–10. Fall, 1982.

735. Shubert, J.F. "Coordinated collection development for the purpose of resource sharing." *Collection Management.* pp. 75–83. Spring, 1985.
736. Simms, M. "Allocating the book fund to departments and branch libraries." *Library Journal.* pp. 1302–1308. October 1, 1946.
737. Sims, E.M. "Selection and reference use in the college and university library." *Library Trends.* pp. 107–116. July, 1966.
738. Sinha, B.K. and R.C. Clelland. "Modeling for the management of library collections." *Management Science.* pp. 547–557. January, 1977.
739. Skipper, J.E. "National planning for resource development." *Library Trends.* pp. 321–324. October, 1966.
740. Slote, Stanley. *Weeding Library Collections.* Littleton: Libraries Unlimited, 1989.
741. Snowball, George and M.S. Cohen. "Control of book fund expenditures under an accrual accounting system." *Collection Management.* pp. 5–20. Spring, 1979.
742. Snyder, C.A. and B.I. Shapiro. "CIC Resource Sharing Project." *College and Research Libraries News.* pp. 21–23. 1990.
743. Sohn, I. "Cooperative collection development: A brief overview." *Collection Management.* pp. 1–9. Summer, 1986.
744. Sowell, S.L. "Expanding horizons in collection development with expert systems." *Special Libraries.* pp. 45–50. Winter, 1989.
745. Spain, F.L. "Selection and acquisition of books for children." *Library Trends.* pp. 455–461. April, 1955.
746. Spangler, E. "Surveyor finds Connecticut libraries avoid controversial books." *Connecticut Libraries.* pp. 6–8. Autumn, 1971.
747. Spiller, D. *Book Selection: An Introduction to Principles and Practice.* Shoestring Press, 1971.
748. Spiller, D. "Book selection in hard times." *Library Association Record.* pp. 297. September, 1982.
749. Stam, D.H. "Collaborative collection development: Progress, problems, and potential." *Collection Building.* pp. 3–9. No. 3, 1985.
750. "Stanford and University of California commit $560,000 to shared acquisition program." *Library Journal.* pp. 2210. December 1, 1982.
751. Stankus, Tony. "Making the scientist a library ally in the

real research journal funding wars." *Library Acquisitions, Practice and Theory.* pp. 113–119. 1990.

752. Stankus, Tony. " You know more than you think - Making your initial contribution to the subject collection literature." *Science Technology and Libraries.* pp. 93–101. Spring, 1990.

753. Stebelman, S. "The role of subject specialists in reference collection development." *RQ,* pp. 266–73. Winter, 1989.

754. Steinbrenner, I. "Cost effectiveness of book rental plans." *Ohio Library Association Bulletin.* pp. 5–6. April, 1979.

755. Stevens, N.D. "Innovative approach to collection management." *Collection Management.* pp. 25–28. Spring, 1978.

756. Stevens, R.E. "Problems of acquisition for research libraries." *Library Trends.* Complete Issue. January, 1970.

757. Stiffler, S.A. "Core analysis in collection management." *Collection Management.* pp. 135–149. Fall–Winter, 1983.

758. Stiffler, S.A. "Footnote on confusion: Book selection in the smaller college library." *Ohio Library Association Bulletin.* pp. 17–18. July, 1970.

759. Stiffler, S.A. "Librarian, the scholar, and the book collection." *Library College Journal.* pp. 37–41. Summer, 1970.

760. Stiffler, S.A. "A philosophy of book selection for smaller academic libraries." *College and Research Libraries.* pp. 204–208. May, 1963.

761. Strauss, L.S. "Books and other publications - selection and acquisition," in *Scientific and Technical Libraries.* New York: Interscience, 1964.

762. Streit, Sam. "Acquiring rare books by purchase: Recent library trends." *Library Trends.* pp. 189–211. Summer, 1987.

763. Strom, Folke. "Interlibrary cooperation in Sweden and the medical part of the Scandia Plan." *MLA Bulletin.* pp. 287–293. January, 1964.

764. Stueart, Robert. *The Area Specialist Bibliographer: An Inquiry Into His Role.* Metuchen: Scarecrow Press, 1972.

765. Stueart, Robert and George Miller. *Collection Development in Libraries: A Treatise.* Greenwich: JAI Press, 1980.

766. Sullivan, David. "Books aren't us? The year's work in collection development 1990." *LRTS.* pp. 283–293. July, 1991.

767. Swanick, E.L. "Building a collection of *New Brunswick-ana* at the New Brunswick Legislative Library." *Collection Management.* pp. 109–121. Nos. 1–2, 1990.

768. Sylvestre, J.J. "Cooperative acquisition plan for Canada." *Canadian Library Journal.* pp. 433–38. November, 1969.
769. Talmadge, R.L. "Farmington Plan." *Canadian Library Association Bulletin.* pp. 209–212. March, 1960.
770. Tanis, N.E. "The departmental allocation of library book funds in the junior college - developing criteria. *Library Resources and Technical Services.* pp. 321–327. Fall, 1961.
771. Tauber, Maurice. "Faculty and the development of library collections." *Journal of Higher Education.* pp. 454–458. November 8, 1961.
772. Taylor, David. *Managing The Serials Explosion - The Issues for Publishers and Librarians.* White Plains: Knowledge Industry, 1982.
773. Tenopir, Carol. "Collection development - CD-ROM." *Library Journal.* pp. 194+. September 1, 1990.
774. Teo, Elizabeth. "Audiovisual materials in the college and community college library: Basics of collection building." *Choice.* pp. 487–501. June, 1977.
775. Ternberg, M.G. "Selecting and acquiring business materials." *Collection Building.* pp. 22–31. 1988.
776. Thakore, A.V. "Practice of book selection in a university library." *Indiana Librarian.* pp. 71–75. September, 1960.
777. Thom, Ian. "Duplicates exchange: A cost analysis." *Library Resources and Technical Services.* pp. 81–84. Spring, 1957.
778. Thomas, A.F. "Book selection in an economic recession." *Catholic Library World.* pp. 299–300. February, 1976.
779. Thomas, L.C. "Building school library media collections." *Bookmark.* pp. 16–19. Fall, 1982.
780. Thompson, I.H. "The system of allocation from the book budget at UNC-Greensboro." *North Carolina Libraries.* pp. 17–19. Spring, 1985.
781. Thompson, Laurence. "The dogma of book selection in university libraries." *College and Research Libraries.* pp. 442–445. November, 1960.
782. Thorcen, B. "Mysterious art of book selection: Magic for magic." *Synergy.* pp. 26–27. Autumn, 1971.
783. Tolliver, B.J. "Collection development problems and opportunities." *Catholic Library World.* pp. 223+. March–April, 1987.
784. Trump, A.G. "Book selection in a college library." *South Dakota Library Bulletin.* pp. 156–158. October, 1962.

785. Tucker, C. "Selection power-starting and maintaining a materials review group." *Ohio Media Spectrum*. pp. 26–29. Spring, 1990.
786. "Tucson makes client development central to collection development." *Library Journal*. pp. 586. March, 15, 1982.
787. Tuttle, Marcia. *Introduction to Serials Management*. Greenwich: JAI Press, 1983.
788. Van Jackson, W. "Role of the college library - the academic core." *Virginia Librarian*. pp. 6–11. Summer, 1967.
789. Van Orden, Phyllis. *Collection Program in Elementary and Middle Schools*. Littleton: Libraries Unlimited, 1982.
790. Van Orden, Phyllis and Edith Phillips. *Background Readings in Building Library Collections*. Metuchen: Scarecrow Press, 1979.
791. Vandergrift, K.E. "Are we selecting for a generation of skeptics." *School Library Journal*. pp. 41–43. February, 1977.
792. Veit, Fritz. "Book order procedures in the publicly controlled colleges and universities of the Midwest." *College and Research Libraries*. pp. 33–40. January, 1962.
793. Vinson, L. "Students, systems, and selection." *Library Journal*. pp. 205–207. January 15, 1970.
794. Vosper, R.G. "Allocation of the book budget." *College and Research Libraries*. pp. 215–218. July, 1949.
795. Wall, C. "Collection development and the formula driven budget allocation." *Library Acquisitions, Practice and Theory*. pp. 311–313. No. 4, 1986.
796. Walton, C.C. "Modest proposal for cooperation collection development." *Colorado Libraries*. pp. 45–48. March, 1984.
797. Warner, Edward and Anita Anker. "Utilizing library constituents perceived needs in allocating journal costs." *Journal of the ASIS*, pp. 325–28. November, 1979.
798. Weber, David. "A century of cooperative programs among academic libraries." *College and Research Libraries*. pp. 205–221. May, 1976.
799. Weech, Terry. "Collection development and state publications." *Government Publications Review*. pp. 47–58. 1981.
800. Weinstein, F.D. "Book selection in the sciences." *ALA Bulletin*. pp. 509–519. July, 1958.
801. Weintraub, Karl. "The humanistic scholar and the library." *Library Quarterly*. pp. 22–39. January, 1980.
802. Weitzel W.T. "Why and how of a book selection policy." *North Country Libraries*. pp. 1–4. March, 1963.

803. Welch, Helen. "Publications exchange." *Library Trends.* pp. 423–431. April, 1955.

804. Welsch, Erwin. "Back to the future - a personal statement on collection development in an information culture." *Library Resources and Technical Services.* pp. 29–36. January, 1989.

805. Welsch, Erwin. "Collection development model for foreign literature." *Collection Management.* pp. 1–11. Spring, 1985.

806. Welsch, Erwin. "Price vs. coverage: Calculating the impact on collection development." *Library Resources and Technical Services.* pp. 159–63. April, 1988.

807. Welsch, Erwin. "Resources: The year's work in 1982." *LRTS.* pp. 315–329. 1983.

808. Welsch, Erwin. "Social scientific view of collection development: A review article." *Collection Management.* pp. 71–84. Fall, 1982.

809. Welsch, Erwin et al. "Microcomputer use in collection development." *Library Resources and Technical Services.* pp. 73–79. January, 1985.

810. White, Herbert. "Library materials prices and academic library practices: Between Scylla and Charybdis." *Journal of Academic Librarianship.* pp. 20–23. March, 1979.

811. White, Herbert. "Publishers, libraries and costs of journal subscriptions in times of funding retrenchment." *Library Quarterly.* pp. 359–77. October, 1976.

812. Wiemers, E. et al. "Collection evaluation: A practical guide to the literature." *Library Acquisitions, Practice and Theory.* pp. 65–76. No. 1, 1984.

813. Wiener, P.B. "Acquisition of first novels in academic libraries." *Collection Management.* pp. 25–36. Fall–Winter, 1983.

814. Wiener, P.B. "Media managers and the myth of collection building." *Catholic Library World.* pp. 321–22. March, 1985.

815. Willett, C. "International collaboration among acquisition librarians." *IFLA Journal.* pp. 289–98. No. 4, 1985.

816. Williams, D.E. "Midwest Collection Management and Development Institute." *RTSD News.* pp. 56. No. 6, 1989.

817. Williams, Gordon. "The function and methods of libraries in the diffusion of knowledge." *Library Quarterly.* pp. 58–75. January, 1980.

818. Williams, Gordon. "The librarian's role in the develop-

ment of library book collections." *Library Quarterly.* pp. 374–86. October, 1964.

819. Willison, I.R. "The American research library system in a period of constraint." *Journal of American Studies.* pp. 21–34. April, 1975.

820. Wilson, Louis and Maurice Tauber. *The University Library.* New York: Columbia University Press, 1956.

821. Wilson, Patrick and Mona Farid. "On the use of the records of research." *Library Quarterly.* pp. 127–45. April, 1979.

822. Wing, D.G. and R. Vosper. "The antiquarian book market and the acquisition of rare books." *Library Trends.* pp. 385–392. April, 1955.

823. Witten, L. "Collecting medieval and Renaissance manuscripts today." *Library Trends.* pp. 398–405. April, 1961.

824. Wolf, H.C. "Library board's responsibility for book selection." *Library Journal.* pp. 209. January 15, 1960.

825. Woods, L.B. and C. Perry-Holmes. "Libraries practice prior-censorship to avoid the flak." *Library Journal.* pp. 1711–1715. September 15, 1982.

826. Wortman, W.A. *Collection Management: Background and Principles.* Chicago: ALA, 1989.

827. Wortman, W.A. "Collection management 1986." *Library Resources and Technical Services.* pp. 287–305. October, 1987.

828. Yaple, H.M. "Gunfight at the O.K. Corral - Holding your own with collection development." *Library Acquisitions, Practice and Theory.* pp. 33–37. No. 1, 1991.

829. Zigrosser, C. and C.M. Gaehde. *Guide to the Collecting and Care of Original Prints.* New York: Crown, 1965.

830. Zimmerman, L. "Reference problems; the Farmington Plan and Florida." *Florida Libraries.* pp. 7–8. September, 1954.

831. Zimmerman, W.E. "Technical book selection and survey of practice in public libraries - a bibliographic essay." MA thesis. Western Reserve University, 1957.

832. Zwartz, E. "International Book Exchange: British National Book Centre." *New Zealand Librarian.* pp. 131–134. June, 1962.

PART TWO

COLLECTION EVALUATION

The process of evaluating library collections has grown into one of the most important functions of collection development librarians; indeed, it has been argued that "Every librarian would like to be able to answer the question: 'How good is my collection?' . . . Most librarians are interested in discovering some objective, qualitative measure of the value of their book collections, but that is a difficult task."[833]

Collection evaluation is by no means a recent innovation; however, present trends have tended to accelerate attempts to analyze the strengths and weaknesses of library resources. Among these trends are the general reduction of acquisition budgets during the preceding decade, and the expansion of cooperative planning among libraries, which has required careful scrutinization of collection development plans and "careful assessment of existing collections."[834] The literature of collection evaluation, though of relatively recent origin, is extensive and estimable. A survey of this literature follows, concentrating on what are generally recognized as the seminal works—those by Bonn,[835] Lancaster,[836] and Mosher,[837] followed by the works of more recent writers.

George Bonn's work was one of the earliest major treatments of collection evaluation, and he set forth the purposes and techniques of this topic.

> Over the years several quite different techniques have been developed to evaluate library collections for a number of purposes. They have been applied in varying configurations, sometimes independently but more often in conjunction with one or more other techniques, and with varying degrees of success, depending on how well the chosen methods covered really get at the intended purpose of the evaluation. For example, the quantity of a collection—its numerical size—has always been relatively easy to ascertain assuming accuracy, objectivity, and the use of standard units of measurement on the part of the enumerator. The quality of a collection—its relative excellence or its value or worth in a particular situation—has always been more difficult to judge objectively.[838]

Bonn lists and describes five distinct methods for evaluating library collections currently in use at the time of his publication.

1. Compiling statistics on holdings, use, and expenditures.
2. Checking lists, catalogs, and bibliographies.
3. Obtaining opinions from regular users.
4. Examining the collection directly.
5. Applying standards (using various of the foregoing methods), plus testing the library's document delivery capability and noting the relative use of several libraries by a particular group.

The first of these, quantitative evaluations conducted by compiling statistics, is widely practiced in nearly all types and sizes of libraries. Bonn believes the main advantages of this method "are that statistics are easily available, easily understood, and easy to compare; the main disadvantages are lack of standard definitions of units, possible lack of distinction between titles and volumes, difficulty in counting nonprint material, and possible inaccuracy or inconsistency of published data."[839]

One of the most frequently used evaluations is that of determining gross size of collections. A widely held assumption is that quantity does equate to quality,[840] and that shelf list counts, etc., can provide statistics that will supply meaningful insights into library quality, or useful benchmarks to be compared to institutions of like design or purpose.[841] Indeed, voluminous standards have been developed over the years by professional organizations and accrediting agencies in an attempt to specify minimum and ideal levels of collection size among academic libraries. The efficacy of shelf list comparisons, and, to a lesser extent, standards for adequacy, will be examined in greater detail later. For now it is important to note the various counting stratagems librarians have used to determine the total number of volumes in the library, the volumes added per year, dollars spent on materials annually, circulation figures, interlibrary loan requests, unfilled queries, volumes available per field of academic discipline, and volumes available per individual course of instruction—all such counts have been utilized by librarians with varying results and degrees of success. Sheer counts of collection size have their value. E.E. Williams makes the point that "there is normally a high correlation between the size of a library, its usefulness, and (if it is an academic library) the quality of the institution it serves,"[842] and Jordan claims a direct correlation between size of an academic library and its "academic excellence."[843] Mosher also cites the "straightforwardness and clarity in gathering, representing, and interpreting data"[844] from numeric counts of library shelf lists.

> Shelf list measurement data acquire meaning when compared with like data from other similar libraries: for example, it is easy to say, and to understand, that if library X has 10,000 titles in LC class J and Library Y has 15,000, library Y has a better (larger) collection in political science. Furthermore, the data can be manipulated as finely as the capacity of a classification system to define its subjects. Data acquired in this way, if accurately interpreted— which is not always as easy as it seems—can be of use in ascertaining collection areas which need more, or less, collection effort, for justifying book-budget requests, for acquiring a general, or descriptive, view of a library's collections, and for planning cooperative collection development ventures.[845]

There are drawbacks to the numeric count method, however. Mosher lists confusion arising from historical use of more than one classification system, inability of subject classification to represent programs or courses accurately, unreliability of data if book selection was erratic, duplication of titles, and erroneous or obsolescent data.

While emphasizing the positive aspects of numeric counts, Lancaster[846] too points out the dangers of comparing the collections of various libraries simply on the basis of size. He claims that most libraries report size in number of volumes, whereas the number of unique titles may be a better representation of the quality of the collection. Lancaster also believes that both absolute size and rate of growth must be taken into account. "Percentage rate of growth alone could present a somewhat distorted picture of the quality of a collection. A library may show a high percentage rate of growth if it fails to discard obsolete items while collecting new ones. Such a library, however, is performing a great disservice to its users. In addition to creating chronic storage problems such a policy is likely to lead to diminution in the quality of the collection."[847] Ultimately, compiling statistics on collection size is widely perceived as an essential activity for evaluators. However, consultants frequently advise librarians to combine a mixture of evaluation techniques to obtain more useful estimations of collection quality. One time-honored method for this purpose is the second of Bonn's five methods—checking lists, catalogs, and bibliographies. This is the most widely reported technique of acquiring qualitative data.

> A standard method of evaluating the quality of all or part of a collection is to compare holdings to an authoritative list—either a list of principal works for a library or field, or a list chosen or compiled by the evaluator for the purposes of assessing a particular collection. There are advantages to evaluating with lists. Once an appropriate list is chosen or compiled, the task of doing the checking can be done by nonprofessional staff, making the method relatively inexpensive. The method provides a direct qualitative assessment of collection strength, rather than a merely quantitative one. The results are easily summarized and suited to comparisons among similar collections, so an estimate of the strength of each collection can be added to the size and growth estimates discussed above. As a result, such an evaluation yields a measure of the 'quality' of the collection as well as a list of items which could be added to directly improve the collection. A sequence of tests can be designed using general and specialized lists to investigate in depth the strengths and weaknesses of a collection. The result is a check on quality to any desired depth and a plan for strengthening the collection.[848]

Bonn saw the main advantages of using lists as a method of evaluation in the large number of general and specialized lists available in published formats, their topicality, the fact that most are produced by competent librarians, and that most can be applied to individual libraries or types of libraries. Bonn, however, saw significant dangers to look for when using lists for evaluation. Among the disadvantages are that "published lists may have been used previously as buying guides by the very library being evaluated; lists are arbitrary samples; published lists soon become outdated unless systematically revised; published lists bear no necessary relationship to a given library's community or to its interests or needs; and lists assume that a core of works exists for every group of libraries.[849]

Bonn points out even more damning shortcomings of the ways in which list checking may be applied. Lists used as evaluation instruments are not always standards of quality. Thus, a list cannot signify collection quality any better than sheer statistics can. Some lists will ignore books that a library owns that are as good or even better for local needs than cited books. In addition, a list will not automatically rate or grade the quality of library collections according to established norms for numbers or percentages of titles owned. Grading a collection based on the percentage of titles owned by the library in any special list checked is essentially a subjective and arbitrary judgment; however, while urging caution Bonn does highly recommend the use of checklists, especially when combined with other evaluating techniques.

Mosher has fewer reservations about utilizing checklists, bibliographies, and catalog comparisons in order to ascertain collection quality or excellence (quality here defined as the "long term utility of or need for library materials").[850] The author advocates this method for focusing materials budgets on areas most needful of development, while restricting funds for materials in areas of lower priority, and it is especially advantageous in libraries building retrospective collections. Mosher cites four basic techniques for evaluation based on bibliographic checking:

a. A check of a sampling chosen from one or more accepted, important subject or field bibliographies, or bibliographies which would support the particular programs under examination;

b. a check of one or more monographic or journal article bibliographies, or citation lists from works of significance to local users or programs;

c. checks of basic lists of most used, most cited titles— from reading lists, graduate field reading lists, or departmental bibliographies to determine basic collection adequacy; and

d. more comprehensive searches of titles in bibliographies or lists in areas where weaknesses were revealed by any of the above methods.[851]

Lancaster advocates evaluation of a library collection in toto by checking it against another authority like *Books for College Libraries*[852] (a selected list of about 50,000 titles designed to support college teaching programs that depend heavily upon the library and to supply the necessary materials for term papers and suggested and independent outside reading), or Winchell's *Guide to Reference Books*,[853] or the Brandon[854] list for small medical libraries. Bonn[855] also provides an excellent compilation of titles for collection evaluation, as does Weimers.[856]

Lancaster believes list checking has greater utility in the small or mid-sized library than in research institutions, although even large collections can be checked against a variety of checklists ranging across many subject areas. However, like Bonn, Lancaster is cautious in extolling the virtues of list checking. Their reservations are shared by Coale,[857] who points out that strengths and weaknesses of research collections lie in printed and manuscript primary sources, and that checklists are not widely available for scholarly research needs; also by Hirsch,[858] who warns that lists become dated quickly and that use of standard lists may lead to conformity among collections of various institutions; by Goldhor,[859] who warns that titles checked against a list in a special subject may represent only a small percentage of the library's total holdings in that field, with the checking revealing nothing more about the other books owned by the library (this danger can be mitigated by taking a complete list of the library's collection in a special subject and comparing it with several selection and book-reviewing sources); and by McInnis,[860] who maintains that few comprehensive lists are available for any subject, and their utility is limited anyway by the fact that the scope of one specific subject defined by one particular individual or organization may not be appropriate to the needs of other particular individuals or libraries.

Those critics who warn about placing too much faith in the efficacy of list checking favor an approach that shies away from universal tools. Instead, they believe that evaluation of coverage in a special subject area does not depend on locating a single comprehensive checklist. Rather, evaluation should develop "carefully constructed samples of bibliographic references."[861] Thereby, the evaluation should more accurately reflect the strengths and weaknesses of individual collections.

There is one other technique that is closely related to list checking and is receiving much wider attention for collection evaluation than other methods. This technique is citation analysis, which draws a special list of references from published works; these references (or a sample from them) are checked against library holdings. The heart of the approach is its reliance on published research and other writings to establish quality and quantity of collections.

There are two possible sources for the population of items being checked. Which one is to be used is determined by the purpose of the study. A pool may be generated from references in locally written pieces of research-dissertations, for example. These could then be checked to see what proportion of the items cited were held by the library. This would then provide management information for decisions on adding new titles or acquiring backfiles. On the other hand, a population may be derived from a work or group of works done at another institution to determine whether or not the research reported could have been carried out at the collection being evaluated.

A number of assumptions underlie this method. Many of these are generally accepted in library research. Others may need rethinking in light of today's conditions. These assumptions include: 1) the notion that researchers are effective exploiters of library resources, and therefore, the cited references are a reasonable proxy for all the materials which might be used, 2) the library or collection being rated and the one used by the author are similar in purpose, size and subject matter, 3) the works being checked are the kind that could be and ought to be written in the library being evaluated (in fact, it may be appropriate for similar institutions to emphasize different aspects of a discipline and collection in order to meet the needs of these different sets of users), 4) the library used by the author of the research providing the citation pool actually owned these items—this will become more and more a questionable assumption as formalized plans for interlibrary loan and cooperative collection development proliferate, 5) finally, that the author actually used items he/she cited.[862]

Citation analysis is very valuable for collection developers in providing information about "patterns of dependency among subject disciplines."[863] *Science Citation Index* and *Social Science Citation Index* are tools with which researchers can analyze how much writers in various subjects depend for their sources on other fields. Metz lists a variety of levels wherein citation techniques are useful in delineating relationships among interest areas:

1) *In studying how small groups of researchers emerge and how their work reflects the mutual influence of their members, bibliographic coupling and, more recently, cocitation analysis have yielded objective evidence of the relationships among individual papers or networks of papers.* Coupling infers the relationship between two papers from the number of references they make to identical sources. Co-citation analysis reverses this, assessing relationships by counting subject papers that cite both of the publications under consideration.

2) *Citation analysis has been used to illustrate the relationships among subject disciplines.* Considerable research has been completed that establishes a dependent

relationship among the physical sciences; less attention has been devoted to the life sciences and social sciences.

3) *At the most general level of analysis, bibliometric techniques have helped to suggest larger congeries which share unique traditions in their approaches to knowledge and are reasonably independent of one another.* Garfield, Pierce, Vickery, et al., have researched possible relationships among various fields of knowledge, about whether the social sciences can be seen as separate from the humanities and natural sciences, or whether science and technology are mature and self-sufficient enough to constitute separate areas of knowledge.

4) *In some respects citation studies are ideally suited for examining interdisciplinary relationships. They provide a highly quantified measure of the extent to which one discipline finds another's literature significant enough to acknowledge in its own research.*[864]

One handicap in the use of citation analysis for collection evaluation is that the bulk of research on bibliometrics is in the area of the natural sciences, and especially in periodical literature, whereas the social sciences and the humanities have received much less attention.[865] Then, too, there are reservations about citation analysis that question the evaluative use of citations on the point that no one knows why authors provide references. Brooks said that

> there is no social psychology of citation behavior . . . An extensive list of citations may mean no more than, for example, zealous self-citation, collusive arrangements between researchers, or universal condemnation by peers. As a result, current attitudes towards citation analysis seem confused.[866]

Brooks surveyed a sample of academic writers at the University of Iowa in order to assess their motivations in giving references. Each faculty writer in the study was asked to assess his or her motivations for providing references by using seven separate scales. These were currency, negative credit, operational information, persuasiveness, positive credit, reader alert, and social consensus. The results of Brooks's study revealed that persuasiveness achieved prominence as a motivator. It was first of the seven possible motivators in both Brooks's full data set and the humanities subset, and was very close to the top in the science subset.

It is necessary to point out some of the limitations of citation analysis for collection evaluation. Citation analysis is not very useful for broad fields encompassing many subdisciplines such as history or literature. It is better suited to clearly defined subtropics. Larger scrutiny would require enormous expenditure of time and staff.

Another disadvantage of citation analysis is the tendency for many writers to overlook materials that are used in consultation or background work, and to fail to cite such sources. Relying on this technique also means that research clienteles are emphasized to the detriment of other library users.

In addition, when studying the use of a collection by library clienteles, there is the danger of a closed circle of data. Evaluators learn about sources cited by researchers that may have arrived via interlibrary loan rather than having been owned by the library under evaluation, and such evaluations will not pinpoint sources writers would have liked to read but did without in favor of other sources close at hand.

The third of Bonn's five primary methods for the evaluation of collections—obtaining opinions from regular users—may occur more frequently through informal librarian contacts with students, administrators, and faculty than through rigorously designed surveys by collection development librarians. Bonn thought this method was highly advantageous because users of the faculty, researcher, and professional variety were likely to be knowledgeable or expert in the literature of their fields, and that trends in research and changes in interests could be pinpointed. Furthermore, "of all the ways in which to evaluate a library's collection, finding out what its users think of it comes closest to an evaluation in terms of the library's objectives or mission."[867] He recommended the use of questionnaires so that users could rate adequacy of collections to meet needs, and such surveys have been reported from many institutions, especially from research libraries.

Bonn listed the main disadvantages of this method of evaluation as being a time-consuming activity since users usually must be approached individually, parts of the collection may not be covered adequately because of restricted user interest at the time of the survey, and the caliber of current users and their demands may be too high or too low for the intended or expected level of the collection.

Mosher, on the other hand, advises that personal contact should be emphasized in a regular program of liaison with library users in order to establish how well collections are meeting needs, for this approach is much more successful in most cases than sending out questionnaires whose return rate may be very low.

Lancaster and Hirsch categorize these attempts to acquire user input as "impressionistic," non-quantitative procedures, that in the academic library may well be entirely subjective but nonetheless of considerable value if conducted by faculty possessing extensive knowledge of their disciplines. Lancaster points the reader to instructions by E.E. Williams in this regard.

> Fortunately there are faculty members whom the surveyor of college and university libraries can consult by means of questionnaires or interviews or both. Ideally, he can hope to base his findings on the expert opinion of men who know their subject, have a broad knowledge of its literature, have intensively used both the library he is surveying and many others, and have also kept themselves well informed of the degree to which the library is meeting the needs of their students, undergraduate and graduate. In practice, of course, the surveyor does not find such men in every subject, and the individuals he consults do not always agree. Even in the largest university there will be some important segments of the collection in which, temporarily, no one is particularly interested. If one man in a

department has been depended upon to build up the relevant collections, he will probably know more about the library's holdings in his area than anyone else, but may well be unconscious of deficiencies or indifferent to them; indeed, there will be deficiencies that have developed because of his lack of interest in certain subdivisions of the subject.[868]

More recent recommendations for obtaining user input shifts the center of attention away from faculty to students, and is more important for a small or mid-sized academic library than for a research institution. Miller and Rockwood argue that "university-centered theories of collection development are inappropriate for the college library; yet they still constitute much of the theoretical basis for college collection development."[869] The authors contend that students, not faculty, are the college library's primary clientele, and as undergraduate teaching institutions colleges must avoid placing significant portions of their materials budgets into specialized research categories for individual faculty. Miller and Rockwood believe, as does Evan Farber,[870] that college libraries must concentrate on developing materials to directly satisfy students, including cultural and recreational items to broaden horizons rather than to merely serve basic curricular needs. Thus, evaluators would shift the focus of attention in acquiring user input away from faculty in the college. Instead, students would be queried for their impressions of collection strengths and weaknesses, and advice from this segment of the academic community would strongly influence collection development programs.

Bonn's fourth element—"Direct Observation"— combines aspects of the preceding activity of obtaining user input; however, observation of the collection is an evaluation technique that is distinct and invaluable when conducted by qualified evaluators.

The main advantages of direct observation are that it is practical and immediately effective. The main disadvantages are that it requires a subject or materials expert and is not very scientific. To the surveyor who knows the literature, an examination of the bookshelves will quickly reveal the size, the scope, the depth, and the significance of the collection. He can tell at once if duplicate copies or superseded editions inflate the collection, and he can tell if journal runs are substantial and complete. He can estimate the proportions of various parts of the collection and the recency of the material. Later checking of circulation files can verify or revise any preliminary judgments.[871]

George Bonn's final element of collection evaluation is "Applying Standards," by which he means a bewildering array of criteria developed by educational organizations as diverse as the National Council for Accreditation of Teacher Education and the Council on Social Work Education, which developed standards for adequacy of library collections. Early standards promulgated by the type of accrediting agencies just mentioned were helpful in relating library needs to the goals and objectives of parent institutions and accrediting organizations. But many of these early standards were vague, and so general as to bear little value for present-day evaluators, an example of which is the 1972 American Library Association's "Standards for Accreditation."

> The general and special collections, staff, and services of the institutional library should be adequate to meet the general educational purposes and needs of the library school. The collection of materials in the field of library science should be adequate in scope, size, content, and availability to support the goals and objectives of the school.[872]

On the other hand, the National Association of Schools of Art issued standards in 1971 that called for very specific quantities of material:

> Five thousand volumes on art and related subjects, plus at least twenty-five periodicals, and should be staffed by an adequate number of professionally qualified personnel. The slide collection should provide at least ten thousand items. These figures apply to institutions with relatively small enrollments. Larger schools or schools with more

complex offerings should have proportionally larger library collections.[873]

Summaries of early standards established by accrediting organizations can be found in Eli Oboler's *College and University Library Accreditation Standards—1957*,[874] in Signe Ottersen's "Bibliography on Standards for Evaluating Libraries;"[875] and in the *Library Trends* issue on "Standards for Libraries" in 1972.[876] Bonn points out the changes that have occurred over recent years, especially the shift in emphasis away from quantity, per se, to quality in more recently established standards. Then, too, there is much more stress placed on institutional goals and objectives as a frame of reference in which standards are to be applied. Bonn cautions against placing undue emphasis on the latter orientation, because goals and objectives may not be suitable for objective evaluations, they may not be easy to interpret, and experts from similar accrediting agencies may disagree about specific goals and objectives. Lancaster refers to another disadvantage, that of the danger of "trying to compare the collections of various libraries simply on the basis of size, either absolute—total number of volumes—or in volumes per individual served."[877] However, accrediting bodies continue to be undeterred by the difficulty of creating meaningful standards.

The earliest attempts to establish concepts of collection adequacy were more concerned with annual growth rate than with total size of collection. A method of calculating annual growth rate was devised so that enrollment was tied to expenditures for library materials, and the ratio was considered to be the minimum desirable growth rate for a given library's collection. In 1928 the American Library Association recommended that universities should make a fixed expenditure per student for library funding that "should not be less than 4% of the university budget."[878] During the 1930's, the North Central Association of Colleges and Secondary Schools cited a standard of $5.00 per student. This standard was subsequently altered to the vague statement: "Expenditures should be sufficient to cover needed replacements of and additions to the present holdings." Also in the early 1930's, the United States Office of Education said that schools allocating less than 4% of their funds for library purposes should carefully examine the adequacy of their book collections.

These early standards for collection adequacy are examples of rudimentary formula budgeting, which makes no predictions about desirable and necessary collection size, but merely fixes a dollar figure for library support and assumes that the necessary number of volumes will be acquired. Only much later would professional library organizations begin to specify quantitative standards for collection size.

In 1959, the Association of College and Research Libraries (ACRL) adopted *Standards for College Libraries* that decreed:

> The size of the library collections is largely determined by the following major factors: (1) The extent and nature of the curriculum, (2) The number and character of graduate programs, (3) The methods of instruction, (4) The size of the undergraduate and graduate student body, both full time and extension, and (5) The need of the faculty for more advanced materials which can not be met conveniently by the use of research libraries in the area. An analysis of small college library statistics suggests that no library can be expected to give effective support to the instructional program if it contains fewer than 50,000 carefully chosen volumes.[879]

It was not long until the ACRL standards received severe criticism, especially by Clapp and Jordan, who believed strongly in a different approach.

Clapp and Jordan promulgated new standards for the adequacy of library collections based on what they termed essential controlling factors. These were the size, composition, and background of the college's student body; the size and character of the teaching departments; methods of instruction; geography of the campus; and the intellectual climate of the school. In turn, the controlling factors produced formulas for minimum adequacy that are dependent on many variables. First, the authors stated that all books contained in basic bibliographies should be part of any academic library, and the optimum minimum size of a basic undergraduate library collection should be 50,750 volumes. This total was produced by calculating the variables of a given number of volumes for each faculty member, for each student, for each honors student, for individual major subject fields, and so on. The resulting formulas, the authors believed, provided a better method for estimating minimal adequacy than the standards then in existence produced by the American Library Association and other organizations.[880] Clapp-Jordan emphasized the qualitative as well as quantitative virtues of their formulas, for the criteria were based on titles drawn from outstanding book selection lists and specialized subject bibliographies. Clapp and Jordan also emphasized the difficulty of applying these checklists for collection evaluation; in fact, they were remarkably prescient in anticipating present-day methods that do much to remove such difficulties.

Here is Clapp and Jordan's prediction:

> The best yardsticks of adequacy are therefore those to which we have become accustomed—the book-selection list and the specialized subject bibliography, frequently reviewed and brought up to date by experts and in the light of use. But to apply these yardsticks is, at the present time, something else again; manual checking and searching procedures are involved—slow, tiresome and costly.
>
> Yet it may be foreseen that, with the advent of electronic catalogs the checking of a book-selection list or bibliography will become the mere routine of a mechanical process. Not only will evaluation of collections be simplified thereby, but collection-building procedures will be assisted. The end result will be gains in the quality of collections.[881]

Clapp-Jordan earned widespread credence among academic librarians. The formulas were adopted by program-planning-budgeting (PPB) systems in Texas, Washington, Florida, New York, and other states. PPB budgeting practices mandate the careful setting out by libraries of what they need in order to perform their missions. Ordinarily, formulas are set forth to establish adequacy of performance, and the Clapp-Jordan formulas were convenient for targets on collection size. Michael Moran argues that "the program statements of a PPB system may be stated in terms of absolute needs in order to satisfy budgeting agencies, but in reality and in relation to the library's role as an educational agency of the university these needs are arbitrary. The only honest and valid argument that the library can make to the budgeting authority is that it wishes to have additional money in some arbitrary amount in order to increase the quality of education it offers . . . library budget requests do not lend themselves to a PPB system."[882]

Clapp and Jordan were careful to point out that using their formula to establish minimum adequacy could be achieved only if all material was chosen carefully with a view to the purpose to be served, and the weeding program was as realistic in relation to needs as was the acquisition program. When the authors tested the formula on three groups of libraries of varying size they discovered some research libraries with very large collections were below minimum adequacy, and five of the seven junior college libraries tested did not satisfy the threshold for adequacy as set forth in the formula.

R.M. McInnis attempted to verify the Clapp-Jordan formula by comparing it with a regression analysis applied to library data from prominent graduate institutions, but failed to do so.[883] The regression equations produced higher figures for the expected number of volumes; thus minimal adequacy as defined by Clapp-Jordan may report a low rather than high level of adequacy. McInnis believed the formula had inherent weaknesses, a major one being the number of doctoral fields in a large university is so sizable, it exerts too much influence on the formula's results. However, McInnis recommended keeping Clapp-Jordan in the assortment of methods librarians use for evaluation because the formula does provide a rough, quickly computed guide to minimum levels of library size.

F.W. Lancaster, too, believed Clapp-Jordan had merit over previous formulas or standards in that "it considers multiple factors affecting the required size of a collection rather than just one single factor such as size of the student body."[884] Lancaster shared some of McInnis's reservations, however, and cautioned that there was a danger that some administrations might interpret minimal standards established by the formula as optimum levels. As a result, library acquisitions could be curtailed. And, in fact, this occurred in the State University of New York library system in the early 1970's, when libraries fought attempts to keep their growth at levels recommended by the formula.

Apart from the skirmishes noted above, action on the standards front was quiet for nearly ten years following publication of the ACRL standards and the Clapp-Jordan formula. Then, in 1975, the ACRL promulgated a new set of "Standards for College Libraries,"[885] the most notable feature of which was the raising of adequacy for a basic collection from about 50,000 volumes to 85,000 volumes. Four years later, the ACRL followed with "An Evaluative Checklist for Reviewing a College Library Program,"[886] which continued a minimum level of adequacy at 85,000 volumes but supplied a practical framework for satisfying library needs of individual departments, graduate fields of study, individual faculty, and so on. Curiously, however, despite the attempt to prescribe minimum levels of adequacy for major areas of need in the college, the new standards, as with the old, failed to address collecting levels for individual courses offered in the college's curriculum. There is no mention of minimum adequacy whatsoever at this level in published standards. The interested reader must go back to 1963 and the work of Robert T. Jordan to find any reference to optimum levels of collection support for courses in the college curriculum.

> There are various possibilities for a 'common sense' inspection of the conclusion that a minimum of 50,000 volumes are required in a college ranking high in academic quality. For example, 250 courses constitute a moderate number for a typical college (10 courses in each of 25

subject fields). If the library has an average of 150 books to support each course, certainly a modest amount, plus 12,500 books not directly related to any specific courses, the total would be 50,000 volumes.[887]

Jordan's suggestions about adequacy levels per course seem to have been ignored in subsequent ACRL standards, and, indeed, in the Clapp-Jordan formula, which was published only two years afterward. Only William McGrath pursued collection evaluation to the final and possibly most relevant level, that of individual course. And his work provided the rationale for many subsequent studies at many different types of libraries.

McGrath began studying ways of matching library resources to college curricula at the University of Southwestern Louisiana in 1969. He believed that the university catalog of course descriptions is the best document to reveal topical departmental interests and needs with a strong degree of continuity. And, in fact, it was argued that a college catalog is a much better record than the card catalog for evaluation purposes because the card catalog reflects the cumulative scholarly interests of the curriculum, while the university catalog represents the current changing curriculum. Acting on this assumption, McGrath began a very ambitious and labor intensive survey of his university's catalog, in which more than 1,300 courses were classified (Library of Congress call numbers) by library catalogers. When this was completed, the call numbers were measured against like holdings in the library's shelf list in order to count the number of books that were available to support individual courses of instruction. McGrath[888] argued that, based on the results of this first experiment, the university catalog clearly was the best guide to current scholarly interests in the campus departments; and libraries could apply universal lessons learned in such analyses with classification groups listed course-by-course and department-by-department. The results of such effort would produce book selection aids, as correlations for curriculum and circulation, and as an aid to weeding and preservation efforts.

McGrath's experiments soon were replicated at other university libraries. Golden[889] reported on an evaluation of the collection at the University of Nebraska at Omaha in which holdings were compared with curriculum structure. Again, LC class numbers were assigned to individual courses. Enrollment in courses also was surveyed and added to total measurements. In a follow-up to the study evaluators claimed that this evaluation was very successful in measuring strengths and weaknesses of collections, although a knowledge of quantity alone was deemed not sufficient. Other qualitative evaluation methods were recommended as well. Individual evaluators cited additional benefits, especially the improved knowledge librarians gained of university programs, which made liaison between teachers and librarians much stronger.

In addition, Whaley reported on similar projects at the State University of New York at Binghamton, where teaching faculty assigned LC class numbers to courses taught, and a supplementary taxonomy was developed to help apply numbers to course descriptions. The evaluation required much time and manpower, but the benefits of identifying gaps in the collection and course needs were deemed important enough to justify the effort. The perceived benefits at Louisiana and Nebraska were replicated at SUNY. In sum, the method:

> provides valuable information for both the librarians and the teaching faculty. The faculty gains better understanding of the book collection and how it supports the curriculum. Bibliographers learn of gaps in the collection before they become embarrassingly visible, the result of unfulfilled demands. Administrators, with a better understanding of course needs and library support, can allocate funds for materials in a more rational fashion, rather than relying on past practices as their principal guide. Finally the contributions of professors and librarians in this collection analysis procedure help to establish and maintain a useful collection that serves the needs of its patrons. And that, after all, is what libraries are all about.[890]

In all the evaluations cited above, one player acted in an uncooperative role throughout. As a result elaborate and expensive countermeasures were necessary in order to obtain desired results. The salient complication consistently fell on attempts to achieve specificity when correlating classification schedules and courses taught. Time after time, enhancements were added—enlisting teaching faculty who interpreted course descriptions and scanned LC schedules for appropriate matches, or involving all the cataloging staff in trying to classify courses, or adding on specially constructed taxonomies to buttress classification schedules. In spite of these efforts, evaluators still were dissatisfied with results. Can this be the reason so few libraries have attempted to classify courses in the university catalog? Few would argue that this method is not an extremely effective method of evaluating a library's direct support of academic curriculum. But attempting to complete a successful evaluation using incommodious classification schedules is akin to laboring over a jigsaw puzzle with half the pieces missing.

Compare the advantages an on-line library catalog brings to collection evaluation. Evaluators can ignore the cumbersome or, at times, impossible chore of matching call numbers to course descriptions. They can forget classification schedules altogether. On-line public catalogs are notable for speed of access and ability to simplify what otherwise may be very complicated subject searches. And when applied to collection evaluation, online catalogs are remarkable tools that simplify and accelerate the tasks of correlating library materials and courses of instruction.

Of all the evaluation techniques available, course related evaluations are extremely valuable for collection development librarians in the small and mid-sized academic library.

Lyle stressed this point many years ago when he said that "first demands on all college library book funds come from courses taught in the curriculum,"[89] as did Wilson and Tauber:

> Despite the emphasis upon research, the university library is confronted with the problem of providing materials which are used in connection with undergraduate and

graduate courses offered in the institution . . . Universities, like colleges, differ in the acquisitions of such materials in relation to their curriculums. In both colleges and universities there is a constant need for careful selection of titles to support the educational program.[892]

McGrath developed the technique of classifying courses in the university catalog in order to ascertain adequacies or deficiencies in library collections. His technique called for the assignment of call numbers to individual courses in the same manner that numbers are assigned to books. Then the number of catalog cards in the shelf list could be measured to determine how many books existed to support each course in the curriculum.

The manual operations required to complete an evaluation of 1,346 courses by McGrath at Southwestern Louisiana in 1969 totaled 560 hours of cataloger effort, the equivalent of 70 eight-hour workdays. McGrath does not include his own hours in this total, nor the hours of teaching faculty and other librarians who contributed to the evaluation. The enormous investment of time and staff discouraged other libraries from attempting such evaluations, regardless of their value. The University of Nebraska and SUNY libraries encountered similar staff demands made especially onerous by the difficulty of interpreting course descriptions and then classifying appropriate call numbers to individual courses. Cassata and Dewey put it well:

> The evaluation of the collection of a large university library is a task seldom undertaken; more likely, it is one which is proposed and discussed, then relegated to a file folder as a good rainy year project. The paucity of articles in the literature on the subject of comprehensive and systematic evaluations of library collections testifies that few libraries have a surfeit of staff, time, energy, or funds to commit to so demanding a problem.[892]

After all the preparatory work, evaluators were forced to turn to the shelf list for an estimation of collection size. And this step is fraught with quicksand. Shelf list measurements can show gross size of a collection fairly well, but they cannot show how accessible the materials are (checked out of the library, for example) or how current and up-to-date the collection is. On-line catalogs can do both.

In addition, some studies have shown that "a specialist's definition of the literature of his field may differ greatly from the definition of that field provided by the Dewey or Library of Congress classification systems," and that "shelflist counts miss anywhere from 30% to 80% of the titles in a given subject."[894] The alarming possibility exists that after spending an enormous investment on course-related evaluations, McGrath and colleagues' results were skewed by this phenomenon.

In any case, few libraries followed McGrath's lead. Such evaluations using manual methods are beyond the means of all but the most ambitious libraries. This situation changes radically, however, when an automated system is introduced. Evaluators can dispense with classification schemes altogether, and ignore counting cards in the shelf list as well. As demonstrated, college catalog course descriptions (buttressed by syllabi and course notes) provide adequate key words to determine how well library collections are supporting the curriculum. Not only is quantity of staff necessary to complete such an evaluation meaningfully reduced, but also quality of staff. No longer are catalogers required to classify courses—nor teaching faculty to interpret course descriptions. Reasonably well-informed collection development librarians can oversee evaluations. By supervising graduate assistants or clerical staff, librarians can complete extensive searches of the on-line public access catalog to determine collection strengths and weaknesses.

Among all the advantages of an on-line catalog, this factor of speed and convenience may be the paramount attraction for collection evaluators. A close second and third are the added inducements that the key word approach can provide greater specificity than broad call number classifications, especially when two or more call numbers are assigned to a course. And the computer makes possible much more discriminating analyses, including date, language, and format of material.

In summing up it should be noted that the on-line catalog is not a panacea for all evaluator problems, despite the effusive claims made above. Occasionally it is necessary to supply additional key words or synonyms beyond those supplied in course catalogs and syllabi whenever such descriptions are insufficient or incomprehensible.

These are minor irritations, however, when compared with all the advantages the computer brings to collection evaluation. Compaigne recently commented on the progress computers have brought to libraries, in general.

> Compunications* makes possible the previously hardly thinkable or unthinkable. Thus, the ability to randomly access information from a vast data base and manipulate it . . . is not new. We can always go to a library and randomly access its stacks. But it has been highly labor intensive and has required considerable skill on the part of the searcher. The trend in computer and communications use has been to lower the labor involved as well as the skill required.[895]

For libraries this statement is nowhere more true than in collection evaluation. George Bonn, too, saw the on-line catalog's potential in 1974 when he said that "libraries with computer capabilities could easily keep running tabs on library holdings . . . and could correlate any or all of them with the academic courses that are offered."[896]

Clapp and Jordan also were prescient, taking the broad view for the future of collection development.

> Yet it may be foreseen that, with the advent of electronic catalogs the checking of a book selection list or bibliography will become the mere routine of a mechanical process. Not only will evaluation of collections be simplified thereby, but collection building procedures will be assisted. The end result will be gains in the quality of collections.[897]

---

*This term seems to be an invention of Compaigne's. I find no reference to it in general or specialized dictionaries.

I admire the authors as much for their foresight as for their development of formulas of collection adequacy and of evaluation methods. The day those authors envisioned, when electronic catalogs would be widely available to collection development librarians, is at hand. Yet, there is scant evidence of evaluators using on-line catalogs to date. Perhaps the flood of articles and books on database searching, cooperative cataloging, and reference works with on-line public access catalogs accurately reflects the trend of computer applications in libraries. I would not be surprised, however, to see emphasis begin to shift away from those areas. Reference librarians, catalogers, instructional and circulation librarians all benefit enormously from the development of electronic catalogs. But of all librarians, collection developers and evaluators may discover they benefit as much or more than their colleagues from the time-saving attributes of on-line catalogs.

Shifting focus away from classifying courses in the college catalog to the use of key word searching simplifies what otherwise are prohibitively expensive and time-consuming analyses of collection strengths and weaknesses, and makes it possible for academic libraries to accomplish productive collection evaluations. The result achieved thereby is to measurably advance the strength and overall quality of library collections.

The late 1980's saw an acceleration of the trend toward automated evaluation of collections, and of the use of the Research Libraries Group (RLG) Conspectus. In 1986, Kruegar[898] summarized the attributes of the Illinois statewide on-line catalog and the uses to which it was put for collection analysis. Also in that year, Atkinson[899] wrote an excellent treatise on evaluation and on standards for preservation, stressing the need for a comprehensive collection development policy to define procedures for weeding, repair, and preservation. Budd[900] completed a citation analysis of American Literature, and reflected that such analyses are less than perfect for the humanities in general. Loertscher[901] developed a collection mapping technique for quantitatively evaluating materials and their relevancy to curriculum, while Hall[902] published a manual for collection assessment. Use of the RLG Conspectus was widespread. Stephens[903] analyzed the use of the RLG Conspectus for regional evaluations in Alaska, while Farrell[904] offered advice on applications of the National Collections Inventory Project (NCIP). Stam[905] also reviewed use of the NCIP and the many cooperative collection development projects based on such models. Reed[906] also provided valuable instructions on use of the NCIP, Mosher[907] examined links between the Conspectus and the NCIP, and Lincoln[908] evaluated collections at the University of Alaska with the Conspectus.

Losee[909] devised a method of retrospective analysis with use of MARC tapes. Palais[910] created a collection development policy for Arizona State University by categorizing courses with Library of Congress call numbers, Burrell[911] developed a system to predict future use of library materials, Warwick's[912] analysis indicated that circulation data were poor predictors of future use, and Futas[913] enumerated the difficulties that complicated precise collection evaluations.

Much additional work was accomplished with the Conspectus during the following year. Stam[914] explored the evolution of the Conspectus and the organizational variables that come into play when evaluations are begun. The limitations of the Conspectus approach were noted, too, especially in regard to plans for cooperative collection development. Ferguson[915] reported on several specific evaluations based on the Conspectus, while Abel[916] used it as a mapping device. Henige[917] warns of overestimating the potential benefits of Conspectus work, and Miller[918] stressed the need for more widespread acceptance of the benefits of the Conspectus. Horrell[919] advocated use of the Conspectus as a means of completing a review of American art holdings nationwide.

Other specialized approaches were undertaken by Nisonger,[920] whose use of the Conspectus was instrumental in evaluating Russian and Slavic collections at Alaska; by Forcier,[921] whose adaptation paved the way for Conspectus evaluations in multi-sized libraries in the Northwest; and by Oberg,[922] whose evaluation methods succeeded in a smaller college setting because of intensive prior training of librarians engaged in the project. White[922] prepared an excellent manual to help librarians undertake projects with evaluations, and Ferguson[924] went back over the previous ten years to review progress with the Conspectus, and asserted that its use had done much more than was commonly believed to further cooperation between and within libraries.

Many writers offered advice on the use of new automated techniques when evaluating library collections. Beaton[925] explained the use of interlibrary loan transactions in the analysis of strengths and weaknesses of general collections; Dillon[926] described the development of an automated collection analysis method at OCLC; Sanders[927] used the OCLC and RLG records in tandem when comparing collections; Piccininni[928] summarized the application of HEGIS data for collection evaluation in New York State; Armbruster[929] provided a detailed overview of the AMIGOS evaluation system; and Cubberly[930] completed analyses of a specialized collection at Florida.

F.W. Lancaster[931] and Mark Grover contributed more general and highly useful treatises on evaluation. Grover addressed the personal management issues that often came into sharp relief when exhaustive, time-consuming evaluations are undertaken by libraries. Although the reasons for undertaking collection analysis seldom provoke conflict among librarians, the necessary measures to ensure success and administrative oversight often engender disagreements, a problem Grover explored in some detail:

> Even though other factors have been involved in stimulating collection evaluation studies, these three elements—to show collection adequacy or deficiencies, determine where growth should occur, and respond to accreditation needs—continue to be the most important reasons assessments are conducted in most college and university libraries. As such, assessment studies are generally in response to administrative and/or nonlibrary pressure to provide supportive information for decisions already made. In so doing, librarians continue to be reactors and not actors within the university community.

Accreditation reports, budget requests, and administrative games are the stimuli for much of the activity occurring in collection assessment. The result is that there continues to be libraries in an unfortunate continuation of the 1950's practice of relegating a disproportionate percentage of collection development duties in the library to nonlibrarians such as faculty, book dealers, approval plans companies, and outside gift donors. Many librarians still appear to be either too insecure or too busy with administrative concerns and/or patron-related reference work to become adequately involved in creative and constructive collection development activities. Librarians allow themselves to be purely information directors and administrators: able to process, maintain, and provide access to physical objects but unwilling to make adequate and important decisions on the qualitative nature of the actual information.

If collection assessment is to become a meaningful and useful management tool, administrators must see librarians not only as processors but creators of information. They need to learn to use assessments as a managerial tool that will provide an ongoing understanding of the library, enabling collection decisions to be made on the basis of adequate understanding and knowledge, and not just personal musings or hunches. By developing a logical organized plan for periodic assessment of all areas of the library, the administrator should be able not just to react to outside demands and pressures, but use that plan as a tool for better management. Collection assessment can become as Paul Mosher has stated, the most potent and promising tools of the collection manager—a cornerstone of collection management.[932]

Another excellent manual is the American Library Association's *Guide to the Evaluation of Library Collections*,[933] which supplies a strong grouping in methodology. Additional works of greater specificity came from Stielow,[934] who showed how to evaluate resources based on stratification of materials, and from Hyman,[935] who provided a method of completing user-based evaluations. Elzy[936] supplied a procedure for using standard bibliographies to check holdings on specific subjects, and Baker[937] developed a system to use microcomputer software to complete collection analyses.

The beginning of the 1990's saw continued contraction of many library budgets, in some cases, extreme in its effect on acquisition of new materials. As a result cooperative collection development and resource sharing attained added importance, and as Atkinson[938] noted in a cogent 1992 article, "In an era of continuously declining resources, interlibrary cooperation has become not only respectable but expected." Also in this article Atkinson provided a counterpoint to Henige's long-standing claim about the negative aspects of NCIP and the alleged subjective factors of Conspectus evaluations in general. Ferguson also supplied a rebuttal to those arguments, stressing that the Conspectus obviously is imperfect, but that all too often evaluation confuses means and ends. The basic problem . . .

> is that we librarians involved with the Conspectus methodology for cooperative collection development purposes have allowed it to become an end unto itself. The creation of the Conspectus, the verification studies, and the supplementary guidelines have become our focus instead of the real problems we face. We have used the Conspectus as a smoke screen to avoid the difficult problems that serve as barriers to cooperation: Interinstitutional competitiveness, our cultural love for autonomy, and the continuance of the ownership paradigm. If we would focus as much attention on these barriers as we have on the Conspectus, we could create an environment in which librarians, faculty members, and administrators could sit down together to use the Conspectus information to help forge subject-based agreements. The problem with the Conspectus is not the data itself, it is that we have done nothing significant with the data for non-Conspectus reasons.[939]

Difficult times also exert a powerful motive toward self-analysis and time management, as evidenced by the recent work of Paul Metz.[940] Looking inward rather than to the expansive horizon of collection building and interlibrary cooperation, the author instead reflects the times with a call for more costing studies and time analysis in libraries. Metz notes:

> There appears to be little, if any, literature relating the environmental and task conditions of subject bibliography to time requirements . . . Among these are the needs of managers to assign workloads which are realistic and reasonably equitable, and the right of collection development staff to know the relative weights of their respective workloads.

Ryan,[941] too, noted the sobering fact that "fewer and fewer dollars will be available for higher education from public and private sources," and the challenge this poses for libraries is one of managing resources efficiently. How well do we measure performance, and how well do libraries communicate the values, standards, principles, and assumptions on which those measures rest? This will be necessary for acquisition of antiquarian materials, and for collection management, in general.

If, as seems likely, the last decade of the 20th century will signal a pronounced shift away from library ownership of materials towards cooperative arrangements encompassing acquisitions and loans, then collection evaluation must receive far greater attention than collection managers have allocated in the past. This may become doubly difficult given the staffing levels anticipated during difficult economic periods. Already overburdened librarians will find their responsibilities increasing even as demands for new services and technologies grow. For many, relegating evaluation to the lower end of goals and objectives will seem prudent, if not unavoidable. However, measuring the strengths and weaknesses of library collections must remain a top priority especially during periods of drought when scarce dollars search out the very best materials for the largest number of users.

NOTES PART TWO

833. Carter, Mary and Wallace Bonk. *Building library collections.* 2nd edition. Metuchen: Scarecrow Press, 1964. p. 131.
834. Wiemers, Eugene, et al. "Collection evaluation: a practical guide to the literature." *Library Acquisitions Practice and Theory* 8:65–78. 1984.
835. Bonn, George. "Evaluation of the collection." *Library Trends* 22:265–304. January 1974.
836. Lancaster, F.W. *The measurement and evaluation of library services.* Washington: Information Resources Press, 1977.
837. Mosher, Paul. "Collection evaluation or analysis: matching library acquisitions to library needs," in *Collection Development in Libraries: a treatise,* edited by Robert Stueart and George Miller. Greenwich: JAI Press, 1980.
838. Bonn, 1974, 266.
839. Bonn, 1974, 267.
840. Bonn, 1974, 268.
841. An interesting example of this technique is the comparative shelf list measurement project sponsored by the ALA Discussion Group of Chief Collection Development Officers of Large Research Libraries. *Titles classified by the Library of Congress classification: national shelflist count.* Berkeley: University of California Library, 1979.
842. Williams, E.E. "Surveying library collections," in *Library Surveys* edited by M.F. Tauber and I.R. Stephens. New York: Columbia University Press, 1967. pp. 23–45.
843. Jordan, R.T. "Library characteristics of colleges ranking high in academic excellence." *College and Research Libraries* 24:369–376. 1963.
844. Mosher, 1980, 535.
845. Ibid.
846. Lancaster, 1977, 167.
847. Lancaster, 1977, 168.

848. Weimers, 1984, 68.
849. Bonn, 1974, 275.
850. Mosher, 1980, 537.
851. Mosher, 1980, 538–539.
852. *Books for College Libraries.* Chicago: American Libraries Association, 1967.
853. Winchell, Constance. *Guide to reference books.* Chicago: American Library Association, 1967.
854. Brandon, A.N. "Selected list of books and journals for the small library." *Bulletin of the Medical Library Association* 61:179–200. 1973.
855. Boon, 1974.
856. Weimers, 1984.
857. Coale, R.P. "Evaluation of a research library collection: Latin-American colonial history at the Newberry." *Library Quarterly* 35:173–184. 1965.
858. Hirsch, R. "Evaluation of book collection," *Library evaluation* edited by W.S. Yenawine. Syracuse: Syracuse University Press, 1959.
859. Goldhor, Herbert. "Analysis of an inductive method of evaluating the book collection of a public library." *Libri* 23:6–17, 1973.
860. McInnis, R. Marvin. "Research collections: an approach to the assessment of quality." IPLO Quarterly 13:13–22. July 1971.
861. Lancaster, 1977, 179.
862. Weimers, 1984, 70.
863. Metz, Paul. *The Landscape of Literatures; Use of Subject Collections in a University Library.* Chicago: American Library Association, 1983. p. 2.
864. Metz, 1983, 2–3.
865. Miller, William. *Collection Development in the Literature of the Humanities: Can Citation Analysis Provide a Rational Guide?* Beaverton, Oregon: Blackwell North America, 1976. p. 1.
866. Brooks, Terrence A. "Private Acts and Public Objects: An Investigation of Citer Motivations." *Journal of the American Society for Information Science.* July 1985. p. 223.
867. Bonn, 1974, 280.
868. Williams, 1967, 23–34.
869. Miller, William and D. Stephen Rockwood. "Collection Development from a College Perspective." *College and Research Libraries* 40:318–24. July 1979.

870. Farber, Evan. "College Librarians and the University Library Syndrome." *The Academic Library: Essays in Honor of Guy R. Lyle.* Metuchen: Scarecrow Press, 1974. p. 22.
871. Bonn, 1974, 283.
872. American Library Association. Committee on Accreditation. *Standards for Accreditation 1972.* Chicago: American Library Association, 1972. p. 12.
873. National Association of Schools of Art. *The Bulletin.* Washington: National Association of Schools of Art, October 1971. p. 8.
874. Oboler, Eli, et al. *College and University Library Accreditation Standards—1957* Chicago: ACRL, 1958.
875. Ottersen, Signe. "A Bibliography on Standards for Evaluating Libraries." *College and Research Libraries* 32:127–44. March 2971.
876. Hirsch, F.E. "Standards for Libraries." *Library Trends* 21: p. 159. 1972.
877. Lancaster, 1977, 167.
878. Moran, Michael. "The Concept of Adequacy in University Libraries." *College and Research Libraries* 39:85–93. March 1978.
879. "Standards for College Libraries." *College and Research Libraries* 20:274–80. July 1959.
880. Clapp, Vernon and Robert Jordan. "Quantitative Criteria for Adequacy of Academic Library Collections." *College and Research Libraries* 26:371–80. September 1965. p. 380.
881. Clapp-Jordan, 1965, 380.
882. Moran, 1978, 88–89.
883. McInnis, R.M. "The Formula Approach to Library Size: An Empirical Study of its Efficiency in Evaluating Research Libraries." *College and Research Libraries* 33:190–98. 1972.
884. Lancaster, 1977, 171.
885. Association of College and Research Libraries. "Standards for College Libraries." College and Research Libraries News. October 1975. pp. 277–79.
886. Association of College and Research Libraries. "An Evaluative Checklist for Reviewing a College Library Program." *College and Research Libraries News.* November 1979. pp. 305–16.
887. Jordan, 1963, 369–76.

888. McGrath, William and Norma Durand. "Classifying courses in the university catalog." *College and Research Libraries* 30:553–39. November 1969.

889. Golden, Barbara. "A method for quantitatively evaluating a university library collection." *Library Resources and Technical Services* 18:268+ Summer 1974.

890. Whaley, John. "An approach to collection analysis." *Library Resources and Technical Services* 25:330–38. July 1981.

891. Lyle, Guy. *The Administration of the College Library.* New York: H.W. Wilson, 1961. p. 239.

892. Wilson, Louis and Maurice Tauber. *The University Library.* New York: Columbia University Press, 1956. p. 367.

893. Cassata, Mary and Gene Dewey. "The evaluation of a university library collection: Some guidelines." *Library Resources and Technical Services.* p. 450. Fall 1969.

894. Saunders, Stewart et al. "Alternatives to the shelflist measure for determining the size of a subject collection." p. 390. Winter 1981.

895. Compaigne, Benjamin. "Information technology and cultural change: Toward a new literacy." Harvard University Center for Information Policy, 1984. p. 31.

896. Bonn, George. "Evaluation of the collection." *Library Trends.* p. 274. January 1974.

897. Clapp, Vernon and Robert Jordan. "Quantitative criteria for adequacy of academic library collections." *College and Research Libraries.* p. 380. September 1965.

898. Krueger, Karen. "Guidelines for collection management," in *Collection Management in Public Libraries.* Chicago: ALA, 1986.

899. Atkinson, Ross. "The language of the levels: Reflections on the communication of collection development policy." *College and Research Libraries* 47:140–49. March 1986.

900. Budd, John. "A citation study of American Literature: Implications for collection management." *Collection Management* 8:49–62. Summer 1986.

901. Loertscher, David. "Collection mapping—An evaluation strategy for collection development." *Drexel Library Quarterly* 21:9–21. Spring 1985.

902. Hall, Blaine. *Collection Assessment Manual for College and University Libraries.* Phoenix: Oryx Press, 1986.

903. Stephens, Dennis. "A stitch in time: The Alaska Cooperative Collection Development Project," in *Coordinating*

Cooperative Collection Development by Wilson Luquire. New York: Haworth, 1986.

904. Farrell, David. "The NCIP option for coordinated collection management." *Library Resources and Technical Services* 30:47–56. January–March 1986.

905. Stam, David. "Collaborative collection development; Progress, problems, and potential." *Collection Building* 7:3–9. 1986.

906. Reed-Scott, Jutta. *Manual for the North American Inventory of Research Library Collections.* Washington: Association of Research Libraries, 1986.

907. Mosher, Paul. "A national scheme for collaboration in collection development: The RLG-NCIP effort." *Coordinating Cooperative Collection Development* by Wilson Luquire. New York: Haworth, 1986.

908. Lincoln, Tamara and C.E. West. "The research value of Siberia content monographs in polar collections of the University of Alaska, Fairbanks." *Collection Management* 8:31–47. Summer 1986.

909. Losee, Robert. "A decision-theoretic model of materials selection for acquisition." *Library Quarterly* 57:269–83. July 1987.

910. Palais, Elliot. "Use of course analysis in compiling a collection development policy statement for a university library." *Journal of Academic Librarianship* 13:8–13. March 1987.

911. Burrell, Q.L. "A third note on aging in a library circulation model: Applications to future use and relegation." *Journal of Documentation* 43:24–45. March 1987.

912. Warwick, J.P. "Duplication of texts in academic libraries: A behavioral model for library management." *Journal of Librarianship* 19:41–52. January 1987.

913. Futas, Elizabeth and David Vidor. "What constitutes a good collection?" *Library Journal* 112:45–74. April 15, 1987.

914. Stam, David. "Development and use of the RLG Conspectus." *NCIP: Means to an End.* Washington: Association of Research Libraries, 1987.

915. Ferguson, A.W. et al. "Internal uses of the RLG Conspectus." *Journal of Library Administration* 8:35–40. Summer 1987.

916. Abel, M.D. "The Conspectus: Issues and Questions" *NCIP: Means to an End.* Washington: Association of Research Libraries, 1987.

917. Henige, David. "Epistemological dead end and ergonomic disaster? The NCIP project." *Journal of Academic Librarianship* 13:209–213. September 1987.

918. Miller, Robert. "NCIP in the U.S." *NCIP: Means to an End.* Washington: Association of Research Libraries, 1987.

919. Horrell, Jeffrey. "The RLG Conspectus and the NCIP Project: A means to a beginning." *Art Documentation* 6:106–07. Fall 1987.

920. Nisonger, Thomas. "Acquisitions and collection development: Cooperation in a changing environment." *Library Acquisitions, Practice and Theory* 12:73–77. 1988.

921. Forcier, Peggy. "Building collections together: The Pacific Northwest Conspectus." *Library Journal* p. 43–45. April 15, 1988.

922. Oberg, Larry. "Evaluating the Conspectus approach for smaller library collections." *College and Research Libraries* 49:187–96. 1988.

923. White, Howard. "Evaluating subject collections." *Annual Review of OCLC Research.* Dublin: OCLC, 1988.

924. Ferguson, Anthony et al. "The RLG Conspectus: Its uses and benefits." *College and Research Libraries* 49:197–206. 1988.

925. Beaton, Barbara and Jay Kirk. "Applications of an automated interlibrary loan log." *Journal of Academic Librarianship* 14:24–27. 1988.

926. Dillon, Martin et al. "Design issues for a microcomputer based collection analysis system." *Microcomputers for Information Management* 5:263–73. 1988.

927. Sanders, Nancy et al. "Automated collection analysis using the OCLC and RLG bibliographic databases." *College and Research Libraries,* 49:305–14. 1988.

928. Piccininni, James. "Using the HEGIS to enhance collection development decisions in academic libraries." *Collection Management* 10:15–24. Nos. 1–2, 1988.

929. Armbruster, Ann. "Library MARC tapes as a resource for collection analysis." *Advances in Library Automation and Networking* edited by Joe Hewitt. Greenwood: JAI Press, 1988.

930. Cubberly, Carol and Barry Centini. "Improving library services for nursing studies in an academic library." *Collection Management* 10:95–106. Nos. 1–2, 1988.

931. Lancaster, F.W. *If You Want to Evaluate Your Library.* Champaign: University of Illinois, 1988.

932. Grover, Mark. "Collection assessment in the 1980's." *Collection Building* 8:23–26. 1988.
933. American Library Association. *Guide to the Evaluation of Library Collections.* Chicago: ALA, 1989.
934. Stielow, Fred and Helen Tibbo. "Collection analysis in modern librarianship: A stratified multidimensional model." *Collection Management* 11:73–91. Nos. 3–4, 1989.
935. Hyman, Ferne. "Collection evaluation in the research environment." *Collection Building* 9:33–37. Nos. 3–4, 1989.
936. Elzy, Cheryl and F.W. Lancaster. "Looking at a collection in different ways: A comparison of methods of bibliographic checking." *Collection Management* 12:1–10. Nos. 3–4, 1990.
937. Baker, Robert. "Using a turnkey automated system to support collection assessment." *College & Research Libraries* 51:360–66. 1990.
938. Atkinson, Ross. "In defense of relativism." *Journal of Academic Librarianship* 17:353. January 1992.
939. Ferguson, A.W. "Philosophical arguments and real shortcomings." *Journal of Academic Librarianship* 17:350–351. January 1992.
940. Metz, Paul. "Quantifying the workload of subject bibliographers in collection development." *Journal of Academic Librarianship* 17:284–87. November 1991.
941. Ryan, Michael. "Developing special collections in the 90's." *Journal of Academic Librarianship* 17:288–93. November 1991.

COMPREHENSIVE BIBLIOGRAPHY ON COLLECTION EVALUATION

942. Aaron, S.L. "The collection developer's link to global education." *School Library Media Quarterly.* pp. 35–43. Fall, 1990.
943. Adalian, P.T. and I.F. Rockman. "Title by title review in reference collection development." *Reference Services Review.* pp. 85–88. Winter, 1985.
944. Aguilar, W. "The application of relative use and interlibrary demand in collection development." *Collection Management.* pp. 15–24. Spring, 1986.
945. Alabi, G. "Bradford's Law and its application." *International Library Review.* pp. 151–158. January, 1979.
946. Allen, Nancy. *Film Study Collections: A Guide to their Development and Use.* New York: Ungar, 1979.
947. Almong, Robert. "The concept of systematic amplication: A survey of the literature." *Collection Management.* pp. 153–165. Summer, 1978.
948. Alt, Martha and Richard Shiels. "Assessment of library materials on the history of Christianity at Ohio State University." *Collection Management.* pp. 67–77. Spring, 1987.
949. American Library Association. "An evaluative checklist for reviewing a college library program." *CRL News.* pp. 305–316. November, 1979.
950. American Library Association. "Standards for college libraries." *College and Research Libraries.* pp. 274–280. July, 1959.
951. American Library Association. "Standards for college libraries." *CRL News.* pp. 277–279; 290–301. October, 1975.
952. Archer, J.D. "Preorder searching in academic libraries: A bibliographic essay." *Library Acquisitions, Practice and Theory.* pp. 139–144. 1983.

953. Ash, L. "Old dog, no tricks: Perceptions of the qualitative analysis of book collections." *Library Trends.* pp. 385–395. Winter, 1985.

954. Ash, Lee. *Yale's Selective Book Retirement Program.* Hamden: Archon Books, 1963.

955. Atkinson, R.W. "Language of the levels: Reflections on the communications of collection development policy." *College and Research Libraries.* pp. 140–149. March, 1986.

956. Atkinson, R.W. "Text mutability and collection administration." *Library Acquisitions, Practice and Theory.* pp. 355–358, No. 4, 1990.

957. Avallone, S. "Receptivity to religion—3rd annual mini-survey on religious books in public libraries." *Library Journal.* pp. 1891–1893. October 15, 1984.

958. Baker, R.K. "Using a turnkey automated system to support collection assessment." *College and Research Libraries.* pp. 360–366. July, 1990.

959. Baker, S.L. "Does the use of a demand-oriented selection policy reduce overall collection quality?" *Public Library Quarterly.* pp. 29–49. Fall, 1984.

960. Banks, Paul. "Environmental standards for storage of books and manuscripts." *Library Journal.* pp. 339–343. February 1, 1974.

961. Barber, Raymond and J.C. Mancall. "The application of bibliometric techniques to the analysis of materials for young adults." *Collection Management.* pp. 229–245. Fall, 1978.

962. Bartolo, L.M. "Automated ILL analysis and collection development - A hi-tech marriage of convenience." *Library Acquisitions, Practice and Theory.* pp. 361–69. No. 4, 1989.

963. Baughman, James. "A structural analysis of the literature of sociology." *Library Quarterly.* pp. 293–308. October, 1974.

964. Baughman, James. "Toward a structural approach to collection development." *College and Research Libraries.* pp. 241–48. May, 1977.

965. Beckerman, E.P. "Administrator's viewpoint: Collection development in an urban setting." *Collection Building.* pp. 35–44. Winter, 1984.

966. Bentley, Stella. "Academic library statistics - a search for a meaningful evaluative tool." *Library Research.* pp. 143–152. Summer, 1979.

967. Bentley, Stella and David Farrell. "Beyond retrenchment: The Reallocation of a Library Materials Budget." *Journal of Academic Librarianship.* pp. 321–325. January, 1985.

968. Berry, John. "Leaning toward quality of book collections." *Library Journal.* pp. 2013. October 1, 1979.

969. Bohem, Hilda. "Regional conservation services - what can we do." *Library Journal.* pp. 1428–1431. July, 1979.

970. Bolgiano, Christina and Mary King. " Profiling a periodicals collection." *College and Research Libraries.* pp. 99–104. March, 1978.

971. Bone, Larry. "Community analysis and libraries." *Library Trends.* pp. 429–643. January, 1976.

972. Bone, Larry. "Future of book selection and collection building." *Catholic Library World.* pp. 66–68. September, 1975.

973. Bone, Larry and Thomas Raines. "The nature of the urban main library: Its relation to selection and collection building." *Library Trends.* pp. 625–39. April, 1972.

974. Bonn, George. "Evaluation of the collection." *Library Trends.* pp. 265–304. January, 1974.

975. Borkowski, Casimir and Murdo MacLeod. "The implications of some recent studies of library use." *Scholarly Publishing.* pp. 3–24. October, 1979.

976. Borlase, Ron. "Nonlinear bimodel model for monitoring the flow of materials fund allocation." *Journal of Academic Librarianship.* pp. 274–276. November, 1979.

977. Boyce, Bert and Mark Funk. "Bradford's law and the selection of high quality papers." *LRTS.* pp. 390–401. Fall, 1978.

978. Boyer, Calvin. "State-wide contracts for library materials: Analysis of the attendant dysfunctional consequences." *College and Research Libraries.* pp. 86–94. March, 1974.

979. Brandon, A.N. "Selected list of books and journals for the small library." *MLA Bulletin.* pp. 179–200, 1973.

980. Britton, W.A. "A use statistic for collection management: The 80/20 Rule revisited." *Library Acquisitions, Practice and Theory.* pp. 183–189. No. 2, 1990.

981. Broadus, Robert. "The applications of citation analyses to library collection building." *Advances in Librarianship.* pp. 299–335. 1977.

982. Broadus, Robert. "Materials of history - saving and discarding." *Collection Building.* pp. 3–6. No. 1–2, 1990.

983. Brooks, Terrence. "Private acts and public objects - An

investigation of citer motivations." *ASIS Journal.* p. 223. July, 1985.

984. Brown, Charlotte. "Deaccessing for the greater good." *Wilson Library Bulletin.* pp. 22–24. April, 1987.

985. Buckland, Michael. *Book Availability and the Library User.* Elmsford: Pergamon Press, 1975.

986. Budd, John. "A citation study of American Literature - Implications for collection development." *Collection Management.* pp. 49–62. Summer, 1986.

987. Burns, Robert. "Library use as a performance measure: Its background and rationale." *Journal of Academic Librarianship.* pp. 4–11. March, 1978.

988. Burns, R.W. *Evaluation of the Holdings in Science and Technology in the University of Idaho Library.* Moscow: University of Idaho, 1968.

989. Burr, Robert. "Evaluating library collections, a case study." *Journal of Academic Librarianship.* pp. 256–260. November, 1979.

990. Buzzard, M. "Writing a collection development policy for an academic library." *Collection Management.* pp. 317–28. Winter, 1978.

991. Buzzard, M.L. and D.E. New. "Investigation of collection support for doctoral research." *College and Research Libraries.* pp. 469–75. November, 1983.

992. Byrd, Gary. "An economic 'Commons' tragedy for research libraries - Scholarly journal publishing and pricing trends." *College and Research Libraries.* pp. 184–95. 1990.

993. Cargill, J.S. "Collection development policies: An alternative viewpoint." *Library Acquisition, Practice and Theory.* pp. 47–49. No. 1, 1984.

994. Carothers, D.F. "Resources of the large academic research library." *Library Trends.* pp. 67–88. Summer, 1983.

995. Carpenter, E.J. "Toward interdisciplinarity in literary research: Some implications for collection development." *Collection Management.* pp. 75–85. No. 1, 1990.

996. Carter, J. "Book auctions." *Library Trends.* pp. 471–482. April, 1961.

997. Caswell, L.S. "Grief and collection development." *Library Acquisition, Practice and Theory.* pp. 195–199. No. 3, 1987.

998. Child, Margaret. "Further thoughts on selection for preservation." *LRTS.* pp. 354–62. October/December, 1986.

999. Childress, B. and N.J. Gibbs. "Collection assessment and development using B/NA approval plan referral slips." *Collection Management.* pp. 137–143. Nos. 1–2, 1989.

1000. Christiansen, Dorothy et al. "Guide to collection evaluation through use and user studies." *LRTS.* pp. 432–440. No. 27, 1983.

1001. Clapp, Verner and Robert Jordan. "Quantitative Criteria for Adequacy of Academic Library Collections." *College and Research Libraries.* pp. 371–380. September, 1965.

1002. Clapp, Verner and Robert Jordan. "Quantitative Critiera for adequacy of academic library collection." *College and Research Libraries.* pp. 154–163. March, 1989.

1003. Cline, H.F. and L.T. Sinnott. *Building Library Collections - Policies and Practices in Academic Libraries.* Lexington: Lexington Books, 1981.

1004. Coale, R.P. "Evaluation of a research library collection - Latin American Colonial history at the Newberry." *Library Quarterly.* pp. 173–184. 1965.

1005. Cochrance, P. "Research library collections in a changing universe: Four points of view." *College and Research Libraries.* pp. 214–24. May, 1984.

1006. Comer, C. "List checking as a method for evaluating library collections. *Collection Building.* pp. 26–34. No. 3, 1981.

1007. Coney, Donelad et al. *Report of a Survey of the Indiana University Library.* Chicago: American Library Association, 1940.

1008. Connell, T.H. "Comparing the circulation of library materials ordered by faculty and librarians." *College Management.* pp. 73–84. Nos. 1–2, 1991.

1009. Cooper, Michael. "Criteria for weeding of collections." *Library Resources and Technical Services.* pp. 339–351. Summer, 1968.

1010. Cooper, Michael. "The economics of library size - a preliminary inquiry." *Library Trends.* pp. 63–78. Summer, 1979.

1011. Crush, Marion. "Deselection policy - how to exclude everything." *Wilson Library Bulletin.* pp. 180–181. October, 1970.

1012. Dannelly, Gay. "The National Shelflist Count - A tool for collection management." *Library Acquisitions, Practice and Theory.* pp. 241–50. 1989.

1013. Darling, Pam. "A local preservation program - where to start." *Library Journal.* pp. 2343–2347. November 15, 1976.

1014. Davis, C.H. and D. Shaw. "Collection overlap as a function of library size - comparison of American and Canadian public libraries." *ASIS Journal.* pp. 19–24. January, 1979.

1015. Davis, Mary. "Model for a vendor study in a manual or semi-automated acquisitions system." *Library Acquisitions, Practice and Theory.* pp. 53–60. 1979.

1016. DeCandido, Robert. "Preserving our library materials." *Library Science.* pp. 4–6. March, 1979.

1017. DeProspo, Ernest et al. *Performance Measures for Public Libraries.* Chicago: A.L.A., 1973.

1018. Diodato, V.P. "Original language, non-English journals: Weeding them and holding them." *Science and Technology Libraries.* pp. 55–67. Spring, 1986.

1019. Dixon, J. "Book selection, racism, and the law of the land." *Assistant Librarian.* pp. 94+. July–August, 1979.

1020. Dolive, M.S. "Focusing on the collection." *Texas Libraries.* pp 84–91. Fall, 1989.

1021. Dorst, T. "Statewide cooperative collection development project." *Illinois Libraries.* pp. 17–18. January, 1987.

1022. Drake, M.A. "Forecasting academic library growth." *College and Research Libraries.* pp. 53–59. January, 1976.

1023. Dudley, C.C. "Microcomputer software collection development." *Choice.* pp. 704–705. January, 1986.

1024. Eaglen, Audrey. "Book wholesalers: Pros and cons." *Library Journal.* pp. 116–119. October, 1978.

1025. Edelman, Hendrik and G.M. Tatum. "The development of collections in American university libraries." *College and Research Libraries.* pp. 222–45. May, 1976.

1026. Elstein, R.S. "Mapping the landscape - Analysis and evaluation of art libraries' collections." *Art Documentation.* pp. 66–67. Summer, 1987.

1027. Elzy, Cheryl and F.W. Lancaster. "Looking at a collection in different ways: Comparison of methods of bibliographic checking." *Collection Management.* pp. 1–10. Nos. 3–4, 1990.

1028. Emery, C.D. "The use of portable barcode scanners in collections inventory." *Collection Management.* pp. 1–17. No. 4, 1990.

1029. Emery, Mark. "Consideration regarding Women's Studies collection development in academic libraries." *Collection Management.* pp. 85–94. No. 1–2, 1988.

1030. Engeldinger, E.A. "Inventorying academic library reference collections: A survey of the field." *Collection Management.* pp. 25–41. Winter, 1987.

1031. Engeldinger, E.A. "Use as a criterion for the weeding of reference collections - A review and case study." *Reference Librarian.* pp. 119–128. No. 29, 1990.

1032. Evans, G. Edward. "Book selection and book collection usage in academic libraries." *Library Quarterly.* pp. 297–308. July, 1970.

1033. Evans, G. Edward and Claudia W. Argyres. "Approval plans and collection development in academic libraries." *LRTS.* pp. 35–50.Winter, 1974.

1034. Evans, G.T. "Cost of information about library acquisition budgets." *Collection Management.* pp. 3–23. Spring, 1978.

1035. Evans, J. "Gardening books for a public library reference collection." *Reference Services Review.* pp. 53–58. No. 2, 1990.

1036. Farber, Evan. "Limiting college library growth - Bane or Boon?" *Journal of Academic Librarianship.* pp. 12–15. November, 1975.

1037. Farrell, David. "The NCIP option for coordinated collection development." *LRTS.* pp. 47–56. January/March, 1986.

1038. Farrell, David and Jutta Reed-Scott. "The NCIP: Implications for the future." *LRTS.* pp. 15–28. January, 1989.

1039. Ferguson, A.W. "Assessing the collection development need for CD-ROM products." *Library Acquisitions, Practice and Theory.* pp. 325–32. No. 3–4, 1988.

1040. Ferguson, A.W. et al. "The RLG Conspectus - its uses and benefits." *College and Research Libraries.* pp. 197–206. May, 1988.

1041. Fletcher, John. "Inflation indexes for academic library purchases." *Library Association Record.* pp. 400–401. August, 1987.

1042. Flynn, Roger. "The University of Pittsburgh study of journal usage: A summary report." *Serials Librarian.* pp. 25–33. Fall, 1979.

1043. Fraley, Ruth. "Publishers vs. wholesalers: The ordering dilemma." *Library Acquisitions, Practice and Theory.* pp. 9–13. No. 1, 1979.

1044. French, Janet. "The evaluation gap: The state of the art in A/V reviewing with special emphasis on filmstrips." *Library Journal.* pp. 1162–1166. March 15, 1970.

1045. Fussler, H.H. and J.L. Simon. *Patterns in the Use of Books in Large Research Libraries.* Chicago: University of Chicago Library, 1969.

1046. Futas, Elizabeth. "Issues in collection development: Collection evaluation." *Collection Building.* pp. 54–55. No. 1, 1982.

1047. Futas, Elizabeth and David Vidor. "What constitutes a good collection?" *Library Journal.* pp. 45–74. April, 15, 1987.

1048. Futas, Elizabeth and Sheila Intner. "Collection evaluation." *Library Trends.* pp. 237–436. Winter, 1985.

1049. Galvin, Thomas and Allen Kent. "Use of a university library collection: A progress report on a Pittsburgh study." *Library Journal.* pp. 2317–20. November 15, 1977.

1050. Gamble, A. and L.G. Wiedrick. "Evaluation of Calgary's basic collection for elementary schools." *School Libraries in Canada.* pp. 16–18. Summer, 1982.

1051. Gardner, C.A. "Book selection policies in the college library - a reappraisal." *College and Research Libraries.* pp. 140–46. March, 1985.

1052. Gardner, Jeff. *CAP: A project for the analysis of the collection development process in large academic libraries.* New York: K.G. Saur, 1979.

1053. Garland, K. "Collections within New York are as varied as the libraries themselves." *Bookmark.* pp. 208–210. Spring, 1990.

1054. Gatten, Jeff et al. "Purchasing CD-ROM products - considerations for a new technology." *Library Acquisitions, Practice and Theory.* pp. 273–81. No. 4, 1987.

1055. Gaver, M.V. *Background Readings in Building Library Collections.* Metuchen: Scarecrow Press, 1969.

1056. Gers, R. "Output measurement in Maryland: Book availability and user satisfaction." *Public Libraries.* pp. 77–80. Fall, 1982.

1057. Goehlert, Robert. "Journal use per monetary unit: A reanalysis of use data." *Library Acquisitions, Practice and Theory.* pp. 91–98. 1979.

1058. Goehlert, Robert. "Periodical use in an academic library." *Special Libraries.* pp. 51–60. February, 1978.

1059. Golden, Barbara. "A method for quantitatively evaluating a university library collection." *Library Resources and Technical Services.* pp. 268–74. Summer, 1974.

1060. Goldhor, Herbert. "Analysis of an inductive method of evaluating the book collection of a public library." *Libri.* pp. 6–17. 1973.

1061. Goldhor, Herbert. "U.S. public library adult non-fiction book collections in the humanities." *Collection Management.* pp. 31–43. Spring, 1979.

1062. Goldstein, M. and J. Sedransk. "Using a sample technique to describe characteristics of a collection." *College and Research Libraries.* pp. 195–202. May, 1977.

1063. Goodwin, J.G. "Applying the Fairfax Plan to reference collection management." *Reference Librarian.* pp. 33–42. No. 29, 1990.

1064. Gore, Dan. "The mischief in measurement." *Library Journal.* pp. 933–937. May 1, 1978.

1065. Gorman, Robert. "Selecting New Right materials: A case study." *Collection Building.* pp. 3–8. No. 3, 1987.

1066. Gosnell, C.F. "Obsolescence of books in college libraries." *Collection Management.* pp. 167–82. Summer, 1978.

1067. Grant, Joan and S. Perelmuter. "Vendor performance evaluation." *Journal of Academic Librarianship.* pp. 366–67. November, 1978.

1068. Grant, Robert. "Predicting the need for multiple copies of books." *Journal of Library Automation.* pp. 64–71. June, 1971.

1069. Grimes, D. "Assessing assessment - a researcher's evaluation of conspectus." *Catholic Library World.* pp. 259–261. May–June, 1989.

1070. Grover, M.L. "Collection assessment in the 1980's." *Collection Building.* pp. 23–26. No. 4, 1987.

1071. Gwinn, Nancy and Paul Mosher. "Coordinating Collection Development - the RLG Conspectus." *College and Research Libraries.* pp. 128–140. March, 1983.

1072. Gyeszly, S. et al. "Collection evaluation and growth at Texas A & M 1978 and 1988 - A comparative statistical analysis." *Collection Management.* pp. 155–172. Nos. 3–4, 1990.

1073. Haar, J. et al. "Choosing CD-ROM Products." *College and Research Libraries News.* pp. 839–41. October, 1990.

1074. Hacken, R.D. "Statistical assumption - masking in library collection assessment: Peccadilloes and pitfalls." *Collection Management.* pp. 17–32. Summer, 1985.

1075. Hall, Blaine. *Collection Assessment Manual for College and University Libraries.* Phoenix: Oryx Press, 1985.

1076. Hall, Blaine. "Writing the collection assessment manual." *Collection Management.* pp. 49–61. Fall–Winter, 1984.

1077. Hamilton, M.J. "Poor condition: Procedures for identifying and treating materials before adding to the collections." *RTSD News.* pp. 19–21. No. 2, 1988.

1078. Hamilton, P.A. and T. Weech. "Development and testing of an instrument to measure attitudes toward the quality vs. demand debate in collection management." *Collection Management.* pp. 27–42. Nos. 3–4, 1988.

1079. Hamlin, A.T. "Book collections of British university libraries - an American reaction." *International Library Review.* pp. 135–73. April, 1970.

1080. Hardesty, L.L. "Use of library materials at a small liberal arts college." *Collection Management.* pp. 61–80. Nos. 3–4, 1988.

1081. Harms, J.M. and L.J. Lettow. "The cupboard is bare: The need to expand poetry collections." *School Library Journal.* pp. 34–35. January, 1987.

1082. Hawks, C.P. "The GEAC acquisitions system as a source of management information." *Library Acquisitions, Practice and Theory.* pp. 245–53. No. 4, 1986.

1083. Hazen, D.C. "Collection development, collection management, and preservation." *Library Resources and Technical Services.* pp. 3–11. January, 1982.

1084. Heaney, Henry. "Western European interest in conspectus." *Libri.* 28–32. 1990.

1085. Heinritz, F.J. "Rate of growth for library collections." *College and Research Libraries.* pp. 95–96. March, 1974.

1086. Heitshu, S.C. "Changing acquisition systems: An evolutionary process." *Technicalities.* pp. 3–7. April, 1984.

1087. Henige, David. "Epistemological dead end and ergonomic disaster: The North American Collections Inventory Project." *Journal of Academic Librarianship.* pp. 209–213. September, 1987.

1088. Henri, I. "The RLG Conspectus Down Under." *Library Acquisitions, Practice and Theory.* pp. 73–80. No. 1, 1989.

1089. Herouz, Marlene and Carol Fleishauer. "Cancellation decisions - evaluating standing orders." *LRTS*. pp. 368–379. Fall, 1978.

1090. Herubel, J.P. "Simple citation analysis and the Purdue history periodical collection." *Indiana Libraries*. pp. 18–21. No. 2, 1990.

1091. Hirsch, R. "Evaluation of the book collection," *Library Evaluation*. Syracuse: Syracuse University Press, 1959.

1092. Hodowanec, George. "An acquisition rate model for academic libraries." *College and Research Libraries*. pp. 439–47. November, 1978.

1093. Hodowanec, George. "Literature obsolesence, dispersion, and collection development." *College and Research Libraries*. pp. 421–443. November, 1983.

1094. Hodson, J. "The use of microcomputers for collection evaluation." *Library Software Review*. pp. 231–32. July–August, 1990.

1095. Horrell, Jeff. "The RLG Conspectus and the NCIP Project: A means to a beginning." *Art Documentation*. pp. 106–107. Fall, 1987.

1096. Howard, I.G. "Synergy for research library collections using RLG Conspectus." *Libri*. pp. 205–209. September, 1988.

1097. Hulbert, Linda and David Curry. "Evaluation of an approval plan." *College and Research Libraries*. pp. 485–91. November, 1978.

1098. Hulser, Richard. "Weeding in a corporate library as part of a collection maintenance program." *Science and Technology Libraries*. pp. 1–9. Spring, 1986.

1099. Hyman, Ferne. "Collection evaluation in the research environment." *Collection Building*. pp. 33–37. Nos. 3–4, 1989.

1100. Intner, Sheila. "Differences between access vs. ownership." *Technicalities*. pp. 5–8. September, 1989.

1101. Johnson, Carol and Richard Trueswell. "The weighted criteria statistic score: An approach to journal selection." *College and Research Libraries*. pp. 287–292. July, 1978.

1102. Jones, A. "Resource sharing in an electronic age-past, present and future." *Catholic Library World*. pp. 104–106. November–December, 1989.

1103. Jordon, Robert. "Library characteristics of colleges ranking high in academic excellence." *College and Research Libraries*. pp. 369–376. 1963.

1104. Kaske, Neal. "Library utilization studies - time for comparison." *Library Journal.* pp. 685–86. March, 15, 1979.
1105. Kennedy, Gail. "Relationship between acquisitions and collection development." *Library Acquisitions, Practice and Theory.* pp. 225–32. No. 3, 1983.
1106. Kent, Allen, et al. *Use of Library Materials - The University of Pittsburgh Study.* New York: Dekker, 1979.
1107. Kilton, Thomas. D. "Out of print procurement in academic libraries: Current methods and sources." *Collection Management.* pp. 113–134. Fall–Winter, 1983.
1108. Knightly, John. "Library collections and academic curricula: Quantitative relationships." *College and Research Libraries.* pp. 295–301. July, 1975.
1109. Koenig, Michael. "Citation analysis for the arts and humanities as a collection management tool." *Collection Management.* pp. 247–261. Fall, 1978.
1110. Koenig, Michael. "Online serials collection analysis." *Journal of the JASIS.* pp. 148–153. May, 1979.
1111. Kohl, D. *Acquisitions, Collection Development and Collection Use: A Handbook for Library Management.* Santa Barbara: ABC-CLIO, 1985.
1112. Kovacs, Beatrice. "Impact of weeding on collection development: SciTech collections vs. general collections." *Science and Technology Libraries.* pp. 25–36. Spring, 1989.
1113. Kreyche, M. "BCL3 and NOTIS - an automated collection analysis project." *Library Acquisitions, Practice and Theory.* pp. 323–28. No. 4, 1989.
1114. Kreyche, M. "Notes on the Books for College Libraries tape format." *Information Technology and Libraries.* pp. 111–112. March, 1990.
1115. Kriz, Harry. "Subscription vs. books in a constant dollar budget." *College and Research Libraries.* pp. 105–109. March, 1978.
1116. Kull, B. "Evaluating materials: Previewing and selection of media materials." *Media Spectrum.* pp. 6+. No. 2, 1982.
1117. Lampe, David. "Your neighbor in the library may be a thief." *Smithsonian.* pp. 140–154. November, 1979.
1118. Lancaster, F.W. "Evaluating collections by their use." *Collection Management.* pp. 15–43. Spring/Summer, 1982.
1119. No entry.

1120. Lancaster, F.W. and M.J. Joncich. *The Measurement and Evaluation of Library Services.* Washington: Information Resources Press, 1977.

1121. Lane, L.M. "Relationships between loans and in-house use of books in determining a use factor for budget allocation." *Library Acquisitions, Practice and Theory.* pp. 95–102.

1122. Lauer, J.J. "Methodology for estimating the size of subject collections using African Studies as an example." *College and Research Libraries.* pp. 380–83. September, 1983.

1123. Leach, S. "Growth rates of major academic libraries." *College and Research Libraries.* pp. 531–42. November, 1976.

1124. Leider, R. "How librarians help to inflate the price of books and what to do about it." *American Libraries.* pp. 559–560. October, 1980.

1125. Lincoln, Robert. "Vendors and delivery." *Canadian Library Journal.* pp. 51–57. Febrauary, 1978.

1126. Line, Maurice. "Obsolescence studies - A plea for realism." *Journal of Documentation.* pp. 46–47. March, 1986.

1127. Line, Maurice, et al. "Practical interpretation of citation and library use studies." *College and Research Libraries.* pp. 393–96. September, 1975.

1128. Loertscher, D.V. "Collection mapping - an evaluation strategy for collection development." *Drexel Library Quarterly.* pp. 9–39. Spring, 1985.

1129. Loertscher, David et al. *Evaluating School Library Media Programs.* New York: Neal-Schuman Publishers, 1986.

1130. Lopez, M.D. "Lopez or citation technique of in-depth collection evaluation explicated." *College and Research Libraries.* pp. 251–55. May, 1983.

1131. Losee, R.M. "A decision theoretic model of materials selection for acquisition." *Library Quarterly.* pp. 269–83. July, 1987.

1132. Losee, R.M. "Theoretical adequacy and the scientific study of materials selection." *Collection Management.* pp. 15–26. No. 3, 1988.

1133. Lucas, T.A. "Verifying the conspectus - problems and progress." *College and Research Libraries News.* pp. 199–201. March, 1990.

1134. Lucker, Jay et al. "Weeding collections in an academic library system." *Science and Technology Libraries.* pp. 11–23. Spring, 1986.

1135. Lukas, J. "Practicing librarian - a no cost, online acquisitions system for a medium size library." *Library Journal.* pp. 684–85. March 15, 1980.

1136. Lundin, A.H. "List checking in collection development - An imprecise art." *Collection Management.* pp. 103–112. Nos. 3–4, 1989.

1137. Lupone, G. "Research methods for analyzing serials budgets." *Serials Librarian.* pp. 153–155. Nos. 3–4, 1988.

1138. Lynden, Fred. "Collection management by automation." *Library Acquisitions, Practice and Theory.* pp. 177–183. 1989.

1139. Lynden, Fred. "Cost analysis of monographs and serials." *Journal of Library Administration.* pp. 19–40. No. 3, 1990.

1140. Lynden, Fred. "Plan of action for collecting statistical data on the prices of library materials." *IFLA Journal.* pp. 422–428. 1990.

1141. McCormick, R. "Ethnic studies materials for school libraries - how to choose and use them." *Catholic Library World.* pp. 339–41. March, 1980.

1142. McDonald, D.R. et al. "Sequential analysis: A methodology for monitoring approval plans." *College and Research Libraries.* pp. 329–34. July, 1979.

1143. MacDonald, Mary. "Weeding the collection." *Unabashed Librarian.* pp. 7–8. Summer, 1975.

1144. McGrath, William. "Correlating the subjects of books taken out of and books used within an open stack library." *College and Research Libraries.* pp. 280–85. July, 1971.

1145. McGrath, William. "Determining and allocating book funds for current domestic buying." *College and Research Libraries.* pp. 269–72. July, 1967.

1146. McGrath, William. "A pragmatic book allocation formula for academic and public libraries with a test for its effectiveness." *Library Resources and Technical Services.* pp. 356–69. Fall, 1975.

1147. McGrath, William. "Relationships between hard-soft, pure-applied, and life-nonlife disciplines and subject book use in a university library." *Information Processing and Management.* pp. 17–28. No. 1, 1978.

1148. McGrath, William. "Relationships between subject characteristics and use of books in a university library." *PhD Thesis.* Syracuse University, 1975.

1149. McGrath, William. "The significance of books used according to a classified profile of academic departments." *College and Research Libraries.* pp. 212–219. May, 1972.

1150. McGrath, William. "Two models for predicting subject circulation: A contribution to the allocation problem." *Journal of the JASIS.* pp. 264–68. September, 1979.

1151. McGrath, William et al. "Ethnocentricity and cross-disciplinary circulation." *College and Research Libraries.* pp. 511–518. November, 1979.

1152. McGrath, William and N.B. Nuzzo. "Existing collection strength and shelflist correlations in RLG's Conspectus for music." *College and Research Libraries.* pp. 194–203. March, 1991.

1153. McInnis, R.M. "Research collections - An approach to the assessment of quality." *IPLO Quarterly.* pp. 13–22. July, 1971.

1154. McInnis, R.M. "The formula approach to library size - An empirical study of its effects in evaluating research libraries." *College and Research Libraries.* pp. 190–98. May, 1972.

1155. McJenkin, V. "Streamlining essential routines." *Wilson Library Bulletin.* pp. 680–681. April, 1963.

1156. McMurdo, G. "Purchasing: The Librarian as loner." *Library Review.* pp. 207–214. Autumn, 1983.

1157. McPherson, W.G. "Quantifying the allocation of monograph funds - an instance in practice." *College and Research Libraries.* pp. 116–127. March, 1983.

1158. Machlup, Fritz. "Our libraries: Can we measure their holdings and acquisitions?" *AAUP Bulletin.* pp. 303–07. October, 1976.

1159. Magrill, Rosemary. "Collection development in 1981." *LRTS.* pp. 240–253. 1982.

1160. Mahar, Mary. "Determining values in instructional materials." *Illinois Libraries.* pp. 286–290. April, 1964.

1161. Maher, W.J. and B.F. Shearer. "Undergraduate use patterns of newspapers on microfilm." *College and Research Libraries.* pp. 254–260. May, 1979.

1162. Mahoney, K. "Weeding the small library collection." *Connecticut Libraries.* pp. 45–47. Spring, 1982.

1163. Mancini, D. "Implementing a collection development policy." *Georgia Libraries.* pp. 92–94. November, 1985.

1164. Matheson, Ann. "The Conspectus experience." *Journal of Librarianship.* pp. 171–182. 1990.

1165. Metz, Paul. *The Landscape of Literatures of the Humanities - Can Citation Analysis Provide a Rational Guide.* Beaverton: Blackwell, 1976.

1166. Metz, Paul. "The use of the general collection in the Library of Congress." *Library Quarterly.* pp. 415–34. October, 1979.

1167. Metz, Paul and B. Foltin. "A social history of madness - or, Who is buying this round? Anticipating and avoiding gaps in collection development." *College and Research Libraries.* pp. 33–39. January, 1990.

1168. Miller, Constance and James Rettig. "Reference obsolescence." *RQ,* pp. 52–58. Fall, 1986.

1169. Miller, Edward and A.L. O'Neill. "Journal deselection and costing." *Library Acquisitions, Practice and Theory.* pp. 173–178. 1990.

1170. Montgomery, K.L. and et al. "Cost benefit model of library acquisition in terms of use. Progress Report." *Journal of the JASIS.* pp. 73–74. January, 1976.

1171. Moran, Michael. "The concept of adequacy in university libraries." *College and Research Libraries.* pp. 85–93. March, 1978.

1172. Mosher, Paul. "Collaborative interdependence - The human dimension of the Conspectus." *IFLA Journal.* pp. 327–31. 1990.

1173. Mosher, Paul. "Collection evaluation in research libraries: The search for quality, consistency, and system in collection development." *Library Resources and Technical Services.* pp. 16–32. Winter, 1979.

1174. Mosher, Paul. "Quality and library collections - New directions in research and practice in collection evaluation." *Advances in Librarianship.* New York: Academic Press, 1984.

1175. Mosher, Paul and Marcia Pankake. "A guide to coordinated and cooperative collection development." *LRTS.* pp. 417–431. 1983.

1176. Mostyn, G.R. "Use of supply-demand equality in evaluating collection adequacy." *California Librarian.* pp. 16–23. April, 1974.

1177. Murray, W.A. et al. "Collection mapping and collection development." *Drexel Library Quarterly.* pp. 40–51. Spring, 1985.

1178. Naylor, Richard. "The efficient mid-size library: Comparing book budget to population to collection size." *Library Journal.* pp. 119–120. February 15, 1987.

1179. New, Doris and Retha Ott. "Interlibrary loan analysis as a collection development tool." *Library Resources and Technical Services.* pp. 275–83. Summer, 1974.

1180. Newborn, D.E. and I.P. Godden. "Improving approval plan performance: A care study." *Library Acquisition, Practice and Theory.* pp. 145–55. No. 2, 1980.

1181. Newhouse, Joseph and Arthur Alexander. *An Economic Analysis of Public Library Services.* Lexington: D.C. Heath, 1972.

1182. Nimmer, R.J. "Circulation and collection patterns at the OSU libraries." *Library Acquisition, Practice and Theory.* pp. 61–70. No. 1, 1980.

1183. Nisonger, T.E. "Editing the RLG Conspectus to analyze the O.C.L.C. archival tapes of 17 Texas libraries." *Library Resources and Technical Services.* pp. 309–327. October, 1985.

1184. Nisonger, T.E. "Test of two citation checking techniques for evaluating political science collections in university libraries." *Library Resources and Technical Services.* pp. 163–76. April, 1983.

1185. Nolan, C.W. "The lean reference collection." *College and Research Libraries.* pp. 80–91. January, 1991.

1186. Nugent, W.R. "Statistics of collection overlap at the libraries of the six New England state universities." *Library Resources and Technical Services.* pp. 31–36. Winter, 1968.

1187. Oberg, L.R. "Evaluating the conspectus approach for smaller library collections." *College and Research Libraries.* pp. 187–196. May, 1988.

1188. O'Connell, J.B. "Collection evaluation in a developing country: A Mexican case study." *Libri.* pp. 44–64. March, 1984.

1189. O'Connor, Dan and E.R. Dyer. "Evaluation of corporate reference collections." *Reference Librarian.* pp. 21–31. 1990.

1190. Orne, Jerrold. "The Place of the Library in the Evaluation of Graduate Work." *College and Research Libraries.* pp. 25–32. January, 1969.

1191. Osburn, Charles. "Collection development: The link between scholarship and library resources." *New Directions for Higher Education.* pp. 45–54. September, 1982.

1192. Osburn, Charles. "Non-use and loser studies in collection development." *Collection Management.* pp. 45–53. Spring–Summer, 1982.

1193. Osburn, Charles. "Planning for a university library policy on collection development." *International Library Review.* pp. 209–224. April, 1977.

1194. Ottersen, Signe. "A bibliography on standards for evaluating libraries." *College and Research Libraries.* pp. 127–144. March, 1971.

1195. Palais, Elliot. "Use of course analysis in compiling a collection development policy statement for a university library." *Journal of Academic Librarianship.* pp. 8–13. March, 1987.

1196. Palincsar, S.F. "Online-assisted collection development in a government depository library collection." *Library Software Review.* pp. 94–96. March/April, 1990.

1197. Pan, Elizabeth. "Journal citation as a predictor of journal usage in libraries." *Collection Management.* pp. 29–38. Spring, 1978.

1198. Pargellis, S. "Book supply and the book market." *Library Quarterly.* pp. 199–204. July, 1953.

1199. Paskoff, B.M. and A.H. Perrault. "A tool for comparative collection analysis." *Library Resources and Technical Services.* pp. 199–215. April, 1990.

1200. Pasterczyk, C.E. "A quantitative method for evaluating approval plans performance." *Collection Management.* pp. 25–38. Nos. 1–2, 1988.

1201. Patterson, Robert. "Organizing for conservation." *Library Journal.* pp. 1116–1119. May 15, 1979.

1202. Payson, E. and B. Moore. "Statistical collection management analysis of OCLC-MARC tape records." *Information Technology and Libraries.* pp. 220–32. September, 1985.

1203. Peccininni, J.C. "Using the higher education general information system to enhance collection development decisions in academic libraries." *Collection Management.* pp. 15–24. No. 1, 1988.

1204. Perrault, A.H. "Humanities collection management - An impressionistic, realistic, optimistic appraisal of the state of the art." *Collection Management.* pp. 1–23. Fall–Winter, 1983.

1205. Perushek, D.E. "Features in managing East Asian Studies collections." *American Archivist Collection Management.* pp. 89–101. Fall–Winter, 1983.

1206. Phelps, D. "Publishers discounts but at what price?" *Library Acquisitions, Practice and Theory.* pp. 289–293. No. 3, 1990.

1207. Pierce, Sydney. *Weeding and Maintenance of Reference Collections.* Haworth Press, 1990.

1208. Pinnell-Stephens, J. "Local conspectus applications." *PNLA Quarterly.* pp. 22–23. Spring, 1989.

1209. "Pittsburgh University studies of collection usage: A Symposium." *Journal of Academic Librarianship.* pp. 60–70. May, 1979.

1210. Popovich, Charles. "The characteristics of a collection for research in business-management." *College and Research Libraries.* pp. 110–117. March, 1978.

1211. Porta, M.A. and F.W. Lancaster. "Evaluation of a scholarly collection in a specific subject area by bibliographic checking." *Libri.* pp. 131–37. June, 1988.

1212. Potter, W.G. "Collection overlap in the LCS network in Illinois." *Library Quarterly.* pp. 119–141. April, 1986.

1213. Potter, W.G. "Modeling collection overlap on a microcomputer." *Information Technology and Libraries.* pp. 400–407. December, 1983.

1214. Reed, Mary. "Identification of storage candidates among monographs." *Collection Management.* pp. 203–214. Summer/Fall, 1979.

1215. Reid, R.C. "Fee based services and collection development in an academic library." *Drexel Library Quarterly.* pp. 54–67. Fall, 1983.

1216. Reidelbach, John and G. Shirk. "Selecting an approval plan vendor: Step by step process." *Library Acquisitions, Practice and Theory.* pp. 115–125. No. 2, 1983.

1217. Rice, Barbara. "Science periodicals use study." *Serials Librarian.* pp. 35–47. Fall, 1979.

1218. Riechel, Rosemarie. "Public libraries - a method of survival through preservation." *Catholic Library World.* pp. 162–165. November, 1979.

1219. Riggsbee, M.S. "Book selection methods in school libraries: A survey of practices in North Carolina." *North Carolina Libraries.* pp. 13–17. Summer, 1981.

1220. Roberts, M. and K. Cameron. "Barometer of unmet demand: ILL analysis and monographic acquisitions." *Library Acquisitions, Practice and Theory.* pp. 31–42. No. 1, 1984.

1221. Robinson, E.J. and S.J. Turner. "Improving library effectiveness: A proposal for applying fuzzy set concepts in the management of large collections." *American Society of Information Science Journal.* pp. 458–62. November, 1981.

1222. Robinson, W.C. "Gift materials in Tennessee academic and public libraries." *Tennessee Libraries.* pp. 12–24. Spring, 1990.

1223. Rochester, M.K. "The ABN Database-Sampling strategies for collection overlap studies." *Information Technology and Libraries.* pp. 190–96. September, 1987.

1224. Rouse, Roscoe. "Within library solutions to book space problems." *Library Trends.* pp. 299–310. January, 1971.

1225. Roy, Loriene. "Does weeding increase circulation? A review of the related literature." *Collection Management.* pp. 141–156. Nos. 1–2, 1988.

1226. Rutledge, J. "Collecting contemporary European literature for a research library." *Collection Management.* pp. 1–13. Spring–Summer, 1983.

1227. Sanders, N.P. et al. "Automated collection analysis using the OCLC and RLG bibliographic databases." *College and Research Libraries.* pp. 305–314. July, 1988.

1228. Sandler, M. "Quantitative approaches to qualitative collection assessment." *Collection Building.* pp. 12–17. No. 4, 1987.

1229. Sargent, Seymour. "The uses and limitations of Trueswell." *College and Research Libraries.* pp. 416–23. September, 1979.

1230. Schad, Jasper. "Allocating materials budgets in institutions of higher education." *Journal of Academic Librarianship.* pp. 328–332. January, 1978.

1231. Schloman, Barbara and Ruth Ahl. "Retention periods for journals in a small academic library." *Special Libraries.* pp. 377–383. September, 1979.

1232. Schofield, J.L. et al. "Evaluation of an academic library's stock effectiveness." *Journal of Librarianship.* pp. 207–27. July, 1975.

1233. Segal, J.A. "Journal deselection - A literature review and an application." *Science and Technology Libraries.* pp. 25–42. Spring, 1986.

1234. Serebnick, Judith. "Using checklists to measure diversity in library collections." *Catholic Library World.* pp. 355–56. March, 1984.

1235. Seymour, Carol. "Weeding the collection - a review of research on identifying obsolete stock." *Libri.* pp. 137–48. 1972.

1236. Shaw, W.M. "A practical journal usage technique." *College and Research Libraries.* pp. 479–484. November, 1978.

1237. Sheridan, Robert. "Measuring book disappearace, how to evaluate need for collection protection." *Library Journal.* pp. 2040–2043. September 1, 1974.

1238. Shipman, John. "Signifying renewal as well as change - One library's experience with the Center for Research Libraries." *Library Acquisitions, Practice and Theory.* pp. 243–48. 1978.

1239. Skelley, G.T. "Characteristics of collections added to American research libraries 1940–1970." *College and Research Libraries.* pp. 52–60. January, 1975.

1240. Sloan, Bernard. "Resource sharing among academic libraries - the LCS experience." *Journal of Academic Librarianship.* pp. 26–29. March, 1986.

1241. Slote, Stanley. "Identifying useful core collections." *Library Quarterly.* pp. 25–34. January, 1970.

1242. Slote, Stanley. *Weeding Library Collections.* Littleton: Libraries Unlimited, 1975.

1243. Smith, H.F. "Agricultural documents - Acquisitions and control." *Special Libraries.* pp. 23–29. Winter, 1991.

1244. Sohn, J. "Cooperative collection development: A brief overview." *Collection Management.* pp. 1–9. Summer, 1986.

1245. Spicer, C.A. "An inventory for the 80's." *Collection Building.* pp. 16–18. No. 3, 1987.

1246. "Standards for College Libraries." *College and Research Libraries.* pp. 274–280. July, 1959.

1247. "Standards for College Libraries." *College and Research Libraries.* pp. 305–316. November, 1979.

1248. Stankus, Tony. "Journal weeding in relation to declining faculty member publishing." *Science and Technology Libraries.* pp. 43–53. Spring, 1986.

1249. Stenstrom, Patricia and Ruth McBride. "Serial use by social science faculty: A survey." *College and Research Libraries.* pp. 426–431. September, 1979.

1250. Stephens, D.J. "The Conspectus in Alaska and how we're using it." *PNLA Quarterly.* pp. 15–16. Spring, 1989.

1251. Stielow, F.J. and H.R. Tibbo. "Collection analysis in modern librarianship - A stratified multidimensional model." *Collection Management.* pp. 73–91. Nos. 3–4, 1989.

1252. Stiffler, S.A. "Core analysis in collection management." *Collection Management.* pp. 135–149. Fall–Winter, 1983.

1253. Stubban, V.C. "Use of the RLG Conspectus as a tool for analyzing and evaluating agricultural collections." *Quarterly Bulletin of the International Association of Agricultural Librarians and Documentalists.* pp. 105–110. No. 3, 1988.

1254. Tauber, Maurice and E.H. Wilson. *Report of a Survey of Montana State University Library.* Chicago: American Library Association, 1951.

1255. Tauber, Maurice and I.R. Stephens. *Library Surveys.* New York: Columbia University Press, 1967.

1256. Taylor, Colin. "A practical solution to weeding university library periodical collections." *Collection Management.* pp. 27–45. Fall–Winter, 1976–77.

1257. Taylor, N. "Dehumanized: The Worst possible time for blind ordering of rubbish." *Library Association Record.* p. 17. January, 1976.

1258. Tezla, K.E. "Reference collection development using the RLG Conspectus." *Reference Librarian.* pp. 43–51. No. 29, 1990.

1259. Thomason, N.W. "Evaluating a school media center book collection." *Catholic Library World.* pp. 87–88. September, 1981.

1260. Thompson, James. "Revision of stock in academic libraries." *Library Association Record.* pp. 41–44. March, 1973.

1261. Tomer, Christinger. "Identification, evaluation, and selection of books for preservation." *Collection Management.* pp. 45–54. Spring, 1979.

1262. Totten, Herman. "Selection of library materials for storage - A state of the art." *Library Trends.* pp. 341–51. January, 1971.

1263. Trueswell, Richard. "User circulation satisfaction vs. size of holdings at three academic libraries." *College and Research Libraries.* pp. 204–13. May, 1969.

1264. Trueswell, Richard. "The uses and limitations of Trueswell; a comment." *College and Research Libraries.* pp. 424–25. September, 1979.

1265. Trueswell, Richard and S.J. Turner. "Simulating circulation use characteristic curves using circulation data." *Journal of the ASIS.* pp. 83–87. March, 1979.

1266. Truett, Carol. "Weeding and evaluating the reference collection - A study of policies and practices in academic and public libraries." *Reference Librarian.* pp. 53–67. 1990.

1267. Turner, S.J. "Trueswell's weeding technique: The facts." *College and Research Libraries.* pp. 134–138. March, 1980.

1268. Turner, Stephen. "A formula for estimating collection use." *College and Research Libraries.* pp. 509–513. November, 1977.

1269. Turock, B.J. "PDQ: Professional Development Quarterly—collection management and bibliometrics in the public library." *Public Library Quarterly.* pp. 3–10. Fall, 1982.

1270. Usdin, Tommie. "Core lists of medical journals: a comparison." *Bulletin of the Medical Library Association.* pp. 212–217. April, 1979.

1271. VanOrden, Phyllis. *The Collection Program in Schools.* Littleton: Libraries Unlimited, 1988.

1272. Voigt, Melvin. "Acquisition rates in university libraries." *College and Research Libraries.* pp. 263–271. July, 1975.

1273. Walker, G.P. "Describing and evaluating library collections." *Journal of Librarianship.* pp. 219–231. October, 1978.

1274. Warncke, Ruth. "Analyzing your community: Basis for building library service." *Illinois Libraries.* pp. 64–76. February, 1975.

1275. Warner, M. and K. Flynn. "Legal collections in small and medium-sized public libraries." *Collection Building.* pp. 25–33. No. 2, 1986.

1276. Watson, P.G. "Collection development and evaluation in reference and adult services librarianship." *RQ.* pp. 143–145. Winter, 1986.

1277. Weaver, James. "Gift appraisal practices in NAPCU." *PNLA Quarterly.* pp. 3–5. Fall, 1978.

1278. No entry.

1279. Welsch, Erwin. "A collection development model for foreign literatures." *Collection Management.* pp. 1–11. Spring, 1985.

1280. Wender, Ruth. "Counting journal title usage in the health sciences." *Special Libraries.* pp. 219–226. May–June, 1979.

1281. Wenger, Charles et al. "Monograph evaluation for acquisitions in a large research library." *Journal of the ASIS.* pp. 88–92. March, 1979.

1282. Whaley, J. "Groping toward national standards for collection evaluation." *Show Me Libraries.* pp. 25–28. March, 1986.

1283. Wiemers, E. "Collection evaluation—a practical guide to the literature." *Library Acquisitions, Practice and Theory.* pp. 65–76. No. 1, 1984.

1284. Wilson, Louis et al. *A Study of the Libraries of Cornell University.* Ithaca: Cornell University, 1948.

1285. Wilson, Patrick. "Limits to the growth of knowledge: The case of the social and behavioral sciences." *Library Quarterly.* pp. 4–21. January, 1980.

1286. Winkel, Lois. "Developing collections to service children: Tools of the trade." *Catholic Library World.* pp. 172–177, January–February, 1986.

1287. Wood, John and Lynn Coppel. "Drowning our kittens—deselection of periodicals." *Serials Librarian.* pp. 317–331. Spring, 1979.

1288. Wyllys, Ron. "On the analysis of growth rates of library collections and expenditures." *Collection Management.* pp. 115–128. Summer, 1978.

1289. Yenawine, W.S. *Library Evaluation.* Syracuse: Syracuse University Press, 1959.

1290. Yerburgh, Mark. "Academic libraries and the evaluation of microform collections." *Microform Review.* pp. 14–19. January–February, 1978.

1291. Zeugner, L.A. "Acquisitions survey—the vendors respond." *Library Acquisitions, Practice and Theory.* pp. 313–315. No. 3, 1990.

PART THREE

COMPREHENSIVE BIBLIOGRAPHY ON ACQUISITIONS

COMPREHENSIVE BIBLIOGRAPHY ON ACQUISITIONS

1292. "Abel operation folds; jobbers vie for business." *Library Journal.* p. 353. February, 1575.
1293. Ackerman, C. "Joys of standing orders." *Wilson Library Bulletin.* pp. 293–294. December, 1974.
1294. "Acquisition of Latin American library materials." *Library Journal.* pp. 2747–2749. August, 1960.
1295. "Acquisition policy: A symposium." *College and Research Libraries.* pp. 363–372. October, 1953.
1296. "Acquisition policy of the Illinois State Library." *Illinois Libraries.* pp. 362–366. May, 1961.
1297. Akinfolarin, W.A. "The acquisition of books and journals in austere times." *Library Review.* pp. 36–40. No. 1, 1990.
1298. Alessi, D.L. and K. Goforth. "Standing orders and approval plans: Are they compatible?" *Serials Librarian.* pp. 21–41. October–November, 1987.
1299. Alford, H.W. "A new concept in serial dealers." *Library Resources and Technical Services.* pp. 259–263. Summer, 1963.
1300. Alldredge, N.S. "Doing business in the West—boom or bust in library acquisitions." *Library Acquisitions, Practice and Theory.* pp. 21–27. No. 1, 1991.
1301. Allen, F.W. "Some notes on the acquisition of old books." *Special Libraries.* pp. 73–76. March, 1947.
1302. Allen, G.G. and C.T. Lee. "The development of an objective budget allocation procedure for academic library acquisitions." *Libri.* pp. 211–221. September, 1987.
1303. Alley, Brian. "Acquisitions, Budgets and Collections: Acquisitions 90 conference." *Technicalities.* pp. 10–11. June, 1990.
1304. Alley, Brian, "BAS: Once more with feeling." *Technicalities.* p. 2. April, 1984.

1305. Alley, Brian. "The information gap, reinventing the wheel, and other tales." *Technicalities.* pp. 1+. July, 1990.

1306. Alley, Brian. "WYSIWYG Acquisitions, we're almost there." *Technicalities.* p. 1. June, 1990.

1307. Alley, Brian and J.S. Cargill. "Automated acquisitions systems, or, does your library acquire materials bit by bit." *Library Acquisitions Practice and Theory.* pp. 113–115. No. 2, 1980.

1308. Allison, B. "Map acquisition: An annotated bibliography." *Western Association Map. Library Information Bulletin.* pp. 16–25. November, 1983.

1309. Altbach, Philip and Keith Smith. "Publishing in the 3rd World." *Library Trends.* pp. 449–599. Spring, 1978.

1310. Altbach, Philip and Sheila McVey. "Perspectives on publishing." *Annals of the American Academy of Political and Social Sciences.* pp. 1–150. September, 1975.

1311. Altman, F. "The antiquarian reprint dealer looks at acquisitions." *Library Resources and Technical Services.* pp. 207–210. Spring, 1967.

1312. Association of Research Libraries. *Approval Plan, SPEC Kit 141.* Washington: American Library Association, 1988.

1313. American Library Association. *Bookdealer - Library Relations Committee Guidelines for Handling Library Orders for In-Print Monographic Publications.* Chicago: ALA, 1984.

1314. American Library Association. *Guidelines for Handling Library Orders for Microfilms.* Chicago: ALA, 1977.

1315. Anand, A.K. and H.R. Chopra. "Books on approval: An analysis with reference to university acquisitions." *Herald of Library Science.* pp. 202–207. July, 1980.

1316. Anderson, M.L. "Lonesome dove, doing business in the West - a librarian's view." *Library Acquisitions, Practice and Theory.* pp. 15–17. No. 1, 1991.

1317. Andriot, J.L. "Documents Expediting Project." *Library Journal.* pp. 693–695. April 15, 1952.

1318. Angoff, Allan. "Know your publishers." *Wilson Library Bulletin.* pp. 156–158. October, 1962.

1319. Anthony, L.J. and J.E. Hailstone. "Use of punched cards in preparation of lists of periodicals." *Aslib Proceedings.* pp. 348–360. October, 1960.

1320. "Approval plans in Ohio grow in popularity." *Library Journal.* pp. 991–992. May 1, 1979.

1321. Archer, B.J. "Acquiring Soviet Literature." *Special Libraries.* pp. 199–200. August, 1960.
1322. Archer, J.H. "Acquisition of Canadian provincial government documents." *Library Resources and Technical Services.* pp. 52–59. Winter, 1961.
1323. Arms, W.Y. and T.P. Walter. "Simulation model for purchasing duplicate copies in a library." *Journal of Library Automation.* pp. 73–82. June, 1974.
1324. Ash, Lee. "Subsidized periodical publishing." *Library Trends.* pp. 302–309. January, 1962.
1325. Ashley, P. "NOTIS in action: Acquiring materials with an integrated system." *Illinois Libraries.* pp. 56–67. January, 1982.
1326. Atkinson, Ross. "The citation as inter text - toward a theory of the selection process." *Library Resources and Technical Services.* pp. 109–119. 1984.
1327. "Audiovisual selection aids." *Wisconsin Library Bulletin.* pp. 180–181. May, 1966.
1328. Auld, L.W. "Compiling school library orders with punched cards in centralized processing." *Hawaii L.A. Journal.* pp. 14–25. Spring, 1964.
1329. Austin, R. "Evaluation of a blanket order plan for French publications." *Collection Management.* pp. 137–148. Nos. 3–4, 1988.
1330. "Automated acquisitions at Georgia Southern." *RTSD News.* p. 39. July–August, 1982.
1331. Axford, H. William. "The economics of a domestic approval plan." *College and Research Libraries.* pp. 368–375. September, 1971.
1332. Bach, H. "Acquisition policy of the American academic library." *College and Research Libraries.* pp. 441–451. November, 1957.
1333. Bach, H. "Why allocate?" *Library Resources and Technical Sources.* pp. 161–165. Spring, 1964.
1334. Bacon, B.L. "Buying around - the economics of library purchasing." *Canadian Library Journal.* pp. 247–49. October, 1979.
1335. Bagshaw, M. "Enter computer." *Top of the News.* pp. 39–42. November, 1966.
1336. Bailey, E.C. "Acquisition and use of general encyclopedias in small academic libraries." *RQ.* pp. 218–222. Winter, 1985.

1337. Ball, Alice. "Costs of serial acquisition through USBE." *Serial Slants.* pp. 11–15. April, 1952.
1338. Bandara, S.B. "Dormant exchanges - a suggestion for less wasteful exchanges." *Libri.* pp. 313–322. 1978.
1339. Banerjea, P.K. "Librarian and the bookseller." *Indian Librarian.* pp. 114–118. December, 1964.
1340. Barber, Joe. "Random vendor assignment in vendor performance evaluation." *Library Acquisition: Practice and Theory.* pp. 265–80. 1986.
1341. Barber, J.W. "Vendor studies redux: Evaluating the approval plan option from within." *Library Acquisitions, Practice and Theory.* pp. 133–41. No. 2, 1989.
1342. Barber, J.W. et al. "Organizing out-of-print and replacement acquisition for effectiveness, efficiency and the future." *Library Acquisitions, Practice and Theory.* pp. 137–163. No. 2, 1990.
1343. Barbman, M.W. "Sheboygan centralized book purchasing for neighboring village libraries." *PLD Reporter.* p. 38. November, 1956.
1344. Barry, J.W. "A study on the long term periodical subscriptions." *Library Resources and Technical Services.* pp. 50–54. Winter, 1959.
1345. Batts, N.C. "Data analysis of science monograph ordering cataloging forms." *Special Libraries.* pp. 538–586. October, 1966.
1346. Baumann, S. "Application of Davis' model for a vendor study." *Library Acquisitions Practice and Theory.* pp. 83–90. No. 2, 1984.
1347. Becker, J. "Automating the serial record." *ALA Bulletin.* pp. 557–558. June, 1964.
1348. Beckman, Margaret. "Political setting of libraries in postsecondary institutions." *Canadian Library Journal.* pp. 145–147. June, 1981.
1349. Belzer, S.A. "Remarks on reprinting." *Reprint Expediting Service Bulletin.* pp. 1–41. Spring, 1964.
1350. Bender, Ann. "Allocation of funds in support of collection development in public libraries." *Library Resources and Technical Services.* pp. 45–51. Winter, 1979.
1351. Bennett, Fleming. "The current bookmarket." *Library Trends.* pp. 376–384. April, 1958.
1352. Bennett, Fleming. "Prompt payment of bookdealers in-

voices - an approach to standards." *College and Research Libraries.* pp. 387–392. October, 1953.

1353. Benson, N.L. "Latin American books and periodicals." *Library Trends.* pp. 589–598. January, 1967.

1354. Berkner, Dimity. "Communications between vendors and librarians." *Library Acquisitions, Practice and Theory.* pp. 85–90. 1979.

1355. Berry, P.L. "U.S. and Canadian government documents on microforms." *Library Resources and Technical Services.* pp. 60–67. Winter, 1961.

1356. Bevis, Dorothy. "Acquisition and resources: Highlights of 1962." *Library Resources and Technical Services.* pp. 142–155. Spring, 1963.

1357. Bevis, Dorothy. "A sampling of the year's work in acquisitions and resources." *Library Resources and Technical Services.* pp. 110–112. Spring, 1962.

1358. Bevis, Dorothy. "The year's work in acquisitions and resources." *Library Resources and Technical Services.* pp. 105–115. Spring, 1961.

1359. Beyerly, E. "Acquisition methods and sources of Soviet medical publications." *Medical Library Association Bulletin.* pp. 124–131. April, 1959.

1360. Biblarz, D. "The growing out-of-print crisis." *Technical Services Quarterly.* pp. 3–12. No. 2, 1989.

1361. Bird, V., et al. *Order Processes: A Manual.* Hackensack: F.B. Rothman, 1960.

1362. Bishop, D. "Publication patterns of scientific serials." *American Documentation.* pp. 113–121. April, 1965.

1363. Blaustein, A.P. "Panel on foreign law: Selection of foreign materials, periodicals." *Law Library Journal.* pp. 350–364. November, 1962.

1364. Bloomberg, Marty and G. Edward Evans. *Introduction to Technical Services for Library Technicians.* Littleton: Libraries Unlimited, 1985.

1365. Boissonnas, C.M. "When we buy books we know what we pay for, or do we?" *Library Acquisitions, Practice and Theory.* pp. 87–101. No. 2, 1989.

1366. Bonk, Sharon. "Toward a methodology of evaluating serials vendors." *Library Acquisitions, Practice and Theory.* pp. 51–60. 1985.

1367. Borlase, Rod. "A nonlinear, bimodal model for monitoring the flow of materials fund allocations." *Journal of Academic Librarianship.* pp. 274–276. November, 1979.

1368. Boss, Richard et al. "Automating acquisitions." *Library Technology Reports.* pp. 479–634. September–October, 1986.

1369. Boss, Richard and J. McQueen. "The uses of automation and related technologies by domestic book and serial jobbers." *Library Technology Reports.* pp. 125–251. March–April, 1989.

1370. Boyer, Calvin. "State-wide contracts for library materials—an analysis of the attendant dysfunctional consequences." *College and Research Libraries.* pp. 86–94. March, 1974.

1371. Bracken, J.K. and J.C. Calhoun. "Profiling vendor performance." *Library Resources and Technical Services.* pp. 120–128. April, 1984.

1372. Broadus, Robert. *Selecting Materials for Libraries.* New York: H.W. Wilson, 1973.

1373. Brown, B.M. "Curriculum: Acquisitions and cataloging." *Drexel Library Quarterly.* pp. 84–91. January, 1967.

1374. Brown, D.R. and K. DeGraff. "Practical Librarian from purchase order to processing slip on OCLC." *Library Journal.* pp. 2173–2174. October 15, 1979.

1375. Bruer, J.M. "Acquisitions in 1972." *Library Resources and Technical Services.* pp. 171–181. Spring, 1974.

1376. Bruer, J.M. "Acquisitions in 1973." *Library Resources and Technical Services.* pp. 239–247. Summer, 1974.

1377. Bruer, J.M. "Acquisitions in 1974." *Library Resources and Technical Services.* pp. 226–241. Summer, 1975.

1378. Brunswick, S.R. "Acquisition of Hebrew and Yiddish books." *Library Resources and Technical Services.* pp. 377–379. Summer, 1965.

1379. Bryan, H. "Order in ordering." *Australian Library Journal.* pp. 120–126. July, 1957.

1380. Bryan, H. "Streamling order and accession routines." *Australian Library Journal.* pp. 121–126. October, 1954.

1381. Bryant, Bonita. "Automating acquisitions. The planning process." *Library Resources and Technical Services.* pp. 285–298. October–December, 1984.

1382. Budd, J. "Allocation formulas in the literature—a review." *Library Acquisitions, Practice and Theory.* pp. 95–107. No. 1, 1991.

1383. Bullard, Scott. "Acquisitions - ache and its relief." *American Libraries*. pp. 857+ November, 1987.

1384. Bullard, Scott. "Booksellers discussion group: Toward standardized formats for electronic purchase orders." *Library Acquisitions, Practice and Theory*. pp. 239–240. No. 3, 1982.

1385. Bullard, Scott. "OLAS—one library's experience." *Library Acquisitions, Practice and Theory*. pp. 73–80. No. 2, 1981.

1386. Burstein, H.M. "Antiquarian books and booksellers." *Bay State Librarian*. pp. 12–15. July, 1961.

1387. Butcher, S.J. "The acquisition of books." *Library Association Record*. pp. 259–262. August, 1952.

1388. Butler, Pierce. *Librarians, Scholars, and Booksellers at Mid-Century*. Chicago: University of Chicago Press, 1953.

1389. Cargill, Jennifer. "Report on the 4th International Conference on Approval Plans." *Library Acquisitions, Practice and Theory*. pp. 109–111. No. 2, 1980.

1390. Cargill, Jennifer and Brian Alley. *Practical Approval Plan Management*. Phoenix: Oryx Press, 1979.

1391. Carney, J.J. "Plumbers, bibliomaniacs, and the library budget." *Improving College and University Teaching*. pp. 178–180. Summer, 1970.

1392. Carpenter, E.J. "Collection development policies: The case for." *Library Acquisitions, Practice and Theory*. pp. 43–45. No. 1, 1984.

1393. Carter, Frances. "Science in the public library: A study in acquisition and use." *MA Thesis*. University of Chicago, 1948.

1394. Carter, J. "Book auctions." *Library Trends*. pp. 471–482. April, 1961.

1395. Carter, M., Bonk, W.J., and Magrill, R.M. *Building Library Collections*. 4th edition. Metuchen: Scarecrow Press, 1974.

1396. Cave, R. "Translations and the book selection problem." *Library World*. pp. 32–35. August, 1960.

1397. Cenzer, P.S. "Decentralized acquisitions—a future trend?" *Library Acquisitions, Practice and Theory*. pp. 37–40. No. 1, 1985.

1398. Chamberlin, C.E. "The impact of institutional change: Opportunities for acquisition." *Library Acquisitions, Practice and Theory*. pp. 153–159. No. 2, 1987.

1399. Chamberlin, D.E. "In-process records." *College and Research Libraries.* pp. 335–338. October 1946.

1400. Chen, W.C. "Small college library acquisition problems." *Library Journal.* pp. 1762–1765. June 1, 1959.

1401. Cherry, Susan. "Booking it big." *American Libraries.* pp. 260–261. May, 1978.

1402. Chicorel, Marietta. "Acquisitions in an age of plenty." *Library Resources and Technical Services.* pp. 19–27. Winter, 1966.

1403. Chicorel, Marietta. "Cost indexes for library materials." *Wilson Library Bulletin.* pp. 896–900. June, 1965.

1404. Chicorel, Marietta. "Highlights in acquisitions." *Library Resources and Technical Services.* pp. 112–125. Spring, 1964.

1405. Chicorel, Marietta. "Trends in book prices and related fields in West Germany 1954–1960." *Library Resources and Technical Services.* pp. 47–56. Winter, 1963.

1406. Chicorel, Marietta. "West German and U.S. book costs as comparative factors in book budgets." *Library Resources and Technical Services.* pp. 328–333. Fall, 1963.

1407. Childress, B. and B. Nelson. "Out of print acquisitions— a duel perspective." *Southeastern Librarian.* pp. 121–124. Winter, 1987.

1408. Chiu, A.K. "Problems of acquiring Far Eastern publications for American libraries." *Special Libraries.* pp. 19–25. January, 1957.

1409. Christ, Robert. "Acquisition work in college libraries." *College and Research Libraries.* pp. 17–23. January, 1949.

1410. Chunn, J. "Birthday book acquisitions." *School Library Journal.* p. 3. January, 1980.

1411. Clack, Mary and Sally Williams. "Using locally and nationally produced periodical price indexes in budget preparation." *Library Resources and Technical Services.* pp. 345–356. No. 27, 1983.

1412. Clark, C.D. and C.L. Feick. "Monographic series and the RLIN acquisitions system." *Serials Review.* pp. 68–72. Fall, 1984.

1413. Clark, S.D. and B.A. Winters. "Bidness as usual—the responsible procurement of library materials." *Library Acquisitions, Practice and Theory.* pp. 265–274. No. 3, 1990.

1414. Clasquin, Frank. "Financial management of seriels and journals through subject core lists." *Serials Librarian.* pp. 287–297. Spring, 1978.

1415. Clasquin, Frank. "Procurement of periodicals on an annual bid basis." *SLA SciTech News.* pp. 10–12. Spring, 1965.

1416. Coe, G. et al. "Book distributors and automation—a complete package." *Library Technology Reports.* pp. 497–501. July–August, 1990.

1417. Colburn, E.B. *Multiple Order Forms Used by American Libraries.* Chicago: ALA, 1949.

1418. Conditt, P. "Rise and demise of Richard Abel and Company." *PNLA Quarterly.* pp. 10–14. April, 1975.

1419. Condon, W.J. and C.E. Dent. "Blank-check-with-book order book purchasing." *Unabashed Librarian.* pp. 8–10. Fall, 1972.

1420. Coney, Donald. "An experimental index for apportioning departmental book funds for a university library." *Library Quarterly.* pp. 422–428. July, 1942.

1421. Cook, Sarah. "The selective purchase of out-of-print books: A survey of practices." *Library Resources and Technical Services.* pp. 31–37. Winter, 1966.

1422. Cookingham, R.M. "Internal Greenaway procedures." *Unbashed Librarian.* p. 16. No. 27, 1978.

1423. Cooper, M.D. "Modeling arrival patterns of library book orders." *Library and Information Science Research.* pp. 237–255. July, 1988.

1424. Coppola, Dominick. "Breakthrough in Latin American acquisitions." *Stechert-Hafner Book News.* pp. 1–2. September, 1962.

1425. Coppola, Dominick. "The international bookseller looks at acquisitions." *Library Resources and Technical Services.* pp. 203–206. Spring, 1967.

1426. Coppola, Dominick. "Library-book trade relations in the field of current books." *College and Research Libraries.* pp. 330–333. July 1956.

1427. Cox, Carl. "Mechanized acquisitions procedures at the University of Maryland." *College and Research Libraries.* pp. 232–236. May, 1965.

1428. Cox, M.A. "Acquisition policies in academic and public libraries." MA Thesis. University of Mississippi, 1963.

1429. Cronquist, C. "Low cost automation of acquisitions in a small academic library." *OCLC Micro.* pp. 20–22. June, 1990.

1430. Culbertson, D.S. "The costs of data processing in university libraries." *Book Acquisitions and Cataloging, Col-*

lege and Research Libraries. pp. 487–489. November, 1963.

1431. Culpepper, J.C. "Recent application of acquisitions survey instrument—a viable alternative." *Kentucky Libraries.* pp. 3–7. Fall, 1981.

1432. Cureton, Jan. "Perspectives on establishing a film collection." *Library Trends.* pp. 93–100. Summer, 1978.

1433. Curran, A.T. "The mechanization of the serials records for the moving and merging of the Boston medical and Harvard medical serials." *Library Resources and Technical Services.* pp. 362–372. Summer, 1966.

1434. Curran, N.E. "Yours for the ordering." *Wilson Library Bulletin.* pp. 342–344. December, 1962.

1435. Dane, Chase. "Recent trends in book buying." *School Library Association of California Bulletin.* pp. 11–13. November, 1961.

1436. Davidson, J.S. "Direct from the publisher." *Publishers Weekly.* pp. 40–41. July 11, 1960.

1437. Davis, Mary. "Model for a vendor study in a manual or semi-automated acquisitions system." *Library Acquisitions, Practice and Theory.* pp. 53–60. No. 1, 1979.

1438. Dawson, J.M. "Acquisitions of university libraries." PhD dissertation. University of Chicago, 1956.

1439. Day, R. and J. Angus. "Off-campus acquisitions at Deakin University Library." *Library Acquisitions, Practice and Theory.* pp. 33–42. No. 1, 1986.

1440. Derthick, Jan and Barbara Moran. "Serial agent selection in ARL libraries." *Advances in Serials Management.* pp. 1–42. 1986.

1441. Desmarais, N. "Nonesuch acquisitions system." *Library Software Review.* pp. 377–387. November–December, 1987.

1442. Desmarais, N. "Unicorn collection management system—acquisitions module." *Library Software Review.* pp. 289–298. September–October, 1987.

1443. Dessauer, John. *Book Publishing: What It Is, What It Does.* New York: R.R. Bowker, 1974.

1444. Dessauer, John. "Introducing the funnel—a regional processing center to handle all book transactions." *Publishers Weekly.* pp. 24–25. November 27, 1972.

1445. Dessauer, John. "Library acquisitions: A look into the future." *Publishers Weekly.* pp. 55–68. June 16, 1975.

1446. Dessauer, John. "Two year colleges and their library

acquisitions: A look into the future." *Publishers Weekly.* pp. 55–58. February 16, 1976.

1447. DeVilbiss, Mary. "The approval built collection in the medium-sized academic library." *College and Research Libraries.* pp. 487–492. November, 1975.

1448. DeVolder, A.L. *Approval Plans: A Survey.* University of New Mexico, 1972. 15p.

1449. DeVolder, A.L. "Approval plans—bounty or bedlam?" *Publishers Weekly.* pp. 18–20. July 3, 1972.

1450. DeVolder, A.L. "Why continue an approval plan?" *Mountain Plains Library Quarterly.* pp. 11–16. Summer, 1972.

1451. Diodato, L.W. "Use of gifts in a medium sized academic library." *Collection Management* pp. 53–71. Spring–Summer, 1983.

1452. Dobbyn, Margaret. "Approval plan purchasing in perspective." *College and Research Libraries.* pp. 480–484. November, 1972.

1453. Doiron, P.M. "Anatomy of acquisitions." *Library Journal.* p. 2981. October 15, 1973.

1454. Dole, W.V. "Librarians, publishers, and vendors: Looking for Mr. Goodbuy." *Library Acquisitions, Practice and Theory.* pp. 125–134. No. 2, 1987.

1455. Donaldson, M. "Book prices surveyed." *Library Journal.* pp. 2388–2389. September 15, 1958.

1456. Dougherty, Richard. "Acquisitions—1965 in review." *Library Resources and Technical Services.* pp. 165–172. Spring, 1966.

1457. Dougherty, Richard. "Year's work in acquisitions." *Library Resources and Technical Services.* pp. 149–156. Spring, 1965.

1458. Dougherty, Richard and A. McKinney. "Ten years of progress in acquisitions 1956–1966." *Library Resources and Technical Services.* pp. 289–300. Summer, 1967.

1459. Dougherty, Richard and Sam Boone. "An ordering procedure using the Xerox 914." *Library Resources and Technical Services.* pp. 43–45. Winter, 1966.

1460. Drury, Francis. *Order Work for Libraries.* Chicago: ALA, 1930.

1461. Drury, Francis. *The Selection and Acquisition of Books for Libraries.* Chicago: ALA, 1928.

1462. Dudley, Norman. "The blanket order." *Library Trends.* pp. 318–327. January, 1970.

1463. Dunlap, Connie. "Automated acquisitions procedures at the University of Michigan Library." *Library Resources and Technical Services.* pp. 192–202. Spring, 1967.

1464. Dykeman, Amy and Bill Katz. *Automated Acquisitions: Issues For the Present and Future.* Haworth Press, 1989.

1465. Eaglen, Audrey. "Automated acquisitions." *Collection Building.* pp. 43–48. No. 2, 1988.

1466. Eaglen, Audrey. "Book distribution—present conditions and implications for the future." *School Library Journal.* pp. 55–59. December, 1979.

1467. Eaglen, Audrey. "Book wholesalers—pros and cons." *School Library Journal.* pp. 116–119. October, 1978.

1468. Eaglen, Audrey. "Library-publishing connection: Too many books?" *Collection Building.* pp. 40–42. Spring, 1983.

1469. Eaglen, Audrey. "More about the discount mess." *School Library Journal.* pp. 105–108. October, 1979.

1470. Eaglen, Audrey. "Out of patience—indefinitely." *School Library Journal.* pp. 23–26. February, 1978.

1471. Eaglen, Audrey. "Short discount shuffles—what it's all about." *School Library Journal.* pp. 30–33. May, 1979.

1472. Edelman, Hendrik. "The death of the Farmington Plan." *Library Journal.* pp. 1251–1253. April 15, 1973.

1473. Edelman, Hendrik. "Selection methodology in academic libraries." *Library Resources and Technical Services.* pp. 33–38. No. 23, 1979.

1474. Edgar, N.L. "Missing issues: One technique for replacement." *Library Acquisitions, Practice and Theory.* pp. 205–304. No. 3, 1982.

1475. Eichinski, G. "Automated acquisitions system—general description." *LASIE.* pp. 1–24. May. 1973.

1476. Ellis, R. and L. Straus. "Electronic ordering at UTLAS: A chronicle of library-book, vendor-bibliographic utility cooperation." *Information Technology and Libraries.* pp. 343–345. December, 1982.

1477. Ellsworth, R.E. "Some aspects of the problem of allocating book funds among departments in universities." *Library Quarterly.* pp. 486–494. July, 1942.

1478. Erlandson, J.A. and Y. Boyer. "Acquisition of state documents." *Library Acquisitions, Practice and Theory.* pp. 117–127. No. 2, 1980.

1479. Eshner, E. "1,713 volumes added for a total cost of $4,304.34." *Unabashed Librarian.* pp. 3–5. Winter, 1973.

1480. Esplin, D.G. "Library as international book buyer." *Scholarly Publishing.* pp. 359–363. July, 1972.

1481. Evans, Edward. "The cost of information about library acquisitions budgets." *Collection Management.* pp. 3–23. Spring, 1978.

1482. Evans, G. Edward and C.W. Argyres. "Approval plans and collection development in academic libraries." *Library Resources and Technical Services.* pp. 35–50. Winter, 1974.

1483. Evans, Glyn et al. *Development of a Responsive Library Acquisitions Formula.* Albany: Office of Library Services, 1978.

1484. Evans, R.W. "O.P. problems." *Choice.* pp. 285–286. July–August, 1965.

1485. Eyman, E.G. et al. "Periodicals automation at Miami-Dade Junior College." *Library Resources and Technical Services.* pp. 341–361. Summer, 1966.

1486. Facente, Gary. "An overview of American publishing for librarians." *Library Resources and Technical Services.* pp. 57–67. January–March, 1986.

1487. Fall, J. "Problems of American libraries in acquiring foreign publications." *Library Quarterly.* pp. 101–113. April, 1954.

1488. Fast, Barry. "Publishing and bookselling—a look at some idiosyncrasies." *Library Acquisitions, Practice and Theory.* pp. 15–17. 1979.

1489. Felland, N. "Periodical aids to map acquisition." *Library Journal.* p. 438. March, 15, 1950.

1490. Fessler, Aaron. "Bring them back alive." *ALA Bulletin.* pp. 559–561. October, 1956.

1491. Fessler, Aaron. "Facing problems of the out-of-print book." *Special Libraries.* pp. 463–465. December, 1957.

1492. Fessler, Aaron. "Reprinted reference books." *Library Journal.* pp. 691–694. March 1, 1958.

1493. Fisher, W.H. "Education for acquisitions—an informal survey." *Library Acquisitions, Practice and Theory.* pp. 29–31. No. 1, 1991.

1494. Flannery, A. "A routine for checking book orders by the cataloging department." *Journal of Cataloging and Classification.* pp. 98–102. September, 1952.

1495. Fletcher, J. "Inflation indexes for academic library purchases." *Library Association Record.* pp. 400–401. August, 1987.

1496. Flowers, J.L. "Acquisitions administrators' discussion group report." *Library Acquisitions, Practice and Theory.* pp. 131–132. No. 1, 1991.

1497. Folcarelli, Ralph and Ralph Ferragamo. "Microform publications—hardware and suppliers." *Library Trends.* pp. 711–725. April, 1976.

1498. Ford, Stephen. *The Acquisition of Library Materials.* Chicago: American Library Association, 1973.

1499. Fouts, J. "Report on the business of acquisitions Regional Institute." *Library Acquisitions, Practice and Theory.* pp. 255–266. No. 3, 1987.

1500. Fraley, Ruth. "Publishers vs. wholesalers—the ordering dilemma." *Library Acquisitions, Practice and Theory.* pp. 9–13. No. 1, 1979.

1501. Frase, R.W. "Economic development in publishing." *Library Trends.* pp. 7–15. July, 1958.

1502. Fraser, Walter. "Publishers vs libraries. Some hidden dimensions in the current debate." *IEEE Transactions on Professional Communications.* pp. 200–206. September, 1975

1503. Fristoe, A.J. and R.E. Myers. "Acquisitions in 1969." *Library Resources and Technical Services.* pp. 132–142. Spring, 1971.

1504. Fristoe, A.J. et al. "Acquisitions in 1971." *Library Resources and Technical Services.* pp. 173–177. Spring, 1972.

1505. Furnham, A. "Book reviews as a selection tool for librarians." *Collection Management.* pp. 33–43. Spring, 1986.

1506. Fussler, Herman. "Acquisitions policy: Larger university libraries." *College and Research Libraries.* pp. 363–367. October, 1953.

1507. Fussler, Herman. "A new pattern for library cooperation." *Library Journal.* pp. 126–133. January 15, 1956.

1508. Futas, Elizabeth. *Library Acquisition Policies and Procedures.* Phoenix: Oryx Press, 1977.

1509. Gabriel, Michael. "Surging serial costs—the microfiche solution." *Library Journal.* pp. 2450–2453. October 1, 1974.

1510. Galvin, Thomas. "Zero based budgeting in libraries and information centers." *Library Acquisitions.* pp. 7–14. 1978.

1511. Gamble, L. "Blanket ordering and the University of

Texas at Austin Library." *Texas Library Journal.* pp. 230–232. November, 1972.

1512. Gardner, R.K. "Selection of library materials." *Choice.* p. 1500. June, 1986.

1513. Garten, E.D. and G. Rummel. "AMOS: Tennessee Tech University Library automated acquisitions system." *Library Acquisitions, Practice and Theory.* pp. 41–45. No. 1, 1983.

1514. Gellatly, P. "Libraries and subscription agencies." *PNLA Quarterly.* pp. 35–40. October, 1966.

1515. Genaway, David. "Percentage based allocation for acquisitions: A simplified method for the allocation of the library materials budget." *Library Acquisitions, Practice and Theory.* pp. 293–313. No. 4, 1986.

1516. Genaway, David. "The Q formula: The flexible formula for library acquisitions in relation to the FTE driven formula." *Library Acquisitions, Practice and Theory.* pp. 293–313. No. 4, 1986.

1517. George, V. "Acquisitions," in *Handbook of Special Librarianship and Information Work.* London: Aslib, 1962. pp. 32–69.

1518. Gibbs, N.J. "LC MARC approval tapes at Auburn University." *Library Acquisitions, Practice and Theory.* pp. 217–219. No. 3, 1987.

1519. Gipson, J.S. "Total cost of acquisitions in a community college." *College and Research Libraries.* pp. 273–276. July, 1967.

1520. Gladstone, J.M. "Marginal punched cards as an order record." *Libri.* pp. 365–369. 1965.

1521. Godden, Irene. *Collection Development and Acquisitions 1970–1980.* Metuchen: Scarecrow Press, 1982.

1522. Goehner, D.M. "Allocating by formula—the rationale from an institutional perspective." *Collection Management.* pp. 161–173. Fall–Winter, 1983.

1523. Goellner, J.G. "The future of university presses." *Library Journal.* pp. 1695–1699. September 15, 1978.

1524. Gorchels, C. "Acquisitions policy statements in colleges of education." *Library Resources and Technical Services.* pp. 157–159. Spring, 1961.

1525. Gorman, G.E. "Collection development and acquisitions in a distance learning environment." *Library Acquisitions, Practice and Theory.* pp. 9–66. No. 1, 1986.

1526. Goyal, S.K. "Allocation of library funds to different

departments of a university: An operational research approach." *College and Research Libraries.* pp. 219–222. May, 1973.

1527. Goyal, S.K. "Systematic method for reducing overordering copies of books." *Library Resources and Technical Services.* pp. 26–32. Winter, 1972.

1528. Grant, J. "The librarian and the purchasing function." *Library Acquisitions, Practice and Theory.* pp. 305–306. No. 4, 1985.

1529. Grant, Joan and Susan Perelmuter. "Vendor performance evaluation." *Journal of Academic Librarianship.* pp. 366–367. November, 1978.

1530. Graziano, Eugene. "Interlibrary loan analysis: Diagnostic for scientific serials backfiles acquisitions." *Special Libraries.* pp. 251–257. May, 1962.

1531. Gregor, J. and W.C. Fraser. "University of Windsor experience with an approval plan in three subjects and three vendors." *Canadian Library Journal.* pp. 227–231. August, 1981.

1532. Grieder, E.M. "The foundations of acquisition policy in the small university library." *College and Research Libraries.* pp. 208–214. July, 1949.

1533. Grieder, Ted. *Acquisitions: Where, What, and How.* Westport: Greenwood Press, 1978.

1534. Groot, E.H. "Comparison of library tools for monograph verification." *Library Resources and Technical Services.* pp. 149–161. April, 1981.

1535. Hadcroft, M.M. "College library orders." *Library World.* pp. 278+. March, 1970.

1536. Haldeman, Michael. "The small press movement." *Library Journal.* pp. 2477–2481. December 15, 1977.

1537. Hale, C.E. "Library consumerism: A need for concerted action saying no to exorbitantly high book and periodical prices." *Technicalities.* pp. 8–9. May, 1984.

1538. Halstead, K. "Price indexes for school and academic library acquisitions." *Bowker Annual of Library and Book Trade Information.* New York: R.R. Bowker, 1984. pp. 389–393.

1539. Hamaker, C.A. and S.F. Grinell. "Cost analysis of monographs and serials." *Journal of Library Administration.* pp. 41–49. No. 3, 1990.

1540. Hamlin, A.T. "Book fund and book orders." *Bookmark.* pp. 14–15. September, 1963.

1541. Hamlin, A.T. "Impact of college enrollments on acquisition policy." *Ohio Library Association Bulletin.* p. 4. October, 1965.

1542. Hand, T.S. "Acquisition and handling of periodicals in ten college libraries in the Philadelphia area." *Serial Slants.* pp. 58–61. April, 1954.

1543. Hardin, W. "Deposit accounts and their economic impact in medium-sized academic libraries." *Collection Management.* pp. 97–106. No. 1, 1989.

1544. Haro, R.P. "Bibliographer in the academic library." *Library Resources and Technical Services.* pp. 163–169. Spring, 1969.

1545. Harrell, J. and G. St. Clair. "Revolutionizing acquisitions productivity with PC's." *Technicalities.* pp. 3–7. October, 1987.

1546. Harrison, K. and D. Summers. "Development of an automated acquisitions system at the University of Lancaster Library." *Program.* pp. 143–162. April, 1988.

1547. Hartz, F.R. "Selection of school/media materials." *Catholic Library World.* pp. 425–429. May, 1976.

1548. Hatch, L. "The book order deadline." *Library Journal.* pp. 1986–1988. November 15, 1953.

1549. Haviland, Virginia. "Book selection, Problem? Pleasure? Privilege?" *Illinois Libraries.* pp. 310–317. April, 1965.

1550. Hawks, C.P. "Internal control, auditing, and the automated acquisitions system." *Journal of Academic Librarianship.* pp. 296–301. November, 1990.

1551. Hawks, C.P. "Report of the ALCTS Midwest Collection Management and Development Institute." *Library Acquisitions, Practice and Theory.* pp. 101–111. No. 1, 1990.

1552. Hayes, S. "On account—Deposit accounts for monograph acquisitions." *Bottom Line.* pp. 28–29. No. 4, 1987.

1553. Hayes, S. "On account: Let me count the ways—information acquisition accounting." *Bottom Line.* pp. 29–31. No. 3, 1989.

1554. Hayes, S. "On account—manager of spending, purchasing trends, and terms in the business and library communities." *Bottom Line.* pp. 36–38. Fall, 1990.

1555. Hayman, L.M. "D Base III for acquisitions department budgets." *Library Software Review.* pp. 372–373. November–December, 1987.

1556. Heitshu, S.C. "Changing acquisition systems—an evolutionary process." *Technicalities.* pp. 3–7. April, 1984.

1557. Helen, S.N. "Book purchasing for small college libraries." *Catholic Library World.* pp. 147–152. December, 1957.

1558. Hellenga, R.R. "Departmental acquisitions policies for small college libraries." *Library Acquisitions, Practice and Theory.* pp. 81–84. No. 2, 1979.

1559. Henderson, J.D. "The public library acquisitions program." *Library Trends.* pp. 448–454. April, 1955.

1560. Henderson, W.T. "Acquisitions policies of academic and research libraries." MA thesis. University of Chicago, 1960.

1561. Henshaw, R.H. and W.H. Kurth. "Dealer rating system at L.C." *Library Resources and Technical Services.* pp. 131–136. Summer, 1957.

1562. Heppel, S.G. "A survey of O.P. buying practices." *Library Resources and Technical Services.* pp. 28–30. Winter, 1966.

1563. Heroux, Marlene and Carol Fleishauer. "Cancellation decisions: Evaluating standing orders." *Library Resources and Technical Services.* pp. 368–379. Fall, 1978.

1564. Heyman, Berna and George Abbott. "Automated acquisitions: A bibliography." *Library Technology Reports.* pp. 195–202. March–April, 1981.

1565. Hingers, Edward. "The audiovisual supplier—dealing with dealers and distributors." *Library Trends.* pp. 737–748. April, 1976.

1566. Hirsch, F.E. "The librarian looks at the publisher." *College and Research Libraries.* pp. 321–327. October, 1951.

1567. Hitchen, H.S. "Booksellers and the libraries." *Library World.* pp. 158–160. January, 1962.

1568. Hodowanec, G.V. "Acquisition rate model for academic libraries." *College and Research Libraries.* pp. 439–447. November, 1978.

1569. Hoffman, Andrea. "Collection development programs in academic libraries: An administrative approach." *Bookmark.* pp. 121–125. Spring, 1979.

1570. Hogan, Walter. "Automated acquisitions systems—a review." *RTSD Newsletter.* pp. 5–7. January–February, 1980.

1571. Hogan, Walter. "Ringgold's Nonesuch acquisitions system one year after installation." *Library Acquisitions, Practice and Theory.* pp. 41–45. No. 1, 1982.

1572. Howrey, M.M. and H.E. Easley. "Design, development, and implementation of an automated library acquisitions system—the Aurora College experience." *Illinois Libraries.* pp. 322–327. May, 1983.

1573. Huff, W.H. and N.B. Brown. "Serial services cost indexes." *Library Resources and Technical Services.* pp. 158–160. Spring, 1960.

1574. Hulbert, Linda and David Curry. "Evaluation of an approval plan." *College and Research Libraries.* pp. 485–491. November, 1978.

1575. Huleatt, R.S. "Rx for acquisition hangups." *Special Libraries.* pp. 81–85. February, 1973.

1576. Hunt, P. "Institute explores library purchasing problems." *Virginia Librarian.* pp. 7–8. May, 1975.

1577. Hunter, Kevil. "The approval plan of smaller scope." *Library Acquisitions, Practice and Theory.* pp. 13–20. 1985.

1578. "Index of book prices by category, selected years." *Library Journal.* p. 578. February 1, 1964.

1579. Jackson, C. "Bookdealer—Library Relations Committee." *Wilson Library Bulletin.* p. 340. December, 1962.

1580. Jacob, E. "The use of TAAB in out-of-print book searching." *College and Research Libraries.* pp. 16–18. January, 1956.

1581. Jacob, E. and B. Salisbury. "Automatic purchase of university press books." *Library Journal.* pp. 707–708. March 1, 1958.

1582. Jenkins, F. "Acquisition of scientific and technological material." *Library Trends.* pp. 414–422. April, 1955.

1583. Johnson, K.S. and Joel Rutstein. *The Politics of Book Fund Allocations: A Case Study.* New York: K.G. Saur, 1979.

1584. Johnson, M.A. "A rose is a rose is a rose, but what is an acquisitions budget when it carries another name." *Technicalities.* pp. 7–8+. July, 1989.

1585. Johnson, R.K. "Some facets of acquisition work in selected military libraries." *Library Resources and Technical Services.* pp. 16–24. Winter, 1958.

1586. Jones, H.W. "Computerized subscription and periodicals routing in an aerospace library." *Special Libraries.* pp. 634–638. November, 1967.

1587. Jordon, R.T. "Eliminate the middleman in book ordering." *Library Journal.* pp. 327–329. January 15, 1961.

1588. Joshi, Y. "Rationalizing library acquisitions policy: A case study." *Quarterly Bulletin of International Associa-*

tion of Agricultural Librarians and Documentalist. pp. 7–13. No. 1, 1985.

1589. Juhlin, Alton. "Use of IBM equipment in order procedures at SIU library." *Illinois Libraries.* pp. 598–602. November, 1962.

1590. Kaatrude, P.B. "Approval plan versus conventional selection—determining the overlap." *Collection Management.* pp. 145–150. No. 1–2, 1989.

1591. Kaiser, J.B. "Library Journal's survey of wholesale book purchasing." *Library Journal.* pp. 365–368. February 1, 1959.

1592. Kaiser, J.B. "What wholesalers think of library customers." *Library Journal.* pp. 369–370. February 1, 1959.

1593. Kandiah, J. "Deakin automated acquisitions: An update." *LASIE.* pp. 12–18. May–June, 1982.

1594. Kaser, D. "Acquisition work in the next 20 years." *Southeastern Librarian.* pp. 90–94. Summer, 1965.

1595. Kaser, D. "Discounts and service." *Missouri Library Quarterly.* pp. 92–95. September, 1958.

1596. Katz, William and Peter Gellatly. *Guide to Magazine and Serial Agents.* New York: R.R. Bowker, 1975.

1597. Kautz, B.A. "Approval plans: A time saver for agriculture bibliographers." *Quarterly Bulletin of the International Association of Agricultural Librarians and Documentalists.* pp. 1–6. No. 1, 1985.

1598. Keder, J. "Using the campus network for interlibrary loan and book orders." *Library Software Review.* pp. 250–251. September–October, 1989.

1599. Keller, Alton. "Book records on punched cards." *Library Journal.* pp. 1785–1786. December 15, 1946.

1600. Keller, D.B. "Acquisition of library materials from East Europe." *Library Resources and Technical Services.* pp. 34–37. Winter, 1963.

1601. Kelley, Mary. "A book is not a bargain." *North County Libraries.* pp. 3–4. November, 1961.

1602. Kennedy, Gail. "The relationship between acquisitions and collection development." *Library Acquisitions, Practice and Theory.* pp. 225–232. 1983.

1603. Kerabian, J.S. "Book appraisals." *Library Trends.* pp. 466–470. April, 1961.

1604. Kevil, L.H. "The approval of smaller scope." *Library Acquisitions, Practice and Theory.* pp. 13–20. No. 1, 1985.

1605. Kflu, T. "Vendor performance evaluation, numeric formula." *Library Acquisitions, Practice and Theory.* pp. 307–312. No. 3, 1990.

1606. Khurshid, Z. "DOBIS/LIBIS acquisitions subsystem in operation." *Library Acquisitions, Practice and Theory.* pp. 325–334. No. 4, 1987.

1607. Kilton, Thomas. "Out-of-print procurement in academic libraries—current methods and sources." *Collection Management.* pp. 113–134. Fall–Winter, 1983.

1608. Kim, David V. and Wilson, C.A. *Policies of Publishers— A Handbook for Order Librarians.* Metuchen: Scarecrow Press, 1989.

1609. Kim, Ung. "Purchasing books from publishers and wholesalers." Library Resources and Technical Services. pp. 133–147. Spring, 1975.

1610. Kim, Ung. "Comparison of two OP book buying methods." *College and Research Libraries.* pp. 258–264. September, 1973.

1611. Kim, Ung. "Purchasing books from publishers and wholesalers." *Library Resources and Technical Services.* pp. 133–147. Spring, 1975.

1612. Knoblauch, M.G. "BATAB at the Chicago Public Library." *Illinois Libraries.* pp. 17–19. January, 1982.

1613. Kohl, David. *Acquisitions, Collection Development and Collection Use.* Santa Barbara: ABC-Clio, 1985.

1614. Kovacic, M. "Gifts and exchanges in U.S. academic libraries." *Library Resources and Technical Services.* pp. 155–163. Spring, 1980.

1615. Kritzer, H.W. "Effect of the introduction of a multiple order form on the technical processing of books in a medium sized university library." MA thesis. Catholic University, 1958.

1616. Krummel, D.W. "Observations on library acquisitions of music." *Notes.* pp. 5–16. September, 1966.

1617. Kruse, P. "Piracy and the Britannica: Unauthorized reprintings of the 9th edition." *Library Quarterly.* pp. 313–328. October, 1963.

1618. Kuntz, Harry. "Serial agents—selection and evaluation." *Serials Librarian.* pp. 139–150. Winter, 1977.

1619. Kurth, William. "Acquisitions from Mexico." *Library Resources and Technical Services.* pp. 96–114. Spring, 1958.

1620. Kurth, William. "Additional price indexes for U.S. books." *Library Journal.* p. 1496. April 15, 1960.

1621. Kurth, William. "U.S. book and periodical prices—a

preliminary report." *Library Journal.* pp. 54–57. January 1, 1960.

1622. Lane, Alfred. *Gifts and Exchange Manual.* Westport: Greenwood, 1980.

1623. Lane, Alfred. "Gifts and exchanges—practicalities and problems." *Library Resources and Technical Services.* pp. 92–97. Winter, 1979.

1624. Lanier, Don. "Library and series books." *Southeastern Librarian.* pp. 169–171. Fall, 1978.

1625. Lanier, Don and Glenn Anderson. "Gift books and appraisals." *College and Research Libraries.* pp. 440–443. September, 1979.

1626. Lawson, S. "Books for schools." *New Library World.* pp. 130–131. July, 1979.

1627. Lazinger, S.S. "Producing a multi-access order file—new books program using dBase III Plus." *Library Software Review.* p. 295. September–October, 1990.

1628. Lee, C.C. "Library acquisitions system—a micro application." *Library Software Review.* pp. 2–7. January–February, 1989.

1629. Lee, C.E. "Selected bibliography of acquisition tools for government publications." *News Notes of California Libraries.* pp. 501–507. October, 1956.

1630. Lefkowitz, A. "Automated acquisitions at UCLA." *RTSD Newsletter.* pp. 29–30. May–June, 1982.

1631. Lehman, J.O. "Choice as a selection tool." *Wilson Library Quarterly.* pp. 957–961. May, 1970.

1632. Leider, R. "How librarians help inflate the price of books and what to do about it." *American Libraries.* pp. 559–560. October, 1980.

1633. Leonard, A. "How to find out-of-print publications." *Special Libraries.* pp. 22–23. January, 1961.

1634. Leonhardt, Thomas. "Collection development and acquisitions: The divisions of responsibility." *RTSD News.* pp. 73–75. 1984.

1635. Leonhardt, Thomas. "Duke University library automated acquisitions system." *Library Acquisitions, Practice and Theory.* pp. 185–191. Nos. 3–4, 1981.

1636. Leonhardt, Thomas. "Gift appraisals—a practical approach." *Library Acquisitions, Practice and Theory.* pp. 77–79. 1979.

1637. Likness, C.S. "The creative use of acquisitions mechanisms in the college library." *Collection Management.* pp. 3–9. Nos. 1–2, 1990.

1638. Lincoln, Robert. "Controlling duplicate orders, or, riding a camel." *Library Acquisitions, Practice and Theory.* pp. 143–150. Nos. 3–4, 1978.

1639. Lincoln, Robert. "Vendors and delivery—an analysis of selected publishers, publishers/agents, distributors, and wholesalers." *Canadian Library Journal.* pp. 51+. February, 1978.

1640. Lindsey, J.A. "Vendor discounts to libraries in a consortium." *Library Acquisitions, Practice and Theory.* pp. 147–1152. Nos. 3–4, 1981.

1641. Loggins, A. "Books—supplies, commodity or capital?" *Unabashed Librarian.* p. 24. no. 77, 1990.

1642. Lowy, G. *A Searchers Manual.* Hamden: Shoe String Press, 1965.

1643. Lucas, R. and G. Caldwell. "Joint Publications Research Service Translations." *College and Research Libraries.* pp. 103–110. March, 1964.

1644. Ludington, F.B. "The increased cost of books." *Library Journal.* p. 151. January 15, 1959.

1645. Lukac, J. "Practicing librarian: A no cost online acquisitions system for a medium size library." *Library Journal.* pp. 684–685. March, 15, 1980.

1646. Lunn, B. "Acquisitions in special libraries." *South African Libraries.* pp. 57–64. October, 1961.

1647. Lynch, B.P. "The future library market for scholarly books." *Scholarly Publishing.* pp. 86–90. January, 1988.

1648. Lynden, Fred. "Cost analysis of monographs and serials." *Journal of Library Administration.* pp. 19–40. No. 3, 1990.

1649. Lynden, Fred. "Resources in 1977." *Library Resources and Technical Services.* pp. 310–334. Summer, 1978.

1650. Lynden, Fred and Arthur Meyerfield. "Library out-of-print procurement—the Stanford University experience." *Library Resources and Technical Services.* pp. 216–224. Spring, 1973.

1651. Lzorick, G.J. and T.L. Minder. "A least cost searching sequence." *College and Research Libraries.* pp. 85–90. March, 1964.

1652. McCann, A. "Applications of machines to library techniques." *American Documentation.* pp. 260–265. October, 1961.

1653. Mack, C. "OLAS at the Des Plaines Public Library." *Illinois Libraries.* pp. 20–21. January, 1982.

1654. Maddox, I. "On my mind: Approval plans: Viable?" *Journal of Academic Librarianship.* p. 22. January, 1976.

1655. Magrill, Rose Mary. *Technical Services: A Selected Annotated Bibliography.* Westport: Greenwood Press, 1977.

1656. McClelland, J.G. "Publishers view of reprinting." *Library Journal.* pp. 183–185. January 15, 1961.

1657. McCullough, Elizabeth et al. *Approval Plans and Academic Libraries: An Interpretive Survey.* Phoenix: Oryx Press, 1977.

1658. McCullough, Kathleen. "Approval plans—vendor responsibility and library research." *College and Research Libraries.* pp. 368–381. September, 1972.

1659. McDonald, David. "Sequential analysis—a methodology for monitoring approval plans." *College and Research Libraries.* pp. 329–334, July, 1979.

1660. McDonnell, T. "Book orders and ISBN's." *Unabashed Librarian.* p. 7. No. 53, 1984.

1661. McGaw, H.F. *Marginal Punch Cards in Colleges and University Libraries.* New York: Scarecrow Press, 1952.

1662. McGinnis, M. "Stretching the monographic budget in the academic library." *Indiana Libraries.* pp. 38–44. No. 2, 1990.

1663. McGrath, William. "Pragmatic book allocation formula for academic and public libraries with a test for its effectiveness." *Library Resources and Technical Services.* pp. 356–369. Fall, 1975.

1664. McLaren, M. "Full acquisitions systems." *Library Acquisitions, Practice and Theory.* pp. 247–250. No. 3, 1990.

1665. MacManus, G.S. "What librarians should know about book buying." *Library Journal.* pp. 3394–3397. October 1, 1960.

1666. McMurdo, G. "Purchasing: The librarian as loner." *Library Review.* pp. 207–214. Autumn, 1983.

1667. McNiff, Philip. "Acquisition of library materials from the Middle East." *Library Resources and Technical Services.* pp. 22–27. Winter, 1963.

1668. McNiff, Philip. "Foreign area studies and their effect on library development." *College and Research Libraries.* pp. 291–296. July, 1963.

1669. McNiff, P.J. "Harvard's position on blanket orders and En Bloc purchases." *Library Journal.* p. 146. January 15, 1961.

1670. Machlup, F. "Our libraries—can we measure their holdings and acquisitions?" *AAUP Bulletin.* pp. 303–307. October, 1976.

1671. Mack, J.G. and S. Finn. "Film and video acquisition at the Library of Congress." *Collection Management.* pp. 25–41. No. 1, 1991.

1672. Maddox, J. "Are the gods listening? Use of approval plans for automated acquisitions." *Library Acquisitions, Practice and Theory.* pp. 209–213. No. 3, 1987.

1673. Magrill, Rose Mary and Doralyn Hickey. *Acquisitions Management and Collection Development in Libraries.* Chicago: American Library Association, 1984.

1674. Maher, W.J. "Measurement and analysis of processing costs in academic archives." *College and Research Libraries.* pp. 59–67. January, 1982.

1675. Malkin, S.M. "Organization and structure of the American antiquarian book trade." *Library Trends.* pp. 483–492. April, 1961.

1676. Mann, S.E. "Approval plans as a method of collection development." *North Carolina Libraries.* pp. 12–14. Spring, 1985.

1677. Marcinko, D. "Automating acquisitions with NOTIS—a southern exposure." *Library Acquisitions, Practice and Theory.* pp. 109–114. No. 1, 1988.

1678. Martin, Murray. *Budgetary Control in Academic Libraries.* Greenwich: JAI Press, 1978.

1679. Martin, Murray. "The series standing order and the library." *Choice.* pp. 1152–1155. October, 1973.

1680. Martin, R.L. "Foreign scientific literature in translation." *American Documentation.* pp. 135–150. April, 1960.

1681. Maryles, D. "Blackwell takes over Abel assets; sets up new firm." *Publishers Weekly.* p. 223. January 27, 1975.

1682. Mason, Harold. "Beating the bush for books: The dealers' source of supply." *College and Research Libraries.* pp. 21–29. January, 1961.

1683. Massman, Virgil and David Olson. "Book selection: A national plan for small academic libraries." *College and Research Libraries.* pp. 271–279. July, 1970.

1684. Matthews, S.E. "Multiple order form slips." *Library Journal.* pp. 635–638. March, 1957.

1685. Matthews, S.E. "Simplifying library acquisitions with university purchasing." *College and Research Libraries.* pp. 331–334, July, 1957.

1686. Maxwell, I.R. "Cost of scientific periodical publications." *Nature*. p. 1052. September 17, 1960.

1687. Maybury, C. "Dealers and documents." *Library Resources and Technical Services*. pp. 184–186. Spring, 1962.

1688. Mays, A.H. "Some design principles for an automated acquisition system." *LASIE*. pp. 7–15. May–June, 1984.

1689. Melcher, Daniel. "Discount diversity." *Library Journal*. pp. 960–962. March 1, 1961.

1690. Melcher, Daniel. "When is the book really O.P.?" *Library Journal*. pp. 4576–4578. October 1, 1966.

1691. Melcher, Daniel and Margaret Saul. *Melcher on Acquisition*. Chicago: American Library Association, 1971.

1692. Melinat, C.H. *Librarianship and Publishing*. Syracuse: Syracuse School of Library Science, 1963.

1693. Merritt, LeRoy. *Book Selection and Intellectual Freedom*. New York: H.W. Wilson, 1970.

1694. Metcalf, Keyes. "Problems of acquisitions policy in a university library." *Harvard Library Bulletin*. pp. 293–303. Autumn, 1950.

1695. Milkovic, Milan. "Continuations: Some fundamental acquisitions concepts and procedures." *Serials Librarian*. pp. 35–41. Spring, 1981.

1696. Miller, E.F. "Automated book ordering and receiving." *Special Libraries*. pp. 96–100. February, 1966.

1697. Miller, H.S. "How not to buy books for libraries." *Library Acquisitions, Practice and Theory*. pp. 275–281. No. 3, 1990.

1698. Miller, William and D.S. Rockwood. "Collection development from a college perspective." *College and Research Libraries*. pp. 318–324. July, 1979.

1699. Millson-Martula, C. "The effectiveness of book selection agents in a small academic library." *College and Research Libraries*. pp. 504–510. November, 1985.

1700. Mitchell, B.J. "Methods used in out-of-print acquisition: A survey of out-of-print book dealers." *Library Resources and Technical Services*. pp. 216–224. Spring, 1973.

1701. Moore, E. "Acquisitions in the special library." *Scholarly Publishing*. pp. 167–173. January, 1982.

1702. Morrissey, E.F. "Mechanized book order and accounting routine." *Southeastern Librarian*. pp. 143–148. Fall, 1965.

1703. Morton, Donald. "Use of a subscription agent's computer facilities in creating and maintaining a library's subscription profile." *Library Resources and Technical Services.* pp. 386–389. Fall, 1978.

1704. Mosher, Paul and Marcia Pankake. "Guide to coordinated and cooperative collection development." *Library Resources and Technical Services.* pp. 417–431. October, 1983.

1705. Mulliner, B.K. "Library of Congress acquisition policies—synopsis covering developing countries." *Library Acquisitions, Practice and Theory.* pp. 103–106. No. 2, 1982.

1706. Mulliner, K. "The acquisitions allocation formula at Ohio University." *Library Acquisitions, Practice and Theory.* pp. 315–327. No. 4, 1986.

1707. Munn, Robert. "The bottomless pit, or the academic library as viewed from the administration building." *College and Research Libraries.* pp. 51–54. January, 1968.

1708. Mycue, David. "University publishing and scholarship—an American confrontation." *Libri.* pp. 31–53. 1977.

1709. Myrick, W.J. "Are library schools educating acquisitions librarians?" *Library Acquisitions, Practice and Theory.* pp. 193–211. Nos. 3–4, 1978.

1710. Neikirk, Harold. "Automated acquisitions and the shared database." *Library Acquisitions, Practice and Theory.* pp. 89–107. 1983.

1711. Neikirk, Harold. "Less does more: Adapting pre-order searching to online cataloging." *Library Acquisitions, Practice and Theory.* pp. 89–94. No. 2, 1981.

1712. Nelson, B.K. "Automated acquisitions in small academic libraries." *Library Acquisitions, Practice and Theory.* pp. 351–359. No. 4, 1989.

1713. Nemeyer, Carol. "Scholarly reprint publishing in the U.S." *Library Resources and Technical Services.* pp. 35–48. Winter, 1971.

1714. Newborn, D.E. and I.P. Godden. "Improving approval plan performance: A case study." *Library Acquisitions, Practice and Theory.* pp. 145–155. No. 2, 1980.

1715. Nicholson, D. and W. Thurston. "Serials and journals in the MIT libraries." *American Documentation.* pp. 304–307. October, 1958.

1716. Nisonger, T.E. "The Library of Congress surplus book program." *Library Acquisitions, Practice and Theory.* pp. 85–94. No. 1, 1991.

1717. Nissley, M. "Handle with care! Delicate package—CD-

ROM's and the acquisition process." *Library Acquisitions, Practice and Theory.* pp. 251–256. No. 3, 1990.

1718. Nzotta, B.C. "Acquisition of publications in indigenous languages in developing countries—the case of Nigeria." *Library Acquisitions, Practice and Theory.* pp. 99–106. No. 2, 1979.

1719. Oboler, E.M. "O.P. and all that." *ALA Bulletin.* pp. 433–434. October, 1953.

1720. Ogburn, J.L. and K.N. Fisher. "Acquiring software for the academic library—new horizons for acquisitions." *Collection Management.* pp. 69–84. No. 3, 1990.

1721. Ogg, H.C. "Writing your own accounting programs." *Computers in Libraries.* pp. 34–38. December, 1989.

1722. Orne, Jerrold. "Resources of foreign scientific literature: Acquisition on a national scale." *American Documentation.* pp. 229–2233. July, 1963.

1723. Orr, R.W. "A few aspects of acquiring serials." *Library Trends.* pp. 393–402. April, 1955.

1724. Osburn, Charles. "Some practical observations on the writing, implementation and revision of collection development policy." *Library Resources and Technical Services.* pp. 7–15. Winter, 1979.

1725. Osgood, T.S. "Let the kids choose their own books." *English Journal.* pp. 57–58. February, 1979.

1726. Ottmers, S.W. "Southwest Texas State College Library— An exploratory study with implications for a library acquisitions program." MA Thesis. University of Texas, 1961.

1727. Overmyer, LaVahn. "An analysis of output costs and procedures for an operational searching service." *American Documentation.* pp. 123–142. April, 1963.

1728. Oyelese, W.O. "Acquisition in university libraries— problems in developing countries." *UNESCO Bulletin.* pp. 81–86. March, 1978.

1729. Packer, D. "Acquisitions allocations—equity, politics, and formulas at Western Washington University." *Journal of Academic Librarianship.* pp. 276–286. November, 1988.

1730. Paige, N. "Goals for service—a survey of school library ordering." *Library Journal.* pp. 937–941. February 15, 1965.

1731. Paige, N. "Is it habit or law? Cutting the red tape of library book buying." *Library Journal.* pp. 909–913. February 15, 1964.

1732. Palmer, P.R. "Reserve book library and the O.P. book."

ALA Reprint Expediting Service Bulletin. pp. 2–9. January, 1957.

1733. Panofsky, Hans. "Acquisition of library materials from Africa." *Library Resources and Technical Services.* pp. 38–46. Winter, 1963.

1734. Pargellis, S. "Book supply and the book market." *Library Quarterly.* pp. 199–204. July, 1953.

1735. Parker, R.H. "Automatic records system at the University of Missouri Library." *College and Research Libraries.* pp. 231–232. May, 1962.

1736. Payne, K.B. "Procuring serials by bid at the USDA library." *Serial Slants.* pp. 71–75. April, 1956.

1737. Pearson, L.R. "Falling dollar imperils research collections." *American Libraries.* pp. 317–318. May, 1987.

1738. Peckham, S. "New book jobber for the Mountain States." *Publishers Weekly.* pp. 34–35. December 9, 1974.

1739. Pemberton, J.M. *Policies of Audiovisual Producers and Distributors.* Metuchen: Scarecrow Press, 1989.

1740. Perdue, A. "Conflicts in collection development." *Library Acquisitions, Practice and Theory.* pp. 123–126. No. 2, 1978.

1741. Perez, Ernest. "Acquisitions of out-of-print material." *Library Resources and Technical Services.* pp. 42–59. Winter, 1973.

1742. Perrault, A.H. "Cooperative acquisitions: Not an easy thing to do." *Louisiana Library Association Bulletin.* pp. 17–21. Summer, 1981.

1743. Perrault, A.H. "New dimensions in approval plan service." *Library Acquisitions, Practice and Theory.* pp. 35–40. No. 1, 1983.

1744. Peterson, Trudy. "The gift and the deed." *American Archivist.* pp. 61–66. January, 1979.

1745. Phelps, D. "Publishers' discounts, but at what price?" *Library Acquisitions, Practice and Theory.* pp. 289–293. No. 3, 1990.

1746. Phillips, R. "University and research section out-of-print survey." *Library Association Record.* pp. 75–81. March, 1966.

1747. Philos, Daphne. "Selection and acquisition of non-print media." *School Media Quarterly.* pp. 179–187. Spring, 1978.

1748. Pickett, A.S. "Experiment in book buying." *Library Journal.* pp. 371–372. Februray 1, 1959.

1749. Pickett, A.S. "Experiment in out-of-print book buying." *Indian Librarian.* pp. 122–123. December, 1960.

1750. Pierce, Thomas. "Empirical approach to the allocation of the university book budget." *Collection Management.* pp. 39–58. Spring, 1978.

1751. "Plan for reducing cost of procuring out of the way books." *Library Journal.* p. 2894. October 1, 1959.

1752. "Plan to speed previewing and ordering of books." *Library Journal.* pp. 2018–2020. June 15, 1959.

1753. Popovich, M. and B. Miller. "Online ordering with Dial-order." *Online.* pp. 63–65. April, 1981.

1754. Posey, Edwin and Kathleen McCullough. "Approval plans one year later." *New Horizons for Academic Libraries.* New York: K.G. Saur, 1979.

1755. Potter, W.G. "LCS for acquisitions." *Illinois Libraries.* pp. 68–70. January, 1982.

1756. Power, Eugene. "O.P. books: A library breakthrough." *American Documentation.* pp. 273–276. October, 1958.

1757. Pretorius, M. "Strengthen your buying power through reviews." *Ohio Media Spectrum.* pp. 18–22. Spring, 1990.

1758. Preuit, R. "Book selection." *Wyoming Library Roundup.* pp. 30–31. December, 1972.

1759. Price, M.O. "Acquisition and technical processing." *Library Trends.* pp. 430–458. April, 1958.

1760. Price, M.O. "Lowest responsible bidder—a legal interpretation." *Library Journal.* pp. 1005–1007. April 1, 1958.

1761. Pritchard, E. "Electronic ordering systems." *Library Acquisitions, Practice and Theory.* pp. 245–246. No. 3, 1990.

1762. Randall, F.S. "Economics in order work." *Illinois Library Association Record.* pp. 71–75. April, 1955.

1763. Randall, G.E. and R.P. Bristol. "PIL or a computer-controlled processing record." *Special Libraries.* pp. 82–86. February, 1964.

1764. Ready, W.B. "Acquisition by standing order." *Library Resources and Technical Services.* pp. 85–88. Spring, 1957.

1765. Ready, W.B. "Acquisitions and collections." *Library Review.* pp. 109–114. Autumn, 1973.

1766. Reichmann, Felix. "Acquisition of library materials from Southeast Asia." *Library Resources and Technical Services.* pp. 13–21. Winter, 1963.

1767. Reichmann, Felix. "Biographical control of reprints."

Library Resources and Technical Services. pp. 415–435. Fall, 1967.

1768. Reichmann, Felix. "Purchase of out-of-print material in American university libraries." *Library Trends.* pp. 328–353. January, 1970.

1769. Reid, M. and Scott Bullard. "Report on the business of acquisitions: Preconference." *Library Acquisitions, Practice and Theory.* pp. 283–295. No. 4, 1985.

1770. Reid, Marion. "Coping with budget adversity—impact of the financial squeeze on acquisitions." *College and Research Libraries.* pp. 266–272. May, 1976.

1771. Reid, Marion. "The pit falls of prepayments." *Louisiana Library Association Bulletin.* pp. 66–67. Winter, 1978.

1772. Reidelbach, John and Gary Shirk. "Selecting an approval plan vendor: Step by step process." *Library Acquisitions, Practice and Theory.* pp. 115–125. 1983.

1773. Revill, D. "Bookfund allocation formula." *New Library World.* pp. 162–163. August, 1974.

1774. Rice, Barbara. "Development of working collections in university libraries." *College and Research Libraries.* pp. 309–312. July, 1977.

1775. Richter, E.A. "Academic library acquisitions policy." *New Mexico Libraries.* pp. 95–99. Winter, 1970.

1776. Rogers, Rutherford. *University Library Administration.* New York: H.W. Wilson, 1971.

1777. Rooks, D.C. "Implementing the automated acquisitions system—staffing considerations." *Library Acquisitions, Practice and Theory.* pp. 423–429. Nos. 3–4, 1988.

1778. Rosenthal, B.M. "The antiquarian reprint trade." *The Antiquarian Bookman.* pp. 1667–1670. April, 19, 1965.

1779. Rossi, Gary. "Library approval plans: A selected, annotated bibliography." *Library Acquisitions, Practice and Theory.* pp. 3–34. 1987.

1780. Rouse, W.B. "Optimal selection of acquisition sources." *Journal of American Society for Information Science.* pp. 227–231.July, 1974.

1781. Ruback, M. "We can get it for you wholesale, with help." *Library Journal.* p. 730. February 15, 1962.

1782. Safran, Franciska. "Defensive ordering." *Library Acquisitions, Practice and Theory.* pp. 5–8. No. 1, 1979.

1783. Samore, Theodore. *Acquisition of Foreign Materials for U.S. Libraries.* Metuchen: Scarecrow Press, 1973.

1784. Sampson, Gary. "Allocating the book budget: Measuring

for inflation." *College and Research Libraries.* pp. 381–383. September, 1978.

1785. Sauer, Tim. "Predicting book fund expenditures—a statistical model." *College and Research Libraries.* pp. 474–478. November, 1978.

1786. Saul, M. "The business of book buying—as special librarians see it." *Library Journal.* pp. 2636–2639. July, 1963.

1787. Schad, Jasper. "Allocating book funds—control or planning?" *College and Research Libraries.* pp. 155–159. May, 1970.

1788. Schad, Jasper. "Fairness in book fund allocation." *College and Research Libraries.* pp. 479–486. November, 1987.

1789. Schatz, B. "Don't shoot the messenger. Discounts and wholesalers." *Library Acquisitions, Practice and Theory.* pp. 85–86. No. 2, 1986.

1790. Schell, M. "Acquisition, handling, and servicing in state libraries." *Library Trends.* pp. 135–142. July, 1966.

1791. Schick, F.L. "Acquiring books from abroad." *Library Resources and Technical Services.* pp. 46–50. Winter, 1959.

1792. Schmid, Thomas. "Libraries and publishers—the uneasy partnership." *Scholarly Publishing.* pp. 3–7. October, 1974.

1793. Schmidt, James. "How to win the budget battle on campus." *American Libraries.* pp. 569–570. November, 1977.

1794. Schmidt, K.A. "The acquisitions process in research libraries: A survey of ARL libraries acquisition departments." *Library Acquisitions, Practice and Theory.* pp. 35–44. No. 1, 1987.

1795. Schmidt, K.A. "Capturing the mainstream: Publisher based and subject based approval plans in academic libraries." *College and Research Libraries.* pp. 365–369. July, 1986.

1796. Schmidt, K.A. "Education for acquisitions—a history." *Library Resources and Technical Services.* pp. 159–169. April, 1990.

1797. Schmidt, K.A. "The education of the acquisitions librarian—survey of ARL acquisitions librarians." *Library Resources and Technical Services.* pp. 7–22. January, 1991.

1798. Schmidt, Karen. "Buying good pennyworths? Review of the literature of acquisitions in the 80's." *Library Resources and Technical Services.* pp. 333–340. October, 1986.

1799. Schmidt, Karen. *Understanding the Business of Library*

Acquisitions. Chicago: American Library Association, 1990.

1800. Schmude, K.G. and R.B. Luxton. "Acquisitions for distance education: An Australian experience." *Library Acquisitions, Practice and Theory.* pp. 25–31. No. 1, 1986.

1801. Schnaars, S.N. "Fourth International Conference on Approval Plans." *College and Research Library News.* p. 34. February, 1980.

1802. Schreiner, K.J. "New use of the OCLC cataloging subsytem: Acquisitions." *Library Acquisitions, Practice and Theory.* pp. 151–157. Nos. 3–4, 1978.

1803. Scoones, M.A. "The mechanization of serial records with particular reference to subscription control." *Aslib Proceedings.* pp. 45–62. February, 1967.

1804. Selsky, D. "Libraries expected to spend $4.5 billion on materials in 1992." *Library Journal.* p. 32. August, 1990.

1805. Sewell, R.G. "Managing European automatic acquisitions." *Library Resources and Technical Services.* pp. 397–405. October, 1983.

1806. Shaw, K.B. "Periodical acquisition policies." *Aslib Proceedings.* pp. 81–86. May, 1953.

1807. Shaw, R.R. "Control of book funds at the University of Hawaii Library." *Library Resources and Technical Services.* pp. 380–382. Summer, 1967.

1808. Shaw, T.S. "Distribution and acquisition." *Library Trends.* pp. 37–49. January, 1962.

1809. Shirk, G.M. and A.L. Miller. "Academic library survey, fall 1988." *Library Acquisitions, Practice and Theory.* pp. 335–341. No. 4, 1989.

1810. Simpson, M.L. "Experiment with acquisitions with the Lamont Library list." *College and Research Libraries.* pp. 430–433. October, 1954.

1811. Skipper, J.E. "The continuing problem of book selection and acquisition." *Library Resources and Technical Services.* pp. 265–271. Fall, 1958.

1812. Smith, E.R. "Out-of-print booksearching." *College and Research Libraries.* pp. 303–309. July, 1968.

1813. Smith, Katherine. "Serials agents—serials librarians." *Library Resources and Technical Services.* pp. 5–18. Winter, 1970.

1814. Smith, P.A. "Impact of automation upon acquisitions and staff at Colorado State University libraries." *Colorado Libraries.* pp. 14+. March, 1984.

1815. Smith, P.A. "Securing out-of-print books." *ALA Bulletin.* pp. 511–512. November, 1948.

1816. Smith, P.A. "What shall we do about OP books?" *Library Journal.* pp. 479–481. May 15, 1945.

1817. Snowball, George and Martin Cohen. "Control of book fund expenditures under an accrual accounting system." *Collection Management.* pp. 5–20. Spring, 1979.

1818. Somers, S.W. "Issues in book and serial acquisitions—all you ever wanted to know about finances." *Technical Services Quarterly.* pp. 69–73. Fall, 1986.

1819. Somers, S.W. "Vendor-library relations—a perspective." *Library Acquisitions, Practice and Theory.* pp. 135–138. No. 2, 1987.

1820. Soupiset, K.A. "College book price information, 1990." *Choice.* p. 1073. March, 1991.

1821. Spaulding, F.W. and R.O. Stanton. "Computerized selection in a library network." *Journal of the ASIS.* pp. 269–280. September–October, 1976.

1822. Spence, Barbara. "The librarian and the procurement problem." *SciTech News.* pp. 6–7. Fall, 1959.

1823. Spence, P. "Library acquisition conference." *Alabama Librarian.* p. 13. November, 1977.

1824. Spigai, F.G. and T. Mahan. "Online acquisition by LOLITA." *Journal of Library Automation.* pp. 276–294. December, 1970.

1825. Stave, D.G. "Art books on approval—why not?" *Library Acquisitions, Practice and Theory.* pp. 5–6. No. 1, 1983.

1826. Steffey, D. "The librarian considers the school library budget." *Illinois Libraries.* pp. 97–100. March, 1952.

1827. Steinbrenner, J. "Cost effectiveness of book rental plans." *Ohio Library Association Bulletin.* pp. 5–6. April, 1979.

1828. Stevens, J.K. and J. Swenson. "Coordinated system of processing gift or exchange serials at the University of Utah Library." *Library Acquisitions, Practice and Theory.* pp. 157–162. No. 2, 1980.

1829. Stevens, Robert. "Library of Congress Public Law 480 Programs." *Library Resources and Technical Services.* pp. 176–188. Spring, 1963.

1830. Stewart, C.C. "Update on ordering standards." *Information Technology and Libraries.* pp. 341–343. December, 1982.

1831. Stokely, Sandra and Marion Reid. "A study of performance of five book dealers used by LSU library." *Library*

Resources and Technical Services. pp. 117–125. Spring, 1978.

1832. Strauch, K. "Issues in book and serial acquisitions—external influences on acquisitions and collection development." *Library Acquisitions, Practice and Theory.* pp. 119–163. No. 2, 1987.

1833. Strauss, L.J. et al. "Books and their publications: Selection and acquisition," *Scientific and Technical Libraries, Their Organizations and Administration.* New York: Interscience, 1964.

1834. Strieby, I.M. "Simplified library-to-dealer purchasing." *Stechert-Hafner Book News.* pp. 81–82. March, 1955.

1835. Sullivan, Robert. "The acquisition of library microforms." *Microform Review.* pp. 136–144. May, 1977.

1836. Sullivan, Robert. "Microform developments related to acquisitions." *College and Research Libraries.* pp. 16–28. January, 1973.

1837. Sweet, A.P. "Forms in acquisition work." *College and Research Libraries.* pp. 396–401. October, 1953.

1838. Taggart, W.R. "Blanket approval ordering: A positive approach." *Canadian Library Journal.* pp. 286–289, July, 1970.

1839. Taggart, W.R. "The pros and cons of blanket approval book acquisition plans." *CACUL Newsletter.* pp. 165–171. February, 1972.

1840. Tate, Vernon. "Microreproductions and the acquisitions programs." *Library Trends.* pp. 432–447. April, 1955.

1841. Taylor, David. *Book Catalogs: Their Varieties and Uses.* Chicago: Newberry Library, 1957.

1842. Taylor, M.M. *School Library and Media Center Acquisitions Policies and Procedures.* Phoenix: Oryx Press, 1981.

1843. Teeple, H.M. "Acquisitions form letter." *Illinois Libraries.* pp. 323–326. April, 1966.

1844. Thayer, M.J. "BIP on CD-ROM, OCLC and dBase III combine to improve acquisitions workflow." *Library Acquisitions, Practice and Theory.* pp. 371–379. No. 4, 1989.

1845. Thibault, Charles. "Survey of specialized acquisitions procedures in a technical documents center." MA thesis. Catholic University of America, 1956.

1846. Thom, Jan. "Some administrative aspects of blanket ordering." *Library Resources and Technical Services.* pp. 338–342. Summer, 1969.

1847. Thompson, Evelyn and G. Forrester. "The automatic ordering of replacement titles for libraries in metropolitan Toronto." *Library Resources and Technical Services.* pp. 215–220. Spring, 1967.

1848. Tiberio, Barbara. "The acquisition of free cartographic materials—request and exchange." *Special Libraries.* pp. 233–238. May–June, 1979.

1849. Tiranti, D. "The pricing of books in the antiquarian book trade." *Antiquarian Bookman,* pp. 1261–1263. 1949.

1850. Tjarks, Alicia. "Coping with Latin American serials." *Serials Librarian.* pp. 407–415. Summer, 1979.

1851. Tree, R.A. "Fashions in collecting and changing prices." *Library Trends.* pp. 476–482. April, 1957.

1852. Treyz, Joe. "O.P. market." *Choice.* pp. 283–285. July–August, 1965.

1853. Tsuneishi, W.M. "Acquisition of library materials from China, Japan, and Korea." *Library Resources and Technical Services.* pp. 28–33. Winter, 1963.

1854. Tyagi, M.S. "Book purchase in Indian university libraries: Some problems." *Library Herald.* pp. 197–209. April–July, 1965.

1855. Van Orden, Phyllis. "Promotion, review, and examination of materials." *School Media Quarterly.* pp. 120–131. Winter, 1978.

1856. Van Pelt, J.D. "Duplication of books: Causes and remedies." *Australian Library Journal.* pp. 42–46. April, 1954.

1857. Veenstra, J. and L.L. Mai. "When do you use a jobber?" *College and Research Libraries.* pp. 522–524. November, 1962.

1858. Veit, Fritz. "Book order procedures in the publicly controlled colleges and universities of the Midwest." *College and Research Libraries.* pp. 33–40. January, 1962.

1859. Verrone, Robert. "Why do books cost so much?" *School Library Journal.* pp. 20–22. February, 1979.

1860. Vickery, B.C. "Periodical sets: What should you buy?" *Aslib Proceedings.* pp. 69–74. May, 1953.

1861. Vinson, M. "Cost finding—a step by step guide to in-house order costs at Southern Methodist." *Bottom Line.* pp. 15–19. No. 3, 1988.

1862. Vogt, Jack. "What is zero-based budgeting." *Library Acquisitions.* pp. 5–6. 1978.

1863. Voigt, Melvin. "Acquisition rates in university libraries." *College and Research Libraries.* pp. 263–271. July, 1975.

1864. Vosper, R.G. "Acquisition policy: Fact or fancy?" *College and Research Libraries.* pp. 367–370. October, 1953.

1865. Vosper, R.G. "Current acquisition trends in American libraries." *Library Trends.* pp. 333–336. April, 1955.

1866. Walch, David. "Budgeting for non-print media in academic libraries." *New Horizons for Academic Libraries.* New York: K.G. Saur, 1979.

1867. Wall, C. Edward. "Budget stretching—remainder books for libraries." *American Libraries* pp. 367–370. June, 1978.

1868. Wallach, K. "Problems of acquisitions and ordering of foreign law." *Law Library Journal.* pp. 365–377. November, 1962.

1869. Waller, T. "Problems of American book publishers." *College and Research Libraries.* pp. 147–150. April, 1952.

1870. Walter, F.K. *The Library's Own Printing.* Chicago: American Library Association, 1934.

1871. Walters, M.D. "Approval plan timing study." *Collection Building.* pp. 14–18. Spring, 1985.

1872. Waltner, Nellie et al. "Periodical prices: A comparison of local and national averages." *Library Acquisitions.* pp. 237–241. 1978.

1873. Weaver, James. "Gift appraisals practices in NAPCU libraries." *PNLA Quarterly.* pp. 3–5. Fall, 1978.

1874. Wedgeworth, Robert. "Brown University Library fund accounting system." *Journal of Library Automation.* pp. 51–65. March, 1968.

1875. Welch, H.M. "Cost of library materials." *Library Trends.* pp. 384–394. April, 1963.

1876. Welch, H.M. "Dealers look at the LC rating system." *Library Resources and Technical Services.* pp. 115–120. Spring, 1958.

1877. Welch, H.M. "The year's work in acquisitions and resources." *Library Resources and Technical Services.* pp. 75–82. Spring, 1958.

1878. Welch, H.M. "The year's work in acquisitions and resources." *Library Resources and Technical Services.* pp. 78–83. Spring, 1959.

1879. Welch, H.M. "The year's work in acquisitions and resources." *Library Resources and Technical Services.* pp. 101–108. Spring, 1960.

1880. Welch, L. "Cost of library materials." *Library Trends.* pp. 384–394. April, 1963.

1881. Welter, R. *Problems of Scholarly Publications in the*

Humanities and Social Sciences. New York: American Council of Learned Societies, 1959.

1882. Werking, Richard. "Allocating the academic library's book budget: Historical perspectives and current reflections." *Journal of Academic Librarianship.* pp. 140–144. July, 1988.

1883. Wernick, A.S. "Computer systems acquisition and the use of letters of credit." *Library HiTech.* pp. 97–99. No. 1, 1988.

1884. West, Stan. "Acquisition of library materials from Latin America." *Library Resources and Technical Services.* pp. 7–12. Winter, 1963.

1885. Weston, L. "Acquisition resources for bibliographic instruction and reference." *Colorado Libraries.* pp. 23–24. March, 1990.

1886. Whitehead, R.J. *A Guide to Selecting Books for Children.* Metuchen: Scarecrow Press, 1984.

1887. Whitten, J.N. and A.L. Fessler. "Hard cover reprint publishing." *Library Trends.* pp. 82–92. July, 1958.

1888. Wiener, P.B. "Acquisition of first novels in academic libraries." *Collection Management.* pp. 25–36. Fall–Winter, 1983.

1889. Wilcox, J.K. "The acquisition of government publications." *Library Trends.* pp. 403–413. April, 1955.

1890. Wilden-Hart, Marion. "Long term effects of approval plans." *Library Resources and Technical Services.* pp. 400–406. Summer, 1970.

1891. Wilkerson, M. "Library purchasing practices." *Special Libraries.* pp. 19–22. January, 1951.

1892. Wing, D.G. and R.G. Vosper. "Antiquarian book market and the acquisition of rare books." *Library Trends.* pp. 385–392. April, 1955.

1893. Winters, B.A. and J.L. Flowers. "Funding future acquisitions—Financial resources for the 1990's." *Library Acquisitions, Practice and Theory.* pp. 125–127. No. 1, 1991.

1894. Wulfekoetter, G. "Background for acquisition work." *Library Journal.* pp. 522–526. February 1, 1961.

1895. Wyllys, Ron. "On the analysis of growth rate of library collections and expenditures." *Collection Management.* pp. 115–128. Summer, 1978.

1896. Wynar, Bohdan. *Library Acquisitions: A Classified Bibliographic Guide to the Literature and Reference Tools.* Littleton: Libraries Unlimited, 1971.

1897. Yonge, Ena. "Map procurement in the special library." *Special Libraries.* pp. 173–174. May–June, 1953.
1898. Zack, D. "Library buys first, borrows second." *Unabashed Librarian.* p. 13. No. 62, 1987.
1899. Zeugner, L.A. "Acquisitions survey—the vendors respond." *Library Acquisitions, Practice and Theory.* pp. 313–315. No. 3, 1990.

PART FOUR

COLLECTION DEVELOPMENT POLICIES

Appearing on subsequent pages are examples of collection development policies, which vary widely in scope and format for different types and sizes of libraries. Some smaller libraries may have a one-page statement setting out the general guidelines to be followed in collecting materials. Other libraries, e.g., research institutions, may prepare a document of many pages that develops extensive details about the goals and objectives of collecting down to narrow subject areas. In any case, every library, no matter how small, is well served by preparation of a carefully reasoned policy that will serve to address user needs, to deter censorship attempts, and to plan for future collection building efforts.

COLLECTION DEVELOPMENT POLICY FOR OHIO STATE DEPARTMENT OF EDUCATION

IV. SUGGESTED CRITERIA FOR SELECTION OF MATERIALS

An important component of the materials selection process is the consistent use of general and specific criteria for evaluating the many different materials and products available. Selecting appropriate and quality instructional materials is dependent upon professionally developed criteria that are clearly defined and defensible.

A. General Criteria

General criteria should be developed that are applicable to all instructional materials, regardless of the type of material being selected or the subject matter content and grade level being considered. Definitive measures should be developed for each general criterion to facilitate the evaluation and selection of materials, which are unique to a given course of study or class of students. The educational issues and factors outlined below should be addressed when developing general criteria.

1. Overall Purpose

Selected instructional materials should address the objectives specified in each course of study and reflect the district's educational philosophy.

2. Student Needs

Selected instructional materials should address general learner needs and individual variances in developmental, physical and emotional maturity, as well as learning styles, skills and interests of all students.

3. Teacher Needs

Selected instructional materials should be compatible with the instructional styles, preferences and priorities of teachers.

185

4. Pluralistic and Nonsexist Representation
   Selected instructional materials should foster respect
   for all people. Women, minorities, ethnic groups, the
   handicapped and aged should be realistically represented and portrayed. The materials should also reflect
   a pluralistic society and global interdependence.
5. Authoritativeness
   Selected instructional materials should reflect the
   competencies of the author, producer and/or publisher. Information on background, education, experience, reputation and previous works are usually taken
   into consideration when questioning authoritativeness.
6. Authenticity
   Selected instructional materials should be valid, reliable, complete and objective. As appropriate, materials
   should have a current copyright or manufacture date.
7. Scope
   Selected instructional materials should be of sufficient
   depth and breadth for coverage of the subject and be
   appropriate for grade and age level use.
8. Format and Technical Quality
   Selected instructional materials should be designed in
   a physical format appropriate to content and intended
   use. The materials should meet acceptable production
   standards, be of sufficient quality and be suitably
   bound or packaged for safety, durability and ease in
   use and storage. Print materials should be readable and
   typographically well-balanced.
9. Content Treatment and Arrangement
   Selected instructional materials should present
   information in a well-organized, challenging and stim-
   ulating style. The content sequence should be logical
   and the style of presentation should be appropriate for
   intended use.
10. Aesthetic Considerations
    Selected instructional materials should have literary,
    artistic and social value and should appeal to the
    imagination, senses and intellect of students.

11. Cost
    Selected instructional materials should have value commensurate with the price, need, potential use and budgetary considerations.
12. Controversial Issues
    Selected instructional materials should present a reasonable balance of opposing sides of controversial issues so that students may develop critical thinking skills. Factual, unbiased instructional materials representing all ideologies, philosophies, religions and political views should be considered. Also, consideration should be given to the literary or social merit of materials addressing sexual topics or containing nonstandard language.
13. Resource Sharing
    Selected instructional materials should complement the existing materials in the school district and community. Given the need and frequency of use, networking, i.e., sharing instructional resources, should be explored prior to purchasing expensive or duplicate items.
14. Trends
    Selected instructional materials should reflect educational, societal and technological trends that increase the effectiveness and usefulness of the materials in meeting student and teacher needs in the present and future.

B. Specific Criteria
   While the general considerations mentioned above are applicable for the evaluation and selection of all types of instructional materials, additional criteria should be considered when evaluating and selecting the following specific categories of materials.
   1. Textbooks
      a. The total series should demonstrate continuity in the presentation of the content with skills taught sequentially. Consideration should be given to the availability of supplemental teaching materials.

    b. The student text should be organized in an appealing manner. Skills and new concepts should be reinforced systematically. The text should facilitate the development of independent study and comprehension.

    c. The teacher edition should be easy to use and should contain practical, flexible options for presenting and testing key concepts. It should also contain a bibliography for student and teacher use.

    d. Materials that supplement the textbook should provide opportunities for students to apply their skills and expand their knowledge beyond the basic textbook.

2. Equipment

    a. A variety of instructional equipment should be selected that can be used with other instructional materials to attain the objectives specified in each course of study.

    b. The equipment should meet desirable performance standards in terms of specific functions.

    c. Consideration should be given to the following properties and factors:

       1) operational ease
       2) durability
       3) dependability
       4) portability
       5) availability of service
       6) maintenance costs
       7) reputation of the manufacturer

3. Library Collection

    a. Reference materials such as dictionaries, encyclopedias, atlases, yearbooks and subject matter reference materials should be current. At least one set of encyclopedia shall have a copyright date within the past five years.

    b. Nonfiction materials should be purposeful and accurate. The materials should supplement and enrich the curriculum, as well as provide additional information of interest to students.

c. Fiction materials should be purposeful and relevant to the interests and needs of students at various levels of maturity. Consideration should be given to such factors as the structural development of the plot, theme and characters; clarity of style; creativity and imaginative appeal; and stereotypes and biases.

d. Nonprint materials, such as films and filmstrips, records and tapes, globes, maps and computer software, should have artistic and technical quality.

e. Periodicals should present various points of view on current issues and ideas, such as political, social and scientific concepts.

f. Newspapers should be of general circulation and report matters of local, state, national and international importance.

g. Vertical files of pamphlets, articles, brochures and clippings of current but limited use and interest should provide timely and valuable information on a given topic or issue.

h. The library collection should contain multiple copies of popular and frequently used materials. Items or books in a series should be examined individually prior to purchasing the entire series. Items subject to renewal subscriptions should be evaluated annually. Significant items or books that are worn or missing should be replaced, and out-of-date or useless items should be withdrawn from the library collection.

4. Supplemental Instructional Resources
Supplemental materials, equipment, activities and services should contribute to the educational philosophy of the district and meet the objectives specified in the course of study. They should be evaluated and selected according to the considerations and criteria noted above.

Gifts, free materials and donated services also should meet established criteria and be of high quality. Consideration should be given to any special conditions requested by the donor or desired by the board of education.

Commercially produced or sponsored materials also should meet accepted criteria and be of high quality. They should not attempt to establish exclusivity for a particular product, service or ideology. The source of funds and sponsoring organization should be known so that the point of view and content may be evaluated critically. Any advertising that appears on or with any material should be in good taste and unobtrusive.

Checklist for School Media Advisory Committee's Reconsideration of Instructional Material—Fiction and Other Literary Forms

Title _____

Author _____

A. Purpose

  1. What is the purpose, theme or message of the material? How well does the author/producer/composer accomplish this purpose?

    _____

    _____

  2. If the story is fantasy, is it the type that has imaginative appeal and is suitable for children?_____ Yes _____ No; for young adults _____ Yes _____ No. If both are marked no, for what age group would you recommend? _____

  3. Will the reading and/or viewing and/or listening to the material result in more compassionate understandings of human beings? _____ Yes _____ No.

  4. Does it offer an opportunity to better understand and appreciate the aspirations, achievements, and problems of various minority groups? _____ Yes _____ No.

  5. Are any questionable elements of the story an integral part of a worthwhile theme or message? _____ Yes _____ No.

B. Content

  1. Does a story about modern times give a realistic picture of life as it is now? _____ Yes _____ No.

  2. Does the story avoid an oversimplified view of life, one that leaves the reader with the general feeling that life is sweet and rosy or ugly and meaningless? _____ Yes _____ No.

  3. When factual information is part of the story, is it presented accurately? _____ Yes _____ No.

  4. Is prejudicial appeal readily identifiable by the potential reader? _____ Yes _____ No.

  5. Are concepts presented appropriate to the ability and maturity of the potential readers? _____ Yes _____ No.

6. Do characters speak in a language true to the period and section of the country in which they live? _____ Yes _____ No.

7. Does the material offend in some special way the sensibilities of women or a minority group by the way it presents either the chief character or any of the minor characters? _____ Yes _____ No.

8. Is there preoccupation with sex, violence, cruelty, brutality, and aberrant behavior that would make this material inappropriate for children? _____ Yes _____ No; young adults? _____ Yes _____ No.

9. If there is use of offensive language, is it appropriate to the purpose of the text for children? _____ Yes _____ No; young adults? _____ Yes _____ No.

10. Is the material free from derisive names and epithets that would offend minority groups? _____ Yes _____ No; children? _____ Yes _____ No; young adults? _____ Yes _____ No.

11. Is the material well written or produced? _____ Yes _____ No.

12. Does the story give a broader understanding of human behavior without stressing differences of class, race, color, sex, education, religion or philosophy in any adverse way? _____ Yes _____ No.

13. Does the material make a significant contribution to the history of literature or ideas? _____ Yes _____ No.

14. Are the illustrations appropriate and in good taste? _____ Yes _____ No.

15. Are the illustrations realistic in relation to the story? _____ Yes _____ No.

Additional Comments

_____
_____
_____

Recommendations by School Media Advisory Committee for Treatment of Challenged Materials

_____
_____
_____

Date _____

Signature of Media Advisory Review Committee

_____   _____

_____   _____

[Adapted from "Policies and Procedures for Selection of Instructional Materials," *School Media Quarterly* (Winter 1977) p. 115–116]

COLLECTION DEVELOPMENT POLICY
WILLIAM PATERSON COLLEGE
Paterson, New Jersey

V. SPECIFIC FORMAT AND COLLECTION POLICIES

In addition to the general guidelines already presented, there are Library policies and procedures that apply only to library materials in specific formats and/or to those housed in specific collections within the Library. These policy statements are presented below.

A. Archives

The Archives Collection Policy is currently under review. Until a new policy is firmly established, the Library is not actively acquiring, organizing, or filing any new materials except for Library archival items. The latter includes, but is not limited to, blueprints, task force reports, and staff meeting reports.

B. Audiovisual Materials

The purpose of the Audiovisual collection is to serve members of the William Paterson College community by providing access to art and information in audiovisual formats that support the curriculum of the College. Although the Audiovisual Collection consists largely of adult-level titles, the collection also includes a representative sampling of juvenile materials that support the curriculum of the School of Education and Community Service.

All requests for the purchase of adult-level, audiovisual materials are sent to the Ordering and Receiving Section, which forwards them to the Audiovisual Department for review. The Head of the Audiovisual Department may modify any media requests to conform to the Audiovisual Department software preference and is responsible for the disposition of any general audiovisual materials funds.

The following types of software are presently included in the Audiovisual Collection. Requests for types of media not included below are considered on a title-by-title basis. In general, however, only software that is compatible with Library-owned hardware is purchased, and preference is given to materials that can be repaired within the Library.

Compact Discs, Cassettes, Records, and Reel-to-Reel Tapes

Compact discs are the preferred audio medium because of their easy storage, portability, and long-term durability. Only those recordings that are unavailable on compact discs are purchased in other audio media. Standard cassettes, open reel-to-reel tapes and 33 1/3 rpm stereophonic records are the only acceptable alternative media.

It is recognized that the Library cannot meet all the audio needs and tastes of the variety of groups constituting the William Paterson College community. However, a representative audio collection has been developed consisting of recordings in the following categories:

a. *Music*—primarily classical music, opera, jazz, folk and children's songs.
b. *Theatre*—primarily show music, plays and dramatic readings.
c. *Spoken Word Recordings*—primarily lectures, seminars, stories, debates and proceedings.

Recordings in other categories, such as comedy and popular music, are considered for purchase and inclusion in the collection on a title-by-title basis by the Head of Collection Development in consultation with the Head of the Audiovisual Department.

8mm Films and Film Loops

The Library does not usually acquire 8mm films or film loops. However, exceptions may be made by the Head of the Audiovisual Department.

Filmstrips and Slides

All slides must be 2" × 2" in size. Whenever a choice of medium is offered, slide sets are preferred over filmstrips.

Microcomputer Software

All requests to purchase microcomputer software must be made on a Microcomputer Software Request Form.

The Library acquires those types of software packages, which supplement the Curriculum Materials Collection (see section IV-C), as well as college-level computer-assisted instruction packages that support the general College curriculum. These include tutorials, educational games, simulations, and drill and practice exercises as well as some multi-purpose packages, such as word processing, data management, spreadsheet, statistical packages, etc. Only software that is compatible, in terms of memory size, language and peripherals, with hardware in the Library will be purchased.

Microcomputer Software, especially software that has not been favorably reviewed or that costs more than $100.00, will be previewed and evaluated by members of the Microcomputer Committee prior to purchase. The committee consists of the following members:

> Librarian in charge of Library software applications, Chair
> Head of the Audiovisual Department
> Curriculum Materials Librarian
> Associate Director for Collection Management
> Associate Director for Readers Services
> Head of Collection Development
> Supervisor of Audiovisual Services

The requestor, and the appropriate Dean and librarian coordinator will also be invited to preview and evaluate the software. A member of the teaching faculty may be called in to provide technical expertise or subject expertise. The Committee follows the general guidelines for nonprint materials (Section III.B) to assure the acquisition of quality of microcomputer programs. Additional factors that will be taken into consideration in the selection of software are:

—Appropriateness of the subject to the curriculum and the collection
—Evidence of field testing and favorable reviews

—Availability of backup copies from the publisher or authorization for the Library to make copies

—Reputation of publisher in terms of providing notification of new versions, replacement copies of damaged programs, and warrantees on program bugs and defects.

The committee may make an affirmative decision even when a requested title does not have all of these characteristics. However, it is unlikely that it would approve the purchase of a title that did not possess the first two characteristics.

The Library will duplicate all uncopyrighted Curriculum Materials software and add these to the circulating collection. In the case of copyrighted materials, the Curriculum Materials Librarian, in consultation with the Collection Development Librarian, will consider cost and desirability of purchase of a second copy on a per item basis at the time of initial purchase.

Motion Picture Films, Videocassettes and Videodisks

In general, 16mm films are rented rather than purchased. The cost of rental is borne by the appropriate academic School. Members of the Audiovisual Department assist faculty in locating titles on specific subjects and ordering information (distribution, price, etc.), and the Department is responsible for processing film/video rental requests.

Teaching faculty members and librarians may request that a film or video title be purchased for the Library from the library materials budget of the requestor's School. Such requests must be made on Film/Video Request Forms. All titles over $125 that are requested for purchase must be previewed and approved by the members of the Film/Video Committee, who preview films as they are received and meet to discuss them. The Committee is composed of the librarians in the following positions:

Head of the Audiovisual Department, Chair
Associate Director for Collection Management

Head of Collection Development
Collection Development Librarian

The Library Coordinator for the subject area of the title being considered for purchase, the requestor, and the appropriate Dean are also invited to preview the title and are asked to evaluate it using the Film/Video Evaluation Form.

Requestors will receive written notification of the Committee's decision. The Film/Video Committee follows the general guidelines for non-print materials (section III.B) to assure the acquisition of quality films and video materials. In addition, the Committee also considers the following characteristics in relation to each title requested:

—Appropriateness of the subject to the curriculum and the collection
—Anticipated high use
—Favorable reviews
—Unavailability of title from easily accessible loan or rental sources
—Cost

The Committee may make an affirmative decision even when a requested title does not have all of these characteristics. However, it is unusual for the Committee to approve requests for titles that do not possess the first two characteristics.

Choice of format is determined on a title-by-title basis. Factors in this decision include price, available hardware and location of classes. In general, the Library does not purchase reel-to-reel video tapes.

Multi-Media Kits

Multi-media kits include any combination of slides of filmstrips with cassettes, reel-to-reel tapes or records. When kits are purchased and a choice of media is offered, cassettes are preferred to tapes and records, and slides are preferred to filmstrips. The Library does not purchase individual parts of multi-media kits.

Transparencies

Transparencies and transparency masters are purchased. Whenever possible, transparencies are acquired framed.

Miscellaneous Media

The following types of materials are usually housed in the Audiovisual Department. Teaching faculty and librarians may submit requests to purchase these materials from their library departmental allocation on a Materials Request Form. With the exception of materials purchased for the Curriculum Materials Department, all acquisitions of these types of materials must have the approval of the Head of Collection Development.

Games and/or Models - globes, maps, and education and simulation games.

Realia - including artifacts, samples, and specimens.

Pictures - including art originals, photographs, post cards, posters, and study prints.

UNIVERSITY OF ILLINOIS
FILM CENTER
MATERIALS SELECTION POLICY

SELECTION POLICY

INTRODUCTION

The purpose of the University of Illinois Film Center materials selection policy is to guide staff members and consultants involved in the selection process and to inform the public about the principles upon which selections are made.

A policy, however detailed, cannot replace the judgment of qualified evaluators, but it can assist evaluators in choosing from the vast array of available materials.

The major goal of the University of Illinois Film Center in materials selection is to secure high-quality films and videotapes for the educational, recreational, and cultural use of the faculty and students of the University and of media users throughout the state and nation.

RESPONSIBILITY FOR SELECTION

The Director of the University of Illinois Film Center is responsible for the content of the Film Center's collections. The selection of materials is coordinated by a film evaluation and selection specialist working with subject specialists from the University and area public schools.

SELECTION CRITERIA

The following criteria are used by the University of Illinois Film Center in judging film and video materials:

—Appropriateness of material to the Film Center collections;
—Needs of clientele;
—Current holdings of the Center in that subject area;
—Potential for cost recovery;
—Distributor reliability and quality of supplementary materials and information;
—Content accuracy, currency, and impartiality;
—Image and sound quality;
—Potential uses, particularly interdisciplinary ties.

WEEDING

The University of Illinois Film Center views selection as an ongoing process that includes the removal of materials from the collection that cease to meet the Film Center's high standards of quality.

CHALLENGED MATERIALS

Despite the quality of the selection process, occasional objections to materials acquired by the Film Center may occur. Intellectual freedom inherent in the First Amendment of the Constitution of the U.S. and expressed in the "Freedom to View" statement of the Educational Film Library Association, the "Library Bill of Rights" of the American Library Association, and the "Statement on Intellectual Freedom" of the Association for Educational Communications and Technology. In the event that materials are challenged, the principles of intellectual freedom must be defended rather than the materials themselves.

If a complaint is made, the following procedures will be followed:

1. The complainant will be informed of the Film Center's selection policy and will be directed to submit a formal request for reconsideration of materials;

2. The challenged material will be kept in circulation during the reconsideration process;
3. The Director will appoint a committee of media utilization and subject specialists to review the challenged material;
4. The committee will determine the extent to which the work meets the standard criteria for selection by consulting reviews and viewing the work and will then submit written reports of its findings to the Director.

UNIVERSITY OF ILLINOIS FILM CENTER
Request for Reconsideration of Materials

Title _____ Order number _____

Request initiated by _____

Address _____

City _____ State _____ Zip _____

Telephone _____

Do you represent:

_____ Yourself

_____ An organization (name) _____

_____ Other group (name) _____

Please answer the following questions and return the completed form to the Director's office. If more space is needed, please use the back or attach additional sheets.

1. To what in the work do you object. Please be specific.
   _____

2. What do you believe is the theme or purpose of this work.
   _____

3. What do you feel might be the result of viewing this work.
   _____

4. Are you aware of judgements of this work as found in reviews? _____
   _____

5. What action do you recommend the Film Center take regarding this work? _____

6. In its place, would you care to recommend another work that you know of?_____

_____   _____
        Signature   Date

7. The Director will make the decision concerning the dispensation of the challenged material and will notify the complainant of his decision;

8. The complainant may appeal the decision.

COLLECTION DEVELOPMENT POLICY
FRONT RANGE COMMUNITY COLLEGE LIBRARY
Denver, Colorado

COLLECTION DEVELOPMENT POLICY

A. Introduction

Front Range Community College is located in the north suburbs of Denver. It is the largest community college in the state, and enrollment has been steadily increasing since the late 1980's.

Many students are beyond the 18–21 age bracket, some are returning to school after long absences, and some already possess degrees.

B. Statement of Standards

The library supports the college curriculum by providing a core of introductory and reference materials in the areas of study. Levels of collection intensity are either at a most basic level, which includes some core titles and one' or two periodical titles, or at a medium level, which includes most recognized standard books, some periodicals and some judicious supplemental coverage as needed.

Area library collections are complementary to this one. There are fine public library collections that fill leisure reading needs. There are college and university collections and regional United States document depository libraries that fill in-depth and retrospective research needs. Because these facilities are accessible to FRCC patrons, the library does not attempt to duplicate services.

C. Intellectual Freedom

The Library adopts as part of its policy the following paragraphs from the *Library Bill of Rights:*

1. As a responsibility of library service, books and other library materials selected should be chosen for values of interests, information and enlightenment of all the people of the community. In no case should library

materials be excluded because of the race or nationality or the social, political, or religious views of the authors.

2.   Libraries should provide books and other materials presenting all points of view concerning the problems and issues of our times: no library materials should be proscribed or removed from libraries because of partisan or doctrinal disapproval.

D.   Responsibility for selection

1.   LMC Selection Committee

It is the professional responsibility of the LMC staff to maintain a collection that fits the needs of the college. For this reason, the LMC staff bears primary responsibility for the selection of materials to be included in the collection.

The Committee consists of members of the Library staff. Media staff is consulted regularly as is other college staff when needed.

The Committee meets formally at irregular intervals to set goals and policy and to review such matters as periodical and microfilm subscription renewals, standing order renewals, and large purchases such as reference books.

Members of the Committee are responsible for scanning review periodicals and making selection suggestions on an informal basis. Selection tools used include:

a.   standard bibliographies:

Books for College Libraries
Core List of Books and Journals in Science and Technology
Sheehy's Guide to Reference Books

b.   review journals:

Bloomsbury Review
Booklist
Library Journal
Science Books and Films
New Technical Books
The New York Times Book Review
Wilson Library Bulletin

c.   other sources:

American Libraries
Book Review Digest
Book Review Index

Books in Print
College and Research Libraries News
Colorado Libraries
Gale's Directory of Publications
Magazines for Libraries
New Books
Ulrich's International Guide to Periodicals

2. Outside input

In addition to the recommendations of the Selection Committee, suggestions from faculty, administrators, students and staff are accepted and given serious consideration.

Recommendations originating from sources beyond the LMC are weighed against the same criteria as those from the LMC Selection Committee; therefore, submission of a request does not guarantee purchase. The LMC staff has the right and professional responsibility to refuse to purchase materials that do not meet the selection criteria.

E. Subject classifications and collection intensity

F. Formats

1. Textbooks

It is the responsibility of the individual student to purchase required class textbooks; therefore, the LMC will not intentionally select these books. In instances where the LMC does own a copy, that book will be placed on Reserve for the duration of the course. The Bookstore provides the LMC with a list of books every semester for this purpose.

2. Fiction

Fiction selections are made by the Selection Committee almost exclusively through Brodart Company's McNaughton book rental program. This program provides patrons with a timely source for leisure reading.

The McNaughton collection is reviewed quarterly by the Acquisitions Librarian. At this time, books may be returned to Brodart or purchased and transferred into the LMC's circulating collection.

Unless there is an exceptional reason to do otherwise, fiction unrelated to class assignments will only be purchased if available through the McNaughton program.

Any greater commitment to fiction is beyond the mission of the LMC.

Children's literature is collected as it is considered class-related material for the Early Childhood Education program.

3. Study guides and workbooks

Study guides and workbooks will not be selected as they tend to be in formats that do not sustain repeated use.

4. Computer software

Computer software and interactive computerized learning materials will not be selected. (See Appendix A)

5. Government documents

United States government publications will be selected. Appropriate deposit accounts exist for this purpose. GPO catalogs are circulated among the Selection Committee. Additionally, Colorado state publications will be selected. Of particular interest are government publications that provide statistics on the economy, crime, poverty, industry, population and publications of current social concern.

6. Periodicals

Periodicals, including newspapers, are selected based on their relevance to the college programs, specific topics covered in program areas, and to provide support for class assignments. No multiple subscriptions of a title will be ordered due to funding constraints.

Highest priority is given to student needs. Specialized titles that are to be used for faculty or curriculum development that departments wish to have routed to staff should be purchased with departmental funds.

The Selection Committee reviews each new title request with the use of the Periodical Review Form (see Appendix B). At the same time, decisions are made for provision of backfiles.

Whenever possible, periodicals selected for the LMC's collection will be those that are indexed, either in a commercial index owned by the LMC, or as part of the publication itself. Non-indexed titles will be selected for the LMC only if they are essential to support a program need or student concern that cannot be filled by an indexed title. This stipulation applies to paid subscription and to complimentary (gift) subscriptions. Both paid and complimentary titles will be reviewed by the Selection Committee and approved by the Director before being added to the collection.

Backfiles of currently received, indexed periodicals are kept indefinitely. Microfilm is the preferred format. If an indexed title is unavailable on microfilm, backfiles will be bound. Volumes prepared for binding will be as complete as possible. Incomplete volumes will be bound after title-by-title approval of the Director. Backfiles of unindexed titles will be kept for two years and then weeded. Newspapers will be weeded more frequently because of space restrictions.

Backfiles of discontinued or cancelled unindexed titles will be weeded as soon as the subscription becomes inactive. Backfiles of suspended or cancelled indexed titles will be retained if the LMC has at least five years of backfiles. Indexed titles with holdings of fewer than five years will be weeded. Microfilm and bound copies of these titles will be weeded as well as the paper copies. Runs of less than five years of both indexed and unindexed titles may be retained if, 1) the title is of local interest or 2) the LMC's holdings constitute a complete run of a title that covers a subject important to the collection. LMC staff has the right to determine retention and/or disposal of individual titles.

All periodicals purchased with LMC funds are housed in the LMC without exception. Periodicals do not circulate to students. Photocopiers are available. Faculty and staff may check out periodicals on a limited basis, but periodicals will not be routed. Routing denies access to students, and periodicals are often lost.

9. Audiovisual

LMC staff will not actively select audiovisual materials, but rather will rely on input from faculty.

The preferred format is 1/2-inch VHS videocassette. Filmstrips, slides, cassettes and 16mm films can be accommodated. Musical recordings will be selected when requested in support of the Music Department. Musical scores will not be selected.

The LMC will not support teleconferences. This is the responsibility of either the Office of Off-Campus Credit/Distant Learning or the individual department that wishes to sponsor such an event. Similarly, the LMC will not purchase production rights, downloading rights or like fees unless the event is selected as an addition to the LMC collection for repeated-use instructional purposes.

United States copyright laws will be strictly followed. Materials will not be duplicated or recorded from a television broadcast without written permission from the producer. Materials will not be duplicated from one format to another (e.g., slides to videocassette) without written permission from the producer. Materials may be used only for educational purposes within this institution or at not-for-profit educational events presented by institutional personnel. Finally, illegal personal copies will not be broadcast from the LMC, nor will they be added to the LMC collection. Other situations require written permission from the producer. The laws will be interpreted by LMC staff as other copyright issues arise. A correspondence file is maintained in the office of the Acquisitions Librarian.

10. Atlases

A representative collection of the major world atlases in addition to United States and western regional atlases is maintained.

11. Pamphlets

Pamphlets are considered monographs under 80 pages in length and are collected for the Vertical File.

12. Phone books

Telephone books produced by the local telephone company are selected for a limited number of Colorado towns only. Commercially produced national business directories and local directories are also purchased.

13. Reserves

The intent of the Reserve collection is to increase students' access to heavily used materials, which may include supplemental reading or items unavailable or inappropriate for student purchase.

Items are placed in the Reserve collection upon the request of faculty. Both library and personal materials are accepted for Reserve. This may include realia, such as skeletons.

14. Reference

The reference collection consists of non-circulating ready-reference and bibliographic materials. The subject coverage of this portion of the LMC collection is not limited to the college curriculum.

Areas of collection intensity include music, biography, literature, medicine, hazardous substances and the sciences.

Selection is performed by the Selection Committee. The collection is weeded continually. Superseded volumes that are still current and heavily used may be put into the circulating collection or given to Larimer.

15. Indices

A small selection of both electronic and printed indices for science, business, health, literature and general studies is maintained. Decisions concerning indices are made by the Selection Committee.

G. Cooperation with other libraries

The LMC maintains institutional memberships with Central Colorado Library System (CCLS) and the Colorado Library Association (CLA). The LMC is an associate member of the Colorado Alliance of Research Libraries (CARL).

H. Duplicates/Multiple copies

Duplicate copies will not be purchased unless there is an extraordinary reason to do so. Duplicate copies currently in the collection should be pulled unless there is evidence that both copies circulate heavily. Pulled duplicates should be considered for Larimer.

I. Replacements, repairs, binding

Simple repairs can be performed in Technical Services. Books may be shipped to a bindery if damage is extensive and content merits the expense.

J. Weeding

Weeding is to be done on virtually a continual basis with the recognition that weeding is an integral part of active library collection maintenance. Weeding helps keep the collection accurate, timely, relevant to current college programs and student needs, and within the mission and changing goals of the library.

Projects will be initiated by the Acquisitions Librarian. Guidelines provided by the American Library Association and other national and local library authorities will be consulted closely in the formulation of these projects.

These guidelines will be modified where necessary to match the needs, goals and mission of this library in the context of the community college. Specifically, this library does not seek to maintain a comprehensive, research-level collection. Book selection criteria given above should be followed when weeding a subject area.

After books have been withdrawn, they are sorted for discard or for storage for a future booksale. Only those books that are popular will be retained for sale; the majority of books are discarded due to storage space and staff time constraints.

K. Gifts

All gifts to the LMC are accepted with the stipulation that gifts become LMC property. As such, books may be discarded, sold through a booksale, or added to either the Westminster or Larimer collection.

Each donor will receive a letter of thanks that states the number of books donated. The LMC will not appraise books for tax purpose because no one on the staff is qualified to do so.

L. Paperback vs. hardcover

Books will be selected in paperback format whenever possible. This action saves money, and students have shown that paperback have a shelflife comparable to hardbacks. (cite) Material in binders or notebooks will be avoided if possible because these formats deteriorate rapidly.

M. O.P. titles

Faculty are notified when requested materials are found to be out of print. Locating out of print materials is a low priority; however, a search is performed when requested.

N. Foreign language materials

Monographs are selected in English only. The LMC does supply current periodical reading material in languages and from countries that have been requested by the current student population. Currently, this includes Korean, Vietnamese, . . .

Additionally, the LMC strives to collect English/foreign language dictionaries for Western European languages and all languages represented by the current student population. Presently this population includes speakers of Vietnamese, Farsi, Arabic, Chinese, Thai, Cambodian and Lao. Student requests in this area are given high priority.

O. Booksale

The booksale is primarily a public relations event held annually if possible. Sale items consist of withdrawn books of interest to students and faculty and items that were donated but not added to the collection. Revenue is set aside for future book purchases.

P. Larimer

Materials that have been withdrawn as duplicates or superseded editions from the Westminster collection will be considered for addition to the Larimer collection.

Because of the geographical distance separating the two campuses and the large size of the student body, it is expected that both collections will contain some of the same titles.

Criteria for selection is much the same as it is for Westminster campus. The librarian at Larimer is responsible for selection. All Larimer faculty requests should be directed to this person.

Q. Budget allocation

Budget allocations are made by program area at the beginning of the fiscal year. Allocations are based loosely on college goals, collection strengths and weaknesses, and specific faculty requests. Because budgeting is a planning activity, these allocations are flexible and may change throughout the year.

R. Standing orders

Standing orders are maintained to ensure prompt delivery of certain desired items. These titles are reviewed annually by the Selection Committee to make sure that all purchases are appropriate.

PART 5

STANDARDS AND GUIDELINES ESTABLISHED BY THE AMERICAN LIBRARY ASSOCIATION THAT GOVERN COLLECTION DEVELOPMENT AND COLLECTION EVALUATION

GUIDE FOR WRITTEN COLLECTION POLICY STATEMENTS

AMERICAN LIBRARY ASSOCIATION
CHICAGO 1989

CONTENTS

PREFACE

The first edition of *Guidelines for the Formulation of Collection Development Policies* was written by Sheila Dowd, Thomas Shaughnessy, and Hans Weber. That 1979 edition of this guide drew on discussions in Collection Management and Development Committee meetings over a period of years; on review of a draft document at the 1977 Collection Development Preconference; and on responses to a draft version published in *Library Resources & Technical Services.*

The 1979 document, published as part of the book, *Guidelines for Collection Development,* served as the basis for discussion at the series of regional Collection Management and Development Institutes sponsored by the Committee since 1981. The Subcommittee on Guidelines for Collection Development, which is responsible for the present version, profited immensely from comments made at these forums.

When the Subcommittee was created in 1984, the urgency to revise the original guidelines was stimulated by librarians across the membership of the American Library Association. They had accepted the premises of the 1979 document but they were aware that a mere five years had created a multitude of changes in technique as well as changes in attitudes toward the value of written collection policy statements. In response, the Subcommittee made extensive use of recent literature on collection development policy statements and their role within a collection management program; the growing number of policy statements produced by many types of libraries; and the work of consortia and cooperative projects, including the

227

Research Libraries Group (RLG), the Association of Research Libraries' North American Collections Inventory Project (NCIP), and the Pacific Northwest Conspectus Database developed by Libraries and Information Resources in the Northwest with the support of the Fred Meyer Charitable Trust, as well as cooperative projects springing up across the country. The Subcommittee also benefited from other collection management guides and manuals produced by the ALA/RTSD Collection Management and Development Committee. And, finally, comments made at a hearing held in San Antonio at the 1988 ALA Midwinter Meeting helped to shape the guide into its final form.

Aware that use of the new guide will prompt further revision and refinement, the Subcommittee has asked the Collection Management and Development Committee to appoint a new group to work on a third edition. All users are encouraged to address queries and suggestions to this group via the Chair of the Collection Management and Development Committee.

1. INTRODUCTION

1.1.   Purpose
    This guide is intended to help librarians who carry out collection development and management programs to write collection policy statements that serve as planning, informational, administrative, and training documents and that further the systematic, rational, and timely selection and deselection of library materials. Because collection policies play an important role in the implementation of coordinated collection development and cooperative collection management arrangements among libraries, this guide prescribes language and measures that promote mutual comprehensibility and comparability of documents guiding such programs.

1.2.   Objectives
    The aims of this document are identification of the essential elements of a written statement of policy

for collection management and development and establishment of a standard terminology and structure for use in preparing comparable policies.

1.3. Need

Every library collection is established for one or more definite purposes. A collection development and management program organizes and directs the processes of acquiring materials, integrating them into coherent collections, managing their growth and maintenance, and deselecting them when appropriate in a cost- and user-beneficial way. Formal planning processes and statements documenting selection and collection development practice are necessary for a number of external reasons: the growth in size and complexity of the publishing universe; fiscal pressures that affect the purchasing power of libraries; and increasing expectations of accountability to library governing boards. Within a library, there is a need to coordinate collection management functions and activities shared by a number of individuals, e.g., planning, analysis or evaluation, selection, and review of collections for preservation, storage, and discard.

The ALA/RTSD Collection Management and Development Committee publishes a series of guides that review the issues and strategies needed to carry out a variety of collection management tasks. Central to their implementation is a written collection policy that clearly describes the library's objectives in developing its collections and the extent to which it has realized those objectives. Additionally, budgetary considerations, the growth of interlibrary cooperation, and expanding service networks have given impetus to the analysis of collection activity in standardization terms. Eventually the full range of collection management functions may be implemented on a broader, geographically and institutionally dispersed scale through formal and informal arrangements for

coordinated and cooperative collection development and management.

Scope
This document will aid librarians at institutions of
all kinds and sizes in formulating statements of
their collection development policies. All elements of the guide may not be equally applicable
to every library. Local variations in policy statements should be planned carefully to describe
local conditions and yet meet the goal of interlibrary comparability and compatibility.

This guide does not address the organizational
environment or planning process used within
libraries in drafting a collection policy statement.
However, examples of data-gathering worksheets
are provided as Appendix 1, sources of published
collection policy documents are provided in Appendix 2, and works that describe and recommend
processes are listed in the Bibliography.

Audience
This guide is designed to assist library administrators and collection development librarians in the
production of a document that serves as both a
planning tool and a communication device. The
resulting policy statement should clarify collection
development objectives to staff, users, cooperating
institutions, funding authorities, and governing
boards. It should enable them to understand the
collection, anticipate what it may or may not contain, and identify levels of strength and weakness in
specific areas of their library collections. The policy
facilitates the coordination of collection development and cooperative services within a single library system or within a geographic region.

Assumptions
**A written collection policy statement is for any
library a necessary tool that:**

(a) defines the scope of existing collections and maps plans for future development of collections (both formats and subjects included and excluded) for library staff, users, administrators, and trustees;

(b) describes collection management and development practice in a systematic way;

(c) provides collection management and development librarians with the means to ensure consistency in the selection and deselection processes, to shape more responsive collections and to use funds more wisely;

(d) provides a yardstick against which to measure progress toward meeting collection goals, using the collection evaluation techniques outlined in the Committee's *Guide in the Evaluation of Library Collections;*

(e) serves as a source of information for librarians with new collection development responsibilities;

(f) fosters better communication between individual collection development librarians;

(g) provides information fundamental to external and internal budgetary preparation and allocation processes;

(h) serves as the basis for identifying areas suitable for interlibrary cooperative collection development;

(i) documents areas in which cooperative programs exist;

(j) establishes useful priorities to guide cataloging, retrospective conversion, and preservation decisions;

(k) provides information on the library's commitment to intellectual freedom.

1.6.2. A library's policies for preservation, for identification of works that may be removed to remote storage locations or discarded, and for cooperative collection development should be coordinated with or incorporated in its collection policy. Libraries should refer to the *Guide to the Evaluation of Library Collections* and the forthcoming *Guide to Review of Collections: Preservation, Storage and Withdrawal* for guidance in developing these policies and meeting their goals.

1.6.3. It is desirable that the form and terminology of collection policy statements be standardized to permit comparison between institutions. This guide adopts a prescriptive approach in that it urges adoption, minimally, of the Elements of a Collection Policy Statement (2.2) and, when using the conspectus approach, the Collection Levels (2.2.3.2) and Language Codes (2.2.3.3).

1.6.4. Librarians acknowledge the impossibility of building totally comprehensive collections and recognize the need for determining which materials should be available on-site in the library's permanent collections and which may be obtained through other means, e.g., resource sharing and other (sometimes commercial) document delivery systems.

2. GUIDE

Principles governing formulation and application of collection policies

Libraries express the long- and short-range needs of their clientele in the form of collection policy statements. These statements guide the development and management of collections. They also serve as the basis for budgetary decision making including establishment of priorities for the allocation of resources.

Collection policy statements should be reviewed at intervals to verify that existing collection goals are being met and to insure that changes in defined goals and user needs are recognized. Staff should be assigned responsibility for regular review and updating.

A library's collection policy statement should be coordinated with those of appropriate other libraries, whether in a hierarchy of dependence or in a division of responsibilities among equals. This will help librarians to select or deselect materials and to assign preservation and cataloging priorities within the context of local, regional, national, or international needs and resources.

Libraries document their collection policies in three ways: using the conspectus approach, a combination of conspectus data and narrative statements, or narrative statements alone.

The conspectus approach has become the standard tool for coordinating collection development and is based upon the library's classification system. To be most useful, data gathered should ultimately be related to the Library of Congress Classification (LCC). Acceptable alternatives to use of the Research Libraries Group/NCIP Conspectus are provided below.

Narrative statements are useful to local librarians and library clientele. These statements may be based upon subject divisions within the library or, for academic or special libraries, upon the several organizational units whose work is supported by the library. When a library determines that the conspectus approach alone does not meet its needs, it is recommended that conspectus data be incorporated in narrative statements. Libraries wishing to express conspectus data in narrative form or choosing not to adopt the conspectus approach should use the narrative format described in 2.2.4.

Elements of a collection policy statement

Introduction to the policy statement

This section of a collection policy statement describes the context of a library's collection management and development programs, lists the mission and goals of the program, and summarizes basic principles common to all aspects of the program.

It includes the following:

A. Purpose of the policy statement and audience to whom it is directed.
B. General description of institution and clientele to be served.
C. Mission statement and goals of collection management and development program.
D. The library's official stance on intellectual freedom and censorship issues.
E. Brief overview of collection:
   1. History of collection;
   2. Broad subject areas emphasized or de-emphasized;
   3. Collection locations.
F. Organization of collection management and development program:
   1. Staffing;
   2. Liaison with user groups.
G. Relationship to policies and programs for the management of collections, such as: preservation, storage, replacement, and deselection.
H. Cooperative collection development agreements.

2.2.2. General collection management and development policies

This section of a collection policy statement describes general policies that transcend subject boundaries and govern the collection of material by format, language, or use.

A. Format of material:
   1. Books
   2. Periodicals
   3. Newspapers
   4. Textbooks
   5. Reprints
   6. Dissertations and theses
   7. Paperbacks
   8. Microforms
   9. Maps
   10. Pamphlets
   11. Art works

    12. Posters
    13. Musical scores
    14. Audio and visual material
    15. Computer software
    16. Electronic formats
    17. Children's materials
    18. Other
B. Special collections of rare books, manuscripts, realia, or archival material.
C. Languages and translations.
D. Local authors' publications.
E. Popular versus scholarly works.
F. Multiple copies.
G. Reserve material.
H. Reference works.
I. Government publications.
J. Acquisition procedures affecting collections policies:
    1. Standing orders;
    2. Approval plans and blanket orders;
    3. Gifts and exchanges.
K. Expensive purchases.

Detailed analysis of subject collections

This section of the policy describes the breadth and depth of subject collections in a standard, uniform, and detailed manner.

Conspectus approach

It is strongly recommended that the conspectus approach to collection evaluation and description be used by libraries of all sizes and that either the Research Libraries Group (RLG) or the Pacific Northwest Conspectus Database (PNW) worksheets be used or adapted. Sample worksheets are included in Appendix I.

    The subject fields used should be those defined by RLG or PNW. The RLG fields are based on the Library of

Congress Classification system (LCC) and are currently being used by the North American Collections Inventory Project (NCIP). Libraries may choose, instead, to adopt the subject fields and worksheets used to compile the Pacific Northwest Conspectus Database, originally developed by Library and Information Resources for the Northwest (LIRN). These worksheets are available at two levels of specificity: the Subject level parallels closely the RLG Conspectus' 3,500 subject fields, while the Category level parallels the National Shelflist Count's more general 500 categories. Smaller libraries may find the Category level most satisfactory for describing their collections. The Pacific Northwest model for conspectus completion permits use of Subject level treatment for some segments of a collection and the Category level for others. This model is being adopted and adapted by many libraries and groups of libraries across the United States.

Libraries using the Dewey Decimal Classification (DDC) or other non-LC classification system may wish to organize the collection descriptions in their policy statements according to their chosen classification. Currently, no satisfactory conversion tables are available, although the LIRN program has developed Dewey Decimal Classification worksheets at both the Subject and Category levels for the Pacific Northwest Conspectus Database. Until tables satisfactorily converting DDC subject fields to LCC are developed, those libraries using DDC will find comparison of their collections with those in libraries using LCC imprecise, even though an analysis using DDC or other classification system may be useful for collection comparison with peer libraries. Several large libraries with collections classified by one or more system other than LCC have satisfactorily used the RLG Conspectus subject divisions.

For each subject category, defined by classification range and subject descriptors, existing collection strength, current collecting intensity and, when the library wishes, desired collecting intensity are described using the collection intensity levels codes in the following section. Languages collected are also described using codes shown below. In addition, scope notes are used to describe special features of the collection, e.g., chronological and geographical parameters, specific subject emphases unique to the institution, and inclusion/exclusion boundaries. Further, library staff responsible for the analysis and development of specific subject collections should be identified. Sample worksheets for the detailed subject analysis section of the policy are found in the Appendixes.

2.2.3.2. Collection levels: Codes, labels, and definitions
The codes in labels, and definitions listed in figure 1 provide an objective method for describing the relative sizes and natures of library holdings in specific subjects. They were developed by the Subcommittee with reference to definitions used by the Research Libraries Group for its Conspectus Online. The "a" and "b" subdivisions of levels 1 through 3 are acceptable expansions of the basic codes and may be especially useful to small libraries.

Existing conspectus databases and worksheets provide for use of commentary on collections in a variety of ways. The RLG database provides three avenues for doing so: Scope Notes are used to make general observations on collections that cut across categories and subjects at the Division and Category level; the Comments field allows libraries to describe particular strengths or limits of a subject collection or collecting activity and to cite special collections at the Subject level; the Preservation Scope Note is used to describe preservation projects encompassing subject areas rather than individual titles. The PNW database also provides a Comments field to be used for the same purposes as RLG Scope Notes and Comments.

Assistance in application of the definitions to collections may be obtained by use of Supplemental Guidelines prepared by RLG member libraries. These subject-oriented documents define the size and nature of a specific discipline's literature. They suggest bibliographies to use in collection evaluation. Ownership of specified proportions of titles in these standard bibliographies help identify the specific level that characterizes the collection.

1	MINIMAL	Very little collecting is done, and items are systematically reviewed for currency of information. Superseded editions are withdrawn.
1a	MINIMAL LEVEL, UNEVEN COVER-AGE	Few selections are made, and there is unsystematic representation of subject.
1b	MINIMAL LEVEL, EVEN COVER-AGE	Few selections are made, but basic authors, some core works, or a spectrum of ideological views are represented.

2	BASIC INFORMA-TION LEVEL	A selective collection of materials that serves to introduce and define a subject and to indicate the varieties of information available elsewhere. It may include dictionaries, encyclopedias, access to appropriate bibliographic databases, selected editions of important works, historical surveys, bibliographies, handbooks, and a few major periodicals. The collection is frequently and systematically reviewed for currency of information.
2a	BASIC INFORMA-TION LEVEL, IN-TRODUCTORY	The emphasis at this level is on providing resources that introduce and define a subject. A collection at this level includes basic reference tools and explanatory works, such as textbooks; historical descriptions of the subject's development; general works devoted to major topics and

figures in the field; and selective major periodicals.

The introductory level of a basic information collection is only sufficient to support patrons attempting to locate general information about a subject or students enrolled in introductory level courses.

2b	BASIC INFORMATION LEVEL, ADVANCED	At the advanced level, basic information about a subject is provided on a wider range of topics and with more depth. There is a broader selection of basic explanatory works, historical descriptions, reference tools, and periodicals that serve to introduce and define a subject.

An advanced basic information level is sufficient to support students in basic courses as well as supporting the basic information needs of patrons in public and special libraries.

3	STUDY OR INSTRUCTIONAL SUPPORT LEVEL	A collection that is adequate to impart and maintain knowledge about a subject in a systematic way but at a level of less than research intensity. The collection includes a wide range of basic works in appropriate formats, a significant number of classic retrospective materials, complete collections of the works of more important writers, selections from the works of secondary writers, a selection of representative journals, access to appropriate machine-readable data files, and the reference tools and fundamental bibliographical apparatus pertaining to the subject.

At the study or instructional support level, a collection is adequate to support independent study and most learning needs of the clientele of public and special libraries, as well as undergraduate and some graduate instruction. The collection is systematically reviewed for currency of information and to assure that essential and significant information is retained.

3a	STUDY OR IN-STRUCTIONAL SUPPORT LEVEL, INTRODUCTORY	This subdivision of a level 3 collection provides resources adequate for imparting and maintaining knowledge about the basic primary topics of a subject area. The collection includes a broad range of basic works in appropriate formats, classic retrospective materials, all key journals on primary topics, selected journals and seminal works on secondary topics, access to appropriate machine-readable data files, and the reference tools and fundamental bibliographical apparatus pertaining to the subject. This subdivision of level 3 supports undergraduate courses, including advanced undergraduate courses, as well as more independent study needs of the clientele of public and special libraries. It is not adequate to support master's degree programs.
3b	STUDY OR IN-STRUCTIONAL SUPPORT LEVEL, ADVANCED	The advanced subdivision of level 3 provides resources adequate for imparting and maintaining knowledge about the primary and secondary topics of a subject area. The collection includes a significant number of seminal works and journals on the primary and secondary topics in the field; a significant number of retrospective materials; a substantial col-

lection of works by secondary figures; works that provide more in-depth discussions of research, techniques, and evaluation; access to appropriate machine-readable data files; and reference tools and fundamental bibliographic apparatus pertaining to the subject.

This level supports all courses of undergraduate study and master's degree programs as well as the more advanced independent study needs of the patrons of public and special libraries.

4	RESEARCH LEVEL	A collection that includes the major published source materials required for dissertation and independent research, including materials containing research reporting, new findings, scientific experimental results, and other information useful to researchers. It is intended to include all important reference works and a wide selection of specialized monographs, as well as a very extensive collection of journals and major indexing and abstracting services in the field. Pertinent foreign language materials are included. Older material is usually retained for historical research and actively preserved. A collection at this level supports doctoral and other original research.
5	COMPREHEN-SIVE LEVEL	A collection in which a library endeavors, so far as it is reasonably possible, to include all significant works of recorded knowledge (publications, manuscripts, other forms), in

all applicable languages, for a necessarily defined and limited field. The level of collection intensity is one that maintains a "special collection"; the aim, if not the achievement, is exhaustiveness. Old material is retained for historical research with active preservation efforts.

Figure 1. Conspectus levels: codes, labels and definitions.

Language codes and definitions

Language codes indicate the language priorities and limitations that govern a library's collecting policies in a given subject. As in the case of the collection level rating, language coverage must be assessed against the universe of resources in the subject. For each collection level assigned, a language code is also assigned.

Label	**Definition**
English	English language material predominates; little or no foreign language material is in the collection.
Selected non-English Language	Selected other language material is included in addition to the English language material.
Wide Selection Languages	Wide selection of material in all applicable languages. No programmatic decision is made to restrict materials according to language.
One non-English Language	Material is primarily in one non-English language. The overall focus is on collecting material in the vernacular of the area.

To facilitate use of the RLG Conspectus by Canadian libraries, the following personal codes were developed by the Canadian Association of Research Libraries. Since 1986 these codes have been used by Quebec libraries.

French	French language predominates. Little or no material in languages other than French is collected.
English/French	English and French materials predominate. Little or no material in languages other than English or French is collected.
Selected non-English	Selected non-English material included in addition to English material.
Selected non-French	Selected non-French material included in addition to French material.
Selected Other Languages	Selected other language material included in addition to English and French.

Since conspectus work is embraced internationally by libraries using other languages for primary collecting, it is anticipated that further adaptations of language s will emerge.

2.2.3.4. Narrative statements

Libraries that choose to document collection policies with narrative statements organized by broad subject descriptor or academic program should include at least the following categories of information about each subject:

A. Purpose or objectives—describes the program or clientele needs met by this segment of the collection.

B. Scope of coverage—describes three characteristics of the collection:

    1. Languages collected and excluded (may be expressed by using codes in 2.2.3.3 above).

    2. Geographical areas covered by the collection in terms of intellectual content or publication sources or both and specific areas excluded, as appropriate.

3. Chronological periods covered by the collection in terms of intellectual content, movements or schools, and specific periods excluded, as appropriate.
4. Chronological periods collected in terms of publication date and specific periods excluded, as appropriate.

C. Types of material (forms) collected in terms of:
1. inclusions;
2. exclusions.

D. Subject description in terms of the library's classification scheme and subject descriptors and, where needed, narrower subject delineations than afforded by the classification scheme. Each subject should be characterized by the collecting level codes prescribed in 2.2.3.2 above.

E. Library unit or selector responsible for this collection. Libraries may wish to provide other categories of useful local information. Such categories might include:
1. Interdisciplinary relationships (between the subject being treated and other segments of the library collection development program or between client populations, such as academic departments).
2. Other resources, including local, regional, or national libraries, other types of organizations and consortial relationships.
3. Policies for (a) purchasing journal article reprints "on demand" for distribution to library patrons without retention of the physical item in the library's permanent collection and (b) other options for acquiring access to information.
4. Other factors so diverse and of such local importance that it would be impossible to specify them here.

2.2.4.   Detailed analysis of special collections
In some libraries, additional policy statements may be written to treat extensive collections of material by their form or location. Policy govern-

ing these collections may differ from policy for subject collections. Some examples of collections for which special policy statements may be needed include:

A. Newspapers
B. Microforms
C. Reference collections
D. Branch library collections
E. Government publications
F. Maps and atlases
G. Archival material
H. Audio and visual material
 I. Computer software
 J. Electronic formats
K. Vertical files
L. Children's materials

Where possible, information about special collections should be incorporated in the detailed subject analyses described in sections 2.2.3.1 and 2.2.3.4 above. However, with some collections it will be useful to use another primary arrangement. For example, a special policy statement for an extensive map collection might be arranged by "general maps," "topographic maps," "raised relief maps," etc., with subdivision by area classification. Elements that should be considered in preparing special collections policy statements are provided in 2.2.3.4 above.

Indexes

Because the information in the collection policy may be used for a wide variety of purposes, an index should be appended correlating policies to user groups, specific programs, and key words and concepts. Libraries using both the conspectus approach and narrative statements should cross-reference classification segments and subject descriptors used as statement titles.

APPENDIXES

1. Conspectus Subject Headings and Worksheets

Research Libraries Group/NCIP Conspectus subject headings

Information about purchase of the manual, worksheets, and software (with hardware specifications) is available from: Association for Research Libraries, Office of Management Services, 1527 New Hampshire Avenue, N.W., Washington, D.C. 20036.

Division Level Subject Headings:

1. Agriculture
2. Art and Architecture
3. Cartographic Materials
4. East Asian Studies
5. Economics and Sociology
6. Education
7. Government Documents
8. History and Auxiliary Sciences of History
9. Law
10. Library and Information Science
11. Linguistics, Languages, and Literature
12. Medicine and Health Science
13. Music
14. Natural History and Biology
15. Philosophy and Religion
16. Physical Geography and Earth Sciences

17. Physical Sciences
18. Political Science
19. Psychology
20. South Asian Studies
21. Technology

A sample RLG Conspectus worksheet is shown in figure 2. Pacific Northwest Conspectus Database subject headings Information about purchase of the manual, worksheets, and software (with hardware specifications) is available from: Project Director, Pacific NW Collection Development Program, State Library Building, Salem, OR 97310-0642; (503) 378-5082.
Division Level Subject Headings:

1. Agriculture
2. Anthropology
3. Art and Architecture
4. Biological Sciences
5. Business and Economics
6. Chemistry
7. Computer Science
8. Education
9. Engineering and Technology
10. Geography and Earth Science
11. History and Auxiliary Sciences
12. Language, Linguistics, and Literature
13. Law
14. Library Science
15. Mathematics
16. Medicine
17. Music
18. Performing Arts
19. Philosophy and Religion
20. Physical Education and Recreation
21. Physical Sciences
22. Political Science
23. Psychology
24. Sociology

RLG CONSPECTUS WORKSHEET

VERSION: 3

ART AND ARCHITECTURE

INSTITUTION:

LC CLASS		SUBJECT GROUP	COLLECTION LEVELS AND LANGUAGE COVERAGE		COMMENTS
			ECS	CCI	
		VISUAL ARTS IN GENERAL			
N61-72, N75	ART1	Theory, Philosophy, Ethics			
N7475-7483	ART2	Art Criticism			
N7810-8199	ART3	Special Subjects in Art—Christian Religious Art			
N8190	ART4	Special Subjects in Art—Non-Christian Religious Art			
N7760-7763	ART5	Special Subjects in Art—Mythology			
N7626	ART6	Special Subjects in Art—Secular Art			
N7575-7624	ART7	Special Subjects in Art—Portraits			
N8210	ART8	Special Subjects in Art—Historical Subjects			
N8213-8214	ART9	Special Subjects in Art—Landscape			
N8217-8266	ART10	Special Subjects in Art—Other (specify)			
N81-390	ART11	Study and Teaching (excluding technique)			
N8350-8356	ART12	Art as a Profession			
N8510-8553	ART13	Art Studios, Materials, Etc.			

Sample Pacific Northwest Conspectus Database worksheets (LCC) are shown in figures 3 and 4.
Sample Pacific Northwest Conspectus Database worksheets (DDC) are shown in figures 5 and 6.

2. Sources of Published Collection Policies

Rather than list citations of individual libraries whose collection policy statements are available for purchase or loan and risk missing references to excellent documents that serve as useful examples of the principles recommended in this guide, the Subcommittee has chosen to offer the sources from which such citations can be obtained:

Library Literature (New York: H.W. Wilson Co.)
Resources in Education / RIE (Washington: Educational Resources Information Center) or ERIC (online database)
American Library Association, Headquarters Library
In addition, information on libraries that have prepared conspectus documents can be obtained from:
Association of Research Libraries
Office of Management Services
1527 New Hampshire Avenue, NW
Washington, D.C. 20036
Pacific Northwest Collection Development Program
Project Director
State Library Building
Salem, OR 97310-0642
Research Libraries Group, Inc.
1200 Villa Street
Mountain View, CA 94041-1100

PACIFIC NORTHWEST CONSPECTUS WORKSHEET - LC

Library:

Date:

By:

Division: ART AND ARCHITECTURE

LC CLASS	LINE NUMBER	DIVISION and CATEGORIES	COLLECTION & LANGUAGE CODES			COMMENTS
			CL	AC	GL	
	ART000	ART AND ARCHITECTURE				
AM	ART001	Museums, Collectors & Collecting				
N1-9211	ART009	Visual Arts in General				
NA1-9425	ART111	Architecture				
NB1-1190	ART144	Sculpture				
NC1-1855	ART151	Graphic Arts, Drawing, Design				
ND1-3416	ART159	Painting				
NE1-2890	ART197	Print Media (Printmaking, Engraving)				
NK600-9955	ART205	Decorative Arts, Applied Arts				
NX280-589	ART223	Arts in General				
TR1-1045	ART250	Photography				
TT	ART266	Handicrafts, Arts & Crafts				

PACIFIC NORTHWEST CONSPECTUS WORKSHEET - LC

Library:
Date:
By:

Division: ART AND ARCHITECTURE

LC CLASS	LINE NUMBER	DIVISION, CATEGORIES and SUBJECTS	COLLECTION & LANGUAGE CODES			COMMENTS
			CL	AC	GL	
	ART000	ART AND ARCHITECTURE				
AM	ART001	*Museums, Collectors & Collecting*				
AM-9	ART002	General Works				
AM10-100	ART003	Description & History of Museums by Country				
AM101	ART004	Description & History of Individual Museums				
AM111-160	ART005	Museology, Museum Methods, Techniques, etc.				
AM200-237	ART006	Collectors & Collecting, Private Cabinets, etc.				
AM301-396	ART007	Collectors & Collecting, by Region or Country				
AM401	ART008	Individual Heterogeneous Collections				

Division: ART AND ARCHITECTURE

Library:
Date: By:

LC CLASS	LINE NUMBER	DIVISION and CATEGORIES	COLLECTION & LANGUAGE CODES			COMMENTS
			CL	AC	GL	
N1-9211	ART009	*Visual Arts in General*				
N61-72	ART009.5	Theory, Philosophy, Ethics				
N81-390	ART010	Study & Teaching				
N400-5098	ART011	Special Museums, Galleries, etc.				
N510-880	ART012	Special Museums, Galleries—United States				
N908-910	ART013	Special Museums, Galleries—Other American Cities				
N1010-3690	ART014	Special Museums, Galleries—Europe				
N3720-3730	ART015	Special Museums, Galleries—India				
N3735	ART016	Special Museums, Galleries—Japan				

Reproduced with the permission of Pacific Northwest Collection Development Program

Figure 4. Sample worksheet for the Library of Congress Classification available for use at the Division, Categories and Subjects level.

PACIFIC NORTHWEST CONSPECTUS WORKSHEET - Dewey

Library:
Date:
By:

Division: ART AND ARCHITECTURE

Dewey CLASS	LINE NUMBER	DIVISION and CATEGORIES	COLLECTION & LANGUAGE CODES			COMMENTS
			CL	AC	GL	
	ARD000	ART AND ARCHITECTURE				
700	ARD010	*Fine & Decorative Arts*				
710	ARD020	*Civic & Landscape Art*				
720	ARD030	*Architecture*				
730	ARD040	*Plastic Arts—Sculpture*				
740	ARD050	*Drawing, Decorative, Minor Arts*				
750	ARD060	*Painting & Paintings*				
760	ARD070	*Graphic Arts, Printmaking & Prints*				
770	ARD080	*Photography & Photographs*				

Reproduced with the permission of Pacific Northwest Collection Development Program

Figure 5. Sample worksheet for the Dewey Decimal Classification available for use at the Division and Categories level.

PACIFIC NORTHWEST CONSPECTUS WORKSHEET—Dewey

Library:
Date: By:

Division: ART AND ARCHITECTURE

Dewey CLASS	LINE NUMBER	DIVISION, CATEGORIES and SUBJECTS	COLLECTION & LANGUAGE CODES			COMMENTS
			CL	AC	GL	
	ARD000	ART AND ARCHITECTURE				
700	ARD010	*Fine & Decorative Arts*				
701	ARD011	Philosophy & Theory of Fine & Decorative Arts				
702	ARD012	Miscellany of Fine & Decorative Arts				
703	ARD013	Dictionaries, Encyclopedias, Concordances				
704	ARD014	Special Topics of General Applicability				
705	ARD015	Serial Publications				
706	ARD016	Organizations & Management				
707	ARD017	Study & Teaching				
708	ARD018	Galleries, Museums, Private Collections				
709	ARD019	Historical & Geographical Treatment				

DDC	ARD Code	Subject			
710	ARD020	*Civic & Landscape Art*			
711	ARD021	Area Planning			
711.1	ARD021.1	Procedural & Social Aspects			
711.2	ARD021.2	International & National, Plans & Planning			
711.3	ARD021.3	Interstate, State, Prov., County Plans & Planning			
711.4	ARD021.4	Local Community Plans & Planning			
711.5	ARD021.5	Plans & Planning for Specific Kinds of Areas			

(Adapted from RLG Conspectus Worksheet Form)

Reproduced with the permission of Pacific Northwest Collection Development Program
Figure 6. Sample worksheet for the Dewey Decimal Classification available for use at the Division, Categories and Subjects level.

GUIDELINES FOR COLLECTION DEVELOPMENT

AMERICAN LIBRARY ASSOCIATION
CHICAGO 1979

CONTENTS

PREFACE

The Collection Development Committee of the Resources Section, Resources and Technical Services Division, American Library Association, was organized to provide a focus in ALA for activities relating to collection development, and, in particular, to: study the present resources of American libraries and the coordination of collection development programs; develop guidelines for the definition of selection policies; evaluate and recommend selection tools for collection development; and recommend qualifications and requisite training for selection personnel. In partial response to these charges, the Committee at its New York meeting of 9 July 1974 appointed task forces comprised of committee members and consultants to prepare guidelines for the following collection development activities: formula budgeting and allocation; the formulation of collection development policies; the development of review programs designed to assist in the solution of space problems; and the description and evaluation of library collections. The guidelines presented here are the result of the work of these task groups. The format and numbering system used in these guidelines have been taken from the American Library Association's Committee on Standards' *ALA Standards Manual* (1976).

Thomas Shaughnessy, Hans Weber, and Sheila Dowd (Chair) prepared *Guidelines for the Formulation of Collection Development Policies.* The *Guidelines* were submitted to the Committee for revision at its meetings of January and July 1975; they were further revised at the Committee's meeting of 19 January 1976 when they were approved for submission to the Executive Committee of the Resources Section. A "preliminary edition," dated March

1976, was approved by the Executive Committee on 19 July 1976 and approved by the Board of Directors of RTSD by a mail ballot in August 1976. The preliminary *Guidelines* appeared in the winter 1977 issue of *Library Resources and Technical Services* (vol. 21, no. 1, pp. 40–46). The version of the *Guidelines* appearing herein is a revision of the *LRTS* draft, which was approved by the RTSD Board of Directors by a mail ballot during the fall of 1978.

Task force members George B. Miller, Jr. (Chair) and Robert W. Butler, with George S. Bonn and Paul Mosher as consultants, prepared *Guidelines for the Evaluation of the Effectiveness of Library Collections.*

Guidelines for the Review of Library Collections was prepared by a task force initially consisting of David Zubatsky and David Perkins and subsequently revised by David Perkins and Paul Mosher. After their approval by the Collection Development Committee, and by the Resources Section Board, both *Guidelines for the Evaluation of the Effectiveness of Library Collections* and *Guidelines for the Review of Library Collections* were approved by the RTSD Board of Directors by a mail ballot during the fall of 1978.

Jean Coberly; Jean Boyer Hamlin; and Elaine Sloan, consultant, wrote *Guidelines for the Allocation of Library Materials Budgets.* This was approved by the Collection Development Committee and the Resources Section Board during the fall of 1978 by mail ballots and by the RTSD Board of Directors at the 1979 Midwinter meeting.

The bibliography on Collection Development Policies was compiled by the 1978 Program-organizing Committee of the Southern California Chapter of the Collection Development Librarian's Chapter of the California Library Association. This bibliography was attached because it lists and annotates important sources. The other bibliographies were compiled by the task groups that drafted guidelines, and the sources listed constituted important elements in the process of guideline formulation.

GUIDELINES FOR THE FORMULATION OF COLLECTION DEVELOPMENT POLICIES

1. INTRODUCTION

1.1   Purpose.

The Committee offers these *Guidelines for the Formulation of Collection Development Policies* in the belief that collection development policy statements must be comprehensible and comparable if they are to prove useful in the implementation of long-range goals for sharing of resources. To promote comprehensibility and comparability, policy statements must employ language that is clearly defined, and measures whose values are commonly understood.

1.2   Objectives.

The immediate aims of the designers of these *Guidelines* are to identify the essential elements of a written statement of collection development policy, and to establish a standard terminology and structure for use in the preparation of such policies.

1.3   Need.

Widespread budgetary constraints and the growth of interlibrary cooperation for shared resources and service networks have given impetus to the pressure to analyze collection activity in universally comprehensible terms.

1.4   Scope.
The Committee has attempted to provide an instrument that will be of use to libraries of all kinds and sizes in formulating statements of their collection development policies. All elements of the *Guidelines,* however, will not be equally applicable to all libraries.

1.5   Audience.
The *Guidelines* are intended to help library administrators and collection development librarians to produce a document that can serve as both a planning tool and a communications device. The resulting policy statements should clarify collection development objectives to staff, users, and cooperating institutions, enabling them to identify areas of strength in library collections; and by this means should facilitate the coordination of collection development and cooperative services within an area or region. The policy statement can itself serve as a communication to some audiences. For other selected audiences, among them library users, funding authorities, and governing boards, the statement should be reviewed as the data file from which interpretative statements can be formulated.

1.6   Methodology.
The *Guidelines* have been submitted to the Committee in open meeting at several Midwinter and Annual Conferences. The group discussions, in which numerous visitors have participated, have resulted in extensive revisions of the initial drafts.

1.7   Assumptions.

1.7.1 A written collection development policy statement is for any library a desirable tool that: (a) enables selectors to work with greater consistency toward defined goals, thus shaping stronger collections and using funds more wisely; (b) informs library staff, users, administrators, trustees, and others as to the scope and nature of existing collections, and the plans for continuing development of resources; (c) provides information that will assist in the budgetary allocation process.

1.7.2 A library's policy for deselection (that is, identification of works that may be removed to remote storage locations or discarded) should be coordinated with its collection development policy. (See below *Guidelines for the Review of Library Collections.*)

1.7.3 It is desirable that form and terminology of collection development policy statements be sufficiently standardized to permit comparison between institutions.

1.7.4 Libraries have acknowledged the impossibility of building totally comprehensive collections, and will increasingly need to rely on cooperative activities. Collection development policy statements will assist cooperative collection building, and will also be of value to users and user-service units in locating materials.

1.8 Definitions.

1.8.1 Levels of collection density and collecting intensity.

1.8.1.1 Assumptions.
Definitions of collecting levels are not to be applied in a relative or *ad hoc* manner (that is, relative to a given library or group of libraries), but in a very objective manner. Consequently, it is quite likely that a large number of libraries will not hold comprehensive collections in any area. Similarly, academic libraries that do not support doctoral programs, or other types of libraries that are not oriented toward special research, may not have any collections that would fall within the research level as defined herein. The definitions are proposed to describe a range and diversity of titles and forms of materials; they do not address the ques-

tion of availability of multiple copies of the same title.

1.8.1.2 Codes.

The codes defined below are designed for use in identifying both the extent of existing collections in given subject fields (collection density) and the extent of current collecting activity in the field (collecting intensity).

A. Comprehensive level. A collection in which a library endeavors, so far as is reasonably possible, to include all significant works of recorded knowledge (publications, manuscripts, other forms) for a necessarily defined field. This level of collecting intensity is that which maintains a "special collection"; the aim, if not the achievement, is exhaustiveness.

B. Research level. A collection that includes the major published source materials required for dissertations and independent research, including materials containing research reporting, new findings, scientific experimental results, and other information useful to researchers. It also includes all important reference works and a wide selection of specialized monographs, as well as an extensive collection of journals and major indexing and abstracting services in the field.

C. Study level. A collection that supports undergraduate or graduate course work, or sustained independent study; that is, which is adequate to maintain knowledge of a subject required for limited or generalized purposes, of less than research intensity. It includes a wide range of basic monographs, complete collections of the works of important writers, selections from the works of secondary writers, a selection of representative journals, and the reference tools and fundamental bibliographical apparatus pertaining to the subject.

NOTE: Some college librarians have expressed a need for further refinement of the "Study level" code for use by libraries without comprehensive or research level collections to enable them to define their collecting policies explicitly enough to meet the needs of network resources planning. We include the following optional subcodes for such institutions.

(1) Advanced study level. A collection that is adequate to support the course work of advanced undergraduate and master's degree programs, or sustained independent study; that is, which is adequate to maintain knowledge of a subject required for limited or generalized purposes, of less than research intensity. It includes a wide range of basic monographs both current and retrospective, complete collections of the works of more important writers, selections from the works of secondary writers, a selection of representative journals, and the reference tools and fundamental bibliographical apparatus pertaining to the subject.

(2) Initial study level. A collection that is adequate to support undergraduate courses. It includes a judicious selection from currently published basic monographs (as are represented by *Choice* selections) supported by seminal retrospective monographs (as are represented by *Books for College Libraries*); a broad selection of works of more important writers; a selection of the most significant works of secondary writers; a selection of the major review journals; and current editions of the most significant reference tools and bibliographies pertaining to the subject.

D. Basic level. A highly selective collection that serves to introduce and define the subject and to indicate the varieties of information available elsewhere. It includes major dictionaries and encyclopedias, selected editions of important works, historical surveys, important bibliographies, and a few major periodicals in the field.

E. Minimal level. A subject area in which few selections are made beyond very basic works.

NOTE: Some subject fields may be completely out of scope for a library's collections. These class numbers can be lined out in the analysis, or "0" can be used to indicate "not collected."

1.8.2 Language codes.
The following codes should be used to indicate languages in which material is collected. Libraries wishing a greater refinement of this data may subcode with the MARC language codes.

F.   All applicable languages (i.e., no exclusions)
G.   English
H.   Romance languages
J.   Germanic languages
K.   Slavic languages
L.   Middle Eastern languages
M.   Asian languages
N.   African languages
P.   Other languages

2. GUIDELINES

2.1 Principles governing formulation and application of collection development policies.

2.1.1 Libraries should identify the long- and short-range needs of their clientele, and establish priorities for the allocation of resources to meet those needs. A collection development policy statement is an orderly expression of those priorities as they relate to the development of library resources.

2.1.2 Collection development policy statements should be reviewed at regular intervals to ensure that changes in defined goals, user needs, and priorities are recognized, and that changing budgetary situations are confronted.

2.1.3   A library's collection development policy should be coordinated with those of appropriate other libraries, whether in a hierarchy of dependence, or in a division of responsibility among equals. A collection development policy statement should assist librarians in selecting and deselecting in conformity with regional needs and resources.

2.2   Elements of a collection development policy statement.

2.2.1   Analysis of general institutional objectives.
This section should include:
A. Clientele to be served
B. General subject boundaries of the collection
C. Kinds of programs or user needs supported (research, instructional recreational, general information, reference, etc.)
D. General priorities and limitations governing selection, including:
   (1) Degree of continuing support for strong collections
   (2) Forms of material collected or excluded
   (3) Languages, geographical areas collected or excluded
   (4) Chronological periods collected or excluded
   (5) Other exclusions
   (6) Duplication of materials (generally treated)
   NOTE: The collection development policy statement addresses the question of breadth and depth of subject coverage. Libraries will need to formulate separate statements of policy relating to duplication of materials; and such additional policy statements must be given consideration in fund allocation.
E. Regional, national, or local cooperative collection agreements that complement or otherwise affect the institutions policy

F. Legal, regulatory, or policy requirements of the institution.

2.2.2 Detailed analysis of collection development policy for subject fields.

It is recommended that this analysis be organized by classification scheme, with a parenthetical subject following the class number for ease of interpretation. The organization by class assures that the library's practice and policy with regard to the entire range of knowledge will be examined; and that the language used in the subject analysis will be as much as possible in a *lingua franca* for internal and interinstitutional discussions. Many libraries have chosen to design their collection development policy statements with an organization by academic program or broad subject descriptor. In such instances an index by class will facilitate cooperative resources planning with other libraries.

Libraries will differ in the degree of detail they will require for the analysis of their collection development policy by class. A suggested minimum refinement of the Library of Congress classification on which to structure the analysis is the breakdown into approximately five hundred subdivisions used in *Titles Classified by the Library of Congress Classification: National Shelflist Count, 1977,* Berkeley, General Library, Univ. of California, 1977 (see Appendix A). For Dewey or other classification schemes a comparably refined breakdown should be attempted. It must be stressed that this recommendation indicates a minimal refinement of classification analysis needed for interinstitutional comparisons. Many libraries will prefer to analyze their collections in greater detail.

For each subject category (i.e., classification number or group of numbers), indicate the following:

    A. Level of collecting intensity codes to indicate
      (1) Existing strength of collection
      (2) Actual current level of collection activity
      (3) Desirable level of collecting to meet program needs
    B. Languages
    C. Chronological periods collected
    D. Geographic areas collected
    E. Forms of material collection
    F. Library unit or selector with primary selection responsibility for the field.

2.2.3   Detailed analysis of collection development policy for form collections.

In some libraries special collection development policy statements are required for certain forms of materials, where policy governing the collection of those materials differs from the library's general policy for subject collections. Some examples of forms for which special policy statements may be needed include:

A. Newspapers
B. Microform collections
C. Manuscripts
D. Government publications
E. Maps
F. Audiovisual materials
G. Data tapes.

Where possible, it is desirable that the basic structure of the policy statement for a form collection follow subject classification; but with some form collections it will be necessary to use another primary arrangement (kind of material, area, etc.). For example, the policy statement for a map collection might be divided first into "general maps," "topographic maps," "raised relief maps," etc., with subdivision by area classification; that for a newspaper collection might be primarily by political division.

Whatever, the basic structure chosen, the detailed analysis of collection development for a

form collection should include the elements identified in 2.2.3.A–F above.

2.2.4   Indexes.
The information in the policy statement should be
made accessible for a wide variety of purposes. To
this end an index should be appended that corre-
lates subject terms to class numbers. Individual
libraries may also wish to index by academic
programs, library units, or other key words or
concepts.

GUIDELINES FOR THE EVALUATION OF THE EFFECTIVENESS OF LIBRARY COLLECTIONS

1. INTRODUCTION

1.1   Purpose.
        This document is intended to provide librarians
        and others with a statement of principles and
        methods to guide them in determining the extent
        to which their library actually did acquire the
        books, journals, or other materials it intended to
        acquire; in other words, whether the library's col-
        lection is fulfilling its purpose.

1.2   Objectives.
        The immediate aims of these *Guidelines* are to
        identify the essential elements of the evaluation
        process and to list the advantages and disadvan-
        tages of each.

1.3   Need.
        Every library collection should be established for a
        definite purpose. The collection may be developed
        for research, recreation, community service and
        development, instruction, support of a corporate
        activity, or a combination of these. In any case,
        evaluations should be made to determine whether
        the collection is meeting its objectives, how well it
        is serving its users, in which ways or areas it is
        deficient, and what remains to be done to develop

the collection. These guidelines are needed to aid in making such an evaluation.

The library administrator should not simply assume that the collection satisfies the research, instructional, developmental, recreational, or corporate needs of the community of users. Rather, subjectivity of judgment should be reduced as much as possible by the use of measurement techniques. Available methods for determining the value of a collection are not completely objective or free of interpretation by the evaluators, nor are they foolproof in their application and outcome. However, procedures are available that can reduce individual interpretation, if that seems advisable. If applied and administered carefully, or if used in combination with one another, the procedures can demonstrate with reasonable assurance how well a collection satisfies the purpose of the library as perceived at any one time. Techniques of measurement should be standardized when possible so that the results of evaluation of different collections might be comparable. Increasingly, libraries are finding that they cannot afford to develop their collections in all areas in which they might wish to do so; therefore, they are considering sharing of resources. If the collection of one library can be shown by reasonable and comparative measurements to be strong in an area or in several areas, another library or other libraries may decide not to be overly concerned about collecting in that area or those areas, perhaps negotiating a cooperative agreement on the use of collections.

1.4   Scope.

These *Guidelines* list various methods to be used in evaluating collections of libraries, indicating the types of library for which each method can be used and advantages and disadvantages of each method. The document is not intended to describe each method in detail, as this has already been done in the literature; it only sets forth a checklist to serve as a guide in considering the most appropriate method(s) of collection evaluation for a specific library or type of library.

1.5   Audience.
These *Guidelines* are intended for library administrators; for collection development officers; for those who adjust collection development (selection) policies as needed to fill in weak areas of the collection; for administrators considering cooperative agreement in the area of collection development; for accreditation boards; or for administrators of the university, corporation, high school, political jurisdiction or other body of which the library is a part.

1.6   Methodology.
Two literature searches were conducted: (1) a computer search of a large number of databases, and (2) a standard manual search. The most valuable published source found was George S. Bonn's article "Evaluation of the Collection," *Library Trends,* 22 (3), January 1974, pages 265–304.

The summary of evaluation methods in these *Guidelines* reflects, to a large extent, those given in the Bonn article and, to a lesser extent, those given in the F.W. Lancaster book, *Measurement and Evaluation of Library Services,* Washington, Information Resources Press, 1977 (cf. section 2.2, measures). "Evaluation of the Collection" and "Evaluation of Document Delivery Capabilities" are the chapters that were used from that book in manuscript. Both of these publications and their extensive lists of references are strongly recommended for further information on collection evaluation. References to more complete discussions are included in the *Guidelines* only when the measure described is set forth basically in one paper.

Following our literature searches, guidelines were drafted and submitted to five successive meetings of the ALA/RTSD/RS Collection Development Committee for revisions. In addition, suggestions were elicited from participants of the ALA Preconference on Collection Development, Detroit, June 1977.

2. GUIDELINES

2.1   Statement of principles.
The value or worth of something is measured by determining how well it is satisfying its purpose. Its purpose, therefore, must be clearly agreed upon and set forth before any evaluation of a library's collection can take place.

The goals and purposes of the collection should be stated in a collection development (selection) policy. Since the development of the collection through selecting can be very subjective, a written policy about what is to be selected or rejected should be developed. Another set of guidelines by the Collection Development Committee sets forth the manner in which such a policy might be formulated and what it should contain. With some evaluation methods, the collection development policy should serve as the yardstick against which the evaluative measurements are made, for instance, when evaluating by searching lists that are chosen on the basis of their appropriateness as set forth in the collection development policy. Some evaluative procedures might show where the policy needs to be changed, for instance, when evaluating the collection on the basis of what the library clientele is actually requesting or using.

Even with a written collection development policy, judgment is still required. In evaluation, judgment is involved more with some techniques than with those that attempt to quantify. Quantitative methods alone may not be completely satisfactory.

The tension between the qualitative and quantitative cannot be fully resolved. The problem is: can the quality of something be measured with quantitative technique? Yet, if no quantitative procedures are involved in the assessment, there may be no basis of comparability with other libraries, less reliability because of the subjective nature of the method. Quantitative methods are more conducive to standardization and comparability, which allows some basis for rating library collections of a similar type for accreditation purposes, for meeting standards, for deciding on sharing of collections, or simply for knowing how one library stands in relation to other libraries.

The presentation of methods that follows is intended to provide sufficient guidance for the evaluator to choose an appropriate method or combination of methods to suit his or her purpose and to make a reasonably reliable evaluation. Some methods may be used in combination with other methods. Often it is advisable to use both quantitative and qualitative techniques. The listings that follow are illustrative rather than exhaustive.

2.2   Measures.

2.2.1   Checking lists, catalogs, bibliographies.
With this procedure the evaluator uses lists of titles or works appropriate to the subjects collected or programs of the library. These lists are then searched in the library files to determine the percentage the library has in its own collection. Presumably a high percentage of items found indicates successful collection development.
Types of lists are:
A. Standard catalogs and basic general lists, such as ALA's basic collections, *Books for College Libraries, Choice's Opening Day Collection*
B. Printed catalogs of the holdings of important and specialized libraries

    C. Specialized bibliographies and basic lists

    D. Current lists, such as best-seller lists, books of selected publishers, annual subject compilations

    E. Lists of reference works

    F. Lists of periodicals

    G. Authorized lists prepared by governmental authorities or professional associations

    H. *Ad hoc* lists compiled for a specific library or type of library or for purposes of matching a certain objective

    I. Citations contained in publications, such as footnotes, bibliographies, references

    J. Lists of most frequently cited journals

    K. Lists, usually in up-to-date journals, of evaluated publications at the forefront of current research

    L. Dealers'/publishers'/auction catalogs

    M. Course syllabi or reading lists

    N. Bibliographies in faculty or staff members' theses or dissertations.

The type of list used to check the collection depends on the type of collection being checked and the purpose of the evaluation. For example, a "basic" collection in an undergraduate library may be checked against "standard" lists developed for this type of collection. The list must match the objectives and type of collection a library has.

2.2.1.1 Advantages.

    A. A variety of published lists is available: comprehensive, specialized, general, popular, or research.

    B. Many available lists are backed by the authority and competence of expert librarians or subject specialists.

    C. Lists of current materials are generally available since many lists are updated regularly.

    D. Lists can be compiled according to the needs of an individual library or type of library.

    E. The procedure of searching lists is easy to apply.

2.2.1.2 Disadvantages.
- A. Available lists may have been used previously as buying guides by the library being evaluated.
- B. Lists representing the viewpoint of one individual or group may not represent the subject well.
- C. Lists even in appropriate subjects may not reflect the interests or purposes of a library.
- D. Many lists are not revised and become out-of-date.
- E. Lists may not be as representative of the library's subjects or purposes as its holdings are.
- F. In some areas lists may be hard to find or compile.

2.2.2 Examining the collection directly.

By this procedure someone, presumably a person familiar with the literature of a subject(s), physically looks over the materials on the shelf. The examination may reveal size, scope, depth, and significance of the collection; recency of material; and physical condition. Furthermore, preservation, conservation, restoration, or replacement of materials may be taken into consideration in the process. For guidance in these matters see below the Collection Development Committee's *Guidelines for Review of Library Collections.*

2.2.2.1 Advantages.
- A. This method can be accomplished quickly.
- B. Strengths and weaknesses of the collection can be evaluated rapidly.
- C. The method can be applied to any library collection.
- D. Cooperative collecting policies can be developed by evaluating strong and weak collection areas of participating libraries.

2.2.2.2 Disadvantages.
- A. Persons knowledgeable in a subject and its literature are required, and they may be difficult to locate.

    B. This method is impressionistic and does not follow quantitative methods.

    C. The materials may not be on the shelf. The shelf list should be used at the same time the shelves are being checked.

2.2.3 Compiling statistics.

By this method statistics of various kinds are collected:

A. Size:

    Number of volumes or titles in the library
    Number of periodical subscriptions
    Measurement of shelf list
    Number of volumes by date of publication.

B. Volumes added in a period of time:

    Measurement of additions to shelf list
    Relationship to circulation statistics
    All measurements preferably by subject or class
    Cataloging statistics.

C. Expenditures for library materials:

    New books
    New periodicals
    Annual or longer time period
    By subject classes
    Percentage of total library budget
    Amount per user or class of user.

D. Formulae:

    Clapp-Jordan. For academic research libraries, measures core collection; volumes per student, per faculty, per graduate field, per undergaduate honors program.[1]

    Cartter "library resources index." For research libraries, measures total volumes, vol-

---

[1]Verner W. Clapp and Robert T. Jordan, "Quantitative Criteria for Adequacy of Academic Library Collections," *College and Research Libraries* 26(5):371–80 (Sept. 1965).

umes added annually, number of current periodicals.[2]

Beasley formula. For potential public library service, measure resources, population, circulation, research capability.[3]

Voigt formula. For university libraries, provides a method for determining an adequate annual acquisition rate of current materials for a university; acquisition rate for graduate fields, for undergraduate students, for research programs as affected by access to other research libraries.[4]

E. Circulation statistics:
   For different classes of users
   For different subject classes of books
   By date of material
   By type of format of material
   At different times of the year
   Compared with acquisition statistics, preferably by subject or class.

F. Unfilled requests and filled requests:
   By subject class, i.e., books or journals
   By form of material
   Compared with acquisition statistics, preferably by subject or class.

G. Interlibrary loan request: how many requests from a library's clientele must go outside?
   By subject class
   By different classes of users
   By form of material.
   Consider cooperative arrangements.

---

[2]Alan M. Cartter, *An Assessment of Quality in Graduate Education* (Washington, D.C.: American Council on Education, 1966), p. 114–15.

[3]Kenneth E. Beasley, "A Theoretical Framework for Public Library Measurement," in *Research Methods in Librarianship: Measurement and Evaluation,* ed. by Herbert Goldhor (Urbana: Univ. of Illinois Graduate School of the Library Sciences, 1968), p. 2–14.

[4]Melvin J. Voigt, "Acquisition Rates in University Libraries," *College and Research Libraries* 36(4):263–71 (July 1975).

    H. Optimum size. Core collection of books or journals most likely to be used:
        Journal-use statistics and Bradford-Zipf Distribution[5]
        Circulation records of books.

2.2.3.1 Advantages.
    A. Some records of statistics may be easily kept.
    B. If proper records have been kept, they are easily available.
    C. If clearly defined, they may be widely understood and comparable.
    D. Formulas take into account multiple factors affecting collection size or growth.
    E. Circulation statistics; requests filled and unfilled and interlibrary loan requests relate directly to the collections' users.

2.2.3.2 Disadvantages.
    A. Statistics may be recorded improperly.
    B. Clear definitions of units may be lacking.
    C. Statistical records may be comparable.
    D. Significance of statistics may be difficult to interpret.
    E. Involved formulas may not be applied consistently and comparably, e.g., in supplying figures and weighting.

2.2.4 Citations from papers of library users.
    This method is most useful for university, special, or other libraries with clearly identified groups of users. It consists of determining the holdings of items cited in footnotes, bibliographies, or references of papers; articles or books written by faculty, research staff, or others writing in areas covered by the library's collection. It is assumed that the writer has found it necessary or desirable to use sources outside the library that serves him or her.

---

[5]B.C. Brookes, "The Derivation and Application of the Bradford-Zipf Distribution," *Journal of Documentation* 24(4):247–65 (Dec. 1968).

2.2.4.1 Advantages.
     A. Lists are easy to come by.
     B. They are tailor-made by the library clientele.
     C. The procedure can be easily applied.
     D. The method relates directly to the interest of the users.
     E. The lists will apply to peripherally related materials of the general collection required by scholars.
     F. The procedure allows for changing interests.

2.2.4.2 Disadvantages.
     A. The author may have limited himself or herself to use of the library being evaluated. Collection bias may also be a problem.
     B. The citations may relate to a limited area of the collection.
     C. Some peripheral areas may be out of scope.
     D. The method is limited to a user group that writes papers.

2.2.5   User opinions.
This procedure requires a survey of users, or user groups, obtaining verbal or written responses in interviews or questionnaires or both.

2.2.5.1 Advantages.
     A. The survey relates directly to the needs of users, and thus to the goals or objectives of the library.
     B. It reflects changing interests and trends.
     C. It can be done for most types of clientele.

2.2.5.2 Disadvantages.
     A. This method requires active solicitation of opinions.
     B. Users are often subjective, inconsistent, uninformed, or passive.
     C. User interests may be focused more narrowly than collection development policies.

2.2.6   Application of standards.
This procedure can be used by those types of libraries for which standards have been devel-

oped. Standards are available for many types of libraries.

2.2.6.1 Advantages.
A. For the appropriate type of library the standard will generally relate closely to the library goals.
B. Standards are generally widely accepted and authoritative.
C. They may be promulgated and used for evaluation by accrediting agencies.
D. They may be very persuasive in engendering support for the library.

2.2.6.2 Disadvantages.
A. Many are stated generally and difficult to apply.
B. They may require a high degree of professional knowledge and judgment.
C. Knowledgeable people may disagree in application or results.
D. Minimum standards may be regarded as maximum standards.

2.2.7   Total resources and document delivery tests.
Increasingly, libraries are becoming interdependent. One library cannot meet all the needs of all its users. Therefore, cooperative systems have developed wherein the use of other libraries may not indicate a collection development problem, but rather an intended result of cooperation and sharing of resources. If the cooperative system fills all requests on a timely basis, regardless of where in the system the material came from, its purpose is accomplished. Statistical methods have been developed for surveys measuring a library's capability of supplying documents. A measure of document delivery capability should consider the varying delivery capability and the varying delivery speed of items available on the shelf or obtained elsewhere. A library's capability of delivering documents to other libraries as well as to its immediate users should be considered.

2.2.7.1 Advantages.
  - A. These tests are not subject to user inconsistency or subjectivity.
  - B. They are based on objective statistical data.
  - C. They can generally be carried out without interrupting normal routines.
  - D. The measurements can be easily understood and can be compared.
  - E. Document Delivery Tests test not only the adequacy of collections but also the ability to deliver to the user.

2.2.7.2 Disadvantages.
  - A. The test procedures may not fit all libraries equally.
  - B. Conditions in a library may invalidate test assumptions.
  - C. Test samples may not be typical of overall document delivery.
  - D. The Document Delivery Test results are meaningful only when compared with Document Delivery Test results in other libraries or in other units or areas of the same library.

2.3 Conclusion.
In any evaluation of a library collection, a combination of these procedures may be used, the one complementing or verifying the other. Some tend to be quantitative, some qualitative, both together possibly producing a reasonable, reliable result. Finally, accurate, detailed records of the evaluation should be kept for future reference; this will avoid unnecessary duplication of effort.

GUIDELINES FOR THE REVIEW OF LIBRARY COLLECTIONS

1. INTRODUCTION

1.1   Purpose.

These *Guidelines* are intended to assist librarians in achieving the goal of selecting material for relegation (see definitions below), preservation, or discard in ways that are consistent with the mission of a particular library. The goals of such a review program may be centered in immediate or long-term local needs or necessities, or may be involved with the sharing of resources by libraries, or a combination of these.

Use of these *Guidelines* should be informed by the Mission and Goals and Collection Development Policy Statements of the library or collection, and by information from collection evaluations or analyses (see the preceding *Guidelines for the Formulation of Collection Development Policies* and *Guidelines for the Evaluation of the Effectiveness of Library Collections*).

1.2   Objectives.

The *Guidelines* are to serve as a tool that will guide librarians in the review of collections for relegation, preservation, or discard, and that will help them clarify objectives to staff, users, and cooperating institutions. A working bibliography has been appended, roughly divided by subject, to extend and elaborate on topics briefly covered below.

1.3   Need.
Most libraries are or will soon be faced by problems of change of institutional goals or programs, space limitation, increasing collection size and cost, the impact of new programs or needs, the problem of accumulation of duplicates or obsolescent materials that may no longer be needed in the active collection, and by the aging and decay of library materials. There is no single, or simple, answer to any of these problems, but most of them can be alleviated or reduced by a systematic, judicious, ongoing program of collection review to identify items that may require conservation treatment, or that—for a variety of reasons—may no longer be required in the active collection. Materials review will provide better collection control, provide easier access to collections, and may achieve economies of space and reduce pressures requiring additional campus facilities.

For purposes of accreditation, evidence of materials review procedures and evidence of the results of review activity may indicate sound library practice despite possible reduction in size of collection.

1.4   Scope.
These *Guidelines* are designed to aid libraries of all kinds and sizes in considering and in formulating review policies, though certain elements of the *Guidelines* will be more applicable to larger libraries.

1.5   Audience.
Library staff and administrators involved in collection development, maintenance, and preservation.

1.6   Methodology.
These *Guidelines* have been developed from review and study of the literature (see bibliography),

from input and comment from committee members and consultants, from professional colleagues, and from comment at workshop sessions of the 1977 ALA Collection Development Preconference.

1.7   Definitions.

Active collections: That portion of a library's total collections immediately available in regular, staffed, campus library facilities.

Compact storage: Storage that will accommodate more books or other library materials in a given area than will a conventional stack arrangement. A density of greater than twenty volumes per square foot is considered compact storage for books. Items so stored must normally be retrieved by paging.

Demand: Request by a patron for specific materials.

Discard: The official removal of an item from either the active or low-use storage collections. Items discarded should be disposed of in an appropriate manner.

Materials: All appropriate library media including books, serials, periodicals, microform, etc. to which the principle of systematic review is applied.

Need: Materials for which there is, or it is anticipated there will be, demand or use by library clientele.

Relegation: Removal of materials from the active collection and consignment thereof to low-use storage.

Review (of library collections): Systematic examination of library collections, which may result in the removal of items from the active collection for low-use storage, discard, or preservation treatment.

Shelf time (time between uses): The period of time a book remains on the shelf between circulations.

Storage: An inactive collection of little-used materials housed in a library or in remote facilities. The low-use storage area may have conventional shelving or compact storage that will accommodate more materials in a given space than conventional stack arrangement.

Use: The removal of a book from the shelf by or for a patron. Use is conventionally measured through circulation, reshelving, or a variety of more sophisticated measures or models described in the literature.

1.8 Assumptions.

A. Perhaps the major question regarding a library's collection is its adequacy in meeting the present and future needs of its clientele. If this adequacy can be increased by review of collections for relegation, preservation, or discard, then it should be done. Mature collections normally require such activity more urgently than do young collections.

B. Institutional mission and goals, size of collection, and rate of collection growth will suggest the need for review for relegation or discard. If a library can identify present or eventual problems of storage or preservation of collections, it may be advantageous to develop goals and plans for a collection review program.

C. Removal of lower priority, less acutely needed, or infrequently used materials from active collection areas may improve accessibility of the collections and reduce overall costs.

D. Reasonably timely secondary access to works seldom needed or used by patrons may not prevent successful research work.

E. For some libraries or fields of study, such as public libraries and undergraduate or science collections, measurement of circulation or demand and in-house use may be the best way to evaluate a book's value to patrons. For other libraries or collections, such as research libraries or humanities collections, assessment of patron need, disciplinary importance as evidenced by citation, or other qualitative criteria may also be significant in evaluating an item's value.

F. It is desirable to standardize terminology so as to allow comparability of practice between libraries.

G. A set of guidelines may speak to the following concerns frequently voiced when review is proposed: (a) unforeseen need for books discarded or stored may arise; (b) if a library's records show a decrease in the number of volumes held, budgets may be cut; (c) cost of a review program may be prohibitive; and (d) suitable means for the transfer or disposal of library materials may be lacking.

2. GUIDELINES

2.1   Principles.
There can be no best way to review collections for relegation, preservation, or discard. Institutional goals and programs, space limitations, and characteristics of the library clientele and collections form a web of circumstances that may be unique for each library. All these principles will be treated in order to clarify the issues involved in collection review so that realistic review goals may be formulated that are based on the combination of principles best suited to local circumstances.

2.1.1 Institutional mission, goals, and programs.
A library decision to review collections and subsequent low-use storage, discard, or treatment of materials should not be an independent activity, but should implement or follow written library

policies and procedures (c.f. sections 1.1, 1.3, 1.8) that are themselves closely related to the mission, goals, programs of the institution or clientele served by the library, available resources, and interinstitutional considerations. Collection review programs, like all library policies and procedures, should be reviewed at regular intervals to insure that they take into account changes in mission, goals, and programs and are consonant with budgetary and space considerations. Collection review programs, for example, must remain compatible with priorities stated by the current version of the library's collection development policy. In addition, it may be desirable for a library to coordinate its review policy with those of other cooperating libraries, whether in a hierarchy or equal division of responsibilities. Such institutions may also share coordinated collection development programs or storage facilities.

2.1.1.1 Institutional goals vary greatly from one kind or size of library to another. While any library wishes its collections to be accessible to its clientele, the means of achieving this goal will vary from library to library. Each library must define accessibility and availability in terms of its goals and capacities before developing a review policy.

2.1.1.2 Support of research is a major goal of many academic libraries, with the result that in certain areas of specialization, such as the Humanities, an academic library may wish to retain a significant percentage of published work in the field; if space becomes limited, this goal of research may conflict with the availability of space.

2.1.1.3 Aging and deterioration of library collections is increasingly recognized as a problem (e.g., Library of Congress and Columbia University have reported that approximately one-third of their collections have become seriously embrittled; the

1959 Barrow Laboratory Study of a sampling of nonfiction books printed in the U.S. between 1900 and 1939 indicated that 97 percent had an expected useful life of 50 years or less). Libraries are consequently initiating programs of conservation and preservation that require long-term systematic review of the condition of library materials so that phased plans of action can be developed over time as funds and staff levels permit. Such review may conveniently coincide with review for low-use storage or discard; indeed, storage review may be part of a conservation program.

2.1.2   External constraints.
Other factors such as physical facilities, local staffing levels and distribution, need for rapid service delivery, methods used for organization of materials, and the materials budget itself will also affect the collection review policy and should be carefully considered before goals are formulated.

2.1.3   Characteristics of clientele.
The major institutional factor determining library policy should be adequate service to library clientele, the latter likely to be determined by factors outside the control of the library. For example, the clientele of a public library may be the taxpayer of the county, city, or state. The clientele of an academic library may be the faculty, staff, and students of the local campus, all faculty and students of sister campuses within the same system; or even all faculty and students within a region or within a state. In case of conflict between service imperatives and internal library goals the areas of inconsistency must be made explicit and resolved as much as possible or the collection review effort may be paralyzed in its beginnings.

2.1.4   When a program of collection review is desirable.
If availability or accessibility of a library collection

can be improved by relegation of materials from the active collection, or if present or anticipated space is or will be inadequate for storing the active collection, or if aging and decay of materials in the active collection will be accelerated by retaining materials in their present condition, then a program of review may be called for.

Many authorities regard a library collection as a living organism, and consider collection review and its results as a way of maintaining a healthy, useful, and goal-centered collection. Generally, mature collections need weeding much more than do young collections. The planned ultimate size of an active collection should be based in part on a process of review. If a library formulates its collection development goals and policy, and combines these with its growth rate, it will be in a position to project goals for a collection review program.

2.2   Criteria.
Assessment of the collection to determine which volumes should be relegated, discarded, or preserved should be based on one or more of the following criteria: use, language or publication/ accession date, value/quality criteria, shelf reading/books slip method, undesirable duplication, or journal relegation criteria. The relative importance assigned each factor will be determined by local need.

2.2.1   Use criteria.
Use criteria should include circulation data, shelf time, in-house use, interlibrary loan circulations, and patron consultation. All of these should probably be included to get an accurate reflection of collection use, although some are difficult to measure. A library may wish to perform a study to determine which, if any, of these measures are useful predictors of the others. In any attempt to measure use, newly published and acquired books

should be excluded from use assessment during their first two years.

2.2.1.1 Circulation counts are a significant measure to be considered in developing review procedures, but circulation represents only a portion of total usage (*See below* shelf time, in-house use, interlibrary loan, patron consultation). Circulations are countable in most libraries and are counted in many, the measure being the number of charge-outs over a period of time. A criterion based on this measure alone would require only the assignment of a cutoff point that would define items circulating less than an assigned number of times during a specified time period as candidates for storage or discard. For example, such a decision might involve storing all books not circulated during a five-year period.

However, the following limitations to using circulation counts should be kept in mind: (a) if a library does not keep consistent circulation records of some sort over an extended period of time, a check on past circulation is extremely difficult, (b) it may be important for libraries to measure browsing and other nonrecorded use and determine its relationship to recorded use, (c) a library could in this way abandon its responsibility to those who need to refer to little-used materials.

2.2.1.2 Shelf time. In heavily used collections it may not be possible to develop use criteria based on circulation counts alone, for very few items may fail to circulate. In this case, shelf time may prove a useful secondary tool to define potential volumes for relegation. When the time between uses exceeds an established standard, those volumes may be considered for relegation. They would still remain available to the patron, but would cease to congest the active collection.

2.2.1.3 In-house use is that aspect of total usage most difficult to measure. If we assume that areas of high circulation will also be areas of high volume in-house use, as McGrath suggested, then criteria based on circulation counts might provide adequate review guides without in-house data. Other studies such as Urquhart and Urquhart, however, suggest that this may not be the case. In a library with large noncirculating collections, in-house use will have to be measured: in such a case reshelving counts are probably the best available approximation of use information, even though studies reveal that as few as 22 percent of titles consulted in a given area may be left on the table for reshelving. In addition, many libraries do not circulate periodicals, and some combination of data derived from reshelving counts, missing issues, mutilation rates, and photocopy records may provide the desired data.

2.2.1.4 Interlibrary loan circulations are seldom recorded either by the circulation system or on the book's date due slip, but records are inevitably maintained by interlibrary loan operation for control of the flow of material. Because libraries may vary widely in the volume of interlibrary loan activity they support (loaning local material) or initiate (requesting unavailable material from other libraries), such data should be incorporated into the use measure chosen.

2.2.1.5 Patron consultation is a way of verifying that review procedures and specific selections for relegation or discard are consonant with the needs and programs of the library. While in most cases librarians are the ultimate authorities in review activities, careful consultation may prevent costly and embarrassing mistakes.

2.2.2   Estimated use.
For libraries that have no records of past circulations, it may be possible to relegate titles to storage based on such factors as language of publication, accession date, publication date, or subject field.

2.2.3   Value/quality criteria method.

Some academic, research, or special libraries may wish to review collections on the basis of the value of individual monograph titles as determined by their appearance on standard lists and/or by the judgment of a specialist or group of specialists. Criteria for value/quality review should be the same as those used initially for book selection, reflecting the goals and objectives of the library. Criteria and methodology may resemble those recommended earlier in the *Guidelines for the Evaluation of the Effectiveness of Library Collections.* In considering a volume the selector may wish to bear in mind such factors as subject matter, historical importance, age, cost, physical condition, citation in other publications, the availability of other material in the field, and the frequency of use.

For example, responsibility for value/quality review for librarians, subject specialists, and teaching faculty in an academic institution might include any of the following: (a) decision by librarian and/or subject specialist only; (b) direct faculty examination of books and production of a call number listing of those that faculty think can be stored or discarded; (c) librarian and/or subject specialist decisions subject to faculty review, which requires display of the books for a designated period of time during which faculty may remove volumes that should remain in the primary working collections; and (d) faculty selection with review by librarians and/or subject specialist.

2.2.4   Shelf reading and book slip method.

This is a method to help research or special libraries that may need to retain material without active circulation records in the active collection.

Librarians or faculty select duplicate, low-use, or little needed titles as candidates for relegation or discard through a systematic shelf-reading program. As this is done, each reviewer places a colored, appropriately labelled, and easily seen slip in each book identified as a candidate for relegation. The slip contains the call number, a legend informing a patron of the intended action, and indicates that a patron who considers the action unwise may remove the slip and turn it in at the circulation desk upon leaving the stack/library. Slips are left in books for a significant period of time (e.g., one or two years), and at the end of the fixed period all titles with slips remaining are pulled and processed for the appropriate action.

2.2.5   Undesirable duplication.
It may be important to monitor duplicates during shelf readings. Multiple copies of obsolete text-books or other superseded books may occupy a significant proportion of badly needed shelf space in stack areas and may be controlled by a program of shelf or shelf list review.

2.2.6   Journal relegation criteria.

2.2.6.1 For journals that circulate, past use and publication date are the major criteria recommended to determine a cutoff point. Use patterns can often determine the "family quality" of journals (the use patterns of all volumes of a journal are often similar, and use is therefore usually distributed throughout a set, rather than being centered on one or two volumes).

2.2.6.2 For noncirculating journal titles, librarians often base decisions on published studies, which have shown that citations of articles may be taken as a measure of use of the journals. Many of these studies show that the number of citations can be linked with the age of the journal in formulae for predicting when a journal can be relegated to storage. To be useful, obsolescence rates must be based on data collected from one's own library, because each library has a unique group of users, a unique purpose, and a unique set of physical facilities (see also 2.2.1.3).

2.2.7   Deteriorating materials criteria.
Any library must ensure that materials acquired for use by its clientele are physically sound. Each library needs a program for the identification and removal over time, as resources permit, of unsound, aged, dilapidated, or embrittled volumes from the shelves for conservation/preservation treatment. As these volumes are identified during collection review processes, a conservation/preservation program can be developed that takes into account the number of items requiring care by type and acuity of need, and time frames and cost projections can be projected for conservation treatment, photocopy, or microform replacement. In some cases, such volumes may be candidates for discard if use and other criteria indicate that they are unused or little used and available through interlibrary borrowing arrangements.

2.3   Conclusion.
Depending on the existence of available facilities for a low-use collection, a library may elect to relegate items to storage, to discard them, or, more commonly, choose some combination of storage and discard considered optimal for local conditions. In developing a review program for relegation and discard, it is important to determine the time frame for review process, and how often the cycle should be repeated. If funds and/or staffing permit, collection review should be made an ongoing program, integrating relegation and discard with the purchase of new materials. In most cases, however, it will be possible to review only at times when the pressures of regular work subside or projected space problems make such a program necessary.

Once a review program has been established, review criteria should be chosen in accordance with the principles, cautions, and criteria discussed above. Whatever the decision, the actual methodology will be influenced by the resources available to implement any review project and the time frame adopted for its accomplishment. Criteria for the use of items in the storage collection should be assigned so as to allow the automatic and rapid return of stored items to the active collection if they receive a minimum level of use.

GUIDELINES FOR THE ALLOCATION OF LIBRARY MATERIALS BUDGETS

1. INTRODUCTION

1.1   Purpose.
These guidelines are offered to assist librarians in allocating funds for library materials, whether through use of a published formula or a method devised locally.

1.2   Objectives.
The Committee has attempted to bring together the elements to be considered in the allocation process. Some published formulas and allocation models that may assist in the process are described, together with a discussion of the advantages and disadvantages of using a formula.

1.3   Need.
Greater accountability for specific budget expenditures and reductions in budget size have created a climate in which the allocation of funds for library materials should be done in a manner that is both understandable and justifiable. An allocation method based on recognized criteria is more likely to meet with acceptance and approval, and it can serve as a valuable planning tool.

1.4   Scope.
The guidelines are designed to aid libraries of all kinds and sizes in determining the most

300

useful way of allocating funds for library materials.

1.5 Audience.
These *Guidelines* are intended to assist library budget officers, collection development librarians, administrators and staff involved in the allocation of the library's materials funds. The guidelines are also intended to aid in communicating the allocation process to library users, to other library staff, and to nonlibrary administrators who have a role in budget allocation and approval.

1.6 Methodology.
These *Guidelines* were drafted by a Subcommittee of the Collection Development Committee and submitted to the full Committee in open meetings at several ALA Midwinter and Annual Conferences. During this same period, the Committee sponsored a program on the allocation of book funds at the Annual Conference in 1974; and at one of its meetings at the Annual Conference in July 1975, it invited several visitors with experience in the development of allocation formulas to share their methods and ideas with members of the Committee. Further revision followed the 1977 Collection Development Preconference in Detroit. These, and subsequent group discussions, led to extensive revisions of the initial draft of the guidelines.

1.7 Definitions.

1.7.1 *Allocation:* Assignment of a portion of the library materials budget to a particular subject field, type of material, administrative unit, etc.

1.7.2 *Allocation unit:* Unit to which an allocation is made; e.g., department, subject LC category. In statistical terms, it is one of the quantities in a variable and is called the *unit of analysis.*

1.7.3   *Approval plans:* Materials are supplied by a vendor or publisher, based upon an individual profile of library needs. Items may be selected or rejected by appropriate library staff.

1.7.4   *Budget:* Funds assigned to the library, usually with a certain portion earmarked for the purchase of library materials.

1.7.5   *Evaluation:* Assessment, preferably periodic, of the effectiveness of a particular allocation method in achieving a library's collection goals.

1.7.6   *Factor:* A concept that may or may not be quantifiable. Generally much vaguer and more difficult to define than variable (see below). A factor may include several variables.

1.7.7   *Formula:* A mathematical model based on prescribed variables for assisting in distribution of library funds.

1.7.8   *Library materials:* All items that make up the holdings of a library. These can include books, manuscripts, serials, government publications, recordings, microforms, pamphlets, maps, etc.

1.7.9   *Monitoring:* Regular checking on the status and use of the allocations provided from the library materials budget.

1.7.10   *Standing order:* An order to a vendor or publisher to supply automatically, as published, all publications in a particular series or in a work-in-parts.

1.7.11   *Test of effectiveness:* Any means used to examine the results of the allocation process and by which an evaluation is made.

1.7.12   *Variable:* A unit that varies quantitatively, such as the number of students enrolled in a department, or the number of books in a subject.

1.7.13   *Weighting:* Assigning a level of value or importance to a specified variable such as the number of full-time equivalency undergraduates. Weights may be assigned arbitrarily to reflect administrative policy. Or they may be determined empirically by computing a variable's relationship to a criterion variable, such as the relationship of enrollment to circulation.

1.8   Assumptions.

1.8.1   A rational method for the allocation of funds for library materials is desirable and achievable. Each institution will need to develop its own method for allocation, which will apply to its own circumstance; however, existing formulas can be (and have been) used as models to assist individual institutions in this process. If properly designed, the allocation method should:

1.8.1.1 Open up the allocation process and identify assumptions.

1.8.1.2 Provide for a planned and logical distribution of available funds, based on the library's goals and priorities.

1.8.1.3 Enable the library to monitor expenditures of funds.

1.8.1.4 Enable the library to demonstrate to both fiscal authorities and patrons how money is being allocated and spent.

1.8.1.5 Provide a method for fulfilling collection goals and needs, as well as institutional goals.

1.8.1.6 Allow increments that will allow desired levels of programmatic support.

1.8.2   In a climate of budget restraints and tighter fiscal control, it becomes increasingly desirable to use some method of allocation, even if one was not used in the past, to insure that all parts of the collection receive consideration and an appropriate share of the funds.

1.8.3   In an era of resource-sharing, a rational method for the allocation of funds can help to insure that the needs of one's institution are being met without the unnecessary overlap or duplication with other institutions.

2. GUIDELINES

2.1   Principles.

2.1.1   Any method used should provide for an effective distribution of available funds, according to agreed-upon priorities.

2.1.2   Librarians, with appropriate consultation, should allocate funds.

2.1.3   The allocation method should be developed in conjunction with the library's goals and collection development policy.

2.1.4   The allocation method should be readily understandable to those who are responsible for the administration and expenditure of such funds.

2.1.5   The allocation method should be flexible enough to respond to changing circumstances or needs within the institution, changes in the publishing industry or book market, and unexpected opportunities for special purchases.

2.1.6   The allocation process should allow for both present needs and anticipated future needs, thus assisting in the planning process.

2.1.7   The allocation method used should be sufficiently well designed and objective not to be readily subject to political pressure.

2.1.8   The allocation process should be one that can provide better program support.

2.2   Factors to be considered in selecting an allocation method.

2.2.1   Whether there is now a formal budgeting process that may place constraints on, or limit the choices of, an allocation method.

2.2.2   Whether the type of accounting procedure or other institutional regulations in use may limit the options, e.g., whether there are encumbrances, whether unspent funds can be carried forward or transferred from one account to another.

2.2.3   Whether an institution is in a "steady state," in a period of growth, or in a period of reduction.

2.2.4   Whether the necessary data are available, e.g., circulation figures.

2.2.5   Whether there exists a formal or informal policy statement and/or statement of priorities.

2.3   Methods of allocating library materials funds.
It is probable that no one method is, or can be, used exclusively within a single institution and that a combination may be necessary. Many budgets provide specific sums of money for certain categories of material (e.g., monographs, serials, newspapers, microforms) for individual units of the library (e.g., a branch library, reference department), or for specific subject fields or language areas.

2.3.1   Allocation units and their advantages and disadvantages.

2.3.1.1 By broad subject field, e.g., humanities, social sciences.
Advantages: Allows flexibility.
Disadvantages: A small subject within the broader one may be overlooked or treated inequitably.

2.3.1.2   By specific subject field, e.g., anthropology.
Advantages: It is easy to monitor behavior in a particular category.
Disadvantages: Interdisciplinary materials cannot be assigned so specifically; specific items may not be identifiable in standing orders or approval plans.

2.3.1.2.1 By major LC or Dewey schedule, e.g., A, B, BC, 010, 020, etc.
Advantages: Acquisition rate could be correlated with largest libraries, such as LC, and thus with national or worldwide publishing rates in each category.
Disadvantages: Could not be correlated readily with institutional policy, curriculum, or academic emphasis.

2.3.1.2.2 By subject profile of academic departments, based on LC or Dewey analysis of courses.
Advantages: Possible to relate acquisitions directly to programs or curriculum.
Disadvantages: Can be difficult to construct profile and collect necessary data.

2.3.1.3   By form of material, e.g., monographs, serials, microform.
Advantages: Statistical data for library and government agencies are usually based on this type of information.
Disadvantages: The subject breakdown possibility may be lost.
Flexibility also may be lost.

2.3.1.4   To units within the library, e.g., reference department, branch.
Advantages: Enables unit to develop an appropriate collection based on user needs since there is a close relationship between the department and its users. Greater accountability is possible.
Disadvantages: Duplication of interdisciplinary materials will be required. While duplication is

not necessarily undesirable, it will be necessary to have a mechanism to insure that unnecessary duplication is avoided.

2.3.1.5   To academic department or programs, e.g., Philosophy, English.
Advantages: Faculty members are involved in the selection process.
Disadvantages: The library risks spotty, unsystematic, and inconsistent development of collections over time.

2.4   Allocation, monitoring, control.
All the individuals and groups mentioned below may be involved to some extent in all parts of the allocation process, but the most usual assignments of responsibility are as follows:

2.4.1   Allocation is done by:
Chief Librarian or other administrative officer
Collection Development Officer
Head of Acquisitions
Staff and/or administrative committee
Cooperative effort between library and faculty
    committee or departments.

2.4.2   Monitoring of expenditures is done by:
Collection Development Officer
Bibliographer
Acquisitions Librarian
Faculty or academic department

2.4.3   Evaluation of the allocation method is done by:
Collection Development Officer
Selection personnel
Users: students, staff, other users. This could
    involve direct or indirect input.

2.5   Problem areas in determining allocations.

2.5.1   Coverage of standing orders, approval, or blanket order plans may be interdisciplinary, thus a subject breakdown is difficult. Also, the required budget amount for these may be difficult to determine in advance.

2.5.2   If there are separate budgets for serials, newspapers, microforms, etc., it may force rigidity on what should be a flexible process.

2.5.3   There is almost always a need for a discretionary fund to take advantage of opportunities or to give aid in a crisis.

2.5.4   The impact of new programs requiring start-up funds can put the budget out of balance, if such funds were not sought or provided in advance.

2.5.5   Duplication in certain categories of materials may be necessary or desirable. Special allowances have to be made for this.

2.5.6   Retrospective material may be needed, but the availability of such materials and their actual costs may be hard to predict.

2.5.7   Inflation factors must be taken into consideration.

2.5.8   The quantity and cost of publications in various subjects or languages may vary widely and should be taken into account in determining allocations.

2.5.9   Gifts and exchange materials can have an impact on allocation funds and may fill the need for certain materials so that purchase is not needed. Budget flexibility to transfer funds from an area where they are not needed will help deal with this situation.

2.5.10   Special funds may have special requirements or limitations on their use. They may even be sufficient to wholly support certain areas of the collection. These must be taken into consideration when regular funds are allocated.

2.5.11   A windfall of funds late in the fiscal year can disrupt the carefully planned allocation process. A procedure for insuring that such funds are wisely spent is essential, e.g., keeping a file of lower priority but approved items to be purchased if additional funds become available.

2.6   Considerations in the development of allocation methods.

2.6.1   Objective factors.

2.6.1.1 External (publishing and book trade) considerations.
   A. The rate and pattern of publishing in various subjects or geographical areas, or for various types of materials
   B. Costs of books and other materials
   C. Differences in costs between various categories of materials
   D. Inflation.

2.6.1.2 Internal (library) considerations.
   A. Size of the collection
   B. Rate of growth of the collection (by subject, department, etc.)
   C. Use of the collection
   D. Unfilled patron needs
   E. Interlibrary borrowing and lending statistics.

2.6.1.3 Nature and size of user group.
   A. Campus:
      Institutional mission
      Method of instruction
      Faculty size, composition, and quality
      Citation level of faculty
      Student enrollment
      Credit hours
      Graduate programs
      Degrees granted
      Off-campus users
      Research programs
      Publications

Remoteness from or proximity to other libraries

Cooperative agreements.

B. Public library:
Library use intensity
Number of users
Composition of users
Literacy level.

C. Special library:
Employees
Outside users
Research staff
Contractors.

D. School library:
Students
Faculty
Staff.

2.6.2   Subjective considerations.
A. Goals of the institution
B. Politics (campus, city, county, state, business, etc.)
C. Historical development of the collection
D. Academic distinction of departments in college or university
E. Extent of reliance of academic department or discipline on library materials.

2.6.3   Weighting of above factors.
There is no generally recognized standard for weighting the above factors. The weight given to a particular factor in a library will be determined by the goals and resources of the library, and will be tailored to the individual library. Many institutions determine their own weightings; e.g., enrollment in upper division units is worth two of lower division units. Others simply weigh all factors in formula equally.

2.7   Published formulas and allocation methods that may be used in the allocation process.

Formulas have been devised to allocate funds among institutions (e.g., the Washington Formula), and within a single institution (e.g., McGrath Formula). Some, such as the Kohut model, address a specific problem—in this case, the balancing of serial and monographic purchases. Brief descriptions and citations to the full texts of the following formulas are provided in Appendix B: Dillehay, Gold, Kohut, McGrath, Pierce.

2.8   Using a formula.
A library may decide to develop its own allocation model or to use one of the models described. It is important to understand what a formula can and cannot do.

2.8.1   Why use a formula?
An appropriate formula may provide for a logical and more equitable distribution of available funds. It can also assist in creating a budget based on programs, priorities, and goals of the institution. It can assist in making choices, so that choosing alternatives and priorities becomes an articulated rather than an unclear process. A good formula can be quite flexible, if properly designed. However, adoption of a formula should not imply rigid acceptance of it.

2.8.2   What can a formula be used for?
It can be used for an initial allocation of funds, for a reallocation of funds, or to allocate supplementary funds to the base.

2.8.3   Benefits of using a formula.
Once a suitable formula has been developed, funds can be allocated easily and quickly. Allocations can be justified on the basis of the formula and objectivity in the allocation process can be demonstrated. The formula itself can be reexamined periodically, if necessary. A for-

mula is equitable, limits variables and factors, and provides structure.

2.8.4   Disadvantages of using a formula.
A formula may not be flexible enough to cover differing needs in various areas, e.g., absolute equity may not be desirable. A formula may not allow for sudden changes in fiscal circumstances. The data necessary for the development of a formula may not be readily available, e.g., library's own book cost figures or data on the rate of publishing in the various subject fields. A formula could be used by budgetary authorities to deny as well as to provide funds. In fact, using a formula may be more difficult and more time-consuming for at least two reasons: (1) if data are plugged in freshly each year, the data must be collected and analyzed in order to determine appropriate weights; and (2) if a departmental subject profile is used, the profile must be revised each year. If the formula is not reviewed each year and the same weights are used, the formula could become stale. A formula may limit variables and thus produce an inappropriate result.

2.8.5   Problems not yet handled by any library budget formula.
A. Retrospective acquisition rates.
B. Built-in recovery from lean years.
C. Recognition of existing collection adequacy.
D. Rates of literature obsolescence in all disciplines. However, half-lives of journal literature, a measure of obsolescence, have been computed for several disciplines.
E. Intuition and knowledge based on experience, e.g., subjective judgment.
F. Multiple copies.
G. Replacement materials.
H. Quality of expenditures.

2.9   Assessment of the efficacy of the allocation process.

Testing the effectiveness of any allocation method should be a regular or periodic operation. Each year's budget preparation should include a review and evaluation of the results of the preceding year's allocations. Methods for evaluation include the use of circulation statistics, interlibrary loan statistics, comparison with bibliographies, user comment and opinion, unfilled patron needs, and the rate and pattern of collection growth.

APPENDIX A
Titles Classified by the Library of Congress Classification: National Shelflist Count

AC	Collections
AE	Encyclopedias
AG	General Reference Works
AI	Indexes
AM	Museums, Collectors & Collecting
AN	Newspapers (if used by campus)
AP	Periodicals
AS	Societies, Academies
AY	Yearbooks, Almanacs, Directories
AZ	History of the Sciences in General, Scholarship, Learning
B 1-68	Philosophy: Periodicals, Societies, Congresses, etc.
B 69-789	Philosophy: History and Systems, Ancient through Renaissance
B 790-5739	Philosophy: History and Systems, Post-Renaissance
BC	Logic
BD	Speculative Philosophy
BF 1-1000	Psychology
BF 1001-1400	Parapsychology
BF 1401-1999	Occult Sciences
BH	Aesthetics
BJ 1-1800	Ethics
BJ 1801-2195	Social Usages, Etiquette
BL	Religions. Mythology, Rationalism

BM	Judaism
BP	Islam, Bahaism, Theosophy, etc.
BQ	Buddhism
BR	Christianity (General)
BS	Bible
BT	Doctrinal Theology
BV	Practical Theology
BX 1-799	Eastern Christian Churches
BX 800-4795	Roman Catholic Church
BX 4800-9999	Protestantism
C	Auxiliary Sciences of History: General
CB	History of Civilization and Culture
CC	Archaeology (General)
CD	Diplomatics, Archives, Seals
CE	Chronology
CJ	Numismatics
CN	Epigraphy
CR	Heraldry
CS	Genealogy
CT	Biography
D 1-900	History (General)
D 901-1075	History of Europe, General
DA	History: Great Britain
DB	History: Austria, Austro-Hungarian Empire, Hungary
DC	History: France
DD	History: Germany
DE	History: Mediterranean Region, Greco-Roman World
DF	History: Greece
DG	History: Italy
DH	History: Netherlands (Low Countries, General and Belgium)
DJ	History: Netherlands (Holland)
DJK	History: Eastern Europe
DK	History: Russia, U.S.S.R.

DL	History: Northern Europe, Scandinavia
DP 1-500	History: Spain
DP 501-900	History: Portugal
DQ	History: Switzerland
DR	History: Eastern Europe, Balkan Peninsula
DS 1-40	History: Asia
DS 41-329	History: Southwestern Asia, Ancient Orient, Near East
DS 330-500	History: Southern Asia, Indian Ocean
DS 501-935	History: Eastern Asia, Southeastern Asia, Far East
DT	History: Africa
DU	History: Oceania (South Seas)
DX	History: Gypsies
E 1-139	History of Americas: General, Indians, North America
E 140-200	United States, Colonial, Special Topics
E 201-299	United States, Revolutionary Period
E 301-440	United States, 1790–1855
E 441-655	United States, Slavery and Civil War
E 656-867	United States Since the Civil War
F 1-205	State & Local History: New England, Atlantic Coast
F 206-475	State & Local History: South, Gulf States
F 476-705	State & Local History: Midwest, Mississippi Valley
F 721-854	State & Local History: The West
F 856-975	State & Local History: Pacific Coast, Alaska
F1000-1170	History: British America, Canada
F 1201-1392	History: Mexico
F 1401-1419	History: Latin America, Spanish America (General)

F 1421-1577	History: Central America
F 1601-2151	History: West Indies
F 2155-2183	History: Caribbean Area
F 2201-3799	History: South America
G 1-922	Geography (General)
G 1001-3122	Atlases
G 3160-9980	Maps
GA 1-87	Mathematical Geography
GA 100-1999	Cartography
GB	Physical Geography
GC	Oceanography
GF	Anthropogeography
GN 1-296	Anthropology
GN 301-686	Ethnology and Ethnography
GN 700-875	Prehistoric Archaeology
GR	Folklore
GT	Manners and Customs (General)
GV 1-200	Recreation
GV 201-555	Physical Training
GV 557-1198	Sports
GV 1199-1570	Games and Amusements
GV 1580-1799	Dancing
GV 1800-1860	Circuses, Carnivals, etc.
H	The Social Sciences in General
HA	Statistics
HB	Economic Theory
HC	Economic History & Conditions: National Production
HD 1-100	Economics: Production
HD 101-1395	Economics: Land
HD 1401-2210	Agricultural Economics
HD 2321-4730	Economics: Industry
HD 4801-8942	Labor
HD 9000-9999	Special Industries and Trades
HE	Transportation and Communication
HF 1-4050	Commerce
HF 5001-6351	Business
HG	Finance

HJ	Public Finance
HM	Sociology: General Works, Theory
HN	Sociology: Social History and Conditions, etc.
HQ	Family, Marriage, Woman, Sexual Life
HS	Societies: Secret, Benevolent, etc.
HT	Communities, Classes, Races
HV	Social Pathology, Welfare, Criminology
HX	Socialism, Communism, Anarchism, Utopianism
J	Official Documents
JA	Political Science: Collections, etc.
JC	Political Theory
JF	Constitutional History, Administration: General, Comparative
JK	Constitutional History & Administration: United States
JL	Constitutional History, Admin.: British and Latin America
JN	Constitutional History & Administration: Europe
JQ	Constitutional Hist., Admin.: Asia, Africa, Australia, Oceania
JS	Local Government
JV 1-5399	Colonies and Colonization
JV 6001-9500	Emigration & Immigration
JX	International Law
K-KC	Law: General
KD	Law: United Kingdom and Ireland
KE	Law: Canada
KF	Law: U.S. (Federal)
KFA-KFW	Law: U.S. States and Territories
KFX	Law: U.S. Cities
KFZ	Law of Individual Territories
KG-KX	Law: Latin America and Old World

L	Education—General
LA	History of Education
LB	Theory & Practice of Education
LC	Special Aspects of Education
LD	Education: Individual Institutions: United States
LE	Education: Institutions: America (Except United States)
LF	Education: Individual Institutions: Europe
LG	Education: Institutions: Asia, Africa, Oceania
LH	College & School Magazines and Papers
LJ	Student Fraternities and Societies
LT	Textbooks
M 1-4	Music: Collections, Manuscripts, Collected Works, etc.
M 5-1490	Instrumental Music, Music Before 1700
M 1495-5000	Vocal Music
ML	Literature of Music
MT	Musical Instruction and Study
N	Visual Arts (General)
NA	Architecture
NB	Sculpture
NC	Graphic Arts (General), Drawing, Design
ND	Painting
NE	Print Media: Printmaking, Engraving, Lithography, etc.
NK	Decorative Arts, Applied Arts, Crafts
NX	Arts in General
P	Philology, Linguistics
PA 1-2995	Classical Philology

PA 3000-3049	Classical Literature
PA 3050-4500	Greek Literature
PA 5000-5665	Byzantine & Modern Greek Literature
PA 6000-7041	Latin Literature
PA 8001-8595	Medieval and Modern Latin Literature
PB 1-431	Modern Languages: General
PB 1001-3029	Celtic Languages and Literatures
PC 1-400	Romanic Philology and Languages: General
PC 601-872	Romanian Language and Literature
PC 890	Dalmation
PC 901-986	Raeto-Romance Language and Literature
PC 1001-1984	Italian Language, Sardinian Language & Literature
PC 2001-3761	French Language
PC 3801-3976	Catalan Language and Literature
PC 4001-4977	Spanish Language
PC 5001-5498	Portuguese Language
PD 1-777	Germanic Philology and Languages: General
PD 1001-1350	Old Germanic Dialects
PD 1501-7159	North Germanic, Scandinavian
PE	English Philology and Language
PF 1-979	Dutch Language
PF 1001-1184	Flemish Language
PF 1401-1558	Friesian Language and Literature
PF 3001-5999	German Language
PG 1-489	Slavic Philology: General
PG 500-585	Slavic Literature: General
PG 601-799	Church Slavic
PG 801-1158	Bulgarian Language and Literature
PG 1161-1164	Macedonian Language and Literature
PG 1171-1798	Serbo-Croatian Language and Literature
PG 1801-1998	Slovenian Language and Literature
PG 2001-2850	Russian Language

PG 2900-3155	Russian Literature: History and Criticism
PG 3200-3299	Russian Literature: Collections
PG 3300-3490	Russian Literature: Individual Authors
PG 3500-3560	Russian Literature: Provincial and Local
PG 3561-3800	Subjects other than Russian Literature
PG 3801-3998	Ukrainian Language and Literature
PG 4001-5198	Czech Language and Literature
PG 5201-5598	Slovak Language and Literature
PG 5631-5698	Sorbian Language and Literature
PG 6001-7498	Polish Language and Literature
PG 7900-7948	Minor Slavic Dialects
PG 8001-9263	Baltic Languages
PG 9501-9678	Albanian
PH 1-79	Finno-Ugrian and Basque: General
PH 91-498	Finnish Language and Literature
PH 501-1109	Other Finnish Languages and Dialects
PH 1201-3718	Hungarian, Ugrian Languages and Literature
PH 5001-5490	Basque Language and Literature
PJ 1-995	Oriental Philology and Literature: General
PJ 1001-1989	Egyptology
PJ 2001-2199	Coptic
PJ 2301-2551	Hamitic
PJ 3001-4091	Semitic Philology, Assyrian, Sumerian
PJ 4101-5809	Hebrew, Aramaic, Syriac
PJ 5901-9288	Arabic, Ethiopian
PK 1-90	Indo-Iranian Philology and Literature: General
PK 101-2891	Indo-Aryan Languages
PK 2901-5534	Indo-Aryan Literature
PK 6001-6599	Iranian Philology and Literature
PK 6701-6996	Afghan, Beluchi, Kurdish, Ossetic, etc.

PK 7001-9601	Dardic, Armenian, Caucasian Languages
PL 1-489	Ural-Altaic Languages
PL 490-495	East Asiatic Languages & Literature (General), Ainu
PL 501-898	Japanese Language and Literature
PL 901-998	Korean Language and Literature
PL 1001-3299	Chinese Language and Literature
PL 3301-3505	Non-Chinese Languages of China
PL 3521-4587	Indo-Chinese, Karen, Tai, etc. Languages
PL 4601-4961	Dravidian Languages and Literature
PL 5001-7107	Oceanic Languages
PL 7501-7893	Unclassed Languages of Asia and the Pacific
PL 8000-8844	African Languages
PM 1-95	Hyperborean Languages of America and Asia
PM 101-7356	American Languages
PM 7801-7895	Mixed Languages, Creole, Pidgeon English, etc.
PM 8001-9021	Artificial Languages, Secret Languages, Esperanto, etc.
PN 1-44	Literature: Periodicals, Yearbooks, Societies, etc.
PN 45-75	Literature: Theory, Philosophy, Esthetics
PN 80-99	Literary Criticism
PN 101-249	Authorship
PN 441-1009	Literary History
PN1010-1590	Poetry, the Performing Arts, Show Biz
PN 1600-1657	The Drama: Periodicals, Yearbooks, General Works
PN 1660-1864	Technique of Dramatic Composition, History of Drama
PN 1865-1989	Historical & Religious Plays, Tragedy, etc.
PN 1990-1992	Broadcasting
PN 1993-1999	Motion Pictures

PN 2000-2081	The Theater: General
PN 2085-2219	The Theater: The Stage, Accessories, History by Period
PN 2220-2298	The Theater in the United States
PN 2300-2554	The Theater in the Americas Except U.S.
PN 2570-2859	The Theater in Europe
PN 2860-3030	The Theater in Asia, Africa, and Oceania
PN 3035	Jewish Theater
PN 3151-3191	The Theater: Amateur and College Theatricals
PN 3195-3300	The Theater: Minstrel Shows, Spectacles, Tableaux, etc.
PN 3311-3503	Prose, Prose Fiction, the Short Story, etc.
PN 4001-4355	Oratory, Elocution, etc.
PN 4390-4500	Diaries, Letters and Essays
PN 4699-5650	Journalism and the Periodical Press
PN 6010-6078	Literature: General Collections
PN 6080-6095	Collections of Quotations
PN 6099-6120	Collections of Poetry and Drama
PN 6121-6146	Collections of Orations, Letters, Essays
PN 6147-6231	Wit and Humor, Satire
PN 6233-6381	Anacreontic Literature, Extracts, etc.
PN 6400-6700	Proverbs, etc.
PQ 1-841	French Literature: History and Criticism
PQ 1100-1297	Collections of French Literature
PQ 1300-1595	Old French Literature, to ca. 1525
PQ 1600-1709	French Literature, 16th Century
PQ 1701-1935	French Literature, 17th Century
PQ 1947-2147	French Literature, 18th Century
PQ 2149-2551	French Literature, 19th Century
PQ 2600-2651	French Literature, 1900–1960
PQ 2660-2686	French Literature, 1961-
PQ 3800-3999	French Literature, Provincial, Local, Colonial, etc.

PQ 4001-4263	Italian Literature: History and Criticism
PQ 4265-4556	Italian Literature to 1400
PQ 4561-4664	Italian Literature, 1400–1700
PQ 4675-4734	Italian Literature, 1701–1900
PQ 4800-4886	Italian Literature, 1901-
PQ 5901-5999	Italian Literature: Provincial, Local, Colonial
PQ 6001-6269	Spanish Literature: History, Criticism, Collections, etc.
PQ 6271-6498	Spanish Literature to 1700
PQ 6500-6576	Spanish Literature, 1700–ca. 1868
PQ 6600-6647	Spanish Literature, 1868–1960
PQ 6651-6676	Spanish Literature, 1961-
PQ 7000-7079	Spanish Literature: Provincial, & in Europe, North America
PQ 7080-7087	Spanish Literature in Spanish America (General)
PQ 7100-7349	Spanish Literature of Mexico, Former U.S. Spanish Provinces
PQ 7361-7539	Spanish Literature of West Indies and Central America
PQ 7551-8560	Spanish Literature of South America
PQ 8600-8929	Spanish Literature of Africa, Asia, Australia, etc.
PQ 9000-9189	Portuguese Literature: History, Criticism, Collections, etc.
PQ 9191-9255	Portuguese Literature to 1700
PQ 9261-9288	Portuguese Literature since 1700
PQ 9400-9479	Portuguese Literature: Provincial & in Europe, U.S., Canada
PQ 9500-9696	Portuguese Literature of Brazil, to 1800
PQ 9697-9699	Portuguese Literature of Brazil, since 1800
PQ 9900-9999	Portuguese Literature of Africa, Asia, Australia, etc.
PR 1-78	English Literature: Literary History and Criticism

PR 81-151	History of English Literature, General
PR 161-479	History of English Literature, by Period
PR 500-978	History of English Literature, by Form (Poetry, Drama, etc)
PR 1098-1395	English Literature: Collections
PR 1490-1799	Anglo-Saxon Literature
PR 1803-2165	Anglo-Norman and Early Middle English Literature
PR 2199-2405	English Renaissance Literature, Prose and Poetry
PR 2411-2416	English Renaissance Drama: Anonymous Plays
PR 2417-2749	English Renaissance Drama: Plays by Playwright A-Shaj
PR 2750-3112	Shakespeare
PR 3135-3198	English Renaissance Drama: Plays by Playwrights Shar-Z
PR 3291-3785	English Literature, 17th and 18th Centuries
PR 3991-5990	English Literature, 19th Century
PR 6000-6049	English Literature, 1900–1960
PR 6050-6076	English Literature, 1961-
PR 8309-9899	English Literature: Provincial, Colonial, etc.
PS 1-478	American Literature: General, Criticism, History
PS 501-690	American Literature: Collections
PS 700-893	American Literature: Colonial Period
PS 991-3390	American Literature: 19th Century
PS 3500-3549	American Literature: 1900–1960
PS 3550-3576	American Literature: 1961-
PT 1-951	German Literature: History, Criticism, Folk Literature
PT 1100-1485	Collections of German Literature
PT 1501-1695	German Literature: 1050–1450/1500
PT 1701-1797	German Literature: 1500–ca. 1700

PT 1799-2592	German Literature: 1700–ca. 1860/70
PT 2600-2659	German Literature: 1860/70–1960
PT 2660-2688	German Literature: 1961-
PT 3701-4899	German Literature: Provincial, Local, Colonial, etc.
PT 5001-5395	Dutch Literature: History and Criticism
PT 5400-5547	Dutch Literature: Collections
PT 5555-5880	Dutch Literature through 1960
PT 5881	Dutch Literature, 1961-
PT 5885-5980	Translations into Dutch, Provincial Dutch Literature, etc.
PT 6000-6471	Flemish Literature since 1830
PT 6500-6590	Afrikaans Literature to 1960
PT 6592	Afrikaans Literature since 1961
PT 7001-7099	Scandinavian Literature: General
PT 7101-7599	Icelandic, Old Norwegian, Faroese
PT 7601-8260	Danish Literature
PT 8301-9155	Norwegian Literature
PT 9201-9999	Swedish Literature
PZ 1-4	Fiction in English
PZ 5-10	Juvenile Literature: American and English
PZ 11-99	Juvenile Literature: Foreign
Q	Science (General) (B)
QA 1-99	Mathematics (General)
QA 101-145	Arithmetic
QA 150-299	Algebra
QA 300-433	Mathematical Analysis (Calculus, etc.)
QA 440-799	Geometry, Trigonometry
QA 801-939	Analytic Mechanics
QB	Astronomy
QC 1-75	Physics (General)
QC 81-119	Weights and Measures
QC 120-168	Experimental Mechanics
QC 170-220	Constitution and Properties of Matter

QC 221-246	Sound
QC 251-338	Heat
QC 350-496	Light, Optics, Radiation (General)
QC 501-798	Electricity, Magnetism, Nuclear Physics
QC 801-999	Geophysics, Meteorology, Geomagnetism
QD 1-69	Chemistry (General)
QD 71-145	Analytical Chemistry
QD 146-199	Inorganic Chemistry
QD 241-449	Organic Chemistry
QD 450-731	Physical and Theoretical Chemistry
QD 901-999	Crystallography
QE	Geology
QH 1-199	Natural History (General)
QH 201-278	Microscopy
QH 301-705	Biology (General)
QK 1-474	Botany (General)
QK 475-989	Botany (Specific Fields)
QL 1-355	Zoology (General)
QL 362-739	Invertebrate and Vertebrate Zoology
QL 750-991	Ethology, Anatomy, Embryology
QM	Human Anatomy (B)
QP 1-348	Physiology (General) (B)
QP 351-499	Nervous System and the Senses (B)
QP 501-801	Animal Biochemistry (B)
QP 901-981	Experimental Pharmacology (B)
QR	Microbiology (B)
R 1-130	Medicine: Periodicals, Societies, General Topics (B)
R 131-687	Medicine: History, Medical Expeditions (B)
R 690-899	Medicine: Special Subjects (B)
RA 3-420	Medicine and the State (B)
RA 421-790	Public Health (B)
RA 791-955	Medical Geography
RA 960-998	Medical Centers, Hospitals, etc. (B)
RA 1001-1171	Forensic Medicine, Medical Jurisprudence (B)

RA 1190-1270	Toxicology (B)
RB	Pathology (B)
RC 1-106	Internal Medicine, Medical Practice: General Works (B)
RC 110-253	Infectious and Parasitic Diseases (B)
RC 254-298	Neoplasma, Neoplastic Diseases (B)
RC 306-320	Tuberculosis (B)
RC 321-431	Neurology (B)
RC 435-576	Psychiatry, Psychopathology (B)
RC 578-632	Allergic, Metabolic, Nutritional Diseases (B)
RC 633-935	Diseases of Organs, Glands, Systems (B)
RC 936-951	Diseases of Regions of the Body (B)
RC 952-1299	Geriatrics, Arctic and Tropical Medicine, etc. (B)
RD	Surgery (B)
RE	Ophthalmology (B)
RF	Otorhinolaryngology (B)
RG	Gynecology and Obstetrics (B)
RJ	Pediatrics (B)
RK	Dentistry (B)
RL	Dermatology (B)
RM	Therapeutics, Pharmacology (B)
RS	Pharmacy and Materia Medica (B)
RT	Nursing (B)
RV	Botanic, Thomsonian, Eclectic Medicine (B)
RX	Homeopathy (B)
RZ	Other Systems of Medicine (B)
S 1-760	Agriculture (General)
S 900-972	Conservation of Natural Resources
SB	Plant Culture and Horticulture
SD	Forestry
SF	Animal Culture, Veterinary Medicine, etc.
SH	Fish Culture and Fisheries
SK	Hunting Sports

T	Technology - General
TA	Engineering - General, Civil Engineering
TC	Hydraulic Engineering
TD	Environmental Technology, Sanitary Engineering
TE	Highway Engineering
TF	Railroad Engineering and Operation
TG	Bridge Engineering
TH	Building Construction
TJ	Mechanical Engineering and Machinery
TK	Electrical Engineering, Electronics, Nuclear Engineering
TL	Motor Vehicles, Aeronautics, Astronautics
TN	Mining Engineering and Metallurgy
TP	Chemical Technology
TR	Photography
TS	Manufactures
TT	Handicrafts, Arts and Crafts
TX	Domestic Arts
U	Military Science (General)
UA	Armies: Organization, Distribution, etc.
UB	Military Administration
UC	Military Science: Maintenance and Transportation
UD	Infantry
UE	Cavalry, Armor
UF	Artillery
UG	Military Engineering
UH	Military Science: Other Services
V	Naval Science (General)
VA	Navies: Organization, Distribution, etc.
VB	Naval Administration

VC	Naval Maintenance
VD	Naval Seamen
VE	Marines
VF	Naval Ordnance
VG	Minor Services of Navies
VK	Navigation, Merchant Marine
VM	Naval Architecture, Shipbuilding, etc.

Z 4-15	History of Books and Bookmaking
Z 40-115	Writing, Paleography
Z 116-550	Printing
Z 551-661	Copyright, Intellectual Property
Z 662-1000	Libraries: Library Science
Z 1001-1121	Bibliography, General
Z 1201-1212	National Bibliography: America
Z 1215-1361	National Bibliography: United States (B)
Z 1365-1401	National Bibliography: Canada
Z 1411-1945	National Bibliography: Mexico, Central & South America
Z 2000-2959	National Bibliography: Europe
Z 3001-4980	National Bibliography: Asia, Africa, Australia, Oceania
Z 5051-5055	Subject and Personal Bibliography: Academies, Societies, etc.
Z 5056-8999	Subject and Personal Bibliography: Other

STANDARDS FOR UNIVERSITY LIBRARIES: EVALUATION OF PERFORMANCE

PREPARED BY
ACRL UNIVERSITY LIBRARIES SECTION'S
UNIVERSITY LIBRARY STANDARDS REVIEW
COMMITTEE
KENT HENDRICKSON, CHAIR

Approved June 1989

Association of College
and Research Libraries
A Division of the
American Library Association

Standards for university libraries: Evaluation of performance

Prepared by the ULS University Library Standards Review
Committee
Kent Hendrickson, Chair

Approved by the ACRL Board at the 1989 Midwinter Meeting and
the ALA Standards Committee at the 1989 Annual Conference.

The initial "Standards for University Libraries" were
adopted by ACRL in 1979. This new revision was prepared by ACRL's Ad Hoc University Library Standards
Review Committee. The members are Patricia L. Bril,
California State University, Fullerton; Murray S. Martin,
Tufts University; Richard W. Meyer, Clemson University;
Maxine Reneker, Arizona State University; Jack A. Sig-
gins, Yale University; and Kent Hendrickson, University
of Nebraska-Lincoln (chair).

Foreword

The 1979 Standards were the product of a joint effort by
ACRL and ARL and the cumulation of eleven years of
work by several committees of both organizations. An
excellent background on the development of standards for
university libraries may be found in Beverly Lynch, "University Library Standards," *Library Trends* 31 (Summer
1982): 33–47. Other articles and related documents are
referenced in the appendices to this document. Appendix

1 cites other standards, statements, and guidelines relating to specific aspects of university libraries. Appendix 2 lists materials providing further information on the application of these standards.

As part of the process of reviewing the 1979 Standards the Committee solicited advice from other members of the university library community. First, open hearings were held during the ALA Midwinter Meetings in 1986; and second, a number of guests consulted with the Committee at the ALA Annual Conference in 1986 and the 1987 Midwinter Meeting. Comments were also received from representatives of regional accrediting associations and selected university administrators. Once the decision was made to revise the existing Standards, the Committee continued to seek advice, culminating with an open hearing during the 1988 ALA Annual Conference.

Many of the same issues discussed by the committees responsible for the 1979 Standards were raised again. By far the most important of these was the question of whether standards should be quantitative or qualitative. In the end, based on the information received, we concluded that neither approach was appropriate. A model procedure for determining measurable expectations is the primary need.

This approach was chosen very carefully. In the course of its deliberations the Committee looked at three issues: Who uses Standards? Why do they use them? What do they need? Standards are addressed to library managers, institutional managers, and evaluating bodies such as accreditation teams. While each of these groups may use standards to arrive at an evaluation of a library, they may do so for quite different reasons. Common needs, however, relate to how well the library is doing, how well it is supported, and how well it compares to other libraries. To answer these questions, facts are needed; not the kind that can be set out readily in a series of prescriptive statements or normative figures, but those gathered through the process described by these standards.

Basic to this document is the proposition that each university library system is unique and therefore should determine its own criteria for performance and evaluation. This process should be undertaken within the framework of the university's mission and goals. Another assumption is that, however the library is placed within the governing structure of the university, its relationship should be such that adequate communication flows to it concerning basic shifts in the mission of the university and changes in its programs. This document also assumes that the critical assessment resulting from the defined process will be transmitted appropriately throughout the university.

It is further assumed that within the library, administrators will have achieved the balance of hierarchical and collegial management, which will allow the libraries' goals to be achieved, as well as adequate representation of staff views into the goal-setting and evaluation process, and appropriate development of the staff in the managerial, scholarly, and professional facets of their job responsibilities.

Finally, this document is necessarily prescriptive in several of its concepts. University libraries must become skilled in the process of examining and redefining as necessary their missions, establishing coherent goals whose attainment may be measured, continually and effectively assessing the needs of users, and identifying and applying those measures that will reveal the extent to which it has been successful in fulfilling its mission.

Introduction

These standards are intended to help members of the library and university administration responsible for determining priorities and evaluating performance to optimize the performance of the library in terms of the mission of the university.

While standards are needed, they cannot be stated as absolutes equally applicable to all universities and be useful. These standards are not a series of expectations or prescriptive sets of figures. They set forth the process by which expectations may be established, and enumerate the topics that should be addressed in the evaluation of university library performance. For supporting detail, see the appendices.

These standards begin with a basic statement of purpose, explain the underlying assumptions, and lead to a statement of expectations.

Standards

General Statement of Purpose

These standards set out the role of the university library within the context of the institution's information policies and academic goals. This mission of the university library is to provide information services in support of the teaching, research, and public service missions of the university. The achievement of that mission requires the development of standards to address the ways in which goals should be developed and measured, needed resources estimated, and success in goal achievement evaluated.

Underlying Assumptions

(1) *Centrality of the Library*
The library is of central importance to the institution. It is an organic combination of people, collections, and buildings whose purpose is to assist users in the process of transforming information into knowledge.

Information and knowledge are central to the attainment of any university's goals. The ways in which information is selected, acquired, stored or accessed, and distributed within the institution will, in large measure, determine the level and success of teaching, scholarship, and research. The institution needs clear policies concerning access to and provision of information. The library must take an active role in the development of these policies.

(2) *The Significance of the Investment in the Library*
The library represents one of the largest cumulative capital investments on any campus. Libraries provide

added value as part of all learning and research processes. The concept of the library as an investment is basic to these standards.

(3) *The Individual Nature of Each Institution*

Each institution has a unique mix of goals, programs, and expectations. These are influenced by geographical location, obligations to other institutions, history, and mission.

(4) *The Individual Nature of Each Library*

The library serving the institution is, as a result, unique. The application of prescriptive measures to a group of unique institutions has been rejected as inapposite. It is the use and interpretation of measures that is important in developing a process for managing change. The need is for a mixture of input and output measures, both qualitative and quantitative, but fundamentally process-oriented.

(5) *Technological Change*

The pace of technological change has rendered outmoded any concept of isolation and self-sufficiency. The library now exists within a complex information world, most of whose participants are not on campus. The library must be dynamic and future-oriented. This orientation does not seek change for its own sake, but recognizes the mutable nature of information in the computer age. Libraries will not abandon their traditional roles as collectors and conservators. Rather they will add new ones as facilitators and processors, and these new roles need to be recognized in the evaluation process.

Section A: Setting Goals and Objectives

To determine the appropriate goals for a university library, representative bodies should engage in a continuing dialogue, carried out on several levels, and documented in a memorandum of understanding or a mission statement adopted by the governing board of the institution.

(1) *Participants*

The participants involved in the process of setting goals should include appropriate representatives from the following groups:

(A) University and Library administration
(B) Faculty
(C) Library staff
(D) Students
(E) Trustees or regents
(F) Advisory Boards
(G) State or other governmental units associated with
      the institution.

The roles of these constituencies vary, but their basic purpose is to bring to the discussions information concerning needs, goals, abilities, and points of view, as these affect the library.

(2) *Process*

The process is one of communication, both formal and informal, designed to increase the level of shared understanding concerning the goals and capabilities of the library.

Formal communication includes committee reports, internal memoranda and newsletters, the annual and special reports of the library and the institution, and discussion in the appropriate public forums.

The administrative organization of the university is itself a means of communication and it is essential that the library, through its administration, be placed so as to have access as needed to the appropriate officers and committees of the institution.

Informal communication is the result of daily contact between members of the community. The library staff should be able to participate fully in such contact. Continuous communication through the daily activities of the library also conveys a message about its role within the institution.

(3) *Product*

The object of this dialogue is to establish goals, provide for their measurement, and assess the degree to which they are reached.

The result should be a shared statement that may take various forms and cover various periods as determined by the institutional policies regarding such matters. The library is responsible for developing short- and long-term goals and objectives in response to this statement, again in consultation with the other participants in the dialogue.

A process of review and revision is required to keep current with need and capacity.

Section B: Factors to be Considered in Developing Goals

The development of goals and objectives requires that the resources needed and available to meet those goals be kept in mind. This section sets forth some of those factors.

Definition: The library consists of a combination of three resources: people, collections, and buildings. These resources are paid for from a budget. They need to be in correct proportion to one another to meet the service goals of the library. There are no comprehensive formulas for arriving at these proportions, but there are ways of determining whether the allocation of resources is in line with expectations.

(1) *Budgetary Support and Sources*

The library represents a major capital investment. As such, it requires ongoing annual investment to retain its value.

The sources of funding vary greatly, in accordance with the style of the parent institution. Whatever the source, the library should control its funds. Although there are many different methods of organizing and controlling budgets, the method chosen should make it possible for the library to operate without undue constraint.

(A) *Capital Expenditures.* It is customary to distinguish and separate major capital expenditures, such as new buildings, renovations, or the installation of automated systems from annual operating budgets. Added resources and services needed to keep up-to-date and maintain expanded plant are also needed.

Minor capital investments will be made each year for extensions or renovations. Adequate provision should be made for both kinds of capital expenditure.

(B) *Operating Budget.* The operating budget of the library must be appropriate to the mission of the library within the university, and sufficient to sustain all operations, including the maintenance of automated systems. The budget should be developed interactively by the university and the library in accordance with the general practice of the institution. If it is impossible to meet all expectations or fund specific new programs this should be made clear, and a means for setting priorities established.

(C) *Budgetary Control.* The library must be responsible for the internal allocation and control of the approved budget, with provision for appropriate consultation. Transactions should be carried out in accordance with the accounting ·practice of the university. Those practices should recognize the special needs of the library, particularly in purchasing library materials.

(D) *Maintenance.* The complex modern library requires constant attention to ensure that it continues to function smoothly.

i. The library is responsible for the ongoing maintenance of its resources and services. This includes not only provision for replacement of equipment and library materials, but also keeping adequate statistics and other performance measures to determine whether the standards of service are being maintained.

ii. Appropriate budgetary provision should be made for maintenance, replacement, repair, renovation, and for investment in new and improved means of information access and delivery.

(2) *Human Resources*

The library is dependent on human resources skilled in the knowledge-based disciplines to achieve its goals. People select, acquire, process, and organize the library's collections, and provide access to the information contained in those collections and the collections of other libraries; they direct its activities and provide its services.

(A) *Level of Staffing.* The library should be staffed in such a way as to meet the university's expectations. The numbers required are determined by the programs offered, the number of buildings and service points, and the hours during which service is offered. While there are no absolute requirements, it is clear that the level of service is determined by the availability of staff.

(B) *Kinds of Staff Needed.* The staff should include librarians and other professionals, support staff, clerks, and students to provide services at the appropriate levels. The proportions of each group to the whole are determined by the programs supported and the locations served. The staff should incorporate the needed skills and academic training to meet the academic needs of the university, and to provide management support.

To reflect the library's involvement in the academic programs of the university, librarians should have appropriate educational backgrounds in library and information science as well as in other disciplines. Librarians require the protection necessary to ensure intellectual freedom, so that they may not be subject to improper pressure in matters such as censorship, copyright, instruction, or the selection of materials. They have the right, as professionals, to speak out on behalf of their professional concerns without fear of reprisal or dismissal.

(C) *Relationship to Other Staff.* The director is responsible for all staff within the library and should ensure that the library adheres to the personnel policies and practices of the university. These policies and practices should recognize the special needs of librarians as professionals working in the field of information.

(D) *Organization.* The organization of the library should reflect its nature and purpose. As a service institution its interest is in people as providers of services. There is general agreement that librarians should be able to exercise independent professional judgment, within the rules, policies, and codes governing professional conduct; to participate in research and the work of professional organizations; to undertake consulting and other professional tasks; and to find advancement within the library, without necessarily having to undertake administrative and supervisory duties. Librarians should participate in the formulations of policies, in accordance with the style of the institution.

(E) *Management.* The library, under the director, should be responsible for managing its own affairs.

This autonomy does not abrogate the responsibility of the library for maintaining relationships with administration and faculty to achieve the dialogue recommended in these standards. The library should also adhere to local procedures and practices as they are stated by the appropriate university agencies.

(F) *Staff Development.* Librarians need to keep pace with change in the fields of library and information science, and other disciplines. The staff and the library administration have a joint responsibility for the development of knowledge and skills. The administration should provide the leadership, resources, and management to foster the cooperative process, the goal being to ensure that the library retain the skills needed to provide service to the university community at the proper level. The library staff should contribute to meeting the goal of keeping up-to-date by expanding their own academic and professional knowledge.

(3) *Collections*

The primary goal of the library is to select, collect, organize, and provide access to all varieties of information for users. Library programs should be developed with that goal in mind.

(A) *Collection Management.* The library shall select and acquire materials in all formats to the level required to support academic programs in research, teaching, and public service.

i. Collection management includes not only purchase for retention, but also leasing, renting, deselection, providing access to other collections, including as appropriate, planned resource-sharing and cooperative storage, and electronic access to databases.

ii. The collections should be extensive enough to support the academic programs offered, recognizing that there are instances where reliance can and should be placed on access to other resources rather than on ownership.

iii. There should be provision for adequate funding to ensure the addition of needed new resources, to maintain growth not only in existing areas of study and research, but also in newly added disciplines or extensions of existing disciplines.

iv. Recognition should be given to changes and academic programs. Equally, recognition should be given to library contributions to consortial or other resource-sharing programs.

v. The collection management program of the library should be developed jointly by the library and the university, indicating the depth and breadth of the collections, as set out in an appropriate taxonomy. The policies setting out this program should be in written form, openly accessible, and regularly reviewed.

vi. The library is responsible for relations with vendors, contractors, and other agencies, and for reviewing the efficacy of such relationships.

(B) *Collection Preservation.* The library should have a program for the conservation and preservation of materials, either locally or with other libraries and agencies. Such a program should be integrated with national programs for conservation and preservation.

i. The library requires variable combinations of temperature and humidity control, and a program for fire and damaging prevention. These should be provided and reassessed at regular intervals.

ii. The library should have an emergency plan to cover minor and major disasters and include both damage prevention and damage recovery. It should also provide for alternative service and management, and be coordinated with campus-wide plans.

iii. The library should not only be able to provide for the care and preservation of its own collections, but be able to participate in local, regional, and national preservation plans.

iv. The library should have adequate safeguards against loss, mutilation, and theft. Since the library has a primary goal of maintaining open access to information, it is particularly vulnerable to those who take advantage of the public good that the library represents. To reduce loss and damage the library should exercise appropriate control over use and borrowing.

(4) *Building Resources*

The library should be housed in one or more buildings adequate to its role within the university, and should reflect a coherent planning effort. That plan should be developed with the participation of all affected parties, and should be reviewed regularly to ensure that changes in expectations, academic programs, or the library and information world are taken into account.

(A) *Amount of Space.* The library should provide space to house collections, space for study and research, and space for associated processing and public service functions, including the provision of space for automated services in a properly controlled environment. The relationships between buildings, spaces, and functions should reflect an appropriately developed written program.

(B) *Distribution of Space.* The choice for the physical organization of the university library must be made in terms of its administrative organization, tempered by recognition of the costs involved. Historically, there have been several solutions to the provision of library space, some philosophically based, others based on cost and institutional style. These range from centralization in one library building to dispersal among several faculty, college, or departmental libraries. Whatever the spatial mode chosen, the choice must be made in accordance with programmatic need, and following a careful process of decision. It is essential to provide the resources needed to implement the style of organization chosen.

(C) *Location of Space.* To fulfill their service missions, libraries need to be close to the center of campus activity. The space occupied is likely to be high in value, as is the cost of the building itself. In planning library facilities, consideration should therefore be given to the possibility of using remote or compact storage for lesser-used materials. If shared storage facilities are available and economical, their use should be considered. In any such case, a solution of this kind should not make access for the user onerous. In a similar manner, space planning should take into account advances in electronic storage, transmission, and retrieval of information.

(D) *Planning Needs.* Because the library grows with the addition of resources (not simply books, but people, work space, machines, and other equipment) long-term planning is essential. External changes, such as the effect of

telecommunications, must also be taken into account. The lead time for the accumulation of capital, the reparation of working drawings, and construction require that library projects be built into long-term university space planning.
(5) *Services*

The overarching goal of the library is to provide services to the university community.

The resources considered in the four preceding sections are the tools with which the library staff develops programs of service. Those programs are measured by their effectiveness in meeting user needs.

(A) *Access.* The library should ensure optimal access to its own collection and to needed resources available elsewhere by developing and maintaining appropriate policies and procedures.

The goal is to make library resources accessible to all members of the institutional community, in accordance with their needs and with regard for the preservation of materials, compliance with legal requirements such as copyright, and the right to personal privacy.

i. Catalog and other records should inform the user about what is owned, where it is, and how to find it. They should be comprehensive and up-to-date, and adhere to accepted national international standards.

ii. Collections should be systematically arranged, using a readily understandable taxonomy. The library should not unduly restrict access, but should take account of the need to preserve fragile materials. If storage facilities are used, retrieval should not place an undue burden on the user.

iii. The library should check collection availability at regular intervals.

iv. The rules and regulations for the use of the library and its collections should be readily accessible to users.

v. The library should provide information transfer services of two kinds: the physical transfer of documents and facsimiles of documents, and the transfer of data electronically.

(a) With the development of online catalogs, telefacsimile transmission, and other forms of information transfer, many users are now able to conduct their bibliographic research outside the library. In such instances, providing access implies the delivery of information, whether in printed or electronic format, by the library to the user at the user's location. This process should be reflected in the policies and procedures of the library.

(b) The library should participate in programs for the sharing of bibliographic data.

(c) The library should participate in programs for inter-library loan, telefacsimile, and document delivery and adhere to the codes for the borrowing and lending of materials. The rules and conditions relating to these programs should be clearly explained. Where charges are required, this should be made clear to potential users; similarly, where restrictions apply.

(d) The library should be prepared, wherever appropriate, to facilitate direct transfer to the user of information so available, as, for example, from databanks, or by referral to other agencies capable of meeting the need.

(B) *Explanation of Resources Services.* The library should provide directional, informational, instructional, and reference services. These services include not only the answering of questions and instruction in the use of the library, but also the provision of printed, graphic, or electronic aids. By these means the library staff should seek to create an awareness of the need to understand the ways in which information-seeking has changed and is changing. The program should therefore be dynamic rather than static in its orientation.

i. The library should provide services designed for all levels of user from freshman to faculty member. By teaching, the use of printed guides, bibliographies, the development of electronic aids and personal interactions, the library staff should seek to assist users in finding needed material and developing appropriate search strategies.

ii. Bibliographic instruction, both formal and informal, should play a significant role in helping library users improve their skills.

iii. Library design should also play a role in making the library understandable. Similarly, new services such as online catalogs should be designed with the user in mind.

iv. These services should be provided not only in the library itself but also in the classroom and through public media, both on and off campus, including extension programs.

(6) *University-wide Cooperation*

To fulfill its goals, the library requires support from within the institution, and, in turn, supports other programs. Such interdependence requires clear relationships with other parts of the university.

(A) *General Requirements.* The library should cooperate with and participate in all university services and programs concerned with information and communication. These activities include such functions as admissions, continuing education, development, public relations, computer services, telecommunications, audiovisual services, publishing, copyright, royalty, depository, and exchange arrangements.

(B) *Computer and Telecommunications Services.* The close link between the library's information services and the provision of computer and telecommunications services for the university as a whole requires that a relationship be established and that the development of all such services be seen as a unified university responsibility.

(C) *Other Services.* Other internal relationships are less direct, but equally important to the mission of the library. The library is, for example, a factor in attracting students and faculty. Because the library plays a central role in research and teaching, it should be involved in plans for the development of the university. Where access to library services is made possible for any external community, for example, the surrounding community, students in off-campus courses, or the residents of a state, such policy decisions should be made with full library consultation.

(7) *Cooperative Programs*

The library exists within a network of relationships extending beyond the institution. These relationships may be customary, contractual, cooperative, or symbolic.

In cooperation with other libraries, consortia, networks, vendors, and other agencies, the library should participate in programs that will assist in meeting its goals and are consistent with the mission of the university.

(8) *Responsiveness to Change*

The library should anticipate changes in the field of information. While this need not mean that the library itself should undertake a particular service, the library should bring that service and its implications to the attention of the university community.

(A) *New Technology.* The library should adopt and maintain new technologies as they develop and are useful in meeting its goals. New services do not totally replace older ones, and the institution must be prepared to provide needed support for an increasing range of information technologies, or to make choices between the services that can be provided within the budget.

(B) *Experimentation.* The library should be conceived as existing within and central to a network of information services, rather than as a stand-alone function. The library needs to assess, by testing and experimentation, the role of new information formats as they emerge.

Section C: Measuring Achievements and Forming a Statement of Expectations

The responsibility for the evaluation of the library lies with the university administration.

The university and the library administration together should establish a mechanism to measure the level of achievement of the library.

The mechanism should establish identifiable outcomes, both qualitative and quantitative, using agreed-on criteria, and providing appropriate feedback. The process should be continuous rather than unitary, though it must also fit into any process established by the university for self-evaluation.

The goal is to arrive at a clearly stated set of expectations, which can be matched against the resources needed, in both cases with the support and understanding of the library and the other participants in the process.

There is no single best way of measuring achievement. A variety of procedures should be used. The budgetary process is one of these, in the course of which goals are set and their achievement measured. Annual reports review progress and set new goals. Accreditation visits offer similar opportunities.

Ongoing interactive communication with committees and other advisory groups is a necessary complement. All these activities provide a setting, based on economic and political realities, within which the review process can go forward.

Inevitably, comparisons will be made with libraries in other universities. Although such comparisons are difficult because of major differences among both institutions and libraries, comparative judgments can be made. These should be aided by appropriate quantitative measures and should not be based solely on subjective evaluations. The critical point is that, if the institution determines to use peer evaluation, the library and the university should agree on a list of institutions having similar missions, goals, and programs. This enables the evaluator to avoid comparing dissimilar libraries.

All these procedures recognize that the library is not static but dynamic and needs to be evaluated from that perspective. As the goals and needs of the university change, so do those of the library. Past measures may no longer be important and new ones may need to be found. An example that has emerged over recent years is the use of access rather than ownership of materials as a criterion.

Any evaluation requires that the responsibility for the evaluation be clearly assigned, the procedure to be followed be understood by all participants, and the goal be defined.

(1) *Participants*

The participants will vary, depending on whether the review is annual, in which case they are likely to be internal to the institution, or if the review is periodic, when the review team is likely to be external. Such external review may also be linked to accreditation or other mandated reviews of the whole institution. Whatever the basis for the review, the membership of the review team should be agreed on by the library and university administrations. The reviewers should be informed of the procedures to be followed, and provided with appropriate documentation. Reports and testimony from both library and non-library sources are proper, in particular from those intimately concerned with the setting of goals.

The report resulting from the review should be made available to both library and university administrators, but acceptance, rejection, and any subsequent implementation of recommendations are the responsibility of the university administrator who is responsible for the library.

(2) *Process*

The procedure followed should parallel that for any major academic or administrative unit.

(A) *Annual Review.* This kind of review is usually associated with the development of the library budget, and will, therefore, consist principally of a dialogue among those responsible for that process. There should be provision for review and discussion of the library's budget presentation, together with review of goals and objectives. The dialogue should give all parties the opportunity to examine the relationships between resources and expectations without preconditions.

Similarly, the annual reporting process provides an opportunity for review of success and failures, and for the development of new goals. These processes can be as formal or informal as required by the university.

(B) *Periodic Review.* Reviews of this nature, whether carried out by internal or external review teams, should include self-assessment, examination by the review team, and review of any reports and recommendations by the university and the library.

The process of self-assessment should provide adequate time for the preparation of the necessary information, and for preliminary review within the university. If the review team requires further information, time should be allowed for its preparation. This process should involve all parties concerned with the university library.

The review should allow for consultation with the appropriate persons concerned with the library and should not be subject to prior decisions as to results.

The resulting reports and recommendations should be reviewed by the appropriate library and university administrators, and there should be an opportunity to clarify misunderstandings and supply further evidence.

Criteria for the evaluation of library resources and services are set out in the following section of these standards. All criteria need to be adapted to the circumstances of each institution, as part of the process of review. Whatever the criteria, they should reflect the views of all participants and be stated clearly.

(3) *Product*

The results of any review or evaluation should be made available in written form to those responsible for administering the library, who should be given the chance to respond or to amplify. The final review should then become the basis for future action by the institution.

The outcome of reporting and discussion should be a reassessment of the library's goals and objectives. It should take into account budgetary and operational limitations, and should establish realistic expectations for the future. By this process the university and the library can maintain a practical balance between resources and mission.

Section D: Evaluative Criteria

The questions that follow are suggested as a means of reaching a proper assessment of the library. There may be other questions that are more appropriate for any individual university library and all libraries should use any measures that are available locally.

(1) *Planning*

(A) Does the institution include library participation in its planning process?

(B) Are there plans for future library development?

(C) Is the mechanism for making these plans adequate?

(D) Do the plans show appropriate consultation within the university?

(E) Is the library staff properly involved in planning and decision-making?

(F) Are there appropriate strategies for reaching stated goals?

(G) Are the goals and timetables realistic?

(2) *Adequacy of Budget*

(A) Are the budgetary resources sufficient to support current activities and to provide for future development?

(B) Does the budget support the purchase of or provision of access to the necessary range of library materials?

(C) Does the budget support the appropriate numbers and kinds of staff for the programs offered?

(D) Is the salary and benefits program adequate and designed to foster retention and recognize achievement?

(E) Does the budget provide adequate support for other operating expenses, including automated services?

(F) Does the budget provide adequate support for new programs and innovations?

(G) Does the process by which the budget is developed allow for appropriate consultation?

(H) Does the library director have the appropriate level of discretion and control over the expenditure of the allocated budget?

(3) *Adequacy of Human Resources*

(A) Are the numbers of staff adequate for the services provided?

(B) Is the distribution of staff among programs appropriate?

(C) Are the proportions of professional and support staff appropriate to the functions served?

(D) Is there an established staff development program for maintaining and improving the education and skills of the library staff?

(E) Are staffing needs properly taken into account in planning new ventures or expansion of existing programs?

(F) Are the policies and procedures for handling staff matters properly formulated and available to staff members? Are they in written form? Do they facilitate performance or hinder it?

(G) Is there a means for staff utilization/job analysis to assure that positions are properly assigned by level and that the staff are performing work appropriate to the level?

(4) *Adequacy of Collection*

(A) Is there a written policy for managing the collection?

(B) Does this policy address issues of user satisfaction?

(C) Is there provision for considering change in academic needs?

(D) What basis is used for determining collection levels and sizes?

(E) Is there evidence of areas of undersupply?

(F) Is there evidence of areas of oversupply?

(G) Does current collecting reflect an appropriate level of program support?

(H) Is there appropriate provision for the review of the current collections?

(I) Is there provision for the transfer and relocation of collections or portions of collections if and when appropriate?

(J) Is there provision for the consideration of consortial and other relationships?

(5) *Adequacy of Buildings and Equipment*

(A) Are the buildings sufficient to house staff and collections?

(B) Are the buildings adequately maintained?

(C) Are there appropriate space plans?

(D) Is there appropriate provision for use by the handicapped?

(E) Is the range, quantity, and location of equipment adequate to the programs offered?

(F) Is the equipment adequately maintained?

(G) Is there budgetary provision for upgrading, repair, or replacement?

(H) Is there evidence of planning for the use of new and improved technologies?

(6)*Access and Availability of the Collections*

(A) Are the policies governing access to and use of the collections clearly stated and readily available?

(B) Are the collections properly housed?

(C) Are the collections actually accessible and available?

(D) Are the bibliographic records appropriate?

(E) Is the staff that is provided for automation, technical services, and other collection-related functions sufficient for the task?

(F) How readily can the library provide materials not owned?

(G) What kinds of cooperative programs are in place?

(H) Is the level of staff support adequate?

(7) *Preservation and Conservation*

(A) Does the library have proper environmental controls?

(B) Does the library have an emergency plan?

(C) Does the library budget have adequate provision for the preservation and repair of damaged, aged, and brittle books?

(D) Does the library have adequate safeguards against loss, mutilation, and theft?

(8) *Resource Usage*

(A) What are the library policies for resource use?

(B) How much is the collection used?

(C) How well is the collection used?

(D) What is the fulfillment ratio?

(E) What is the relationship between collection size, collection growth rate, and collection use?

(9) *Adequacy of Services*

(A) What range of services is offered? Over what range of time?

(B) Are these services appropriate to the mission of the library?

(C) Are the locations where services are offered adequate to the purpose?

(D) What statistics and other measures of quality and quantity are maintained?

(E) Are the size and distribution of public service staff adequate for the numbers and kinds of users?

Appendix 1: Standards, Statements, and Guidelines

Standards, statements, and guidelines relating to specific aspects of university libraries may provide additional valuable guidance in evaluation. Due to size differences and variations in the programs of universities, all of the following standards may not be useful for any individual library. For example, "Standards for College Libraries" may provide relevant guidance to smaller universities in establishing minimal standards for collections and facilities, but will be less meaningful for large research libraries. The reader is referred to the *ALA Handbook of Organization* for a fuller listing of standards and guidelines. Offprints of many of these are available from the American Library Association.

Items listed are sorted according to the major topics of the standards in Section B.

Budgetary Support

ALA. ACRL. "Standards for College Libraries." *College and Research Libraries News* 47, no. 3 (March 1986): 189–200.

Human Resources

ALA. ACRL. "Guidelines and Procedures for the Screening and Appointment of Academic Librarians." *College and Research Libraries News* 38, no. 8 (September 1977): 231–33.

ALA. ACRL. "Model Statement of Criteria and Procedures for Appointment, Promotion in Academic Rank, and Tenure for College and University Librarians." *College and Research Libraries News* 48, no. 5 (May 1987): 247–54.

ALA. ACRL. "Standards for Ethical Conduct for Rare Book, Manuscript, and Special Collections Librarians." *College and Research Libraries News* 48, no. 3 (March 1987): 134–35.

ALA. ACRL. "Standards for Faculty Status for College and University Librarians." *College and Research Libraries News* 35, no. 5 (May 1974): 112–13.

ALA. ACRL. "Statement on Collective Bargaining." (1975). Photocopy.

ALA. ACRL. "Statement on Terminal Professional Degree for Academic Librarians." (1975). Photocopy.

ALA. ACRL. Association of American Colleges, and American Association of University Professors. "Statement on Faculty Status of College and University Librarians." *College and Research Libraries News* 35, no. (February 1974): 26.

ALA. Office for Library Personnel Resources. "Comparable Rewards: The Case for Equal Compensation for Non-Administrative Expertise." Chicago: ALA, 1979.

ALA. Office for Library Personnel Resources. "Guidelines for Affirmative Action Plans." Chicago: ALA, 1976.

ALA Office for Library Personnel Resources. "Library Education and Personnel Utilization." Chicago: ALA, 1976.

Collections

ALA. ACRL. "Guidelines on Manuscripts and Archives." Compilation of policy statements prepared by the ACRL Rare Books and Manuscripts Section's Committee on Manuscripts Collections. 1977. Photocopy.

ALA. Resources and Technical Services Division. *Guidelines for Collection Development.* Edited by David L. Perkins. Chicago: ALA, 1979.

ALA. Resources and Technical Services Division. *Guidelines for Handling Library Orders for Imprint Monographic Publications.* 2d ed. Chicago: ALA, 1984.

ALA. Resources and Technical Services Division. *Preparation of Archival Copies of Theses and Dissertations,* by Jane Boyd and Don Etherington. Chicago: ALA, 1986.

Building Resources

ALA. ACRL. "Access Policy Guidelines." *College and Research Libraries News* 36, no. 10 (November 1975): 322–23.

ALA. ACRL and Society of American Archivists. "Joint Statement on Access to Original Research Materials."

College and Research Libraries News 40, no. 4 (April 1979): 111–12.

ALA. ACRL. "Guidelines for the Security of Rare Books, Manuscripts and Other Special Collections." *College and Research Libraries News* 43, no. 3 (March 1982): 90–93.

Programs and Services

ALA. ACRL. "Guidelines for Audiovisual Services in Academic Libraries." *College and Research Libraries News* 48, no. 9 (October 1987): 533–36.

ALA. ACRL. "Guidelines for Bibliographic Instruction in Academic Libraries." *College and Research Libraries News* 38, no. 4 (April 1977): 92.

ALA. ACRL. "Guidelines for Branch Libraries in Colleges and Universities." *College and Research Libraries News* 36, no. 9 (October 1975): 281–83.

ALA. ACRL. "Guidelines for Extended Campus Library Services." *College and Research Libraries News* 43, no. 3 (March 1982): 86–88.

ALA. ACRL. "The Mission of an Undergraduate Library: Model Statement." *College and Research Libraries News* 48, no. 9 (October 1987): 542–44.

ALA. Reference and Adult Services Division. "A Commitment to Information Services: Developmental Guidelines." Chicago: ALA, 1979.

Cooperative Programs

ALA. Reference and Adult Services Division. "Interlibrary Loan Code for Regional, State, Local, or Other Special Groups of Libraries." *RQ* 20, no. 1 (Fall 1980): 26–28.

International Federation of Library Associations and Institutions. Section on Interlibrary Lending. "International Lending Principles and Guidelines for Procedure (1978)." *RQ* 20, no. 1 (Fall 1980): 32–36.

ALA. Reference and Adult Services Division. "National Interlibrary Loan Code, 1980," *RQ* 20, no. 1 (Fall 1980): 29–31.

Appendix 2: Supporting Materials

The items listed here provide further information relating to the application of these standards to libraries. They were selected with a view to augmenting the standards, by providing additional guidance in evaluating university libraries or in establishing criteria. The items cited are those considered to provide the best entry to the subject. In a few instances, journal articles were cited when no monograph was available on the issue of concern. The annotations are intended only to suggest the means by which each item may supplement the standards.

The reader is also reminded that the statistics collected by the Association of College and Research Libraries (ACRL) of the American Library Association and by the Association of Research Libraries (ARL) contain a wealth of comparative data useful for developing profiles of peer institutions. In addition, the *SPEC Kits* published by the ARL and the *CLIP Notes* published by ACRL can be helpful in synthesizing a profile of the generic research library.

Items listed are sorted according to the major topics of the standards in Section B.

Budgetary Support

College & University Business Administration. Edited by Lanora F. Welzenbach. 4th ed. Washington, D.C.: National Association of College and University Business Officers, 1982.

This is the authoritative reference manual for university administrators involved in establishing business procedures, including budget development. Although it contains little information directly relevant to library evaluation, the organizational structure, budgeting process, and administrative procedure recommended for and typical of most campuses is covered clearly. This work facilitates an understanding of the process that results in placement of the library within the institutional setting. It also describes the accounting practices often required of libraries.

Ratio Analysis in Higher Education: A Guide to Assessing the Institution's Financial Condition. New York: Peat, Marwick, Mitchell, 1980.

This book attempts to provide explicit guidance in obtaining information from financial reports of an institution about its condition. The work explains the fundamentals of the balance sheet and recasts it into ratios designed for comparative evaluation of the health of the institution relative to its peers.

Human Resources

Riggs, Donald E. *Strategic Planning for Library Managers.* Phoenix:Oryx Press, 1984.

In order to develop mission, goals, and objectives, substantial planning is required. This work provides an overview of the strategic planning process so that library managers may better understand the current state of their libraries, where they are going, where they should be going, and how best they may get there.

Collections

Christiansen, Dorothy E., C. Roger Davis, and Jutta Reed-Scott. *Guide to Collection Evaluation through Use and User Studies.* Chicago: ALA, 1983.

"This document was prepared by the Subcommittee on Use and User Studies, Collection Management and Development committee of RTSD . . . to provide librarians and others with a summary of the types of methods available to determine the extent to which . . . library materials are used. It is not intended to readily equip librarians to do use or user studies for collection evaluation but rather to allow them to identify the kind of study best suited to their needs."

Hall, Blaine H. *Collection Assessment Manual for College and University Libraries.* Phoenix: Oryx Press, 1985.

This manual is designed to provide the reader with tools to plan collection assessment, apply the right measurement techniques, analyze the results, and report findings in order to determine effectiveness in meeting collection goals.

National Enquiry into Scholarly Communication. *Scholarly Communication: The Report of the National Enquiry.* Baltimore: Johns Hopkins University Press, 1979.
"Report of a comprehensive three-year research effort conducted under the auspices of the American Council of Learned Societies." This assessment of the state of modern communication through scholarly journals and books provides relevant guidance to librarians attempting to understand the methods used by researchers to document and share their work.

Reed-Scott, Jutta. *Manual for the North American Inventory of Research Library Collections.* Washington, D.C.: Office of Management Studies, Association of Research Libraries, 1985.
The analytical framework developed by the Research Libraries Group, referred to as the RLG Conspectus, was expanded into a broader based North American inventory project by ARL. This manual documents the methodology codified by the Office of Management Studies of ARL for comparative evaluation of collections against profiles of other libraries. Collection strengths can be identified by means of a standard tool for description and assessment with the use of this manual.

Stubbs, Kendon. *Quantitative Criteria for Academic Research Libraries.* Chicago: ALA, 1984.
Using statistical techniques, the author developed quantitative guidelines from the HEGIS survey statistics to distinguish research libraries from non-research libraries. On the basis of this research, minimal criteria for research libraries are suggested. This information may be useful for some libraries that fall under the guidelines of these standards and desire quantitative criteria to articulate their mission.

Use of Library Materials: The University of Pittsburgh Study. New York: M. Dekker, 1979.
This study attempts to determine "the extent to which library materials are used and the full cost of such use" with

the intent of developing a model useful in predicting the return on increasing library expenditure. Although widely criticized, this is one of the few quantitative approaches ever made to model collection development efforts.

Building Resources

Metcalf, Keyes DeWitt. *Planning Academic and Research Library Buildings.* 2nd ed. by Philip D. Leighton and David C. Weber, Chicago: ALA, 1986.

An update to Metcalf's 1956 edition, which served as the bible for building guidelines, this work is designed to be used by librarians and architects. Tables provide formulas and other information relevant to standards for space, lighting, equipment, organization, and other factors.

Programs and Services

ALA. ACRL. *Evaluating Bibliographic Instruction: A Handbook.* Chicago: ALA, 1983.

As well as providing an introduction to the basic precepts of evaluation, this manual is designed to provide the reader with tools to evaluate the effectiveness of bibliographic instruction programs. Chapters are contributed by several authors.

Cronin, Mary J. *Performance Measures for Public Services in Academic and Research Libraries.* Washington, D.C.: Office of Management Studies, Association of Research Libraries, 1985.

"Quality of service in academic libraries . . . is defined in terms of the needs of the library user, and the skills of the library staff in assessing and meeting those needs." This paper pulls together the theory, application and potential of performance measures for academic libraries. It provides a starting point for evaluating library effectiveness in meeting user needs and academic goals.

Determining the Effectiveness of Campus Services. Robert A. Scott, editor. San Francisco: Jossey-Bass, 1984.

Includes six papers covering the major aspects of determining the effectiveness of campus services. Designed to be a sourcebook for those selected to conduct evaluations of campus services such as the library, computer services, public relations, and student services. While not covering libraries exhaustively, the information relevant to other services provides useful insights into overall evaluation methodology.

Dougherty. Richard M. "Libraries and Computing Centers: A Blueprint for Collaboration." *College and Research Libraries* 48, no. 4 (July 1987): 289–96.

For the institution attempting to articulate the mission of the library, this article provides a useful pattern for determining the relationship of the library to the computer center for the individual campus.

Kantor, Paul B. *Objective Performance Measures for Academic and Research Libraries.* Washington, D.C.: Association of Research Libraries, 1984.

Libraries operating within an environment that "constrains, supports, and evaluates" requires some means to determine achievement of objectives. Three measures of performance provided in this manual give concrete means for library staff to determine the effectiveness of library programs in fulfilling the mission of the library. The model covers the areas of availability, accessibility, and delay analysis.

Lancaster, F. Wilfrid. *The Measurement and Evaluation of Library Services.* Washington, D.C.: Information Resources Press, 1977.

This is a general manual of procedures and techniques to use in evaluating the various service functions of the library where evaluation is defined as comparison of performance with objectives.

Reference Policy and Administrative Documents. Edited by Paula D. Watson, Chicago: ALA, 1985.

Reference services policies, online service policies, and reference collection development policies collected in response to the survey conducted by RASD were edited by Paula Watson. These policy statements, along with accompanying organization charts and job descriptions, provide comparative information on the organization of reference departments.

Watson, Paula D. *Reference Services in Academic Research Libraries.* Chicago: ALA, 1986.

The results of sixty-six medium and large research libraries surveyed on the organization, staffing, and functional operations of research library reference departments are reported. Analysis of bibliographic instruction and online search services provides additional comparative information.

University-wide Programs

Boyer, Ernest L. *College: The Undergraduate Experience in America.* New York: Harper & Row, 1987.

A cogent analysis of the condition of undergraduate education in the United States in the 1980s, this report provides many useful insights into changing directions that will affect the mission and organization of libraries. Based on visits to twenty-nine representative campuses along with exhaustive surveys conducted at hundreds more, this work makes numerous recommendations for changing the program approach typically followed by today's colleges. Those changes will affect the organizational setting of libraries.

Flower, Kenneth E. *Academic Libraries on the Periphery: How Telecommunications Information Policy Is Determined in Universities.* OMS, ARL Occasional paper, no 11. Washington, D.C.: Office of Management Studies, Association of Research Libraries, 1986.

Developments in twenty-six universities were examined to reveal that libraries tend to be outside the decision-making process that determines telecommunications policy on research campuses.

Garvin, David A. *The Economics of University Behavior.* New York: Academic Press, 1980.

This analysis by an economist describes the university with a model characterizing it as a prestige-maximizing organization subject to market forces, which helps to explain the behavior of the university community. It provides useful insights into the issues that shape the institution.

Hardesty, Larry L., Jamie Hastreiter, and David Henderson, *Mission Statements for College Libraries.* CLIP Note #5. Chicago: ALA, 1985.

This is a collection of actual mission statements from twenty-six institutions ranging in size from small colleges to moderately large universities. It also includes statements from six regional accrediting agencies.

Responsiveness to Change

Moran, Barbara B. *Academic Libraries: The Changing Knowledge Centers of Colleges and Universities.* Washington, D.C.: Association for the Study of Higher Education, 1984.

The impact of new technology, rising costs, physical preservation problems, and new management approaches requires clear articulation to university administrators of the problems facing libraries. This work attempts to codify in one place those issues driving the restructuring of academic libraries during a period of substantial change and provides a synthesis essential to communicating the options to university administrators.

Priorities for Academic Libraries. Thomas J. Galvin and Beverly P. Lynch, editors. San Francisco: Jossey-Bass, 1982.

This collection of papers by librarians and university administrators, edited by Thomas Galvin and Beverly Lynch, provides an overview of the changes that have caused libraries to be moved from the realm of benign neglect to the center of administrative attention. That attention often requires librarians to re-articulate the rationale behind their enterprise. The goal of this work is to assist with that task.

STANDARDS FOR COLLEGE LIBRARIES, 1986

PREPARED BY THE COLLEGE LIBRARY
STANDARDS COMMITTEE
Jacquelyn M. Morris, Chair

The final version approved by the ACRL Board of Directors.

The Standards for College Libraries were first prepared by a committee of ACRL, approved in 1959, and revised in 1975. This new revision was prepared by ACRL's Ad Hoc College Library Standards Committee. Members are Jacquelyn M. Morris, University of the Pacific (chair); B. Anne Commerton, State University of New York at Oswego; Brian D. Rogers, Connecticut College; Louise S. Sherby, Columbia University; David B. Walch, California Polytechnic State University; and Barbara Williams-Jenkins, South Carolina State College.

Foreword

These Standards were approved as policy by the ACRL Board of Directors at the ALA Midwinter Meeting in Chicago on January 19, 1986. They supersede the 1985 draft Standards published in *C & RL News,* May 1985, and the 1975 Standards published in *C & RL News,* October 1975.

The Ad Hoc Committee was appointed in 1982 to examine the 1975 Standards with particular attention to the following areas:

a. Non-print collections and services;

b. Collections (Formula A) Staff (Formula B), and Budget (% of Education & General);

c. Networking and cooperative associations; and to recommend revisions that would bring them up to date and make them more generally useful.

The Committee studied each standard in terms of the charge and reviewed several recent studies on the subject of Standards, including;

Larry Hardesty and Stella Bentley, *The Use and Effectiveness of the 1975 Standards for College Libraries: A Survey of College Library Directors* (1981).

Ray L. Carpenter, "College Libraries: A Comparative Analysis in Terms of the ACRL Standards," *College & Research Libraries* (42) (January 1981): 7–18.

"An Evaluative Checklist for Reviewing a College Library Program. Based on the 1975 Standards for College Libraries," *C & RL News,* November 1979, pp. 305–16.

The Committee also published a call for comments on the 1975 Standards (*C &RL News,* December 1983) and held hearings at the 1984 ALA Midwinter Meeting and the 1985 ALA Annual Conference.

One of the primary issues with which the Committee has dealt is the effect of new technology on the Standards. While no one predicts the immediate demise of books as we know them, one cannot ignore the multiplicity of formats in which information appears. For example, will the emerging body of online reference tools eventually make it possible for libraries to provide comparable or improved service with smaller book collections?

Access to the major bibliographic utilities is another issue related to technology and libraries. In an information-rich society, does lack of access to these utilities have a detrimental effect on the scholarly programs college libraries are attempting to support? How should the Standards address this lack of concern?

A similar related issue centers on resource sharing and networking. Through access to the emerging "National Database" (defined as the totality of OCLC, RLIN, WLN, and LC) we have greatly increased our knowledge of other libraries' collections. Online identification and location of needed material has shortened the retrieval time. Electronic mail will have a similar impact on resource sharing. Since even the largest libraries find it difficult to collect comprehensively, resource sharing has become an increasingly common fact of life. The 1975 Standards placed a very high value on browsability and immediate access to materials, whereas resource sharing is somewhat contradictory to this concept. On the other hand, cooperative agreements allow for exposure and access to vastly more extensive resources than was hitherto possible.

The Committee discussed extensively the topic of performance measures. While the library directors surveyed and reported in the Hardesty-Bentley article stressed the need for performance measures in the College Library Standards, the Committee concluded that providing them *at this point* is beyond the scope of its charge. Obviously, however, this is a concept whose time has come: the ACRL Ad Hoc Committee on Performance Measures for Academic Libraries, chaired by Virginia Tiefel, has received a five-year appointment, which gives some indication of the complexity of the task. The library profession should monitor and support the work of this ad hoc committee.

Some sentiment has been expressed for standards with less emphasis on quantitative measures, patterned after the more abstract "Standards for University Libraries" (*C & RL News,* April 1979, pp. 101–10). While there are certain advantages to standards written in this way, the vast majority of those expressing opinions to the Committee supported the quantitative measurements provided for in the College Library Standards. Most who expressed this view cited Carpenter's findings, noting that a very large percentage of college libraries fail to meet minimum standards in terms of collection size, staff size or budget. Consequently, prescribed goals continue to be regarded by librarians as an important component of the Standards.

While many statements have been modified in these Standards, certain important points should be noted. For example, while the 1975 Standards addressed collection size, they did not address serial subscriptions, on which it is not unusual now for a library to spend half or more of its annual materials budget. Each Standard has been reviewed in light of library technology, networking, and resource sharing, and audiovisual materials. The inclusion of these aspects of libraries has been addressed in Standard 2, Collections; Standard 3, Organization of Material; Standard 6, Facilities; and Standard 8, Budget.

Introduction to the standards

Libraries have long been considered an integral and essential part of the educational programs offered by colleges. Their role has included collecting the records of civilization and documentation of scientific pursuit. An equally important role is to offer various programs to teach or assist users in the retrieval or interpretation of these records and documents. These information resources are essential for members of the higher education community to pursue their academic programs successfully. Total fulfillment of these roles is, however, an ideal goal that continues to be sought and is yet to be attained. Expectations as to the degree of success in achieving this goal vary from institution to institution, and it is this diversity of expectations that prompts the library profession to offer standards for college libraries.

The Standards seek to describe a realistic set of conditions, which, if met, will provide a college library program of good quality. Every attempt has been made to synthesize and articulate the library profession's expertise and views of the factors contributing to the adequacy of a library's budget, resources, facilities, and staffing, and the effectiveness of its services, administration, and organization.

These Standards are intended to apply to libraries supporting academic programs at the bachelor's and master's degree levels. They may be applied to libraries at universities that grant a small number of doctoral degrees, say, fewer than ten per year. They are not designed for use in two-year colleges, larger universities, or independent professional schools.*

The eight sections of the 1975 College Library Standards have been retained, and include:

1. Objectives
2. Collectives
3. Organization of Materials
4. Staff
5. Services
6. Facilities
7. Administration
8. Budget

Each standard is followed by commentary intended to amplify its intent and assist in its implementation.

Whenever appropriate, the terminology and definitions in the ANSI Z39.7 Standards published in 1983 have been used.

Standard 1: Objectives

1 *The college library shall develop on explicit statement of its objectives in accord with the goals and purposes of the college.*

Commentary

The administration and faculty of every college have a responsibility to examine the educational program from time to time in light of the goals and purposes of the institution. Librarians share this responsibility by seeking ways to provide collections and services that support those goals and purposes. Successful fulfillment of this

---

*Specifically these Standards address themselves to institutions defined by the Carnegie Commission on Higher Education as Liberal Arts Colleges I and II and Comprehensive Universities and Colleges I and II. See the revised edition of *A Classification of Institutions of Higher Education* Berkeley, Calif.: The Council, 1976.

shared responsibility can best be attained when a clear and explicit statement of library objectives is prepared and promulgated so that all members of the college community can understand and evaluate the appropriateness and effectiveness of the library program.

1.1. *The development of library objectives shall be the responsibility of the library staff, in consultation with members of the teaching faculty, administrative officers, and students.*

Commentary

The articulation of library objectives is an obligation of the librarians, with the assistance of the support staff. In developing these objectives the library should seek in a formal or structured way the advice and guidance of its primary users, the faculty and students, and of the college administration, in particular those officers responsible for academic programs and policies.

1.2 *The statement of library objectives shall be reviewed periodically and revised as necessary.*

Commentary

In reviewing the objectives of the library, careful attention should be paid to ongoing advances in the theory and practice of librarianship. Similarly, changes occurring within the education program of the parent institution should be reflected in a timely way in the program of the library.

Standard 2: The collection

2 *The library's collections shall comprise all types of recorded information, including print materials in all formats, audiovisual materials, sound recordings, materials used with computers, graphics, and three-dimensional materials.*

Commentary

Recorded knowledge and literary or artistic works appear in a wide range of formats. Books represent extended reports of scholarly investigation, compilations of findings, and summaries prepared for instructional purposes. The journal communicates more recent information and is particularly important to the science disciplines. Reports in machine-readable form are an even faster means of research communication. Government documents transmit information generated by or at the behest of official agencies, and newspapers record daily activities throughout the world.

Many kinds of communication take place primarily, or exclusively, through such media as films, slide-tapes, sound recordings, and videotapes. Microforms are used to compact many kinds of information for preservation and storage. Recorded information also exists in the form of manuscripts, archives, databases, and computer software packages. Each medium of communication transmits information in unique ways, and each tends to complement the others.

The inherent unity of recorded information and its importance to all academic departments of an institution require that most, if not all, of this information be selected, organized and made available for use by the library of that institution. In this way the institution's information resources can best be articulated and balanced for the benefit of all users.

2.1 *The library shall provide as promptly as possible a high percentage of the materials needed by its users.*

Commentary

While it is important that a library have in its collection the quantity of materials called for in Formula A, its resources ought to be augmented whenever appropriate with external collections and services. A library that meets part of its responsibilities in this way must ensure that such activities do not weaken a continuing commitment to develop its own holdings. There is no substitute for a strong, immediately accessible collection. Moreover, once a collection has attained the size called for by this formula, its usefulness will soon diminish if new materials are not acquired at an annual gross growth rate of from two to five percent. Libraries with collections that are significantly below the size recommended in Formula A should maintain the 5% growth rate until they can claim a grade of A (see Standard 2.2). Those that meet or exceed the criteria for a grade of A may find it unrealistic or unnecessary to sustain a 5% growth rate.

The proper development of a collection includes concern for quality as well as quantity. A collection may be said to have quality for its purposes only to the degree that it possesses a portion of the bibliography of each discipline taught, appropriate in quantity both to the level at which each is taught and to the number of students and faculty members who use it. While it is possible to have quantity without quality, it is not possible to have quality without quantity defined in relation to the characteristics of the institution. No easily applicable criteria have yet been developed, however, for measuring quality in library collections.

The best way to preserve or improve quality in a college library collection is to adhere to rigorous standards of discrimination in the selection of materials to be added, whether as purchases or gifts. The collection should contain a substantial portion of the titles listed in standard bibliographies for the curricular areas of the institution and for supporting general fields of knowledge. Subject lists for college libraries have been prepared by several learned associations, while general bibliographies such as *Books for College Libraries* are especially useful for identifying important retrospective titles. A majority of the appropriate, current publications reviewed in scholarly journals and in reviewing media such as *Choice* or *Library Journal* should be acquired. Careful attention should also be given to standard works of reference and to bibliographical tools that describe the broad range of information sources.

Institutional needs for periodical holdings vary so widely that a generally applicable formula cannot be used, but in general it is good practice for a library to own any title that is needed more than six times per year. Several good lists have been prepared of periodical titles appropriate or necessary for college collections. Katz's *Magazines for Libraries* describes 6,500 titles, of which approximately ten percent may be regarded as essential to a broad liberal arts program for undergraduates. To this estimate must be added as many titles as are deemed necessary by the teaching faculty and librarians to provide requisite depth and diversity of holdings. It may not be necessary to subscribe to certain less frequently used titles if they are available at another library nearby, or if needed articles may be quickly procured through a reliable delivery system or by electronic means.

The library collection should be continually evaluated against standard bibliographies and evolving institutional requirements for purposes both of adding new titles and identifying for withdrawal those titles that have outlived their usefulness. No title should be retained for which a clear purpose is not evident in terms of academic programs or extra-curricular enrichment.

Although the scope and content of the collection is ultimately the responsibility of the library staff, this responsibility can be best fulfilled by developing clear selection policies in cooperation with the teaching faculty. Moreover, the teaching faculty should be encouraged to participate in the selection of new titles for the collection.

2.2 The amount of print material to be provided by the library shall be determined by a formula (see Formula A) that takes into account the nature and extent of the academic program of the institution, its enrollment, and the size of the teaching faculty. Moreover, audiovisual holdings and annual resource sharing transactions should be added to this volume count in assessing the extent to which a library succeeds in making materials available to its users.

Commentary

A. PRINT RESOURCES

A strong core collection of print materials, augmented by specific allowances for enrollment, faculty size, and curricular offerings, is an indispensable requirement for the library of any college. The degree to which a library meets this requirement may be calculated with Formula A.

B. AUDIOVISUAL RESOURCES

The range, extent and configuration of nonprint resources and services in college libraries varies widely according to institutional needs and characteristics. Although audiovisual materials may constitute an important and sometimes sizable part of a library collection, it is neither appropriate nor possible to establish a generally applicable prescriptive formula for calculating the number of such items that should be available.

Audiovisual holdings may be counted as bibliographic unit equivalents and this number should be added to that for print volumes and volume-equivalents in measuring a library's collection against Formula A. These materials include videocassettes, films, and videodisks (1 item = 1 BUE), sound recordings, filmstrips, loops, slide-tape sets, graphic materials including maps, and computer software packages (1 item = 1 BUE); and slides (50 slides = 1 BUE). If some or all of this material is housed in an administratively separate media center or audiovisual facility, it may be included in the grade determination if properly organized for use and readily accessible to the college community.

C. RESOURCE SHARING

The extent of resource sharing through formal cooperative arrangements among libraries should be recognized in any assessment of the ability of a library to supply its users with needed materials. Annual statistics of resource sharing should be added to print and audiovisual holdings for purposes of grade determination, as follows:

FORMULA A—

1. Basic collection	85,000 vols.
2. Allowance per FTE faculty member	100 vols.
3. Allowance per FTE student	15 vols.
4. Allowance per undergraduate major or minor field*	350 vols.
5. Allowance per master's field, when no higher degree is offered in the field*	6,000 vols.
6. Allowance per master's field, when a higher degree is offered in the field*	3,000 vols.
7. Allowance per 6th year specialist degree field*	6,000 vols.
8. Allowance per doctoral field*	25,000 vols.

A "volume" is defined as a physical unit of a work that has been printed or otherwise reproduced, typewritten, or handwritten, contained in one binding or portfolio, hardbound or paperbound, that has been catalogued, classified, or otherwise prepared for use. Microform holdings should be converted to volume-equivalents, whether by actual count or by an averaging formula that considers each reel of microfilm, or ten pieces of any other microform, as one volume-equivalent.

*For example of List of Fields, see Gerald S. Malitz, *A Classification of Instructional Programs*. Washington, D.C.: National Center for Education Statistics, 1981.

1. Number of books or other items borrowed through ILL channels or from other sources, including film and videocassette rental agencies.

2. Number of items borrowed from a nearby library with which a formal resource sharing arrangement is in effect.

D. DETERMINATION OF GRADE

The degree to which a library provides its users with materials is graded by comparing the combined total of holdings (volumes, volume-equivalents, and bibliographic unit equivalents) and resource sharing transactions with the results of the Formula A calculation. Libraries that can provide 90 to 100 percent of as many volumes as are called for in Formula A, augmenting that volume count with figures from Section B and C, shall be graded A in terms of library resources. From 75 to 89 percent shall be graded B; 60 to 74 percent shall be graded C; and 50 to 59 percent shall be graded D.

Standard 3: Organization of materials

3 *Library collections shall be organized by nationally approved conventions and arranged for efficient retrieval at time of need.*

Commentary

The acquisition of library materials comprises only part of the task of providing access to them. Collections should be indexed and arranged systematically to assure efficient identification and retrieval.

3.1 *There shall be a union catalog of the library's holdings that permits identification of items, regardless of format or location, by author, title, and subject.*

Commentary

The union catalog should be comprehensive and provide bibliographic access to materials in all formats owned by the library. This can best be accomplished through the development of a catalog with items entered in accord with established national or international bibliographical conventions, such as rules for entry, descriptive cataloging, filing, classification, and subject headings.

Opportunities of several kinds exist for the cooperative development of the library's catalog. These include the use of cataloging information produced by the Library of Congress and the various bibliographic utilities. It may also include the compilation by a number of libraries of a shared catalog. Catalogs should be subject to continual editing to keep them abreast of modern terminology and contemporary practice.

3.1.1. *The catalog shall be in a format that can be consulted by a number of users concurrently.*

Commentary

A public catalog in any format can satisfy this Standard if it is so arranged that the library's users normally encounter no delay in gaining access to it. While this is rarely a problem with the card catalog, the implementation of a microform, book, or online catalog requires that a sufficient number of copies (or terminals) be available to minimize delay in access at times of heavy demand.

3.1.2 *In addition to the union catalog there shall also be requisite subordinate files to provide bibliographic control and access to all library materials.*

Commentary

Proper organization of the collections requires the maintenance of a number of subordinate files, such as authority files and shelf lists, and of complementary catalogs, such as serial holdings records. Information contained in these files should also be available to library users. In addition, the content of library materials such as journals, documents, and microforms should be made accessible through indexes in printed or computer-based format.

3.2 *Library materials shall be arranged to provide maximum accessibility to all users. Certain categories of materials may be segregated by form for convenience.*

Commentary

Materials should be arranged so that related information can be easily consulted. Some materials such as rarities, manuscripts, or archives, may be segregated for purposes of security and preservation. Materials in exceptionally active use, reference works, and assigned readings, may be kept separate as reference and reserve collections to facilitate access to them. Audiovisual materials, maps, and microforms are examples of resources that may be awkward to integrate physically because of form and may need to be segregated from the main collection. Fragmentation of the collections should be avoided wherever possible, however, with the bulk of the collections shelved by subject in open stack areas to permit and encourage browsing.

3.3 *Materials placed in storage facilities shall be readily accessible to users.*

Commentary

Many libraries or groups of libraries have developed storage facilities for low-use materials such as sets or backruns of journals. These facilities may be situated on campus or in remote locations. The materials housed in these facilities should be easily identifiable and readily available for use in a timely fashion. If direct user access is not possible, a rapid retrieval system should be provided.

Standard 4: Staff

4 *The staff shall be of adequate size and quality to meet the library's needs for services, programs, and collection organization.*

Commentary

The college library shall need a staff composed of qualified librarians, skilled support personnel, and part-time assistants to carry out its stated objectives.

4.1 *Librarians, including the director, shall have a graduate degree from an ALA accredited program, shall be responsible for duties of a professional nature, and shall participate in library and other professional associations.*

Commentary

The librarian has acquired through education in a graduate school of library and information science an understanding of the principles and theories of selection, acquisition, organization, interpretation and administration of library resources. It should be noted that the MLS is regarded as a terminal professional degree by ALA and ACRL. Moreover, developments in computer and information technology have had a major impact on librarianship requiring further that librarians be well informed in this developing area.

Librarians shall be assigned responsibilities that are appropriate to their education and experience and that encourage the ongoing development of professional competencies. Participation in library and other professional associations on and off campus is also necessary to further personal development.

4.2 *Librarians shall be organized as a separate academic unit such as a department or a school. They shall administer themselves in accord with ACRL "Standards for Faculty Status for College and University Librarians" and institutional policies and guidelines.*

Commentary

Librarians comprise the faculty of the library and should organize, administer, and govern themselves accordingly. The status, responsibilities, perquisites and governance of the library faculty shall be fully recognized and supported by the parent institution.

4.3 *The number of librarians required shall be determined by a formula (see Formula B) and shall further take into consideration the goals and services of the library, programs, degrees offered, institutional enrollment, size of faculty and staff, and auxiliary programs.*

Commentary

Formula B is based on enrollment, collection size, and growth of the collection. Other factors to be considered in determining staff size are services and programs, degrees offered, size of the faculty and staff, and auxiliary programs. Examples of services and programs include reference and information services, bibliographic instruction, computer-based services, collection development, and collection organization. In addition, auxiliary programs, e.g., extension, community, and continuing education, as well as size and configuration of facilities and hours of service, are factors to be considered for staff size.

4.4. *The support staff and part-time assistants shall be assigned responsibilities appropriate to their qualifica-*

FORMULA B—

Enrollment, collection size and growth of collection determine the number of librarians required by the college and shall be computed as follows (to be calculated cumulatively):

For each 500, or fraction thereof, FTE students up to 10,000	1 librarian
For each 1,000, or fraction thereof, FTE students above 10,000	1 librarian
For each 100,000 volumes, or fraction thereof, in the collection	1 librarian
For each 5,000 volumes, or fraction thereof, added per year	1 librarian

Libraries that provide 90–100 percent of these formula requirements can, when they are supported by sufficient other staff members, consider themselves at the A level in terms of staff size; those that provide 75–89 percent of these requirements may rate themselves as B; those with 60–74 percent of requirements qualify for a C; and those with 50–59 percent of requirements warrant a D.

tions, training, experience and capabilities. The support staff shall be no less than 65% of the total library staff, not including student assistants.

Commentary

Full-time and part-time support staff carry out a wide variety of paraprofessional, technical, and clerical responsibilities. A productive working relationship between the librarians and the support staff is an essential ingredient in the successful operation of the library. In addition student assistants provide meaningful support in accomplishing many library tasks.

4.5 *Library policies and procedures concerning staff shall be in accord with institutional guidelines and sound personnel management.*

Commentary

The staff represents one of the library's most important assets in support of the instructional program of the college. Its management must be based upon sound, contemporary practices and procedures consistent with the goals and purposes of the institution, including the following:

1. Recruitment methods should be based upon a careful definition of positions to be filled and objective evaluation of credentials and qualifications.

2. Written procedures should be developed in accordance with ACRL and institutional guidelines, and followed in matters of appointment, promotion, tenure, dismissal and appeal.

3. Every staff member should be informed in writing as to the scope of his/her responsibilities.

4. Rates of pay and benefits of library staff should be equivalent to other positions on campus requiring comparable backgrounds.

5. There should be a structured program for orientation and training of new staff members, and career development should be provided for all staff.

SUPPLEMENTARY STAFFING FACTORS TO BE CONSIDERED

Organizational and Institutional

The individual library's organization and institutional factors also influence its staffing needs. Additional factors to be considered are as follows:

Library	*Institutional*
Services and Programs	Degrees Offered
Size and Configuration of Facilities	Size of Faculty and Staff
Hours of Service	Auxiliary Programs

Examples of Services and Programs	*Examples of Institutional Factors*
Reference and Information	Undergraduate Programs
Bibliographic Instruction	Graduate Programs
Computer Based Services	Research
Collection Development	Community
Collection Organization	Continuing Education
Archives	
Audiovisual Services	

---

6. Supervisory staff should be selected on the basis of job knowledge, experience and human relations skills.

7. Procedures should be maintained for periodic review of staff performance and for recognition of achievement.

For references, the following documents may be consulted: "Guidelines and Procedures for the Screening and Appointment of Academic Librarians." *C & RL News,* September 1977, pp. 231–33; "Model Statement of Criteria and Procedures for Appointment, Promotion in Academic Rank, and Tenure for College and University Librarians," *C & RL News,* September and October 1973, pp. 192–95, 243–47; "Statement on the Terminal

Professional Degree for Academic Librarians," Chicago: ACRL, 1975.

Standard 5: Service

5 *The library shall establish and maintain a range and quality of services that will promote the academic program of the institution and encourage optimal library use.*

Commentary

The primary purpose of college library service is to promote and support the academic program of the parent institution. Services should be developed for and made available to all members of the academic community, including the handicapped and non-traditional students. The successful fulfillment of this purpose will require that librarians work closely with classroom faculty to gain from them a clear understanding of their educational objectives and teaching methods and to communicate to them an understanding of the services and resources that the library can offer. While research skills and ease of access to materials will both serve to encourage library use, the primary motivation for students to use the library originates with the instructional methods used in the classroom. Thus, close cooperation between librarians and classroom instructors is essential. Such cooperation must be a planned and structured activity and requires that librarians participate in the academic planning councils of the institution. They should assist teaching faculty in appraising the actual and potential library resources available, work closely with them in developing library services to support their instructional activities, and keep them informed of library capabilities.

5.1 *The library shall provide information and instruction to the user through a variety of techniques to meet differing needs. These shall include, but not be limited to, a variety of professional reference services, and bib-*

liographic instruction programs designed to teach users how to take full advantage of the resources available to them.

Commentary

A fundamental responsibility of a college library is to provide instruction in the most effective and efficient use of its materials. Bibliographic instruction and orientation may be given at many levels of sophistication and may use a variety of methods and materials, including course-related instruction, separate courses (with or without credit), and group or individualized instruction.

Of equal importance is traditional reference service wherein individual users are guided by librarians in their appraisal of the range and extent of the library resources available to them for learning and research. Professional services are optimally available all hours the library is open. Use patterns should be studied to determine those times when the absence of professional assistance would be least detrimental. The third major form of information service is the delivery of information itself. Although obviously inappropriate in the case of student searches, which are purposeful segments of classroom assignments, the actual delivery of information—as distinct from guidance to it—is a reasonable library service in almost all other conceivable situations.

Many of the services suggested in this commentary can be provided or enhanced by access to computerized forms of information retrieval. In fact many information sources are available only in computerized format, and every effort should be made to provide access to them. Services may be provided in person or by other measures such as videocassette, computer slide tape, or other appropriately prepared programs.

5.2 *Library materials of all types and formats that can be used outside the library shall be circulated to qualified users under equitable policies without jeopardizing their preservation of availability to others.*

Commentary

Circulation of library materials should be determined by local conditions, which will include size of the collections, the number of copies, and the extent of the user community. Every effort should be made to circulate materials of all formats that can be used outside the library without undue risk to their preservation. Circulation should be for as long a period as is reasonable without jeopardizing access to materials by other qualified users. This overall goal may prompt some institutions to establish variant or unique loan periods for different titles or classes of titles. Whatever loan policy is used, however, it should be equitably and uniformly administered to all qualified categories of users. The accessibility of materials can also be extended through provision of inexpensive means of photocopying within the laws regarding copyright.

5.2.1 *The quality of the collections shall be enhanced through the use of interlibrary loan and other cooperative agreements.*

Commentary

Local resources should be extended through reciprocal agreements for interlibrary loan according to the ALA codes. Access to materials should be by the most efficient and rapid method possible, incorporating such means as delivery services and electronic mail in addition to, or in place of, traditional forms of delivery. First consideration must always go to the primary users, but strong consideration should be given to fostering the sharing of resources.

5.2.2 *Cooperative programs, other than traditional interlibrary loan, shall be encouraged for the purpose of extending and increasing services and resources.*

Commentary

The rapid growth of information sources, the availability of a myriad of automation services, and the development of other technologies such as laser beam, videodiscs, microcomputer systems, etc., make new demands on budgets. Cooperation with other institutions, and particularly with multi-type library organizations, often becomes a necessity. It must be recognized that this does not only involve receiving but demands a willingness to give or share on the part of each library. This may mean a commitment of time, money, and personnel, but it is necessary if it is the only way to provide up-to-date services to users. Careful weighing of costs and benefits must be undertaken before such agreements are put into effect.

5.3 *The hours of access to the library shall be consistent with reasonable demand.*

Commentary

The number of hours per week that library services should be available will vary, depending upon such factors as whether the college is in an urban or rural setting, teaching methods used, conditions in the dormitories, and whether the student body is primarily resident or commuting. In any case, library scheduling should be responsive to reasonable local need. In some institutions users may need access to study facilities and to the collections, in whole or in part, during more hours of the week than they require the personal services of librarians. However, during the normal hours of operation the users deserve competent, professional service. The high value of the library's collections, associated materials, and equipment, etc., dictates that a responsible individual be in control at all times. The public's need for access to librarians may range upward to one hundred hours per week, whereas around-the-clock access to the library's collection and/or facilities may in some cases be warranted.

5.4 *Where academic programs are offered at off-campus sites, library services shall be provided in accord with ACRL's "Guidelines for Extended Campus Library Services."*

Commentary

Special library problems exist for colleges that provide off-campus instructional programs. Students in such programs must be provided with library services in accord with ACRL's "Guidelines for Extended Campus Library Services." These guidelines suggest that such services be financed on a regular basis, that a librarian be specifically charged with the delivery of such services, that the library implications of such programs be considered before program approval, and that courses so taught encourage library use. Services should be designed to meet the different information and bibliographic needs of these users.

Standard 6: Facilities

6 *The library building shall provide secure and adequate housing for its collections, and ample well-planned space for users and staff and for the provision of services and programs.*

Commentary

Successful library service presupposes an adequate library building. Although the type of building will depend upon the character and purposes of the institution, it should in all cases be functional, providing secure facilities for accommodating the library's resources, sufficient space for their administration and maintenance, and comfortable reading and study areas for users. A new library building should represent a coordinated planning effort involving the library director and staff, the college administration, and the architect, with the director responsible for the preparation of the building program.

FORMULA C—

The size of the college library building shall be calculated on the basis of a formula that takes into consideration the size of the student body, the size of the staff and its space requirements, and the number of volumes in the collections. To the result of this calculation must be added such space as may be required to house and service nonprint materials and microforms, to provide bibliographic instruction to groups, and to accommodate equipment and services associated with various forms of library technology.

  a. *Space for users.* The seating requirement for the library of a college where less than fifty percent of the FTE enrollment resides on campus shall be one for each five students. That for the library of a typical residential college shall be one for each four FTE students. Each study station shall be assumed to require 25 to 35 square feet of floor space, depending upon its function.

  b. *Space for books.* The space allocated for books shall be adequate to accommodate a convenient and orderly distribution of the collection according to the classification system(s) in use, and should include space for growth. Gross space requirements may be estimated according to the following formula.

	Square Feet/Volume
For the first 150,000 volumes	0.10
For the next 150,000 volumes	0.09
For the next 300,000 volumes	0.08
For holdings above 600,000 volumes	0.07

  c. *Space for staff.* Space required for staff offices, service and work areas, catalogs, files, and equipment shall be approximately one-eighth of the sum of the space needed for books and users as calculated under a) and b) above.

This formula indicates the net assignable area required by a library if it is to fulfill its mission with maximum effectiveness. "Net assignable area" is the sum of all areas (measured in square feet) on all floors of a building, assignable to, or useful for, library functions or purposes. (For an explanation of this definition see *The Measurement and Comparison of Physical Facilities for Libraries,* American Library Association, 1970.)

Libraries that provide 90 to 100% of the net assignable area called for by the formula shall be graded A in terms of space; 75–89% shall be graded B; 60–74% shall be graded C; and 50–59% shall be graded D.

The needs of handicapped persons should receive special attention and should be provided for in compliance with the Architectural Barriers Act of 1968 (Public Law 90-480) and the Rehabilitation Act of 1973, Section 504 (Public Law 93-516) and their amendments.

Particular consideration must be given to any present or future requirements for equipment associated with automated systems or other applications of library technology. Among these might be provision for new wiring, cabling, special climate control and maximum flexibility in the use of space. Consideration should also be given to load-bearing requirements for compact shelving and the housing of mixed formats including microforms.

6.1 *The size of the library building shall be determined by a formula (see Formula C) that takes into account the enrollment of the college, the extent and nature of its collections, and the size of its staff.*

6.2 *In designing or managing a library building, the functionality of floor plan and the use of space shall be the paramount concern.*

Commentary

The quality of a building is measured by such characteristics as the utility and comfort of its study and office areas, the design and durability of its furniture and equipment, the functional interrelationships of its service and work areas, and the ease and economy with which it can be operated and used.

6.3 *Except in certain circumstances, the college library's collections and services shall be administered within a single structure.*

Commentary

Decentralized library facilities in a college have some virtues, and they present some difficulties. Primary among their virtues is their convenience to the offices or laboratories of some members of the teaching faculty. Primary among their weaknesses is the resulting fragmentation of the unity of knowledge, the relative isolation of a branch library from most users, potential problems of staffing and security, and the cost of maintaining certain duplicative services or functions. When decentralized library facilities are being considered, these costs and benefits must be carefully compared. In general, experience has shown that decentralized library facilities may not be in the best academic or economic interest of a college.

Standard 7: Administration

Matters pertaining to college library administration are treated in the several other Standards. Matters of personnel administration, for example, are discussed under Standard 4, and fiscal administration under Standard 8. Some important aspects of library management, however, must be considered apart from the other Standards.

7 *The college library shall be administered in a manner that permits and encourages the fullest and most effective use of available library resources.*

Commentary

The function of a library administrator is to direct and coordinate the components of the library—its staff, services, collections, buildings and external relations—so that each contributes effectively and imaginatively to the mission of the library.

7.1 *The statutory or legal foundation for the library's activities shall be recognized in writing.*

Commentary

In order for the library to function effectively, there must first be an articulated understanding within the college as to the statutory or legal basis under which the library operates. This may be a college bylaw, a trustee minute, or a public law that shows the responsibility and flow of authority under which the library is empowered to act.

7.2 *The library director shall be an officer of the college and shall report to the president or the chief academic officer of the institution.*

Commentary

For the closest coordination of library activities with the instructional program, the library director should report either to the president or the chief officer in charge of the academic affairs of the institution.

7.2.1 *The responsibilities and authority of the library director and procedures for appointment shall be defined in writing.*

Commentary

There should be a document defining the responsibility and authority vested in the office of the library director. This document may also be statutorily based and should spell out, in addition to the scope and nature of the director's duties and powers, the procedures for appointment.

7.3 *There shall be a standing advisory committee comprised of students and members of the teaching faculty that shall serve as a channel of formal communication between the library and its user community.*

Commentary

This committee—of which the library director should be an ex officio member—should be used to convey both an awareness to the library of its users' concerns, perceptions and needs, and an understanding to users of the library's objectives and capabilities. The charge to the committee should be specific and in writing.

7.4 *The library shall maintain written policies and procedures manuals covering internal library governance and operational activities.*

Commentary

Written policies and procedures manuals are required for good management, uniformity, and consistency of action. They also aid in training staff and contribute to public understanding.

7.4.1 *The library shall maintain a systematic and continuous program for evaluating its performance, for informing the community of its accomplishments, and for identifying needed improvements.*

Commentary

The library director, in conjunction with the staff, should develop a program for evaluating the library's performance. Objectives developed in accordance with the goals of the institution should play a major part in this evaluation program. Statistics should be maintained for use in reports, to demonstrate trends, and in performance evaluation. In addition, the library director and staff members should seek the assistance of its standing library advisory committee and other representatives of the community it serves.

7.5 *The library shall be administered in accord with the spirit of ALA "Library Bill of Rights."*

Commentary

College libraries should be impervious to the pressures or efforts of any special interest groups or individuals to shape their collections and services. This principle, first postulated by the American Library Association in 1939 as the "Library Bill of Rights," (amended 1948, 1961, 1967 and 1980 by the ALA Council) should govern the administration of every college library and be given the full protection of the parent institution.

Standard 8: Budget

8 *The library director shall have the responsibility for preparing, defending, and administering the library budget in accord with agreed upon objectives.*

Commentary

The library budget is a function of program planning and defines the library's objectives in fiscal terms. The objectives formulated under Standard 1 should constitute the base upon which the library's budget is developed.

8.1 *The library's appropriation shall be six percent of the total institutional budget for educational and general purposes.*

Commentary

The degree to which the college is able to fund the library in accord with institutional objectives is reflected in the relationship of the library appropriation to the total educational and general budget of the college. It is recommended that library budgets, exclusive of capital costs and the costs of physical maintenance, not fall below six percent of the college's total educational and general expenditures if it is to sustain the range of library programs required by the institution and meet appropriate institutional objectives. This percentage should be greater if the library is attempting to overcome past deficiencies, or to meet the needs of new academic programs. The six percent figure is intended to include support for separately established professional libraries, providing the budget for those schools is incorporated into that of the University.

Factors that should be considered in formulating a library's budget requirements are the following:

1. The scope, nature and level of the college curriculum;

2. Instructional methods used, especially as they relate to independent study;

3. The adequacy of existing collections and the publishing rate in fields pertinent to the curriculum;

4. The size, or anticipated size, of the student body and teaching faculty;

5. The adequacy and availability of other library resources;

6. The range of services offered by the library, for example, the number of service points maintained, the number of hours per week that service is provided, the level of bibliographic instruction, online services, etc.;

7. The extent of automation of operations and services, with attendant costs;

8. The extent to which the library already meets the College Library Standards.

8.1.1 *The library's appropriation shall be augmented above the six percent level depending upon the extent to which it bears responsibility for acquiring, processing, and servicing audiovisual materials and microcomputer resources.*

Commentary

It is difficult for an academic library that has not traditionally been purchasing microcomputer and audiovisual materials to accommodate such purchases without some budgetary increase. The level of expenditure depends upon whether or not the institution has an audiovisual center separate from the library that acquires and maintains both audiovisual materials and hardware as well as a computer center that absorbs all costs related to microcomputer resources, even those included in the library.

8.2 *The library director shall have sole authority to apportion funds and initiate expenditures within the library budget and in accord with institutional policy.*

Commentary

Procedures for the preparation and defense of budget estimates, policies on budget approval, and regulation concerning accounting and expenditures vary from one institution to another. The library director must know and conform to local procedure. Sound practices of planning and control require that the director have sole responsibility and authority for allocation—and within college policy, the reallocation—of the library budget and the initiation of expenditures against it. Depending upon local factors, between 35% and 45% of the library's budget is normally allocated to acquisition of resources, and between 50% and 60% is expended for personnel.

8.3 *The library shall maintain internal accounts for approving its invoices for payment, monitoring its encumbrances, and evaluating the flow of its expenditures.*

Commentary

Periodic reports are necessary and provide an accurate account of the funds allocated to the library. They should be current and made accessible for fiscal accountability.

Other works cited

American Library Association, Ad Hoc Committee on the Physical Facilities of Libraries. *Measurement and Comparison of Physical Facilities for Libraries.* Chicago ALA, 1970.

[ACRL] Guidelines and Procedures for the Screening and Appointment of Academic Librarians." *C & RL News,* September 1977, pp. 231–33.

"[ACRL] Guidelines for Extended Campus Library Services." *C & RL News,* March 1982, pp. 86–88.

"[ACRL] Model Statement of Criteria and Procedures for Appointment, Promotion in Academic Rank, and Tenure for

College and University Librarians." *C & RL News,* September and October 1973, pp. 192–95, 243–47.

"[ACRL] Standards for Faculty Status for College and University Librarians." *C & RL News,* May 1974, pp. 112–13.

"[ACRL] Statement on the Terminal Professional Degree for Academic Librarians." Chicago: ALA/ACRL, 1975.

"Library Bill of Rights" (ALA Policy Manual, Section 53.1). In the *ALA Handbook of Organization 1984/85.* Chicago: ALA, 1984, pp. 217–18.

Library Education and Personnel Utilization: A Statement of Policy. Adopted by ALA Council. Chicago: ALA/OLPR, 1970.

[RASD/IFLA] *Interlibrary Loan Codes, 1980; International Lending Principles and Guidelines, 1978.* Chicago: ALA, 1982.

GLOSSARY OF TERMS ASSOCIATED WITH COLLECTION DEVELOPMENT AND LIBRARY TELECOMMUNICATIONS FOR NETWORKING AND RESOURCE SHARING

Allocation: Assignment of a portion of the library materials budget to a particular subject, type of material, administrative unit, or other category.

Application level: The areas of a computer system that concern user processes, as distinguished from communications and housekeeping functions. In library networks, application level refers to the computer processes in support of specific library operations, such as acquisitions, cataloging, serials control, reference, etc.

Authentication: Certification that the data content and content designation of a given bibliographic record have been reviewed by an appropriate center of responsibility and that the record meets the established bibliographic standards of a network. See also: Center of Special Authorization.

Authoritative record: A record that is judged by a designated center of responsibility to conform to a network's standards.

Authority control: The functions involved in establishing, maintaining, and using authority files.

Authority files: A set of records that identifies the established or authoritative forms for headings or access points for a set of bibliographic records. Authority files include cross references from variants to the preferred forms of headings, and links from earlier to later forms and between broader and narrower terms and related terms. An authority file may represent the authoritative forms of headings for an individual institution, a group of related institutions, or a network of related and/or unrelated institutions.

Authority record: A record of an individual heading in an authority file. An authority record may include heading variants, cross references to and from the heading, cataloging notes, historical information, and references to the source of a heading.

Bibliographic control: The functions necessary to generate and organize records of library materials for effective retrieval.

Bibliographic data: Data representing individual bibliographic attributes of an item, typically including descriptive and subject cataloging, element, indexing elements, authority elements, and abstracts.

Bibliographic group: A set of functionally related bibliographic data.

Bibliographic information: The meaning assigned to bibliographic data.

Bibliographic item: A uniquely identified work or part of a work.

Bibliographic (processing) services: Activities that assist libraries in establishing bibliographic control over their materials and in gaining access to mechanisms for their identification and retrieval. See also: Bibliographic service center.

Bibliographic record: A collection of bibliographic data fields treated as one logical entity that describes a specific bibliographic item. See also: Cataloging Record.

Bibliographic reference: The set of bibliographic data needed for unique identification of an item.

Bibliographic service center: An organization that serves as a broker or distributor of computer-based bibliographic (processing) services. A service center gains access to national library network resources through the facilities of a bibliographic utility. It does not necessarily contribute records directly to or maintain portions of the national library network data base.

Bibliographic strip: A coded summary of bibliographic data, especially as printed on the cover of a periodical, used for rapid identification of an item.

Bibliographic utility: An organization that maintains online bibliographic data bases, enabling it to offer computer-based support to any interested users, including national library network participants. A bibliographic utility will maintain components of the national library network data store and provide a standard interface through which bibliographic service centers, and individual national library network participants, may gain access to the nationwide network.

Catalog: A set of bibliographic records generally under control of authority files that describes the resources of a collection, library, or network. It is the instrument by which bibliographic control is maintained for a collection, library, or network, and by which the relationship between individual bibliographic records can be indicated. See also: Library catalog.

Cataloging record: A bibliographic record that describes a specific item and relates it to other items described in the file.

Center of excellence: An institution with the designated responsibility for collecting, cataloging and providing bibliographic records for materials in special subject, geographic or language areas. See also: Resource library.

Center of responsibility: An organization(s) with designated responsibility for establishing and maintaining the authoritative form of data elements to be used within a network. See also: Center of special authorization.

Center of special authorization: An organization, other than a
center of responsibility, that is empowered to authenticate
specific data fields in certain bibliographic records. Authentication by these centers of special authorization can be over-
ridden by decision of a center of responsibility.

Centralized (computer) network: A computer network configuration in which one computer or a group of centrally located
computers provides computing power and maintains control
of application level programs and telecommunications. See
also: Decentralized (computer) network.

Centralized processing:
1) Computer processing in which one computer or a group of
   centrally located computers provides computing services
   and maintains network control.
2) A system for ordering library materials, preparing them for
   use, and preparing cataloging records for them in one
   library or agency for a group of libraries. See also: Bibliographic (processing) services.

Channel:
1) The connection between a message source and a message
   sink in a communications system.
2) A means of one-way transmission of data.

Code: A systematically arranged and comprehensive set of
letters used to refer to defined library collection characteristics, notably collection levels and the extent of various languages' representation in a library collection.

Collecting Intensity: Measures of the effort expended in developing library collections; two are used in Conspectus work.

Collection aspects: The state of a collection at a specific time
and the state of collection building. There are traditionally
three collection aspects: collection strength, current collecting intensity, and desired collecting intensity. The primary
collection aspect is collection strength. Collecting intensity,
whether current or desired, is always expressed in terms of
the collection strength that would ultimately result were such
intensity continued over time.

Collection development: The process of planning, building and
maintaining a library's information resources in a cost-
efficient and user-relevant manner. Principle activities include the identification, selection, and sometimes procurement of locally appropriate materials; the allocation of the
resources budget among different subjects and formats; collection management, analysis, and evaluation; liaison with
library users; planning and implementation of resource shar-

ing and related programs; and the determination and coordination of policies and procedures governing these functions.

Collection development and management program: The formal organization of a library's collection development and management activities in a systematic manner; explicitly linked to the parent agency's mission, administratively structured around corresponding goals and objectives, and supported by appropriate policies, governance structures, training programs, and other administrative arrangements.

Collection levels: A set of abstract collection qualities or characteristics used as a scale to describe or categorize collection strengths (and by extension, current and desired collecting intensities).

Collection management: Activities that are designed to optimize the use of existing information and fiscal resources to assure maximally effective collection development. Techniques employed are collection analysis and evaluation; collection review for preservation, protected access, remote storage, or discard; use and user studies; vendor and dealer assessments; and other methods of study and measurement.

Collection strength: The current condition of a subject collection in a particular library as defined by collection levels. The collection strength may be temporarily at a higher or lower level than that of the current or desired collecting intensity. Termed existing collection (ECI) or Collection Level (CL) when used in conspectus work.

Common carrier: A telecommunications company that is regulated by an appropriate government agency and that offers services to the general public via shared circuits.

Communications computer: A special-purpose computer used to control or format data transmitted between network nodes.

Communications format: A format for the transmission (as opposed to the processing) of machine-readable bibliographic data.

Communications network: The physical means for a group of nodes to intercommunicate data.

Configuration: The arrangement of components or functions within a system.

Consortium: A community of two or more libraries that have formally agreed to coordinate, cooperate, or consolidate certain functions. Consortia may be formed on a geographical, type of library, or subject basis.

Conspectus: A comprehensive survey; a tabulation of particulars representing a general view of them. The term as used here means an overview or summary of collection strengths and collecting intensities, arranged by subject, classification scheme, or a combination of either, and containing standardized codes for collection or collecting levels and for languages of materials collected. Such a conspectus is a synopsis of a library's collection or of a consortium's or network's coordinated collection development overview or policy. First developed by the Research Libraries Group and subsequently adapted by other groups.

Content designator: A means of specifying the data elements in a given field or a machine-readable record.

Control character: A character whose occurrence initiates, modifies or terminates a control function.

Control field: A field that supplies parameters that may be required in the processing of a bibliographic records. See also: Data field.

Control function: An operation that affects the recording, processing, transmission, or interpretation of data.

Coordinated or cooperative collection development: Coordination, cooperation, or sharing in the management and development of library collections by two or more libraries entering into an agreement for this purpose.

Copy-specific data: Data sufficient to identify multiple copies and to describe unique bibliographic attributes among those copies of an item described by a single bibliographic record, where the copies are owned by a single organization. Copy-specific data do not indicate an actual site where an item is located within the organization. See also site data.

Current collecting intensity (CCI): The relative degree of effort presently expended on the development of a subject collection; the current collecting intensity is expressed as the collection strength (defined by collection levels), which will result if the present effort continues over time. Also termed Acquisition Commitment (AC).

Data: A representation to which meaning can be assigned.

Data base:
1) A structured collection of data developed according to uniform standards.
2) An entire set of data available to a computer system.

Data base access services: Organizations that offer access to one or more data bases. The services may provide direct access to data bases they develop and maintain, or through a royalty arrangement provide access to data bases developed and maintained by others.

Data base management: The control processes for the formatting, inputting, storing, retrieving, modifying, and outputting of data in large computer data files.

Data communication: The transfer of data from one point to another over communications channels.

Data element: A defined unit of data within a system.

Data field: A field containing bibliographic or other data not required as parameters for the processing of a bibliographic record, as distinguished from a control field.

Data link: The assemblage of communications equipment and interconnecting circuits that allows data to be exchanged between two or more stations.

Decentralized (computer) network: A computer network configuration in which computing power and/or control functions are distributed over several network nodes. See also: Centralized (computer) network.

Decentralized input: A system in which data for input are accepted from various nodes. In terms of the national library network, decentralized input will allow bibliographic records and authority records to be originated and authenticated by designated centers of responsibility and communicated via telecommunications, magnetic tape or hard copy for inclusion in the national library network data base.

Deselection: The official removal of titles from a library's collection, as a result of systematic weeding or the withdrawal of missing or physically damaged materials.

Desired Collecting Intensity (DCI): The relative degree of effort that should be maintained for the development of a subject collection in order for the library to achieve its mission. Most conspectus work has not included the DCI, but its use for local collection policy statements is deemed important by some libraries. Also termed Collection Goal (CG).

The extent to which a library is successful in achieving its mission is partially apparent at any time by comparing the Current Collecting Intensity and the Desired Collecting Intensity.

Disposition policy: A policy that states the options for disposing of unwanted materials acquired by purchase, gift, deposit, or other means, as governed by local, parent agency, legal, and other restrictions. These options include using for exchange, giving to other agencies, sale, and discard.

Distributed (computer) processing:
1) Computer processing systems in which the control functions and/or computing functions are shared among several network nodes.

  2) A single logical set of processing functions implemented across a number of computers.

Distributed data bases: Logically interconnected data bases or portions or data bases (indexes, locations, etc.) that reside in separate physical locations in a network.

Distributed network:
  1) See: Decentralized (computer) network.
  2) A network design in which each node is connected to every other node either directly or through intermediate nodes.

Extension bit/byte: A bit/byte coding scheme used to designate an extended range of characters, commonly called "escape characters," typically including upper case and lower case alphabets, special characters, and numerals.

Field: A specified set of contiguous characters in a record, used for a particular category of data.

File: A collection of related records.

Fixed field: A field that always has a specific number of character spaces allocated, regardless of the data contents. See also: Variable field.

Format recognition process: A computer process for construction of machine-readable bibliographic records from a stream of date, utilizing a specific format that facilitates identification of content designators.

Front end computer: A subsidiary computer that performs the control and conversion functions necessary for data transmission between host computers and the communications network. See also: Host front end processor, network front end processor.

Fully connected network: A network in which each node is directly connected for communications purposes with every other node.

Header: The control data that precede a message text; for example, source or destination code, priority, message type.

Heading: The form of a name, subject, uniform title, series, etc., used as an access point to a bibliographic record or authority record. The totality of headings in an authority file is indicative of the organization of an entire catalog and the rules used to structure the catalog.

Heterogeneous (computer) network: A network that has dissimilar host computers, such as those of various manufacturers. See also: Homogeneous (computer) network.

Hierarchical (computer) network: A computer network in which processing and control functions are delegated to several levels of specially suited computers.

Holdings data:
1) Data sufficient to identify a number of items owned by an organization, where the several items are described jointly by a single bibliographic record, commonly used with respect to serials (volumes, issues, etc.). Not to be used interchangeably with locations data.
2) Data that indicate the scope of the entire collection, or a specific part of the collection, of a library or group of libraries.

Homogeneous (computer) network: A network with similar host computers, such as those of one model of one manufacturer. See also: Heterogeneous (computer) network.

Host: A system or subsystem in a network that performs actual processing operations against a data base and with which other network nodes communicate.

Host computer: A network computer that performs the primary processing services such as computation, data base access, and data manipulation. See also: Communications computer.

Host front end processor: A front end computer at a host site. It provides the interface between the host computer and the logical network front end processor. Host front end processor functions encompass message formatting, character conversion, operating system control and input/output supervisor control.

Host site: A network location that receives communications from their network nodes, performs operations on them (via a host computer) and sends communications to their nodes.

Information retrieval: The process of selecting from data bases relevant citations to bibliographic items or other pieces of data, using a variety of access points (subjects, names, dates, etc.) and often employing logical operations to define the search strategy.

Interface: The point or process that joins two system components.
1) Shared boundary, defined by common physical, signal and logical characteristics, across which data travel.
2) A device that facilitates interoperation of two systems, as between data communications equipment and data processing equipment or terminal installations.
Interfaces between computers and communications systems may be divided into various classes of functions; e.g., physical, electrical, logical and procedural.

Interstate network: A network with nodes in more than one state.

Intrastate network: A network that exists wholly within one state; it may, however, be a regional network at the same time.

Library bibliographic component: That portion of the national library network encompassing its bibliographic service system and segments of its communications system, and exclusive of the resource library system.

Library catalog: A set of bibliographic records that describes the collection of a library. Generally characterized by conformity to a given set of cataloging standards with respect to choice and form of entry, description and subject analysis. A library catalog represents an attempt to maintain a coherent organization of a library's bibliographic records and to show the interrelationship of the bibliographic items represented.

Link: A communications path between two nodes or points. See also: Interface, data link.

Local authority record: A record in an authority file that conforms to purely local catalog requirements. In a quadraplanar structure, this type of record is held at the "institution level."

Locations data: Data that identify the organization(s) holding one or more items described by a specific bibliographic record. Locations data do not include copy-specific data or site data for those items associated with an organization. See also: Copy-specific data, site data.

Message:
1) A single transmission in one direction, consisting of a header and data.
2) A unit of information transmitted from one node to another on a network.

Message delivery system: The communications computers and network front end processors that control the transmission of messages between network hosts, and the telecommunications facilities used for message transmission. See also: Message processing system.

Message processing system: The host computers and host front end processors in a network that perform operations on network messages. See also: Message delivery system.

Message switching: A telecommunications technique in which a message is received, stored (usually until the best outgoing line is available), and then re-transmitted toward its destination. No direct connection between the incoming and outgoing lines is set up as in line switching.

Message text: The substantive portion of a network transmission; i.e., blocks of data exclusive of control characters. See also: Header.

Message text format: Standardized format for messages in a network. Types of message text formats include query text, bibliographic text, reply text, error text. A message text format for a network could be 1) header length, 2) header, 3) data length, 4) data.

Modem: Modulator-demodulator: a device that modulates and demodulates digital signals so that they may be transmitted by an analog communications transmission medium, such as a telephone line.

Multitype network: A network that serves more than one type of organization, such as a library network with both academic and special libraries as participants. This refers to types of network participants and not to geographical coverage.

National bibliographic center: An organization that provides bibliographic control at the national level, contributing bibliographic records and authority records to the national library network data base.

National bibliographic control:
1) The systematic and nationally coordinated organization and provision of bibliographic data on all materials available in the nation's libraries.
2) A subsystem of the universal bibliographic control system.

National bibliographic service: Bibliographic service emanating from a national bibliographic center; e.g., the Library of Congress, to support the nation's libraries with tools for consistent and uniform cataloging, and for nationwide interlibrary loan.

National library and information service network: A system to facilitate access to the nation's library and information resources. The proposed network is to consist of three coordinated parts: a resource system, a bibliographic service system, and a communications system.

National library network: The library-oriented components of the national library and information service network, in all three of its proposed parts: bibliographic, resource and communications. The national library network will include the contributors to the national library network data store, and will encompass several hierarchical levels: centers of responsibility, centers of special authorization, bibliographic utilities, and bibliographic service centers or major resource libraries.

The national library network is expected to provide services to support the identification of items, the location of items, the transfer of items shared by the network's participants (interlibrary loan), and the acquisition of such items.

National library network data base: A compatible set of machine-readable files of bibliographic data constructed according to network standards and designed to support national library network services.

National library network data store: The aggregate of machine-readable files of bibliographic data possessed by the national library network's contributors. The data store provides the data from which the national library network data base is built.

Since the data store comprises records of only the library sector of the information community, it represents only one facet of the nationwide library and information service data store.

National library network union catalog: A union catalog or set of union catalogs derived from the national library network data base.

A national library network union catalog will provide a non-redundant, sorted index to the network's resources, and interface with a larger, international network. Summary locations data will direct requests to network participants where more specific locations statements are maintained for an item.

Network:
1) Two or more organizations engaged in a common pattern of information exchange through telecommunications links, for some common objectives.
2) An interconnected or interrelated group of nodes.

Network authority record: An authority record created according to standards for content and content designation agreed to by network participants.

Network control program: A subsystem of a host computer in a network, which controls the operations of the communications computer.

Network coordinating agency: An agency responsible for coordinating the development of the library bibliographic component of the national library and information service network.

Network front end processor: A front end computer that acts as the interface between the host or the host front end processor and the network. Its responsibilities include the reliable routing of messages to and from the associated host front end processor and the transmission of messages from other network nodes.

Network library resource system: One of the three components of the national library and information service network. The resource system will designate responsibility to information facilities for providing access to needed library materials and coordinate support from collection development.

Network node: A station, terminal or communications computer in a computer network.

Network operations center: A center that controls, manages, and maintains a network.

Network redundancy: Additional links beyond the minimum number necessary to connect all network nodes.

Network security: The measures taken to protect a network's equipment, communications, and files from unauthorized access, accidental or willful interference, and damage or destruction.

Network topology: The configuration of links and nodes in a network.

Network transaction: A transaction between nodes in a network.

Originating host:
1) The initiator of a network session.
2) The host computer at the source of a message transmitted to a target host in a network.

Preservation: A broad range of activities intended to extend the life of deteriorating library materials. Preservation includes selection of replacement copies, identification of items for retention in storage or protected access, and the selection of materials for conversion to alternate formats such as microforms.

Preservation selection: The selection of items to be preserved from among those identified as in need of physical treatment or reformatting.

Protocol: The conventions used in communicating between nodes and levels in a network, specifically a formal set of conventions governing the format and relative sequencing of message exchanges. (Note: the use of "protocol" for communications conventions between nodes at the same level, and "interface" between nodes at adjacent levels has been suggested.)

Real time system: A computer system that receives and processes data, and can utilize the results immediately to guide subsequent processing operations.

Regional network: A network with nodes in a defined geographical area. A regional network may operate wholly within a state (intrastate network), or have participants across state lines (interstate network).

Registry: A conceptual entity designed to function as a depository for message text format standards and the current and correct version of network protocol for the national library network, and as an assigner of control codes for inclusion in the header field.

Reliability: The ability of a system to perform its intended functions under stated conditions for a stated period of time. See also: Vulnerability.

Remote input: A method of input in which data are entered for processing via an input device that has access to a computer through a telecommunications link. See also: Decentralized input.

Resource library: A library designated as responsible for developing collections in special groups of materials and for providing access to these materials to other libraries. See also: Center of excellence.

Resource sharing:
1) Sharing of materials among cooperating libraries.
2) Sharing of bibliographic data.
3) Sharing of library processing services and the computer facilities, programs, and telecommunications to provide these services.

Response time: The elapsed time between an indication of the end of a query and the display of the first character of the response.

Ring network: A computer network in which each computer is connected to two adjacent computers in a circular pattern.

Scope notes: Descriptions of local holdings or policies that provide information in addition to the codes specified for each subject in a conspectus. Descriptions of preservation projects may be included.

Site data: Data sufficient to identify the actual physical location and shelving position of an item. For example, site data may specify special collection sites in a single-branch, collections and branch sites in multiple-branch collections, and may include call number data.

Source:
1) A computer or terminal that enters data into a connected channel.
2) The point of entry of data into a network. See also: sink.

Station: An input or output point in a telecommunications system.

Telecommunications: Transmission and reception of data by electromagnetic means.

Teleprocessing: Automated data processing that utilizes telecommunications facilities for data transmission.

Terminal:
1) A device for entering data into or receiving data from a computer system or computer network.
2) A point in a communications network at which data can either enter or leave.

Text:
1) The part of a message that contains the substantive information; the body of a message, exclusive of control characters. See also: Message text.
2) The accepted format for a standardized network communication; e.g., query text, reply text, error text, etc. See also: Message text format.
3) A sequence of characters forming part of a transmission from a data source to a data sink, preceded by a header and followed by an "end of text" signal.

Transaction:
1) An operational unit of processing at the application level; a complete step of data processing.
2) A logical grouping of messages in both directions between originating hosts and target hosts in a network.

Union catalog:
1) A catalog that describes the contents of physically separate library collections, indicating by means of locations data the libraries in which a given item may be found.
2) Subsets of the national library network data base.
   a) See: National library network union catalog
   b) Other union catalogs that coexist in the data base, with headings that conform to standards of various specialized centers of special authorization or centers of responsibility.

Universal bibliographic control (UBC): An international system for handling bibliographic data that describe bibliographic items produced anywhere in the world.

Validation: A machine or manual process in which the data and the content designators of a record are matched against standards, and notification is given of any errors or inconsistencies detected. Not only is the record itself checked (verification) but it is also checked against existing files. No data are changed during validation. Examples of validation processes include using a check digit to confirm the accuracy of numeric data and checking a record against existing files for possible record duplication.

Value-added network: A network operated by a private company that is authorized by a government agency to lease basic communications services from common carriers and specialized common carriers, to augment the services through additional facilities, such as switching centers and store-and-forward devices, and to resell the enhanced service to end users. *Telenet* and *Tymnet* are examples of value-added networks.

Variable field: A field in a record the length of which is determined by the number of characters required to store the data in a given occurrence of that field. The length may vary from one occurrence of a variable field to the next. See also: Fixed field.

Verification: A process in which a record is proofread to determine whether it is complete and error-free. See also: Validation.

Verification study: A collection assessment carried out by two or more libraries, using specially prepared evaluative instruments to verify that collection level codes for existing collection strength (ECI) have been assigned accurately and consistently.

Virtual circuit: A telecommunications path that uses a number of point-to-point circuits connected through switching by communications computers. Data transfer is accomplished by forwarding data in blocks from node to node toward the destination, such that the circuit appears as a single physical transmission path.

Vulnerability: The extent to which a system is susceptible to malfunctions under stated conditions. See also: Reliability.

SUBJECT INDEX

Each bibliographic citation in COLLECTION DEVELOP-
MENT AND COLLECTION EVALUATION: A SOURCE-
BOOK is arranged alphabetically by author in the compre-
hensive bibliographies, so that readers searching for a
specific writer should turn to those sections following
Parts 1,2, and 3.

Subject access to entries in this Sourcebook is provided
in the following pages. Readers searching for works about
"Intellectual Freedom," for example, would discover the
following:

INTELLECTUAL FREEDOM
222, 315

The above reference is to entry number (not page number) 222. Entry numbers run consecutively from 1 to 1899
in the margins of pages of bibliographic citations. Cross
references are provided from terms not used to accurate
subject headings in order to ensure rapid and convenient
access.

318–19, 330, 350, 355, 381, 399, 406–7, 432, 441, 478–79, 497, 500, 507, 523, 543, 546, 560, 583, 590–91, 608, 631, 640, 670, 690, 714, 734–35, 743, 798, 905, 1021, 1175, 1240, 1244, 1704
Copyright: 282

Deposit accounts: 1543, 1552
Deselection see Periodicals, cancellation; Weeding
Duplicates exchange: 777

Electronic publishing: 77, 94–95, 97, 99, 209, 285, 301, 395, 418, 430, 463, 1102
Enright Report: 594
Evaluation of collections: 207, 394, 404, 502, 599, 757, 812, 834–43, 857–63, 878, 893–94, 896, 901–2, 913, 923, 927–28, 931–36, 953, 966, 974, 988–89, 1048, 1060, 1091, 1119–20, 1129, 1144, 1154, 1173–74, 1278, 1283
Evaluation of collections, circulation data: 911, 944, 962, 975, 1008, 1028, 1042, 1145, 1151–52, 1182, 1225, 1263, 1265
Evaluation of collections, citation analysis: 865–66, 900, 961, 981, 986, 1090, 1109, 1127, 1130, 1165, 1184, 1197
Evaluation of collections, computer assisted: 926–27, 937, 958, 1094, 1110, 1213
Evaluation of collections, course-related: 888–91, 910, 991, 1001–02, 1059, 1108, 1122, 1149–50, 1153, 1195
Evaluation of collections, list checking: 943, 948–49, 1006, 1027, 1136, 1211, 1234
Evaluation of collections, user studies: 20, 357, 408–11, 568, 980, 985, 987, 1000, 1031–32, 1045, 1049, 1056, 1058, 1080, 1104, 1106, 1118, 1148, 1170, 1176, 1192, 1209, 1268, 1280
Extension see Off-campus services

Faculty participation in selection: 645, 771
Farmington Plan: 135, 248, 277, 303, 370, 469, 603, 769, 830, 1472, 1829
Film collections: 1432, 1671

Gifts: 188, 518, 627, 639, 1222, 1277, 1451, 1614, 1622–23, 1625, 1636, 1744, 1828, 1873

ABOUT THE AUTHOR

Michael R. Gabriel (B.A., University of Maryland; MLS, University of Illinois; Specialist, University of Wisconsin) is Coordinator of Branch Libraries at Northern Illinois University. He has worked in collection management positions at several academic libraries, including the University of California and Mankato State University, where he developed a method of evaluating collections with the aid of online catalogs. He has published extensively on the topic of use of new technologies in libraries, especially applications of electronic media and their impact on library operations such as collection development.